Praise for *When One Room Fit All*

Helen Boertje has dedicated her life to the education of others and this passion for teaching and learning is evidenced in *When One Room Fit All*. It is thoroughly researched and extensively documented, a process that has taken a number of years, a painstaking effort that can be characterized as a true labor of love.

–Marion County Historical Society Board of Directors

With *When One Room Fit All*, Helen Boertje delivers, using her gifted and perceptive writing style to create a unique and original contribution to the history of Marion County, Iowa, and education in general.

–Michael Van Natta, Author of *Leo's Birds*

About the Author

Helen (Van Zante) Boertje received her elementary education in the North Porterville Country School, southeast of Pella. A retired English and biology teacher, she lives in Pella with her two unteachable cats. Helen is a freelance writer whose weekly column "From a Small Farm" appeared in the Pella Chronicle for several years. She currently writes essays for www.towncriernews.com.

When One Room Fit All

When One Room Fit All

The Country Schools of Marion County, Iowa

by Helen Boertje

When One Room Fit All. Copyright © 2012 by Helen Boertje. All rights reserved. No part of this book may be used or reproduced in any manner whatsoever without written permission from the author, except in the case of brief quotations embodied in critical articles or reviews.

ISBN: 978-0-9831961-5-0

Published and printed in the United States of America by The Write Place. Cover and interior design by Alexis Thomas, The Write Place. For more information, please contact:

The Write Place
709 Main Street, Suite 2
Pella, Iowa 50219
www.thewriteplace.biz

Copies of this book may be ordered from The Write Place online at www.thewriteplace.biz/bookplace.

Table of Contents

The number in parentheses after each school name represents the section within the township in which the school was located.

About the Author _____ i
Locations of Marion County Country Schools _____ ix
Preface _____ xi
Acknowledgements _____ xiii
Museum Schools _____ 15

Clay Township
Bethel (27) _____ 17
Clay Center (16) _____ 18
Des Moines Valley (10) _____ 19
Durham (8) _____ 21
Eureka (4) _____ 22
Fairview (20) _____ 23
Iola (31) _____ 25
Lincoln North and South _____ 26
McMillan (18) _____ 27
Union (32) _____ 29
Vigilance (30) _____ 31

Dallas Township
Chicago (17) _____ 35
Dallas Center (21) _____ 35
Fairview (29) _____ 36
Freedom (13) _____ 37
Horstman (8) _____ 38
Marion (27) _____ 39
Newbern (31) _____ 40

Franklin Township
Caloma (31) _____ 43
Empire (36) _____ 44
Fairview (3) _____ 45
Franklin Center (15) _____ 46
Hazel Ridge (22) _____ 48
Highland (13) _____ 48
Pleasant Ridge (5) _____ 51
Springdale (17) _____ 51
Sunnyside (2) _____ 52

Indiana Township
Carlysle (1) _____ 55
Cedar Valley (27) _____ 55
Coal Ridge (25) _____ 56
Indiana (23) _____ 57
Prairie College (9) _____ 57
Robuck (7) _____ 58
Round Grove (20) _____ 58
Simmons (32) _____ 59
Springfield (21) _____ 60
Union (7) _____ 62
Willow Grove (7) _____ 62

Knoxville Township
Brownlee (19) _____ 65
Buckeye (23) _____ 66
Bunker Hill (26) _____ 67
Burr Oak (21) _____ 67
Donley (4) _____ 69
Elm Ridge (4) _____ 69
Fairview (29) _____ 71
Fee (2) _____ 72
Flagler (2) _____ 74
North Flagler (35) _____ 76
South Flagler (11) _____ 78
Georgia Ridge (2) _____ 79
Highland (13) _____ 80
Liberty (22) _____ 80
Lincoln (4) _____ 82
Maple Grove (14) _____ 83
Pleasant Grove (31) _____ 84
Pleasant Hill _____ 85
Pleasant Ridge (29) _____ 85
Rising Star (17) _____ 86
Salem (33) _____ 88
Scott (33) _____ 89
Spring Hill (36) _____ 90
Sumpter (35) _____ 93
Victory (24) _____ 93
Washington (28) _____ 94

Lake Prairie Township
East Amsterdam (20) _____ 97
West Amsterdam (18) _____ 99
Battle Ridge (19) _____ 100
Bunker Hill (17) _____ 102
European #1 (22) _____ 103
European #2 (10) _____ 105
European #3 (23) _____ 107
Oak Grove (33) _____ 108
Plainview (1) _____ 109
Pleasant Grove (22) _____ 111
North Porterville (25) _____ 112
South Porterville (2) _____ 115
Rock Island _____ 116
Sand Ridge (12) _____ 118

Table of Contents, continued

Lake Prairie Township, cont.
East Silver Grove (5) ____ 119
Silver Grove West (6) ____ 121
Valley School (13) _____ 122

Liberty Township
Black Oak (6) _____ 127
Cedar Valley (1) _____ 128
Liberty North (10) _____ 128
Liberty South (16) _____ 128
Shiloh (17) _____ 129
Virginia (11) _____ 131
Weir City _____ 131

Perry Township
Bennington (10) _____ 133
Collins (6) _____ 133
Pleasant Hill (1) _____ 134
Valley (11) _____ 136

Pleasant Grove Township
Conn (19) _____ 139
Hawkeye (2) _____ 140
Ladoga (33) _____ 140
Pleasantville North (9) __ 141
Pleasantville South (22) __ 141
Spalti (8) _____ 141
Stringtown (14) _____ 141
Thorntown (31) _____ 142
Weston (36) _____ 142
Wheeling (5) _____ 142

Polk Township
Bend (17) _____ 145
Coal Ridge (14) _____ 146
Fairview (8) _____ 148
Mt. Vernon (21) _____ 149
East River Ridge (24) ____ 150
West River Ridge (14) ___ 151
Rousseau (9) _____ 153
White Breast (3) _____ 153

Red Rock Township
Brush Creek (24) _____ 157
Cordova (31) _____ 158
Fairview (5) _____ 158
Hickory Grove (2) _____ 159
Liberty Corner (11) _____ 159
Oak Ridge (18) _____ 160
Pleasant Valley (9) _____ 161
Red Rock (36) _____ 163
White Walnut (21) _____ 164

Summit Township
Cincinnati (6) _____ 169
Fair Oaks (29) _____ 170
Liberty Corner (26) _____ 171
Otley (22) _____ 173
Pleasant Grove (18) _____ 175
Pleasant View (4) _____ 176
Richland (24) _____ 177
Summit (9) _____ 178
Valley View (1) _____ 179

Swan Township
Burr Oak (27) _____ 183
Bunker Hill (31) _____ 183
O.K. (15) _____ 184
West Pella (25) _____ 184

Union Township
Blaine (12) _____ 189
Burch (16) _____ 191
Clark (18) _____ 192
Core (6) _____ 193
Oradell (31) _____ 193
Rees (4) _____ 194
Union (11) _____ 195

Washington Township
Columbia (34) _____ 199
Elm Grove (13) _____ 201
Fillmore (9) _____ 203
Gosport (22) _____ 204
Liberty (30) _____ 206
New Albany (11) _____ 206
Pleasant Ridge (25) ____ 208
Union (19) _____ 208
Washington (6) _____ 209

Teachers of Marion County Country Schools_ 213
Photo Enlargements ____ 255
Bibliography _____ 286

Locations of Marion County Country Schools

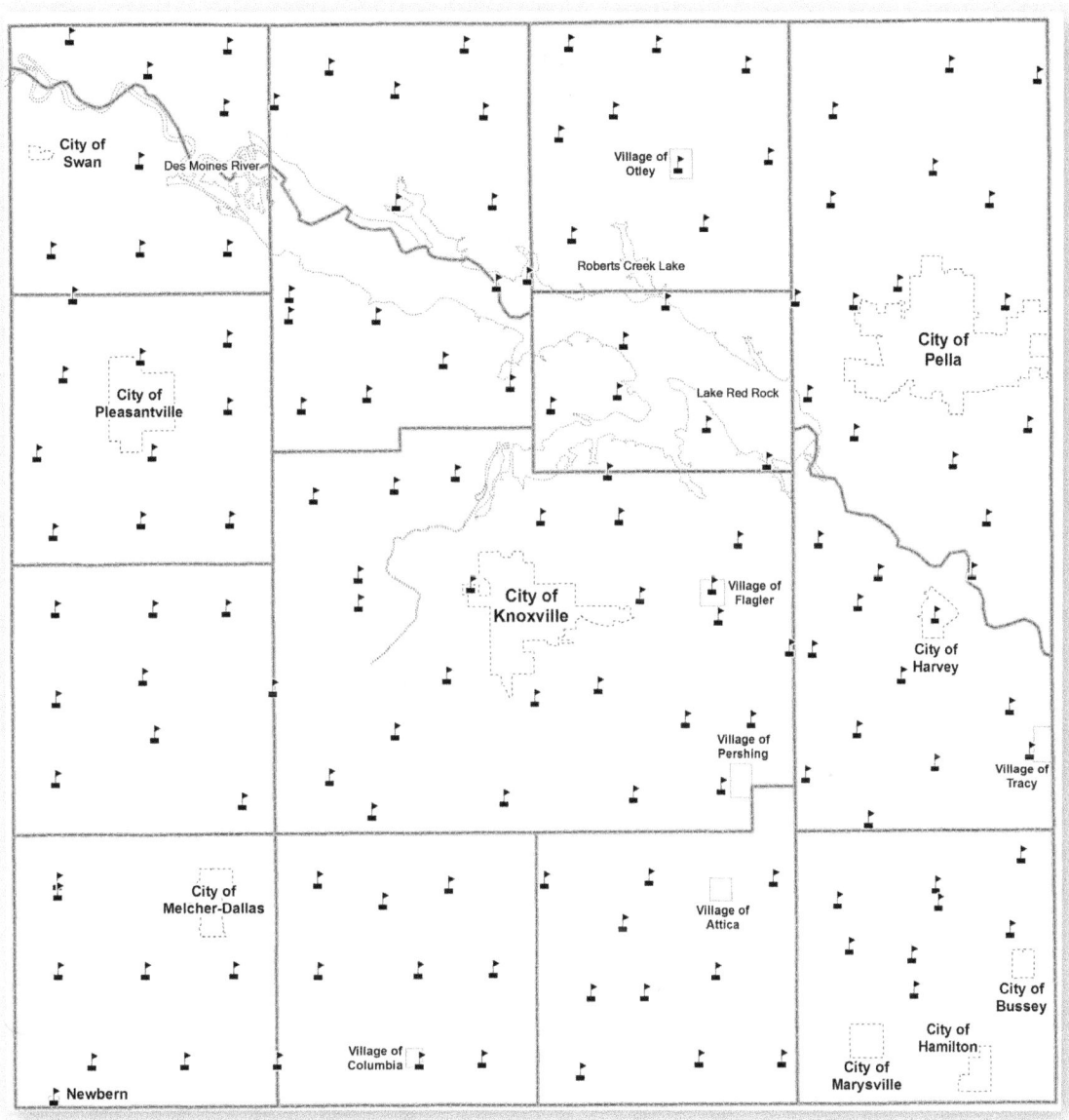

Preface

From the time the first settlers arrived in Marion County in 1843 until the mid-20th century, most rural children received their elementary education in a one-room school within walking distance of their homes. Even before the first log cabin schools were built, many parents persuaded the best-educated person in the neighborhood to set up a school in that person's home. Parents paid a small tuition fee for these schools, which were called subscription schools.

Later districts were divided into two-by-two mile units with the intent that a school be built in the middle so that no student need walk more than a mile to school. From 1890-1930, Iowa led the nation in the largest number of country schools.

Early schools divided the year into three terms, often hiring a different teacher for each term. A high school graduate who was at least eighteen years old could become a teacher. Because of the large number of students, some of whom were older and larger than the teacher, some district directors preferred to hire a man to maintain discipline. Before the 1940's, many districts did not allow married women to teach.

Country schools helped maintain strong neighborhood bonds. After the school day was done, the buildings were used for various events. Several rural churches got their start by meeting in the school on Sunday.

A country school teacher was kept very busy doing janitorial work as well as teaching classes from primary through eighth grade. These teachers carried out an ideal education model that fostered both cooperation and independence and allowed individual students to advance at their own pace. Almost every former student I talked to is grateful for the experience of attending country school.

From township to township, *When One Room Fit All* pinpoints the location of each school and lists the teachers who taught there. At the beginning of each school's entry, the number in parentheses behind the school name represents the section location within the township. Through excerpts from old newspapers and interviews with former teachers and students, the book provides a glimpse of what life was like in the country schools of Marion County, Iowa. At the end of the book, an appendix lists the teachers alphabetically with the names of schools where they taught. A special section with enlarged photos from some of the schools is also included there.

Acknowledgements

Thank you to my editor Hannah Crawford, my graphic designer Alexis Thomas, and my map designer William Buttrey. Thanks also to my daughter Carlyn Wei Marron, Linda Porter, Artie Van Zee, and Marcie Vander Leest for the many hours spent copying the names of teachers from the official records at the Newton AEA. As a member of the Marion County Writers Workshop, I have received much encouragement and helpful suggestions from my colleagues and our facilitator Mike Van Natta. This group meets weekly to read and critique each other's writing.

Thank you to the many former country school students and teachers who shared their experiences. When I began working on this project in 2008, there were two binders of pictures and information at the schoolhouse museum in the Marion County Historical Village. Now, because of information from this group, there are six binders of pictures and personal stories. Thank you to the Knoxville Library for allowing access to the genealogy society room where I gathered much information from early county newspapers. I am also grateful to the Pella Historical Society and the Marion County Historical Society for the use of pictures and other information from their archives.

Many of the school stories and pictures were previously published in the *Pella Chronicle* and the *Knoxville Journal*. Their publication awakened an interest in country schools that prompted many former students and teachers to share their stories, adding a rich personal touch to *The History of Marion County*'s rural schools.

Museum Schools

East Amsterdam on its original location at 198th Place, southwest of Pella. Owned by the Pella Historical Society.

Pleasant Ridge moved to the Marion County Historical Village at 402 Willets Drive, Knoxville. Owned by the Marion County Historical Society.

Map of Clay Township

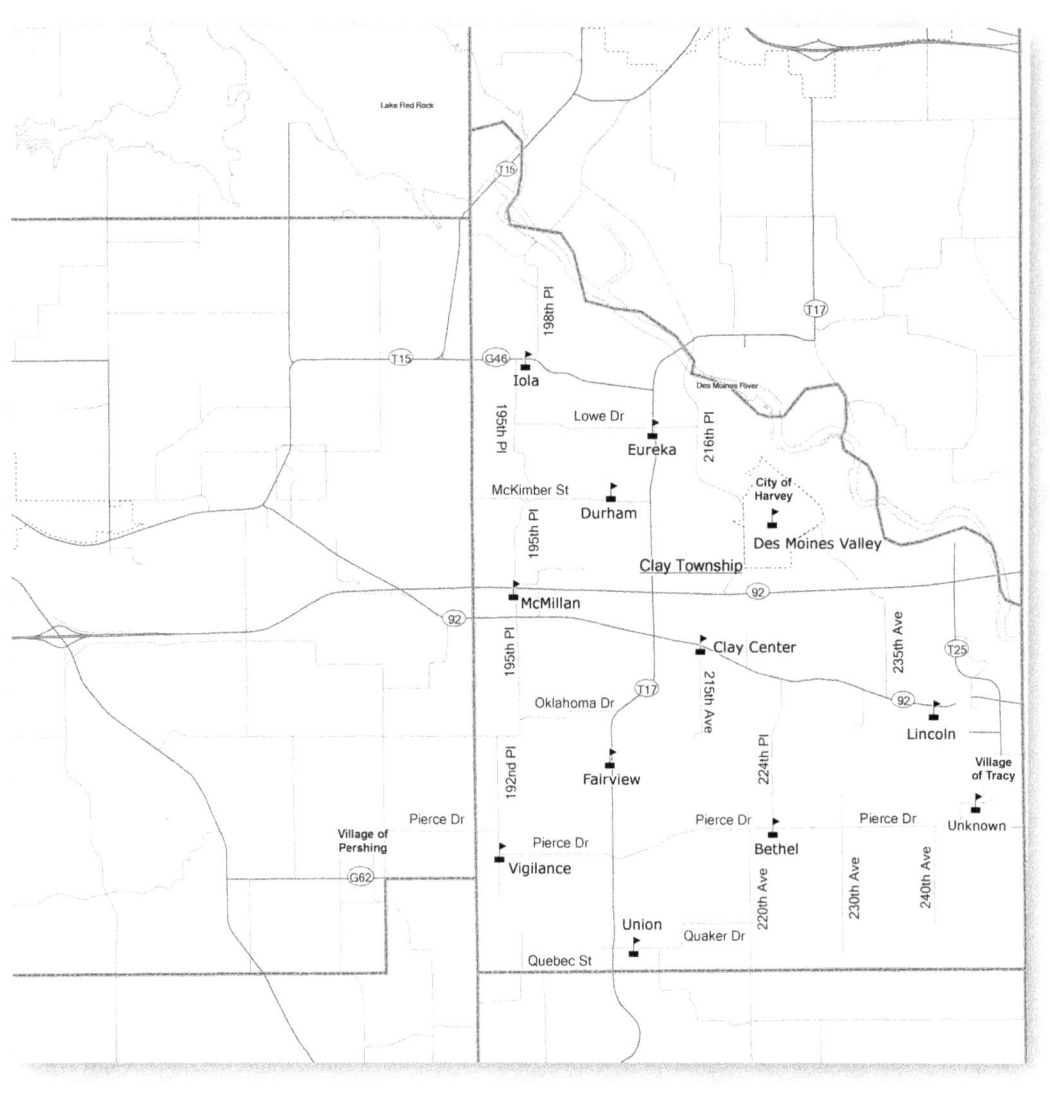

THE SCHOOLS OF
Clay Township

Bethel School (27)

Bethel – This photo is from a postcard taken some time after 1915, when the children at Bethel gathered to ride to Tracy. They rode to their new school in what was called a kid wagon drawn by horses.

THE BETHEL COUNTRY School was southwest of Tracy. The old records indicate there were once two schools known as East Bethel and West Bethel. It appears that they had merged into one school by 1898.

According to *The Knoxville Journal* of July 1882 the neighborhood came with food and music of accordion, organ, and violin at the close of the term as a surprise for teacher Hollie Harrington. In September 1882, *The Journal* reported that H. N. Rouze had removed the old school building from Bethel to his farm.

In 1914, after building a new schoolhouse, Tracy became the first consolidated school in the county. Bethel was part of that consolidation. The picture to the left shows students in front of the old Bethel School. They rode to their new school in what was called a "kid wagon," drawn by horses. The driver was Worth Bruere, the tallest man in the picture. Some families represented were Sarver, Cade, McCarty, Fridlington, Cox, and Leiby. (The picture was provided by Dorothy Vande Kieft whose mother was school teacher Ruth Fridlington)

Teachers designated by (E) for East Bethel and (W) for West Bethel were: Alice Grant (E) 1878; G. Glenn (E), Miss Durham (W) 1879; Miss Hollie Harrington (E), Miss Mary Durham (E), Jeanie Glen 1882; Miss Sarah Waln (W) 1885; Clara Hamilton (E), Etta Owens (W) 1886; Miss Kate Brennen (W) 1890; Charlie Brodigum (E) 1892; Miss Rose Mann (W) 1894; Charles Brodigum (W), Etta Bevins (W), H. T. Curtis (E), C. T. Brodigum (E) 1895; Ida C. Hall, T. L. Vernon 1898; Alta Marsh, Ellen Elder 1900; Mella Rankin, Alta Marsh 1903; Berneice Rolfe, Claudia Herny, H. H. Van Benthuysen 1904; Thomas Cooper 1905; Pauline Avery 1906; Mella Rankin, Katherine Sturgeon 1907; Katherine Sturgeon, Thomas Cooper 1908; Jennie Coon 1909; Junior Conner, Fern Collins, Cecil F. Way 1910; Bertha Surder 1911; Grace Ruple 1912; Marjorie Cooper 1913; and Grace Ruple 1914.

At the opposite end of the county on February 2, 1915, an election was held to consolidate Pleasantville and Pleasant Grove Township. This consolidation closed the country schools of Conn, Hawkeye, Ladoga, Spalti, Stringtown, Thorntown, Wesson, and Wheeling.

Clay Center (16)

Clay Center, 1935 – Front row: Nelson Roozeboom, Hubert Harrington, Wallace Harvey, and Katherine Hoksbergen. Row two: Albert Hoksbergen, Wendell Harvey, Marie Harrington, Henrietta Hoksbergen, and Winifred Harvey. Row three: Robert Harrington, Pat Riggens, Forest Harrington, Teacher Hattie Harvey, Virginia Harrington, Eugene Harrington, and Charles Harrington.

LIKE THE SCHOOLS in Franklin and Dallas Townships that also have the word "Center" in their names, the name of Clay Center School helped establish its location. Although townships are generally divided into neat squares, when a river as large as the Des Moines runs diagonally through a county it results in some oddly shaped townships, making it difficult to exactly pinpoint the center of the township. Clay Center School was a mile or two southwest of Harvey, near the center of section 16, north of old Highway 92 and west of the road connecting Harvey to old 92.

A March 1875 *Knoxville Journal* noted that interested people gathered at the Clay Center School for railroad meetings with an average attendance of 41. This was the period when every small community was hoping to attract a railroad. And schoolhouses served as good places to assemble.

In January 1882, *The Knoxville Journal* reported that Miss Tillie Hamilton couldn't teach because of rheumatism and had been replaced by Beatrice Reichard. In September of 1883, it stated that Miss Mollie McKee had given up and gone home with a toothache. (One wonders if she stayed home a few days or the rest of the year.)

I talked with Henrietta Roozeboom Vander Hart about her school days (in the 1930s) at Clay Center. She said the schoolhouse and yard were on the property of the Dale and Mary Harrington family, situated between their house and barn. She remembers walking through the barnyard to get to the school. Old Highway 92 was paved during the time she attended school.

There were times when the snow drifts completely covered the fences. This did not close the school but caused her dad to take the precautionary measure of walking her to school. She could barely see through the scarf wrapped around her face. On one occasion her feet were so cold that the teacher filled a pan with snow and made her sit by the stove. At the time she thought this was dumb, since she wanted hot water to thaw out her feet. One day when sleet fell all day, the children slipped their way home through about four inches of sleet.

Most of the children who attended Clay Center were the children of farm families. The Riggens, however, had a coal mine south of 92, and one of the Harringtons (there were three in the neighborhood) ran a drag line for strip mines as well as farmed. Henrietta often stopped at one of the Harringtons' on the way home, where she enjoyed an after school snack of fresh baked bread with peanut butter. A real treat, as her mother only put jelly, not peanut butter on her sandwiches.

The students went sledding, played ball, and participated in group games such as Annie-Annie Over. During one game, she and Albert Hoksbergen collided as they ran around a corner of the schoolhouse. This collision left a memorable impression on her and, at the time, an even more memorable impression on him—an egg on his head. Ouch!

Mary Ann Systma Gruber attended only one year. She and her sister Audrey were the only two students in school that year. They did all their work in the morning and played Rook in the afternoon.

The teacher Irene Vriezelaar made some kind of "prune thing" (from surplus commodities) and enticed them into eating it by telling them they wouldn't get the mumps.

Teachers at Clay Center included Miss Fannie Hammond, G. A. Durham 1874; Miss Amanda Waln 1875; Mr. Hammond 1876; Miss A. E. Waln 1877; Miss Clara Banks 1880; Miss Alice Zugg, Miss Ida Hanks 1881; Miss Tillie Hamilton, Miss Beatrice Reichard 1882; Miss Mollie McKee 1883; Miss Mattie Reichard 1884; Eva Horney 1886; Miss Mary Vaughn 1892; Edith Harrington, Miss Todd, Miss Eva Dailey, S. McVay 1893; Eva Dailey 1895; Roy Young, Myrtle Sharon 1898; Nellie Cooper 1900; Fessie M. Palmer, Orpha Woody 1903; Inez Ferguson, Nora Davis 1904; Fessie M. Palmer, Myrtle Shaver 1905; Myrtle Shaver 1906; Rosa Brubaker, Mabel De Witt 1907; Bertha Sarver 1908-09; Mary Woody 1910; Bertha Harvey 1911; Beryl O'Dell 1912; Nina Lyons, Beryl O'Dell 1913; Marie Mendenhall 1914-15; Ruth Nicholson 1916-17; Mrs. Nora Houser 1919-21; Mrs. Fay Douglas 1922-23; Dorothy Snow 1930-31; Pauline Harsin 1933; Floyd Nolin 1934; Miss Hattie Harvey 1935; Pauline Rankin 1936; Wilma L. Nicholson 1937; Lorraine Hanrick Rankin 1938; Twylah Coolley 1939-40; and Irene M. Vriezelaar 1941.

Des Moines Valley (10)

NOW A MUSEUM, the Des Moines Valley School stands high on a hill in Harvey. The two-story brick structure was completed in 1902 at a cost of $5,000. At the time, the little settlement of Harvey was enjoying rapid growth with several stores, a hotel, a bank, two churches, a brick yard, an excelsior plant, nearby coal mines, and access to the Wabash rail line. In 1901, there were forty-four students enrolled in the school.

While the average home in Harvey was being

built for around $600, the school board, anticipating continued growth, authorized the building of the grand brick school.

The museum contains many pictures of students, including the years when the 8th grade graduates could continue as high school students. Both the first (1924) and the last graduating class (1946) had only 5 senior graduates.

The first mention I found of this school was from *The Knoxville Journal*, July 6, 1876: "The School of Des Moines Valley closed with a picnic in the grove near the school. This is Miss Alice Glenn's first school. It is due her to say that the duties and responsibilities of her place were discharged with credit to herself. Mr. Hammond's Clay Center also participated to the number of 75 in all. "

In 1893 the topic for debate at Harvey was "…that we can gain more knowledge by meditation than we can by traveling and observation."

Des Moines Valley, 1910 – 8th grade graduates. Row one: Zella Maddy Simmons, Dent Douglas, Leila Bayless Applegate, and Owan Neiswanger. Row two: Herman Maddy, George Dennis, Teacher Bessie Steen, Mary Wilson McCombs, and Richard Neiswanger.

The Harvey Centennial booklet of 1876-1976 notes that in 1928 the entire school was dismissed to walk in a drizzling rain to meet the 10:30 Wabash train in which Charles Curtis, the man who was to become his vice president, was campaigning to elect Herbert Hoover.

Bonnie Geery is the curator of the museum. She came to the Des Moines Valley School as a teacher in the fall of 1948, having had one year of experience teaching in a country school after her graduation from high school. She boarded with Wesley and Jean Bloom. On Valentine's Day in 1949 Jean introduced her to Orbra Geery, a widower whose wife had died in childbirth. Orbra was eleven years her senior and the father of five children. It must have been love at first sight because they married before school was out, and her students feted her with a shower. Later she and Orbra had four children together. When Governor Ray asked for sponsors for Southeast Asians the Geerys sponsored a Laotian family. Because they could find no preschool for one of the Laotian children, Bonnie began her twenty-year career as a preschool teacher.

I talked with former student Joyce Vander Werff about her experiences at Des Moines Valley. She found it a very comfortable school environment because all the kids had grown up together and knew each other. She felt the school board had done a great job in finding good teachers and there was also a closeness between students and teachers. She remains friends with Marilyn Padgett Vander Linden, with whom she started kindergarten.

I also talked with Karen Wardenburg, who echoed her sister's assessments of the quality of their teachers and the closeness of the community.

"No one had better clothing than anyone else," she said. She recalls that each school day was opened with the pledge of allegiance and the Lord's Prayer. Around 1957 the school got inside water and indoor bathrooms. Before that water was carried in and when the well was dry students would bring fruit jars of water to be emptied into the dispenser where they drank from a common cup. One of the most memorable days was when her class watched the inauguration of President Eisenhower at her parents' home. They were only the second family in Harvey to purchase a TV. She said she was thankful for those years in a small school in which children were taught responsibility.

A partial list of teachers includes: Lue Evans 1873; Miss Emily Wiegand 1875; Miss Alice Glenn 1876; Miss Glenn 1878; Miss Hattie Harrington 1880; Alice Durham 1882; Luella Woods, Lillie Workerman 1886; Ella Burke 1890; Lou McLaughlin 1891; Miss Maggie Watkins, Mrs. Warren 1892; Alice Warren 1893; P. E. Adams, Bertha Moore 1895; Maggie Cooper, A. H. Crosby, Lottie McClymond 1898; Eva Wilson, Nora Spalti, Minnie Gaston 1900; Mr. Cochrane 1901; Mrs. Mae Goldizen, Minnie Tysseling, Leta Bennifield, Mary Mathews 1905; Mary Mathews 1906; Nannie Hyatt, Delia Rietveld, Martha Hines 1911; Beulah Stuff, Delia Rietveld, Grace Larew 1912; Beryl O'Dell, Gertrude McCullough 1913; Anna Rose Hamilton 1931; Helen Neyenisch 1932-33; Harvey D. Bruere, Mary J. Bruere 1946; Mrs. Annie M. Cottrell, Mrs. Lucile Morgan, Mrs. Reefa Harvey 1947; Mrs. Norma Reep, Mrs. Bertha Mayberry 1948; Bonnie Cooper, Irene Van Gorp, Violet McDonnell 1949; Nora Lash, Edith Swartz, Dorothy Anderson, Reefa Harvey 1950; Dorothy Anderson, Mrs. Mildred Lundy, Duane K. Williams, Arlys J. Beaver, Mrs. Jean Johnson 1951; Ernest Klinker 1952; Gertrude McCollough 1954; Gertrude McCullogh 1955; Mrs. Maryellen Beaver, Mrs. Cleo Bennett, Mrs. Jean Johnson 1956; Avis Van Zomeren 1957; and Ferol Chamberlain, Isobel Isley 1961.

Durham (8)

DURHAM WAS LOCATED three miles south and one mile east of the Red Rock Dam. The town was laid out in 1875 as a station on the Chicago, Burlington, and Quincy railroad. It was first named Merrill, then English, and in 1877 was renamed Durham in honor of David Durham, an early settler from Maine. He was a prominent farmer who also operated Durham's Ferry. The town once had a hotel, post office, blacksmith shop, harness shop, barber shop, shoe shop, creamery, doctor's office, two general stores, and a school. Its little schoolhouse was so crowded some of the children attended the Eureka School which was less than a mile away (*The History of Pella, Iowa, 1847-1987*, vol. 2, p. 164).

Teachers were Miss Fannie Coffman, Miss Pace 1886; Miss Sallie Wahls 1887; Mary Momyer, C. Preston Durham 1889; Miss Sadie Waln 1890; Miss Rose Mann 1891; Miss Rose Mason 1892; Alice Warren, Albert Crosby 1894; Minnie Redding, W. J. Van Dyke, Mary Sharon, Nora Sullivan 1895; and Minnie Forsythe, Jennie Johnson, Miss Minnie Redding, Mrs. Miller 1896.

Eureka (4)

Eureka, 1912 – Back row: Jeanette Roorda, Luella Millard, Pearl Millard, Ollie Parson, Reifa Lancaster, Beulah Lancaster, Sylvia Millard, Blanche Lerew, and Teacher Faye Cummings. Middle row: Susie Leighton, Violet Lancaster, Milton Redding, Marion Toom, Ilo Roberts, Gertrude Roorda, Bessie Millard, (small girl behind Bessie not identified), Gertrude Parson, Oral Adair, and Jennie Van Engelenhoven. Front row: (unidentified), Robert Roorda, David Roorda, Lester Redding, Lizzie Millard, Ester Redding, John Van Engelenhoven, Lloyd Parson, Arie Van Engelenhoven, and Lester Bryant.

EUREKA—I LOVE THAT WORD. I learned it from John W. Groenendyke, science teacher at Pella High, who explained that it was from the Greek, "I've found it!" Archimedes figured out a way to calculate the purity of gold by applying the principle of specific gravity. Supposedly he was in the bathtub when he realized measuring the amount of water his body displaced would be a way of doing this. "Eureka," he shouted. (The idea may not have occurred to Archimedes while bathing but it was a way for students to learn about it—see how many years I've remembered it!) Eureka was a name given to many early settlements and I imagine this school was a place where students had many eureka moments.

The first Eureka School was a red brick one constructed shortly after the Civil War. It was replaced with a frame building in 1929. In 1958 the school was closed due to reorganization, and some students were sent to Pella while others were sent to Knoxville. The building remained in place as a community center until 1961 when it was moved to Knoxville. The flagpole was moved to the Eureka cemetery which is on the other side of the road where the Eureka School once stood. Turn off T17 on Lowe Drive to reach the building site.

For many years it was the custom for local newspapers to carry columns about local neighborhoods. The writers told about local weather conditions, births and deaths, visitors, and occasionally mentioned the school. Here are excerpts from the Eureka columns:

Knoxville Journal of March 1874: "The Eureka School taught by Professor Reeves has an average attendance of 50."

Knoxville Journal of February 1875: "A new stove was put in the school at a cost of $25. The average attendance is 40."

Knoxville Journal of November 1884: "The Eureka Literary is dead." (That's too bad. Apparently the adults of the community didn't have time to participate in these "intellectual" meetings at the school house.)

Knoxville Journal of September 15, 1938. "Miss Reefa Holdsworth has these beginners, little Marion

Vander Heiden, Edna Kersey, and Eugene Beaver." The next month the Barnett family moved into the neighborhood as an October column tells us that there were three new students: Cathryn, Patty, and Betty Barnett.

Country schools were still going strong that year. *The Knoxville Journal* of October 6, 1938, said that Marion County was one of the leading counties in the matter of country school enrollment with 5,608 enrolled. There were 101 school boards and an average attendance of 18.8 at each school.

Larry Toom, who graduated from 8th grade in 1955, recalls that a neighborhood community club met monthly at the school for potlucks, singing, and visiting. In addition to the traditional Christmas program, students from Eureka also went caroling in the neighborhood. The covered bridge just to the south of the Eureka cemetery was the gathering place for students after school and during vacation time.

Here are many of the teachers that served Eureka School: Prof. J. H. Reeves 1874; Miss M. Wiegand 1875; Miss Mattie Richard, Miss Mary Parks 1885; A. Whaley 1886; Cora D. Wolf 1887; Mr. Osborn 1888; A. H. Crosby 1895; Flora Kester, Belle Henby 1896; Bula Stuff, Stella Winegardner 1898; Belle Henby 1899; Anna Sullivan, Belle Henby 1900; Marnie Belvill, Maud Laummer 1903; Ethel Welcher 1904; Effie Haines, Ethel Curtis 1905; Mella Rankin 1906; Delia Rietveld 1907-08; Faye Cummings 1909; Grace Larew 1910; Eva Worstell 1911; Aura Dickey, Aletha Lemmon 1912; Ruth Hill 1913; Govert Hackert, Mrs. C. T. Larew 1914; Hazel Conant, Sara Sorenson, Belle Robertson 1915; Pansy Tellet, Odessa Maiter 1916; Mildred Hause 1917; Helen Harrington 1919; Dorothy Clark 1920; Alta Miller 1921; Pearl Bonifield 1922-23; Georgia Roorda 1925; Alta Miller Sarver 1926; Dorothea Bean 1927-28; Hilda Palmquist 1929; Mabel Ray 1930; Helen Lancaster 1932-33; Hazel Rowland 1934; Helen Lancaster 1935; Marie Maddy 1936; Reefa Holdsworth 1937-38; Wilma Beaver 1939-40; Wilma Roorda 1941-42; Mrs. Emily De Witt 1943; Ada De Haan 1944; Hazel Worrall 1945; Darlene McDonnell 1947-51; Edgar Van Arkel 1950-51; Mrs. Arlys Beaver 1952; Mrs. Lucile Morgan 1953-55; Mrs. Jean Johnson 1956; and Mrs. Reefa Harvey 1957.

Fairview (20)

FAIRVIEW STANDS ON its original site, three miles southwest of Harvey on the west side of Highway T17. It is being used for hay storage.

I talked with Maryellen Beaver, who taught school there in the school years 1943 and 1944. She was asked to fill a vacancy as soon as she turned eighteen in the fall of 1943. She described her ten pupils as all good kids with good parents. While teaching there she roomed with a family in the neighborhood even though her parents lived in the adjacent Union School District. It was war time and they did not have an extra car, which would have meant she had to ride four miles to school on a horse. When she got married she stopped teaching. Thelma Hohl took her place as the next teacher at Fairview. She roomed with Maryellen and her husband and the two women kept in touch until Thelma died at age one hundred.

In 1948 Maryellen was again called upon to fill a vacancy at the Union School, the one she had attended. This time she had twenty students in all grades. There was a special challenge to prepare six students for their 8th grade exams. That year, she said, she did many of the things her grade school teacher Bessie Kenney had done. Good teachers were good mentors for many of us.

Fairview closed in the early 1950s and then reopened because McMillan had become too crowded. McMillan student Joan Anderson attended Fairview in the 3rd and 4th grade, getting there by a yellow school bus. Janet Westberg, also from the McMillan School District, attended Fairview from 4th through 8th grade. She recalls lunch of potatoes wrapped in foil and baked on the school heating stove. Water was provided by Don and Jennie Harsin. She said that teacher Mrs. Mott always carried a hanky as she was subject to hay fever and that sometimes she was so tired she needed to lie on a bench for a while. Although Mrs. Mott had health problems, it did not prevent her from teaching for thirty years.

Maryellen Beaver said that at one time the districts of McMillan, Victory, Union, Clay Center, and Vigilance had considered building a high school to serve the students of the area. She felt that was not necessary as both Knoxville and Tracy were close by. However, she said it was a sad time when reorganization came and all these country schools closed.

Teachers included Miss Jennie Glenn 1882; Miss Masteller 1893; Miss Daisy Clarke 1894; Mary Clark 1895; Mary Simmons 1896; Ollie Davis, Minnie Savage 1898; Mary Sarver 1900; Maude Inskeep, Rosa Rice 1903; Lula Townsend 1904; Eugenia McKenzie, Bertha Hughes 1905; Stella Brubaker 1906; Pauline Sarver 1907; Bertha Woody 1909-10; Faye Cummings 1911; Edna Townsend 1912; Helen Cooper 1913; Helen Osborne 1914; Velma E. Wilkins, Pearl Bonifield 1916; Ve Lola Blair 1917; Flora McKinzie 1919; Jennie Leuty 1920; Daisy Musgrove 1921-22; Amy E. Norris 1924; Ruth Fridlington 1925; Malvina Neely 1927; Hester H. Hazen 1928-29; Zelma Crozier 1930; Edna M. Zeigler 1931-32; Arlene Beaver 1934-1935; Laura Belle Overton, Catherine Larew 1937; Harold O'Dell, Pearl Bonifield Poe 1938-40; Helen Beary 1936; Miss Loreen Harvey 1941; Mrs. Dorothy Mae Furgy 1942; Maryellen Johnson 1943; Mrs. Maryellen Beaver 1944; Thelma Hohl 1945; Minnie McDonnell 1950; Jennie Evans 1951; and Evelyn Mott 1957.

Fairview, spring 1947 – Teacher Thelma Hol with students Phillip Maddison, Lyla Harvey, Larry Harson, Kay Harsin, Larry Harvey, John David Lee, Lois Harvey, Norman Milledge, Louis Harvey, and Larry Milledge. Toddler with bat is Leslie J. Beaver, son of Maryellen Beaver.

Iola (31)

Iola, 1929-30 – Row one: Martin Van Veen, Antonie Van Veen, Harold Van Veldhuizen, Joe Woods, and Maurice Verros. Row two: Lester Durham, Jean Woods, Charles Breuklander, Edward Beaver, Arthur Breuklander, and Beulah Beaver. Row three: Marion Verros, Telida Verros, Ruby Matthews, Pauline Verros, and Teacher Bertha Augustine.

IOLA SCHOOL WAS about five miles southwest of Pella on the old Knoxville road near the turnoff to Harvey. According to information supplied by J. P. Durham in an unidentified newspaper article, this school was organized in 1863 and built on ground given by D. T. Durham. His father was David Durham, who was among the first settlers in Marion County in 1843. The family had settled near the Wabash Bridge on what was afterwards known as Durham's Ford.

In 1906 a newer building replaced the one built in 1863. On the night of January 21, 1926, fire destroyed this building. A temporary structure costing $138.79 was put up. A permanent modern structure served the needs of the district until the school was closed at the end of the 1955-56 school year. This building was moved to Harvey and remodeled into a home.

Old school records indicate that before 1903 when an eight months' term was ordered the school was held for only six months equally divided between a winter and spring term. The lowest salary paid was $18 per month. One of the teachers was charged with "inflicting cruel and unusual treatment" and for his neglect to give blackboard exercise in arithmetic for a period of five weeks. A trial date was set so both sides could be heard but he solved the matter by resigning.

When brothers Gerrit, Bert, and Dave Verros attended school in the early 1900s, a teacher from Knoxville drove a mule-driven cart to school. One evening, as she was giving the boys a ride home from school, they met a noisy steam engine pulling a threshing machine. The alarmed mule began twitching his ears back and forth as he edged towards the ditch. The driver jumped down from the engine and grabbed the mule's bridle to avert an accident. The teacher blushed as he asked, "What's the trouble, ma'am, is your ass a little nervous?" (Now isn't that just the kind of talk that a school boy of that day would find scandalous enough to pass down to the next generation?)

From the official records comes this list of teachers: Mary Parks 1886; Mary Stout 1895; Jessie Brown, Grace Stuenenberg 1896; Julia Hocking 1898; Myrtle Sharon 1900; Leona Vander Linden 1903; Orpha Woody, Ethel Ghrist 1904; Mary E. Woody 1906-08; Faye Cummings 1910; Maude

Wilson, Beulah Worsted 1911; Lois Kutz 1912; Mrs. Mair, Nellie Smith 1913; Duinnie Gregory 1914; Christina Leffler 1915; Erma Barker 1916; Lora Flanders 1917; Hazel Gibson 1919; Grace Toom 1920-21; Annette Vander Hart 1922-23; Glen Holllingshead 1924; Vera Covey 1925; Vera Covey 1927; Bertha Augustine 1928; Bertha Augustine 1930-32; Kenneth Durham 1933-34; Grayce Anna Richards 1935-40; Twylah Coolley 1941; Bertha Augustine 1943-44; Bertha Augustine Johnson 1945-47; Mrs. Velda Dunn 1948-50; and Ceola Liebhart 1951-55. From an undated article written during the time Bertha Augustine was teacher comes this additional list: F. M. Harsin, Almeda Weigand, Mary E. Durham, Mollie Ellinwood, Elizabeth Black, W. F. Moore, Fannie Lindley, Jennie Simpkins, Sallie Martin, Florence Durham, E. E. Brown, G. A. Durham, Nannie Bingaman, Phena McCollum, Mary McClymond, Mattie J. Durham, Nora White, Mary Momyer, Nellie Wright, A. L. Amsberry, Nettie Simpson, Eva Scott, Jessie E. Brown, Fannie Eberhart, Ella Decker, Delia Rietveld, Suska Woody, Miss Fellers, June Metcalf, J. P. Durham, Luella Evans, and Mary Davenport.

Lincoln North and South

Lincoln North and South – Student in window.

BUILT SOON AFTER the Civil War, the original Lincoln School was a mile northwest of Tracy on Highway 92. At the time there was no school in the town of Tracy, so some children attended Lincoln while others attended the Bethel School. Because several children who attended Lincoln lived on the island, a school was built there. The island schoolhouse became North Lincoln while the original building was called South Lincoln. Surnames of families who attended school on the island were Benscoter, George, Long, McIntosh, Bixler, Lundy, McCarty, Greenland, Brubaker, McCombs, Grahan, Kline, Current, Marsh, De Koning, Miller, Moleman, Norris, Nossaman, Reed, Ryan, Simmons, Spears, Sweem, and Willis. When Leo Brubaker was the only school-age child left, he was sent to Tracy. The school building was moved to a hillside near the Island Bridge and converted to a family home.

After the consolidation of schools in 1915, the South Lincoln building was moved to Tracy and remodeled as a home. Pupils who attended this school came from the families of Barnes, Brubaker, Cooper, Converse, Current, Crozier, Davis, Doughman, Fitzsimmons, Gladson, Guillion, Hill, Himes, Hubbard, Kline, Lyman, Marsh, Masterson, Mathews, McCarty, Morris, Plate, Ryan, Sherman, Utter, and Solver (*Tracy Centennial—100 Years of History from Tracy and Surrounding Area*, pp. 91-92).

An 1891 *Knoxville Journal* story reported that the following North Lincoln class A students averaged 95: Valera Stafford, Mary Cooper, Bertie Gilchrist, and Eddie Benscoter. The writer went on to say that there had been no school at South Lincoln for six months and patrons were inquiring.

Lincoln North teachers were Mr. D. W. Lamb 1874; Mr. Kline 1881; Mrs. Jennie Delaplaine 1883; Miss Bertha Moore 1884; Mattie Durham 1886; Mrs. T. F. Doughman 1889; Miss Sadie Waln 1890; Miss Edith Wright 1891; Bertha Moore, Rosa Rice 1895; P. Edgar Adonis 1896; Maude Inskeep, Lizzie Coster 1898; Minnie Tysseling, Blanche Taggart, Mary Mathews 1900; Hilda L. Bowman 1910-11; and Gertrude Miller 1912.

Lincoln South teachers were Josie Mann, Alice Warren 1895; Mary Roller, Miss Vivian Berley 1896; Bertha Coster 1898; Jennie K. Johnson, W. H. Lucas 1899; Anna Ridenour, Minnie Tysseling 1900; Miss Estella Laughlin 1902; Sylvia Woody, Beatrice Smith, Mary Roller 1904; Mella Rankin 1905; Ruby B. Miller, Mrs. Susie N. Dolan 1906; Mae Hamilton 1907; Alleta Cunningham 1908; Alice Phelps, Mary Roller 1909; and Nora M. Wesner 1912-13 (North or South?).

McMillan (18)

McMillan North and South, 1955 – First day of school with the Oldsmobile school bus. Left to right: Tom Loynachan, driver Don Harsin, Bob Loynachan, and Nancy Loynachan.

MCMILLAN SCHOOL WAS originally located a few hundred feet northeast of the southwest corner of Highway 92 and 195th place. After the school closed, it was moved to 1934 Old Highway 92 and converted into a farm building.

In the early days, the country school was the center of community life as well as a place where children were taught. For several decades, one of the popular activities was "the literary." The January 12, 1901 *Journal* reported that the question for the McMillan Literary was if "the present method of paying road tax in labor should be abolished and the same be paid in money and the supervisors asked to hire the work done." There would have been two or three debaters on each side and then a panel of judges would declare the winner.

Nancy Loynachan Johansen sent a letter describing an incident that happened to her while she was in 2nd grade at the McMillan School. Driver Don Harsin used an old gray Oldsmobile (1938 or 39 model) which they called the school bus to transport Nancy, her brother Bob, and cousins Ted and Tom Loynachan to and from school. One evening after being dropped off she walked around behind the car and was hit by a pickup and knocked unconscious. She spent two days in the hospital. For years after the accident her mother kept her two-toned green dented lunch box because the doctor told her it had saved Nancy's life. When she first saw the pickup, Nancy threw her hands in the air and the lunch box came down right between her head and the pickup. Not long after that, the parents of the students decided to paint the Oldsmobile yellow and put a sign on top with big letters which said SCHOOL BUS.

Another student, Dixie Loynachan, remembers the time she got locked in the toilet at recess and no one missed her. She also said one of her teachers used cement blocks as steps to get across a fence where she had her trailer parked. The students liked to tease her by taking away the blocks so she couldn't cross the fence. One day when the 8th grade boys were helping a teacher move a piano it tipped over and almost fell on the teacher. No one was hurt but the piano did ruin the baby buggy that one of the girls had brought to school.

I also talked with Joan Anderson, retired Knoxville teacher, who attended this school. Joan, Linda Bachman, and Jewel Woody all started school there and graduated together from Knoxville in 1967. She recalls that in 2nd grade someone helped her cheat because she couldn't keep "two, too, and to" straight. She remembers that on days when it was really cold, one of their teachers would gather the students around the stove and read to them all day.

No one seems to remember this, but at one time there were two schools called McMillan North and McMillan South.

Teachers at the North School included Miss Emily Copland 1875; S. E. Moore 1878; Miss Clara Banks 1882; Emma Jones, Alice Ran 1886; Miss Alice Waln 1891; Mrs. Alice Warren, Miss White 1892; W. H. Lucas 1894; Marye Sharon 1895; Delia J. Rietveld 1898; Ollie Gelderblom, Alta Marsh, Mrs. Hettie Britton 1900; Mella Rankin 1904; Emma Gilchrist, Orpha Woody 1905; Mella Rankin, Ethel Curtis 1906; Susky Woody 1907; Chester A. Metz, Eva M. Cory 1908; Armina Ferguson, Bertha Woody, Eva Cory 1909; Nellie Wilson 1910; Mary Woody 1911; Faye Cummings 1912; Beulah Jones 1913; Edna Townsend 1914; Mrs. Ollin Freeman, Erma Kinser 1915; Myrtle Sharon 1916; Helen Osborne 1917; Mary Sims 1919; Frances Conrey 1920; Helen Harrington 1921; Dorothy Clark 1922-25; Paulina Stittsworth 1925; Bertha Augustine 1926-27; Susie Orcutt 1928; Mary Ghrist 1930; Ruby Seaman 1931-32; Miss Ruby Penland 1933; Helen Harsin 1935-38; Helen Adair 1939-40; Ruth Thomas 1941; Martha Louise Whaley 1943; Barbara Coffman 1944; Rena Fee Welch 1945; Norma Jean Emerson 1947; Norma Jean Cummings 1948; Miss Elizabeth Blackman 1949; Mrs. Evelyn De Joode 1950; Gene McCombs 1951; Mrs. Gene McCombs 1952; Gene McCombs 1953; Maxine Adams 1954; and Mrs. Mildred Gurney 1955-57.

Teachers at McMillan South were G. L. Hackert 1898; Myrtle Sharon 1903; Myrtle Sharon, Lucy Ward 1904; Lillie Mick, Mella Rankin 1905; Mollie B. Nolan, Mary Rogers, Helen McConahey 1908; and Anna McMillen, Myrtle M. Sharon 1907.

Union (32)

Union School, May 10, 1935 (last day of school) – Some preschool children were visitors. Row 1: Martin Johnson, Leona Schimmel, Kenneth Knox, Aaron Knox, Shirley Fridlington, Junella Harkness, Dale Vos, and Gilbert Schimmel. Row 2: Dora Schimmel, Melvin Vos, Herbert Laird, William Schimmel, James Schimmel, and Teacher Daisy Fridlington holding Henry Dirk Schimmel. Row 3: Marguerite Knox, Faith Fridlington, "Little Bertha" Schimmel, Jacob Vos, and Loren Johnson. Row 4: Helen Laird, Jennie Schimmel, Gertrude Vos, "Big Bertha" Schimmel, Lucille Johnson, and Pete De Jong.

UNION SCHOOL WAS about three miles southwest of Tracy on the east side of T17. The earliest records I have found for this school are in a teacher's record book for the years 1913-23. Each teacher rates the coal house and out houses as being in good condition while the schoolhouse takes a downhill slide from fair to poor. The book shows the flexibility teachers had in moving students through the grades. In 1920 there were six beginners, four of whom were only four years old while the other two were five years old. There were also six 2nd graders ranging in age from five to ten years old. Teachers had some difficulty in consistently spelling the Dutch names correctly. Starting as little Henry Roozeboom, he becomes Henry Rosenbaum in first grade and then reverts back to Roozeboom. I'm sure it was very confusing when there were also Roozenbooms in the neighborhood. The traditional subjects were taught, except the year Miriam Fletcher added agriculture for the boys and sewing for the girls.

According to Marguerite Knox, a former student, Union, McMillan, Victory, Vigilance, and Fairview were a part of the Victory Consolidated District, which at one time was so large they considered building a high school in the area.

Marguerite especially enjoyed the holidays. In her first year of school, her teacher baked Valentine cookies. She got one of the larger cookies but one of the older girls persuaded her to exchange it for her smaller one. Marguerite had never seen a decorated cookie, so she took it home to show her little brother who, of course, ate part of it. Almost all of the Valentines were handmade, she said.

At Christmas time, the students exchanged ten-cent gifts and were visited by Santa Claus, played by Neal Schimmel. Even though he didn't have the traditional red coat, the little ones were sure he was the real deal. There was the sound of bells as the sleigh arrived. The teacher would invite Santa Claus to come in and stand near the stove because he was so cold having come from the North Pole. When he got ready to leave, the teacher told the students not to look out the window because they might scare the reindeer.

One day while walking home, Marguerite got stuck in the mud. When fellow student Pete De Jong was unable to pull her out, he got neighbor Willie Van Hall to assist.

Marguerite walked a mile to school. Her schoolmate Bill Schimmel had a very short walk as the school was located on his father's farm. Bill would wait until he heard the five-minute bell and would then start to school. He also had the advantage of being able to go home for lunch. Bill laughed about the time that a groundhog took up residence under the schoolhouse, and every afternoon at about 1:30 they could hear it gnawing under the teacher's desk. (A memorable distraction, but better a groundhog than a beaver.)

When the students hadn't finished their work, they were supposed to stay after school to complete it. One day when Bill hadn't finished his arithmetic, he tried to sneak out but was caught by the teacher. When students needed punishment they were sent by the teacher to cut their own switch from the elderberry bush. There were as many as thirty students during the time that Bill attended and sometimes they would hassle the teacher. Bill must have behaved himself most of the time because he graduated from the 8th grade in 1936 with an honor "I." (This recognition was given to the top ten percent of the country school graduates.)

In the 1942-43 school year, when Edgar Van Arkel was teacher, a new family moved into the neighborhood bringing lice to the school. Marguerite was in high school and picked up lice from her younger siblings. Her mother used a comb dipped in kerosene to kill the lice. Edgar recalls the Friday afternoon that his only kindergarten child was standing at the blackboard when her bloomers dropped. He hunted frantically for a safety pin in the desk. Finding none, he sent the girl along with two others to the outhouse with paper clips. Upon returning, the bloomers stayed up! On Monday before school she proudly lifted her dress and said to him. "Mr. Van Arkel, we went to Oskaloosa on Saturday and Mom got me new bloomers with elastic in them. See?" She pulled them out from her waist to show him they wouldn't fall!

Donna De Jong Blevins, who lives in Tyler, Texas, sent me some pictures and information about the school. Her most memorable event was the time she and her sister Alice got caught in a blizzard walking home from school. They couldn't tell whether they were walking in the road or in the ditch. They sat down in the road and cried. Then they remembered that they were told to keep moving and to listen for the sound of Dad's voice coming to get them. They stopped at Uncle John De Jong's farm but were sent back to the road to continue walking because Uncle John had no telephone to let her grandparents know where they were. Donna's mother had died when Donna was only two and the family had moved in with the grandparents, Don and Betsy De Jong. The girls kept walking and soon they heard their dad's voice calling. He had indeed come to meet them and lead them safely home.

Teachers of the Union School included Alice Maddy 1886; Nellie Carr, Arthur Pea 1891; Wilbur Collins 1892; Miss Dinwiddie 1894; Anna Young, May Johnson 1895; Viola Goering, Floyd Stotts 1896; Edith Stroud 1898; Jean Rogers 1899; Jean Rogers, Stella Jenkins 1900; Mattie Rankin, Ethel

Rice 1903; Anna Funk 1904; Stella Brubaker, Atha Wolfe 1905; Ruth Rose, Pauline Sarver 1906; Pauline Sarver 1907; Burch Doughman 1908; Ve Lola Blair 1909; Bertha Sarver 1910; Mabelle Curry, Beulah Jones 1911; Odessa Spaur 1912; Ivey Brubaker, Vera Crippen 1913; Lucille Grace Murphy 1914; Helen Rankin, Ella McKillip 1915; Sylvia Barnes 1916; Margaret Houser 1917; Wilma Vande Kieft 1919; Miriam Fletcher 1920; Garnet Musgrove, Hazel Gibson 1921; Hazel Gibson 1922; Flora Mckinzie 1924; Daisy Musgrove 1925; Leona Bogaard 1927-28; Ray Vander Linden 1929; Mary V. Smith 1930; Mrs. Daisy Fridlington 1931-32; Leona Bogaard Vriezelaar 1933; Daisy Fridlington 1934-35; Phyllis Fairley 1937; Bessie Robuck 1938-39; Ruth Harrison 1940; Edgar Van Arkel 1942; Minnie McDonnell 1943; Miss Colleen Bridges 1944; Mary Ellen Johnson Beaver, Wilma Noah 1947; Jennie Evans 1949-50; Jennie Evans 1952; Mrs. Mary Osborn Carlson 1952; and Jennie Evans 1954-56.

Vigilance (30)

Vigilance, 1899 – Teacher Susie Norris. Students in no particular order: Ollie Stroud Reed, Gladys Blair Cooley, Myrtle Smith Welch, Forest Kendrick, Clella Jenkins, Ada House Brause, Miriam Rankin Mark, Iva Houser Snow, Ve Lola Blair Norris, Stella Harrington, Herman Hammond, Delmar Kendrick, Minnie Blair McClain, Ival Jenkins, Fred Houser, Helen Rankin Maddy, and Rena Jenkins.

VIGILANCE SCHOOL, EAST of Pershing, was originally located at the northeast corner of 192 Place and Pierce Drive. After the school closed, Harold Loynachan purchased the building and moved it to his farm at 1723 192 Place, where he converted it into a shop. The three windows on opposite sides of the building and the blackboards inside still give a clue to its original use. In a letter, Martha Sherwood Shivvers said she thinks Vigilance was probably built in the late 1800s near the Stroud family farm home.

"This area had been homesteaded earlier by the Loynachans, Stroud and Sherwood families, who moved west from Eastern States. Our father, John Sherwood, who was born in 1885, along with his two older sisters Mae and Nora and a younger half-sister Stella Harrington attended this school. Our father was part of the School Board in later years."

I talked with Frances Sherwood Kirkwood, Martha's younger sister in this family of eight children. Because she was large for her age, the boys picked her rather than choosing other boys for the ball team. Frances had planned to teach but graduated at sixteen and was married before eighteen, so she never realized that dream.

Some excerpts from Martha's letter:

"As with all of the rural schools, some of the

desks were large for two students to sit together; middle-sized desks were for the 'in between' and small desks near the front of the room were for the small folk. East and west windows allowed sunlight to furnish enough lighting for studying, but cloudy days were sometimes difficult. I've never learned of a teacher lighting the kerosene lamps in brackets on the walls, but they were always kept filled with fuel and the chimney clean. But these lights were needed when school programs were given at night or for a social gathering. One Thanksgiving that I remember was a community affair for all of the neighbors who were invited to share the meal and friendship and neighborliness.

Methods of teaching usually followed the same rituals unless a teacher wove in interesting features. One ritual I remember was when calling a particular class to come to the front to recite—let's say for the fourth grade reading: 'Fourth grade reading, turn, rise, and pass.' If someone did not proceed quietly, there were reprimands. Discipline was sternly practiced, but within reason, and parents respected the teacher. There was to be no whispering, no excessive noises, no note passing. I learned this the hard way when caught and my hands were spanked with a ruler."

In February of 1920, Martha turned five and after much pleading was allowed to join her two older brothers as a student at Vigilance. At age eighteen, Martha began teaching at the Victory School north of Pershing. A cluster of homes had been built near the town to accommodate the influx of miners. Their children were either sent to Victory or Vigilance rather than to Pershing which was closer. In 1933, when Martha started teaching at Victory, there were fourteen neighboring children, nine Italians, and all nine grades. She taught two more years at North Flagler before getting married. Henrietta Roozeboom Vander Hart also attended this school for a time. She recalls that the boyfriend of teacher Marie Ream was working with the CCC. The workers would come into the schoolhouse and drink all the water from the water jug and it would have to be refilled by the students. The students practiced their penmanship in time to music. (I had an intense dislike for penmanship practice, especially the idea of holding your hand and arm above the paper. Maybe music would have helped.)

Teachers who taught at Vigilance included Emma Jones 1886; Lizzie Henry 1895; Minnie Kendall, Nellie Rogers 1896; Grace Sterenberg, Florence Inskeep, Edith Stroud 1898; Mrs. Martha Weyman, A. H. Crosby, Susie Norris 1899; Mrs. Martha Weyman, Victoria Noftsger, W. H. Lamme, Jennie M. Kester 1900; Art Betterton, Lydia Sanders 1903; Edythe Hartness, Rosa Brubaker 1904; Rosa Brubaker, Nora F. Davis 1905; Ruth Rose, Mollie Doran, Ella Ridenour 1906; Della Ridenour, Maude Brubaker, Mary L. Auspach 1907; Cora B. Davis 1908; Maude Wilson, Bertha Woody 1910; Anna King 1911; Ethel Tandy 1912; Orba L. Moore, Ve Lola Blair 1913; Ve Lola Blair 1914-16; Helen Rankin 1917; Margaret Leonard, Helen Rankin 1919; Margaret Leonard 1920; Mrs. Jennie Patten 1921; Lillian Neifert 1922; Edith McVay 1925; Mrs. Lillian Rowland 1926; Leona M. Rowland 1928; Helen L. Rowland 1929; Helen Rowland, Zelma Crozier 1930; Helen Rowland 1931; Helen Stroud 1932; Kenneth Ranking 1933-34; Vera Kincaid 1935; Marie Ream 1937; and Wilma L. Nicholson 1939-40.

Map of Dallas Township

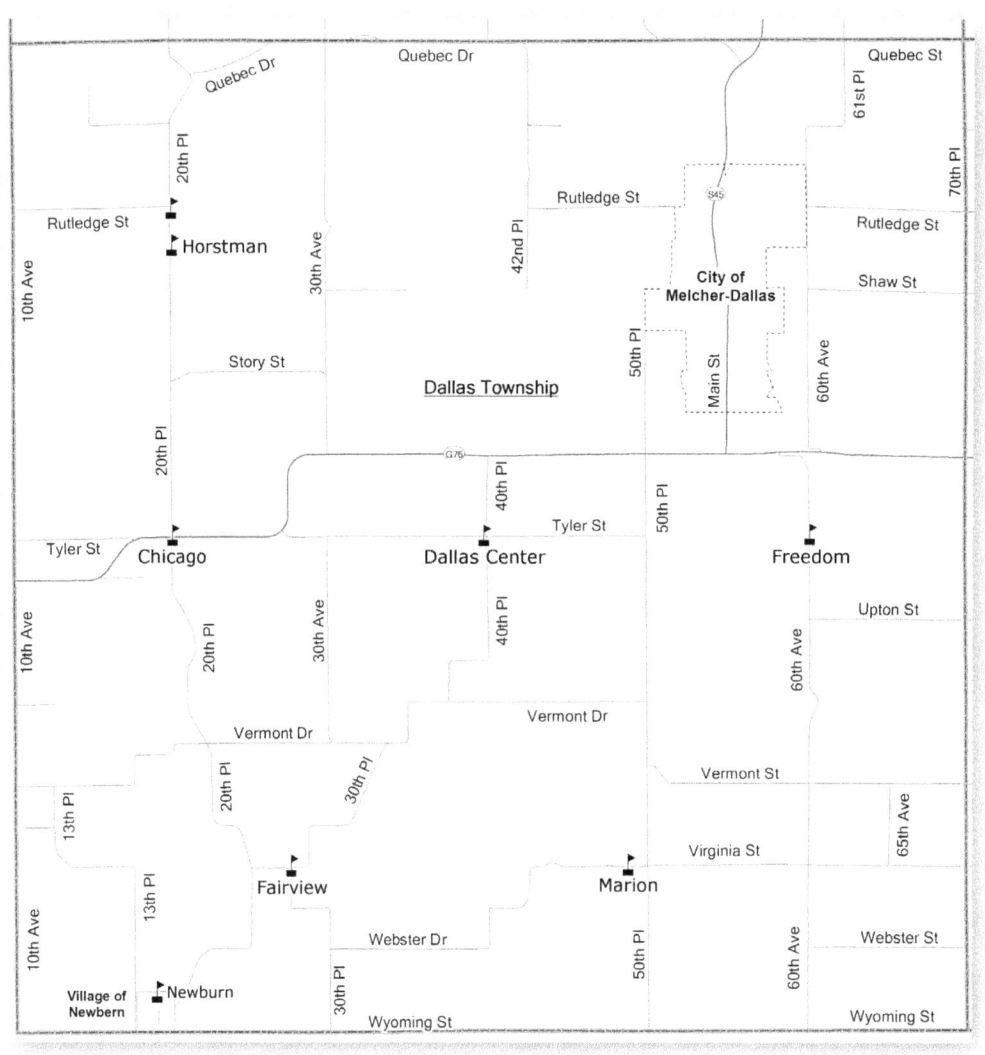

THE SCHOOLS OF
Dallas Township

Chicago (17)

THE CHICAGO COUNTRY School was in the southwestern corner of section 17 along what is currently Highway G76. This part of the county was primarily settled by Germans who were Catholics or Lutherans. Directly north of the school in the northwestern part of section 17 was the small hamlet of New Chicago established in 1867. Since nuns dominate the list of teachers we can conclude that this was a Catholic neighborhood.

Teachers included Wm. Kirraden 1886; Mary Hartnet 1895; Marguerite Noesges 1898-99; Beatrice Harkin 1900; Mary T. Harlan 1903; Mary E. Westphalia 1904; Sister M. Columba 1905; Sister M. Martha Bell 1906-07; Sister Mary Laurence 1908; Sister M. Iowina 1909; Mabel Bush, Mayme Murphy 1910; Sister Mary Lawrence 1911-13; Sister Mary Blanche 1914-20; Sister Mary Concepta 1921-30; Sister M. Scholastica 1931; Sister M. Serena 1932-35; Sister Juventine 1936-41; Sister M. Serena 1942-50; Sister M. Estella 1951-56; and Sister M. Floreberta 1957-59.

Dallas Center (16)

DALLAS CENTER, southwest of Melcher, was in the center of Dallas Township, south of present-day Highway G76. Former student Duane Seuferer says that he and his five brothers all attended this school. He remembers a bit of confusion over the name as there is also an Iowa town called Dallas Center.

The Knoxville Journal of August 11, 1879, commented that J. W. Elder began teaching, which would keep him out of mischief for awhile. (The records show that Mr. Elder taught at five other schools, so he must have kept out of mischief for quite awhile.)

In February of 1892, *The Journal* reports that teacher W. H. Miller closed with the following students neither absent, nor tardy: Ed Wadle; Harry and Ora Clingman; Jos. Griesbaum; Frank Gee; Roy, Guy, and Nettie Wilson; Lizzie Miller; Elmer Tukle; and Nancy Feight. There was an average attendance of twenty-six from the middle of January to the middle of February.

Fairview (29)

Fairview, 1904 – Back row: Dora Frueh, Rena Riggs, Letta Mason, Dora Mason, Alma Pearl Wilson, Emma Smith, Mary Frueh, Sade Graves, Elsie Mason, Nora Smith, Myrtle Smith, Oliver Hunnerdosse, Clara Mason, Ollie Wilson, Katherine Dinwiddie, Robert Riggs, Harry Poush, Edgar Smith, and Grant Riggs. Middle row: Loren Riggs, Lloyd Riggs, Thomas Merl Graves, Ernest Hunnerdosse, Walter Mason, Mathew Smith, John Whitemy, (unknown), Edward ___, (unknown), and Giles Smith. Front row: (unknown), Vera Mason, Ruth Smith, Avis Mason, and Pearl ___.

ONE OF SIX schools in the county named Fairview, this school was located on the southern edge of section 29. The school was on the north side of that short section of Virigina Street, which connects 20th Place with 30th Place.

I talked with former student Robert Gruebel, who graduated from high school in 1951. He was a bus driver for the Melcher Dallas system for many years. There were twelve to fifteen children in school when he attended Fairview. Teacher Aletha Shore stayed with his family during the winter and he walked across fields with her to get to school. The students called themselves the Fairview Cardinals and published a newsletter each month called the *Cardinal Chatterbox*.

Teachers were Carrie Burt 1889; Kate Dinwiddie 1893-94; Kate Dinwiddie, V. M. Bearden 1895; V. M. Bearden, Emma Bearden 1896; Roy M. Porter 1898; G. W. Morrison 1899; Katie Dinwiddie 1900; Katie Dinwiddie 1903-04; M. C. Campbell 1905; Bertha Clingan 1906; Sarah Write, Chester A. Metz 1907; Mattie Porter 1908-09; Pearl Maddy, Juno Caffrey 1910; Mabel Bush, Oneida Badgley, Bertha Williams 1911; Kate Dinwiddie, Laura Mason 1912; Vera Crippen 1913; Nellie Neuman 1914; Mamie Chambers 1915; Velma E. Wilkins, Pearl Bonifield 1916; Laura Mason 1917; Amy Norris 1918; Genevieve Harding, Luella Wright 1919; Clinna Duncan 1920; Beulah Hawkins 1921; Ila Parks 1922; Mabel Kirton 1924; Amy Norris 1925; Faye Stuart 1926; Cleo Poush, Hester Hazen 1929; Myrtle Durham 1930; Marjorie Murray 1932; Mary Carson 1933; Miss Lavon Abrahamson 1934; Wilma Crawford 1935; Irene Hancock 1937; Raymond E. Shore 1938-39; Kenneth Mitchel 1940; Arlene Crowley 1941; Aletha Shore 1942-44; Clinna O. Duncan 1945; Clinna Duncan 1947; Clinna Duncan 1949-54; Clarice Taylor 1955; and Mrs. Anna L. Graves 1956.

Freedom (13)

Freedom, 1935 – Row one: Dwayne Damon, Darwin Damon, and Josephine Gotta. Row two: Mary Gotta, Mary Jane Vroegh, and Joe McCulley. Row three: Teacher Thelma Straup and Wayne Nolte.

FREEDOM, SOMETIMES CALLED Electra, was south of the overhead bridge south of Melcher.

The Knoxville Journal of September 1883 reported that Miss Lydia Little didn't teach because the school house was not in good condition. She gave up and went home with a headache.

According to *The Knoxville Journal* of January 28, 1884, there was a spelling bee at Freedom with five or six schools participating. Miss Mary McCory of Freedom was champion.

From the writings of Thelma Straup who taught at Freedom in the 1930s:

"When the mine started operation and a mining camp was started two more rooms were added to the building with a basement under the new rooms. A furnace was installed in the basement.

Freedom operated for several years as a three-room school with over 100 students enrolled. But as people began moving out of the mining camp it became a two-room school. Then after a few years it became a one-room school again—using one of the new rooms, and using the other new room as a playroom. The original room became a store room. It was once again a school for farm children as the mine closed."

Teachers were W. J. Reasoner 1883; A. R. Minor, W. A. Graves 1891; Miss Riggs 1892; Cora Jacobs, Agnes Manix 1895; Ora L. Lake, May Harned 1898; Alice Bittenbender, Mary Irons 1899; Esta Sweem, Nina Pringle 1900; Myrtle Brauner 1903-04; Myrtle Brauner, Mattie Long 1905; G. W. Morrison, Emma Smith 1906; Ruby A. Palmer 1907; Hella L. Graves 1908; Neva Wilson 1909-10; Helen Cooper, Laura A. Mason 1911; Helen Cooper, Mabel Wilson 1912; Mabel Wilson 1913; W. E. Albertson, Maude Inskeep 1914; Mabel Wilson, Ferne Rowland 1915; Orba L. Moore, Nytha L. Vernon, Nellie Bissett 1916; Orba L. Moore, Martha Vernon, Faye Deitrich, Hazel Clark, Nytha V. Phillips, Eunice Troutman, Selma Hawkins, Marie Hollingsworth 1917; Selma Hawkins, Agnes Weir 1920; Edith Agan, Jennie Watkins 1921; Bess Williams, Maud

Lang 1924; Bess L. Williams 1925; Susie Orcutt 1927; Icel Miller 1929-30; Thelma Wilson 1931-33; Thelma Straup 1934-36; Icel L. Miller 1937; Harriet L. Hill 1938; Marvel Werts 1939-40; and Marvel Werts 1943.

Horstman (8)

Horstman, 1945-46 school year – Ilene Borchet, Marion White, Larry Borchet, and Gene White jumping rope.

THIS SCHOOL WAS close to St. Paul's Evangelical Church in the hamlet of Germantown. The frame church was built in 1872 on two acres given by Henry and Hannah Horstman.

In her story about her days as a schoolteacher, Fern Welch Jones writes that in 1925-26 she was teaching in a new school building at Horstman.

Teachers did their own custodial work. The room was heated by a large coal stove in the middle of the room. They usually boarded with someone in the community. Board and room was $20 per month. Teachers' salaries were from $40 and up. My lowest salary was $70 per month and my highest was $140. Since all grades were taught in the rural school primary (kindergarten) through eighth, I had as many as 65 classes daily. In the rural schools each was divided into three terms, fall term—3 months, winter term—3 months, and spring term—2 months, total 8 months of school.

Darlene Gehring, who provided the pictures of the students, wrote a letter to me which began, "School was fun! The children were exceptionally well behaved." She said the school board always provided a good supply of corn cobs for starting the fire in the big stove. The stove was fired up on Sunday evening, making a comfortable Monday morning. The water supply came from the Victor Maechen farm which was across the road. A favorite memory for her was the bouquets of wild plum blossoms the children gathered for her on the way to school.

Teachers at Horstman included C. A. Smith 1882; Cordia McCorkel, Aramarta Ingles 1886; Fannie Presser 1890; Annie Quante 1895; Ella Collins, Fanny D. Eberhardt 1898; Leota Tice, Fannie Eberhardt 1899; Loveda Van Doren, Fannie Eberhardt 1900; Loveda Van Doren 1901; Myrtle McDonnell, Mattie Gray 1903; Rena Riggs 1904; Olive Hunnerdosse 1905; Emma Smith, Minna L. Heinke, Anna Ridenour 1906; Emma Smith 1907; Dora Rice, Clara Mason 1908; Marjorie Cooper, Rev. Wm. Schrieber 1909; Rev. Schrieber, Minnie McDowell 1910; Florence Marble, Beulah Marquis 1911; Minna Heinke, Fannie L. Crowley 1912; Margie Shives 1913; Belva Marquis, Grace Conway 1914; Ariel Wright, Ethel McGinnis 1915; Ethel

McGinnis 1916; Florence Willis, Marie McDonald 1917; Joye Black 1918; Mabel Fergison 1919; Iscle Boswell 1920; Lavere White 1921; Nellie Woodyard 1922; Juanita Brown, Etha Mason 1924; Anna Carson, Fern Welch 1925; Fern Welch 1926; Doris Feight 1928; Elsie Frobosa 1929; Ruby Penland 1930; Esther Brown 1931; Mrs. Gladys J. Culbertson 1932; Henry Albertson 1933; Henry Culbertson 1934-35; Glen Hunnerdosse 1936; Glen Hunnerdosse 1938; Oscar Hunnerdosse 1939-40; Esther Burt 1944; Darlene Staley 1945; Nora Marsh 1947; Clinna Duncan 1948; Mrs. Nora Marsh 1949-53; Darlene Gehring 1954; and Edna Johnson 1955 (school closed and records were sent to Melcher-Dallas).

Marion (27)

Marion, late 1930s – Row one: Sam Irving, Howard Smith, and Jim Irving. Row two: Ermigene Cratty (unknown), Carl Irving, and Gene Lang. Row three: Violet Irving and Veda Irving. Row four: Billie Irving, Charles Mason, and Lyle Mason.

MARION SCHOOL WAS south of Melcher-Dallas on the north side of Virginia Street and the west side of 50th Place.

According to *The Knoxville Journal* of December 1889, there was a school exhibition on Saturday night. It consisted of songs, dialogues, declamations, tableaux, and more. There was an immense crowd and good order.

On August 29, 1894, *The Journal* reported that the Marion schoolhouse burned to the ground Saturday night. It is supposed to have been "fired" by someone.

Burline Thron was the teacher in 1941 when sparks caused a roof fire. The Melcher Fire Department answered the call and put out the fire. The fifteen pupils were sent home for the day, the roof was repaired, and school continued as usual (*Melcher and Dallas History Book*).

I visited with former student Winifred Hyatt in her Knoxville apartment (2010). She started kindergarten in the spring of 1920 with teacher Joye Black who had twenty-two pupils that year. All five of the Smith children attended this school walking about a mile and a quarter from home.

On the first day of school, Winifred walked with a neighbor girl, Avis Fortune. She started down the road clutching a "Big Chief" tablet, a new box of crayons, a collapsible tin cup, a pencil box, and a lunch bucket. The boys played marbles and the girls played drop-the-handkerchief. Winifred got in trouble when Avis enticed her into wading in the creek. She said her father was not happy.

Winifred's brother, Howard Smith, graduated from Melcher in 1951. His grade school memories include visiting the neighboring family who had twelve children. They lived in an old square house of four rooms. The boys slept in one bedroom and the girls slept in the second bedroom with their parents. When he visited their home he was served a sandwich of thick homemade bread with soup beans. He did not find this to be a very appetizing meal. (I'd say the mother had found an economical way to provide protein for a large family.)

Teachers included Dora Ruckman 1886; Lizzie Wilson 1889; Lizzie Wilson, Miss Cordia McCorkle, Miss Kate Dinwiddie 1892; Miss Minnie Lang 1893; Elsie Roberts, Larry Morrow 1895; Larry Morrow 1896; Miss Morrow 1897; Kate Dinwiddie 1898; Emma E. Bearden 1899; Emma Bearden, Gertrude Almach 1900; Leota Tice, Gertrude Almach 1903; Myrtle E. Smith 1904; Myrtle E. Smith, Merle Brownfield 1905; Merle Brownfield, L. May Miller 1906; Emma Smith 1907; Nora Willis 1908; Mayme Lahman, Minnie Worley 1909; Ada Mae Riggs 1910-11; L. May Miller 1912; Guy Howard 1913; May Long, Catherine Bruge 1914; Alta M. Keene 1915; Howard Jennison 1916; Nellie Newman 1917-18; Joye Black 1919; Daisy Black 1920-21; Mrs. Esther Agan 1922; Faye Kenney 1924; Etha Mason 1925-26; Mrs. Mabel McNeish 1928; Fern Stevenson 1929; Esther Brown 1930; Mary Giles 1932; Wilma Crawford 1933-34; LaVada Miller 1935; Flossie Hixson 1936; Miss Coline Kenney 1938; Claude C. Wadle 1939-40; Miss Burline Thron 1941; Esther Brown 1942-45; Pauline Crandall 1947; Hazel Perry 1948-50; Mrs. Ruth Kruse 1951-52; and Helen M. Wood 1953-55.

Newbern (31)

Newbern, 1905

THE NEWBERN SCHOOL District is tucked into the far southwestern corner of Marion County. The last building that served as a school was converted into a house. The building was moved north to 1056 80th Avenue, Knoxville.

At the request of Ransome Davis, Newbern was surveyed on September 9, 1861. The town was named by Mr. Davis for a town in Indiana by the same name (*Pioneers of Marion County* by Wm. M Donnel). An 1884 atlas lists its population as 119.

In April 1874, *The Knoxville Journal* reported that a normal school opened last week and scholars seemed interested. (A normal school was an instructional school for persons desiring to become teachers.)

On November 28, 1888, a Newbern correspondent wrote, "Our school teacher was tardy last Monday morning." (Doesn't that make a reader wonder why?)

In February 1889, we learn that Miss Rodgers met with an accident coasting which disabled her for two weeks.

In the spring of 1892, the correspondent observed that "there is some talk of building a new school house as the present one is in a total wreck." According to the September 15, 1900, issue of *The Journal*, "Mr. V. M. Beardon while going to his school was thrown from his horse and badly hurt and not able to assume his school duties on Monday. His sister Anna taught in his place."

Mary Maitre sent me the following information from the *Melcher and Dallas History Book* 1855-1982: Pupils in the term ending February 22, 1907, were Pearl Hancock; Hazel, Johnie, Ferne, Clyde, and Noah Bonebrake; Amy Norris; Harold Hunnerdosse; Ora and Osa Rose; Ruth Victor; Carrie, Glenn, and Blanche Gardener; Elsie, Mildred, and Charlie Sargent; Bertha Inbody; Lester Riggs; and Edna Mae Victor. (Some of these children are probably in the 1905 picture on facing page.)

During the Depression years it was impossible for some children to go on to high school when they finished the 8th grade, so they returned to the Newbern School for another year rather than drop out of school.

Bob Colbert, who was employed by *The Chronicle* a few years ago, told me that when he attended school at Newbern the students helped prepare the noon meal, learning such skills as peeling potatoes.

Teachers included Miss Ella Howard 1873; W. A. Graves, Ed Mathena 1886; David Hodson, Miss Dickey 1887; Miss Mary Rogers 1888; Cora McCorkle 1889; J. H. Curtis 1890; Mr. Curtis, Miss Mary Wilson 1891; Miss Eva Gardner 1892; W. N. Graves 1893; Miss Rosella Riggs 1894; Mrs. Emma Bearden 1895; Emma Bearden, Lora Morrow, V. M. Bearden 1896; Albert Crosby 1897; E. P. Brightwell, Kate E. Dinwiddie, Miss Emma Bearden, V. M. Bearden 1898; Kate Dinwiddie 1899; V. M. Bearden 1900; Kate Dinwiddie, V. M. Bearden 1901; Lulu Gibbons 1903; Lulu Crawford 1904; Mattie J. Porter, Rena Riggs 1905; Rena Riggs 1906; Della Hunnerdosse, S.J.O.G. White 1907; C. Ella Fetters 1908; Emma Smith, Laura Mason 1909; Laura Mason 1910; Maude Caswell, Minnie McDonnell 1911; Maude Caswell 1912; Kathryn Norris 1914; Nellie Newman, W. E. Wellons 1915; Margaret Cuthbertsen 1916; Florence Newman 1917; Minnie McDonnell 1918; Amy Norris 1919; Violet Barton 1920-21; Gerry Newman 1922; Mrs. Anna Graves 1924; Mabel Kerton 1925; Etha Mason 1928-31; Esther Brown 1932; Jennie Oxenrider 1933; Martin Van Dyne, Kathleen Wilson 1934; Max A. McCarty 1935; Wilma Crawford 1936; Darrel D. Needles 1937-38; Betty May Calhoun 1940; and Mable Kirton 1943.

Map of Franklin Township

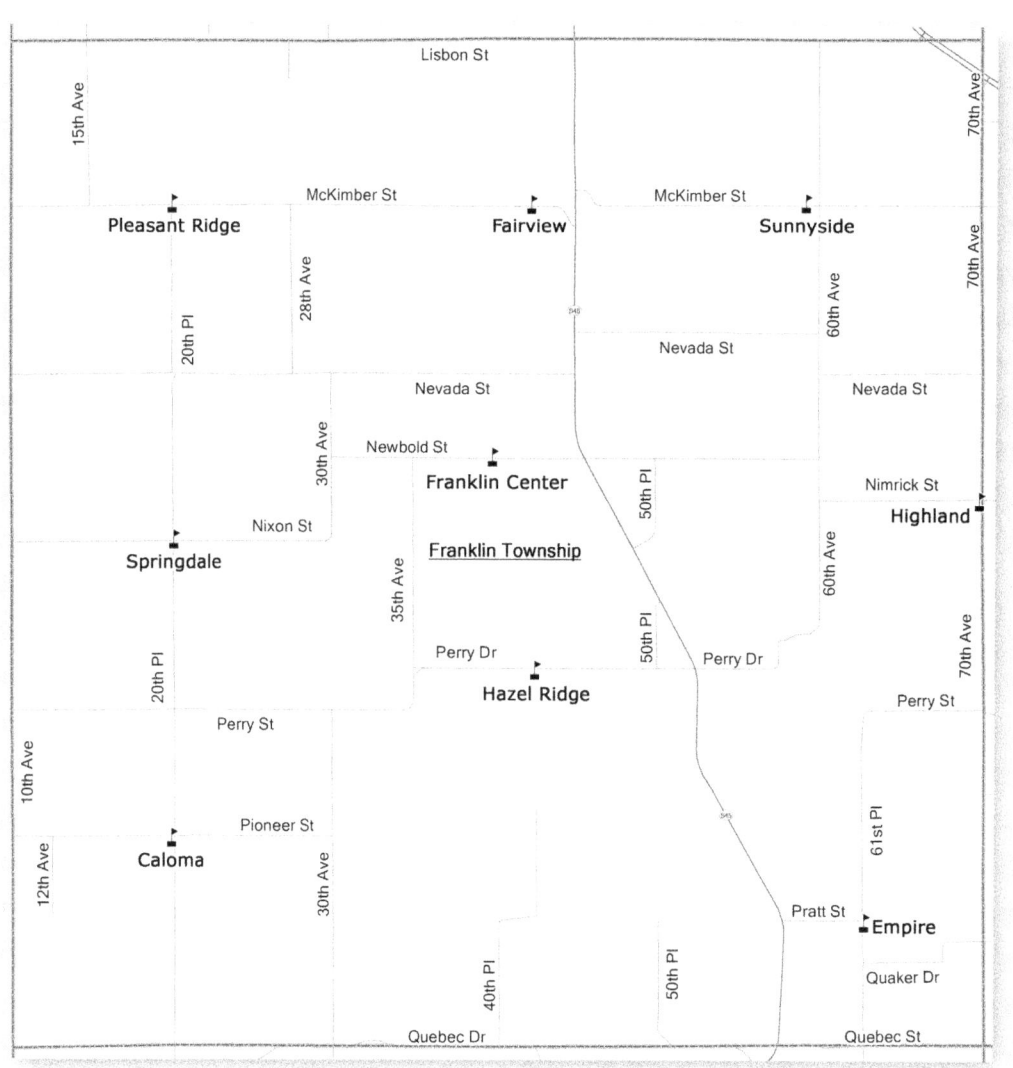

3

THE SCHOOLS OF
Franklin Township

Caloma (31)

Caloma, 1944 – Opal Loynachan, Maxyne Ackerson, (unknown), Billy Gene Schrader, Bobby Ackerson, Gene Stull, and Jerry Schrader.

THE CALOMA SCHOOLHOUSE sat in the southwest corner of the intersection of Pioneer Street and 20th Place. A well can still be found on the school yard although the schoolhouse disappeared long ago. Considered one of the ghost towns of Marion County, the hamlet of Caloma had a post office from 1858 to 1907. An 1884 atlas lists its population as 100.

The Knoxville Journal correspondent for the neighborhood gave high praise to the new teacher in May 1885. "Our school is being taught by Miss E. Crue, a young lady of more than ordinary ability. This is her first term and although it is only two weeks since school commenced she has the esteem of the children and cooperation of the parents. This argues success."

In December of 1889 there was to be a spelling and sack supper at Caloma.

A newspaper clipping (undated) says that Fern Welch Jones started school there in 1911 and finished through 8th grade. Her two sisters and brother attended there and all walked two miles a day to school. She took the 8th grade examinations in twelve subjects and passed them all, which enabled her to enter Dallas High School in the fall of 1919.

I talked with Maxyne Ackerson Chambers, who spent all but the last three months of her grade school years at the Caloma School. Her family moved in March of her 8th grade year and she finished that year at Franklin Center. Although her new school was only a few miles from the Caloma School, Maxyne said she found it hard to adjust.

Maxine's parents had moved to the Caloma district in March of 1938, the year she was eligible to start school in the fall. Teacher Darlene Beven allowed her to attend that spring to get a head start for the fall term. One year, during the war, when the school they called Germantown (Horstman) was unable to find a teacher, the students from that district joined the Caloma students. While reminiscing about what the school looked like—no separate cloak room, windows on the south side only—she suddenly remembered the school ditch thick with violets. "I wonder if they are still there," she said. Probably not, I thought, but they will always be there in her memory.

Teachers included Miss Robinson, Mary Wiegand 1880; Mary Wiegand 1881; Miss S. Robinson 1882; Miss Gertrude Knolten 1883; Miss. E. Crue, Miss Saxson 1885; Minnie Gaston, Sue Stone 1886; Fannie Smith 1888; Mr. Goode, Grant Riggle 1889; Miss Dora Heavener 1890; Samuel T. Ball 1891; Grant Riggle 1892; Grace Collins 1895; Sue Stone 1896; Lora Myers, Cora Hon, Lizzie McKinney 1898; Katie Jones, Myrta Gustin 1899; Myrta Gustin, George W. Newton, Emma Prickett 1900-01; Myrta Gustin, Irmagarde Braun 1903; Clara Langebartles, Myrta Gustin 1904; Myrta Gustin, Minnie L. Heinke 1905; Minnie L. Heinke, Laura A. Mason 1906; Laura Mason 1907; Della Hunerdosse, Jennie Huff, John Williams 1908; Grace Shivvers, Ada Mae Riggs 1909; Cora B. Hon, Laura Mason 1910; John E. Williams 1911; S. T. Biddle 1912-13; Byron Bush, W. D. Campbell, Edna Simpson 1914; Lula McRae, Marjorie Kime 1915; Amy Norris, Ruby Cue 1916; Gracie Palmer 1917; Geraldine Fairley 1918; Caroline Woodyard, Florence Hunt 1919; Bertha Houser 1920; Mrs. Minnie Oldham 1922; Mrs. Minnie Oldham 1924; Fae O. Roe 1925; Helen Hayes 1928; Helen Hayes Roland 1929; Ruth Ridlen 1930; Ruth Hawk 1931; Lila Lukin 1932-33; Berneice Patch 1934-35; Darlene Vinson 1936; Darlene Vinson Bevin 1937; Echo Hukill 1938; Wilma Anderson 1939; Luella I. Shore 1940; Luella Beebout 1941; Elizabeth Ritchie 1942; Frances Brooks 1943; Iantha Bucklew, Grace Daly 1944; Mrs. Elizabeth Lillard 1945; Mrs. Faye Schroder 1947-48; Faye Schroder 1950-52; Mrs. Gladys Bowery 1953; Mrs. Betty Thompson 1954; and Mrs. Faye Schroder 1956-58.

Empire (36)

IT APPEARS THAT THIS SCHOOL was located on 61st Place. The *Melcher and Dallas History Book, 1955 - 1982*, indicates that Empire was added to the Dallas District in 1915.

An 1883 *Knoxville Journal* article comments that attendance was small at Buzzard for the literary. Buzzard was the popular name for this school at one time.

MCHS has a copy of Liza Croft's contract of 1888, in which she agreed to teach for twelve weeks beginning on August 13 for $22 a month. Among other requirements, "She will refrain from all profanity and improper conduct while in their [her pupils'] presence and will institute no cruel or unusual punishment."

The Knoxville Journal of May 1892 says that there will be a stereopticon entertainment at the schoolhouse Thursday evening.

On Columbus Day of that year, *The Journal* reported that the Empire students were on a four-horse wagon to celebrate with the Highland School.

The *Melcher and Dallas History Book* records a monthly report from 1899 in which thirty-two pupils were enrolled with an average attendance of twenty-six. Neither absent nor tardy were Blaine Stillwell, Ezra Campbell, Austin Brown, Maude Donald, Floyd Southward, and Arlie Nichols.

In 1915, Miss Celgo Mylet Toche was hired for eight months at $55 a month to teach and was given an additional $5 for janitor work. (I bet she earned every penny of it.)

Teachers were Lizzie Wilson, Hannah Sexton 1886; Liza Croft 1888; Emma Russell 1889; Miss Agnes Manix, Miss Lizzie Wilson 1891; Miss Agnes Manix, Hiram Curtis 1892; Kate Brennen 1894; Fred Stevenson 1895; Fred Vernon 1896; Minnie Savage, Mary Kelley 1898; Anna R. Bush, Agnes Manix, Mary Rogers, Della Arnold 1899; Agnes Manix, Bernice Stickle 1900-02; Blaine Stillwell 1903; Bernice Stickle, Olive Hunnderdosse 1904; Margaret Conway, Bernice Stickle, Anna Finch 1905; Bernice Stickle 1906-07; Ruby A. Palmer 1908-09; Nora Wills 1910; Ruby Palmer, Myra Nace 1911; Blaine Stillwell 1912-14; Olga Wright, Miss Celgo Mylet Toche 1915; Miss Logan 1916; and Miss Mae Fuller 1917.

Fairview (3)

FAIRVIEW WAS ON the west side of Highway S45. "As the crow flies," it was in a straight line between Pleasant Ridge on the west and Sunnyside on the east. We can assume that like the other five schools in the county it must have been in a great location to merit the name Fairview. Note the ten-year gap where there are no teachers listed. Perhaps there were too few students to support the school between 1925 and 1935.

Marilyn Booth Martin writes that she and her twin sister Marvelyn started school there. The Fairview church was just south of their farm and the school was a quarter mile west of the church. She says they were five in January of 1935 and started school in the fall. Arland Dawson and Duane Kaster were the other two beginners. Other student names were De Moss, Holder, and De Joode. Some students were from families whose dads were working as hired hands for local farmers. Marvelyn and Marilyn took kindergarten and first grade the first year. Helen (their sister with whom they lived) had been like a preschool teacher to them and had taught them the alphabet and how to count as well as reading to them.

When she attended the school, it was small with brand new outhouses built by a WPA project. In 1940, the Pleasantville schools consolidated Franklin Township and the sisters rode the bus to Pleasantville with Charles Van Zee as the driver.

The Fairview Church was organized in 1891 as a branch of the Pleasantville Christian Church. Until 1901, church was held in the Fairview School. The school is gone but the church is still being used, Marilyn said.

Teachers were Ellen Juline 1886; W. M. Graves 1887; W. M. Graves 1890; Ella Collins 1895; Alice Bittenbender, Ella Collins 1898; O. K. Moore, Clara Langebartels, Ella McKinney 1899; Clara Langebartels 1900-01; Clara Langebartels 1903; Sylvia Langebartels 1904; Minnie Heinke 1905;

Mrs. Nora March, Meryl Sterling 1906; Meryl Sterling 1907; Cora M. Van Zee 1908; Bessie Williams 1909; Bessie Williams, Mayme Murphy 1910; Mabel Lemmon, Mabel Woodcock 1911; Bertha Williams 1912-13; Myrtle Glass, Helen Osborne 1914; Hazel Clark 1915; Hazel Kading Anthony, Effie Moss, Liva Barrett 1916; Edna M. Roberts, Liva Barrett 1917; Liva Barrett 1918; Liva Barrett, Olive Freeman 1919; Avis Van Loon 1920; Edris Davidson 1924; Dorothy Shivers 1925; (no school) 1930; Maxine Hukill 1935-36; and Esther Brown 1937-39.

Franklin Center (15)

Franklin Center, mid 1930s

WHERE WAS THE Franklin Center School located? When he was a student there during the 40s, Darrell Gifford of Redland, CA, writes: "Head south from Pleasantville on Highway 60. At the junction with Highway 92, continue south on Highway 181. Turn west at the Kading corner and go past the big round barn. The school will be on the right, across from the Darnell place.

"Sixty years later, I have to rely on Google Earth for this answer: Head south from Pleasantville on Highway 5. At the junction with Highway 92 continue south on S45. Turn right on Newbold Street and proceed west for approximately .6 miles. The county maintenance facility on the right occupies the former site of the school."

The Knoxville Journal of April 18, 1888, tells us that Miss Spence had gone home with measles and her sister was filling her place.

When Miss Lizzie Leonard finished her term in 1891, she received a gift of a photograph album. In May of that year the school burned to the ground (*Knoxville Journal*).

In 1925, long before most schools were considering school reunions, former Franklin Center students were gathering for a basket dinner at Aulds Park. Eighty attended this second reunion but "because of the heat, games were omitted for the greater part. A few of less strenuous were indulged. Dr. A. F. Keeton gave a fine talk" (*Knoxville Journal*). An article from an old Pleasantville newspaper says that at auction there was no bid high enough on the schoolhouse to suit the directors but they did sell the coal shed to Donald Shivvers for $46.00. Presently the school stands in Pleasantville on the site where the maintenance equipment is kept.

Mr. Gifford wrote several delightful "slices of life" about his years as a student in Franklin Center School. These have been placed in the binder at the schoolhouse in the Marion County Park. Here is the one called WET PANTS:

"Harsh winter weather was not considered an excuse for missing school. There were no snow days at Franklin Center. There was, however, a cold weather procedure followed by my mother.

Breakfast was hot oatmeal with milk, a cup of hot cocoa, a glass of water, and, if we could afford it, orange juice.

Clothing began with long underwear and woolen socks. Then a flannel shirt, overalls, and lace-up work shoes were added. Coveralls and overshoes came next. The final layer consisted of a mackinaw coat, a cap with earflaps tied down, a neck scarf, and mittens.

Thus dressed and fed, I would head out for Franklin Center on my trusty pony. After bouncing for the two-mile distance to the school, the first order of business after tying up the pony was to visit the boys' outhouse to eliminate the considerable amount of breakfast fluid.

On one memorable winter day sleet was falling as I left for school. The temperature hovered well below freezing and the sleet was sticking to whatever it touched. Layers of ice were forming on tree limbs.

Once at school, I hastily tied up the pony and headed for the boys' outhouse. Alas, the sleet had frozen the door closed. I removed my mittens and tried to claw the door open with no luck. In desperation I went behind the toilet, out of sight of the schoolhouse, for relief. I managed to undo the large buttons on the mackinaw coat. Then got the zipper of the coveralls down. But I could not manipulate the small metal buttons on the fly of my overalls. My hands were virtually paralyzed from the cold and the sleet.

Nature took its course.

Reluctantly, I entered the schoolhouse. Though the teacher kept a roaring fire in the coal burning stove on cold days, its warmth was hardly noticeable more than a few feet away. On such days, we all kept most of our winter wraps on during school. The many layers of my winter attire absorbed the urine without a telltale outward stain. Fortunately, my desk was on the side of the room opposite the stove. Because I never really thawed out, there was no obvious odor.

If anyone noticed my predicament, nothing was said and I never confessed. To this day, all of my jeans have zippers—not buttons."

Recently, I talked by phone with one of Darrell's classmates, Doran Van Rheenen, who still lives in the area. Doran, Darrell, and Michael Carroll rode their ponies to school and tied them in a shed during school hours. One day, there was a huge windstorm which blew the roof off the shed. When they went out they found the ponies still tied up and (miraculously, I'd say) standing on the roof of the shed.

Doran said that Helen Beem was an especially good teacher. "She knew how to crack the whip. If you misbehaved she grabbed you by the belt and did things to you teachers couldn't do today." He also remembers that when one of the neighborhood girls developed polio the students went to see her in an iron lung.

Teachers at Franklin Center were Emma Blair 1886; Miss Spence, Mr. Williamson 1888; Lizzie Leonard 1891; C.O. Williamson 1894; Viola Goering, Chris Shadle 1895; Mary McNeil 1896; Lizzie Mckinney 1898; Lizzie McKinney, Mary Kelly 1899; Cora Hon, Grace Morris 1900-01; Anna Heller, Myrta Gustin 1903; Myrta Gustin, Sophia Langebartels 1904; Sophia Langebartels, John Williams 1905; Clara E. Heller 1906; Flossie B. Kiefer 1907; John E. Williams, Nora Langebartels 1908; Virgie Shinn 1909; Marie Chrisman, Vera Lukin 1910;

Vera Lukin, Daisy Reeves 1911; Fern Morgan, Catherine Benge 1912; Catherine Benge 1913; Hazel Kading 1914-15; Bessie Williams 1916; Caroline Estes 1917; Ruby Cain 1919; Frances Reiter 1920; Ruth Kading 1922-33; Lela Gifford 1924; Rena Juline 1925; Marie Hixenbaugh 1926; Genevieve Wagner 1927; Grayce Richards 1929-33; Mrs. Lila Lukin Wagner 1934; Kathleen Wilson 1935; Kathleen Wilson, Mary Fedro 1936; Eva Ford 1937-38; Leah Hegwood 1939; Velma Vanden Berg 1940; Grace Richards 1941; Frances Brooks 1942; Frances Brooks 1944-45; Ella Kearney 1947; Mary Hollingsworth 1948; Mrs. Helen Beem 1949; and Mrs. Helen Beem 1951-54.

Hazel Ridge (22)

Hazel Ridge, 1914

THIS SCHOOL was in the southwest corner of section 22 along what is now Perry Street. The name was changed from Gospel Ridge to Hazel Ridge in 1908. A *Knoxville Journal* article states that in 1885 there were thirty students.

Teachers were Miss Ida Rosenberg 1885; Miss Croft 1888; Agnes Manle 1891; Ella Welsher 1895; Jennie D. Barrett; Jennie Bruitt 1898; Fannie D. Eberhardt, Ella McKinney, Villa Parnell 1899; Villa Parnell, Anna Keller 1900-01; Mabel Bush 1903; Lena Shivers 1904; Rena Riggs, Sophia Langebartels 1905; Laura Mason, Fay Tyrrell, Rena Riggs 1906; L. May Miller, Thurman Ward 1907; Faye Tyrrell, Marjorie Cooper, Lulu Stanger 1908; Nora Wills, Mrs. Lisa Welsher 1909; Ida Freeman, Lisa Welsher, Fran Collins 1910; Cora Hon, Fran Cambrion 1911; Fern Cambrion, Hazel Kading 1912; Hazel Kading 1913; Hazel Chivers, Echo Cambrion 1914; Rhea Clark, Ariel Wright, Vera Kading 1915; Edith Sharpe 1916; Bertha Houser, Amy Norris 1917; Mabel Bush, Naureen Donnelly 1918; Iscle Boswell, Nora P. Hartz 1919; Jennie Black, Daisy Metz 1920; Bertha Augustine 1922; Fern Welch 1925; Elizabeth Ritchie 1926; Edna Vinson, Helen Johnson 1930; Elizabeth Ritchie 1932-34; and Elizabeth Ritchie 1936.

Highland (13)

HIGHLAND SCHOOL was about six miles west of Knoxville. It stood on the south corner of the intersection of Maverick Street and 70th Avenue. On the edge of Franklin Township, the district served students in both Franklin and Knoxville Townships. The earliest school for which I have found a record was a log cabin built in the 1870s. When it burned down in 1917, it was replaced by a building of tile blocks covered with stucco. Former student Daryl Jordan told me because there was once a tile factory nearby there are several tile block buildings in that area. He said the only wood in the school building was the framings for the doors and windows and the oak floor of the classroom. Daryl described the building as the Cadillac of schools and regrets that it was torn down rather than being preserved.

For many years, there was a column about the Highland neighborhood in *The Knoxville Journal*. The writers often made comments about the school. Here are some typical examples:

On June 13, 1877, the columnist writes that the school had been closed because of diphtheria. In May 1885, *The Journal* reports that fifty-five were enrolled in the school with fourteen never having been in school before.

In January 1886, the writer says a literary society and debating club had been organized at the Highland schoolhouse.

In the winter term of 1891, there were fifty-eight students enrolled. Hoppy Shivers, age ten, quit for work while twenty-one-year-old Stephan Cleveland left by request of the board. Later records show that Shivers was back in school at age thirteen. That spring, students observed Arbor Day, naming trees and flowers in the morning. In the afternoon, there were songs and recitations.

Pie suppers were a way to raise money for school supplies, but *The Journal* of March 30, 1901, reports that the pie supper was not well attended because of bad roads and threatening weather. (Without modern technology to inform them, the neighbors used common sense and stayed home.)

Jeanne Hudson Bellish, who attended Highland in the 1930s, sent me a letter about her experiences at the school, which was also attended by her three siblings, her father, and her grandfather Hudson. Her grandfather attended school for only three years before going to work pulling trams in the mines south of the school. She doesn't believe he ever returned to school, although he became a very successful man. Later, her grandmother Hudson served as Sunday school superintendent at the schoolhouse. Sunday school classes were just one of the community functions held at the school.

Jeanne, who lives in Indianapolis, Indiana, writes, "I started 1st grade before I was five years old in 1932. My birthday was October 17 and since Benny Brooks (whose birthday was in June) was starting the first grade, Pauline Henning asked my mother if she would be willing to let me start at the same time—I've always said she was probably glad to have me occupied at school—versus having me at home always wanting something to do."

There was some asparagus growing in the schoolyard which Pauline prepared as creamed asparagus for the students' lunch. "In my mind it was the best asparagus I have ever eaten." Margaret Harrington was her 7th and 8th grade teacher who she says always made sure students had tools for learning and brought many books from the library.

Daryl Jordan and Loretta Harkness met with me to discuss their experiences at Highland, bringing with them several pictures of the school which have been placed in the binders at the schoolhouse in the Marion County Historical Village. Daryl graduated in the spring of 1952, while Loretta graduated in 1956, the next year being the last for the Highland School.

Daryl placed great value on his country school education even though he got off to a shaky start in primary when he colored a picture of a sheep purple. His teacher was so concerned that she called on his mother to discuss the matter. That teacher may have thwarted a great artistic career, but she didn't curb his curiosity. That curiosity nearly cost him a finger. On the schoolyard was a heavy cement slab which had been installed as a dry place for students to step on from a horse drawn buggy. He and his buddies attempted to lift the slab to check out the underside when it slipped, nearly cutting off one of his fingers. There was a lot of blood and a lot of excitement. His father took him to see Dr. Dwight Mater, who wanted to cut off the severed part of the finger. His father said no. The finger was stitched together and eventually healed, but the scars are still visible.

His sister Jolene Jordan Harrington told him the story about the teacher who went down one morning to the coal room and surprised a hobo. "I'm sorry," the hobo said, "I thought this was Saturday." The teacher told him he was correct about it being Saturday, but it was also a school day, a make-up snow day. He was very apologetic and left immediately. (I wonder how many others may have taken shelter in these isolated schoolhouses.)

Loretta also feels she received an excellent education at the school. She recalls that both she and her brother Phil were such good hitters that they were never allowed to be on the same ball team. She mentioned that she and some other students helped teacher Mary Truman with routine chores in exchange for rides home after school. This teacher also took the 7th and 8th grade students on a train trip to Chicago. The conversation turned to all the shorter field trips they took to various factories and the state capitol. What great educational experiences the Highland students had both inside and outside the classroom.

Highland – Individual pictures from 1953-54. Top row: Teacher Mary Truman, ____ Brooks, Jolene Jordan, Phillip Bush, Martha Shannon, ____ Overton, and Patsy Goad. Middle row: David McKinney, Loretta Hartness, Sharon Hartness, and Lowell Bush. Bottom row: Barbara Hartness, Joyce Young, Connie Hartness, Jerry Orcutt, Linda Shannon, Elizabeth Overton, and Fern Orcutt.

Teachers included Miss South, Mr. Rolland Wines 1878; Mr. Hase 1879; Miss Wilson 1880; Miss Welcher 1881; Nora Immel, Mr. Lee Curtis 1885; Helen Lanhow, Lorie Dowley 1886; J. K. Butterfield 1887; Mr. Amsberry, R. A. Hardin 1888; Fannie Smith, Lizzie Leonard, Mr. Steel 1889; Claudia Marsh, Mr. J. B. Stanley, Kate Derry, Mr. Metcalf 1891; J. W. Elder 1892; M. G. Metcalf, I. H. McKinney, J. W. Elder, Maggie Watkins, Dow Marsh 1895; Miss Media Watkins, Miss Maggie Watkins, Dow Marsh, M. C. Watson 1896; Gertrude Pritchett, J. H. Woodyard, Thurman Ward, T. L. Vernon, Ollie Gelderbloom 1900; Mary Roller, Grace Morris, Ollie Gelderbloom 1901; Lizzie McKinney, Berneice Stickle 1903; Nellie Rogers 1904; Martha Conway,

Blaine Stilwell, Katherine Sturgeon 1905; Mrs. Nellie McIrea, Grace Orcutt, Katherine Sturgeon 1906; Grace Orcutt 1907; Grace Shivvers 1908; Maude Shook, Jennie McConoughey 1909; Isa F. Houser, Ruby Reese, Ruby Miller, Iva E Stower 1910; Georgia Reichard, Birdie Fast 1911; Cora Rankin, Ina Cummings 1912; Laura Buckley, Birdie Fast, Mary Caffrey 1913; Gertrude Haigh 1914; Nellie Gardener, Merl Witt 1915; Merl Witt 1916-17; Howard Mercer 1918; Sadie Billingsley, Mary Shivvers, Mrs. J. M. Davis 1919; Margaret Curtis 1920; Francis Reiter 1921; Rhoda Culbertson 1922; Ruth Kading 1924; Forest D. Banifield 1925; Georgia Applegate 1926; Fern Welch 1927-28; Pauline Ward 1929; Icel L. Miller 1931; Mrs. Pauline Henning 1932-37; Mildred Harrington 1938-40; Evalyn A. Stevenson 1942; Jessie Hunter 1943; Lucille Hedrick, Mildred Dennison 1944; Mildred Ann Dennison 1945; Elizabeth Ritchie 1947-49; Elretta Burnett 1950-51; Mrs. Dorothy Schell 1952; and Mary L. Truman 1953-57.

Pleasant Ridge (5)

PLEASANT RIDGE SCHOOL DISTRICT was in the northwestern corner of Franklin Township on 20th Place. This places it almost straight west of the Fairview School District and straight north of Sunnyside. There were three Marion county schools named Pleasant Ridge. While much attention has been given to the restored one in the Marion County Park, the other two seem to have been forgotten.

Teachers included Effie Hamilton 1895; R. N. London, Iva Summy 1898; Cleo De Witt, Lulu Miller 1899; A. F. Pense, Mr. Lulu McClymond, Anna Summy 1900; Mrs. Lulu McClymond, Anna Summy 1901; Clara Langebartels, Mrs. Lulu McClymond 1903; Anna Heller, Therza Dyer 1904; John Williams, Myrtle E. Smith 1905; Lulu Stanger 1906; Cora Davis 1907; Vera Lukin; Lula Stanger 1908, Nora Langebartles, Beulah Stuff, Florence Stanger 1909; Ruby Miller 1910; Hallie Swain 1912; Carol Kading 1913-14; Vera Lukin 1915; Thelma Carson 1916; Fern Danity, Mary Weston 1917; Grace Robinson 1918; Inis Smith 1919-20; Pearl Robinson 1922-23; Rena Juline 1924; Florence Kelly 1925; Myrtle Severns 1926-27; Lucille Van Zuck 1929; Elsie Frobosa 1930; Ruth I. Adamson 1932; Bernice Patch 1933; (no school) 1936; and Maxine Hukill 1937-38.

Springdale (17)

MARJORIE ANTHONY DOP provided the pictures and the only information about this school, which was located in the western section of the county at the intersection of 20th Place and Nixon Street. Marjorie writes that her father went to the school and as he got older only attended when there was no field work. Her mother taught there before she was married. Marjorie was the youngest of eight, all of whom went to school at Springdale.

When Marjorie started school she was the only one in her grade. Ella Kearney was her first and only teacher. The school closed after she completed 8th grade. Because the Anthony family lived across the road from the school, they went home for lunch almost every day. For a time, the school received commodities consisting of pork and beans, white cheese, prunes, tomato juice, and grape fruit juice. During that period they would take a sandwich to go with whatever commodities were available. Their drinking water was carried from the nearby Hukill farm with everyone drinking from the same dipper.

They played ball and games such as Red Light-Green Light, Steal Sticks, Mother May I, and Annie-Annie Over. Marjorie speaks for many of us with the words, "I think the country schools provided a good education. I am glad I had a part of that experience."

Teachers included Mr. Harsin 1881; Effie Crew 1886; Lizzie McKinney, Worth Parker 1895; Mable Reynolds, Leora Hon 1898; Cora Hon, Stella Winegardener 1899; Myrtle Spencer, Ernest Lumn, Cora Hon 1900; J. P. MClymond, Myrta Gustin 1901; Nellie F. Flesher, Anna Heller 1903; John Williams 1904; Minerva Heinke, Myrtle H. Flesher 1905; Myrtle Flesher 1906; Lizzie Snyder, Grace K. Shivvers, Cloa Erb 1907; Cloa Erb, Cora Van Zee, Vera Lukin 1908; Vera Lukin, Ethel Truer 1909; Faye Hardin 1910-11; Hazel Kading, Lola B. Haas 1912; Lola B. Haas, Bertha Wlliams 1913; Hazel Conant 1914; Echo Cambrion 1915; Hazel White, Amy Norris 1916; Blanche Norris 1917; Blanche Norris, Olive Freeman 1918; Gertrude Feight, Hallie Black 1919; Amy Norris 1920; Mary Stone 1922; Minta Savage, Ruth Woodle 1924; Mary Kirby 1925; Oma Hukill 1927-28; Leona Cambrion 1929-30; Edna Vinson 1931-32; Leona Cambrion 1933; Darlene Vinson 1934-35; Echo Hukill 1936-37; and Ella Kearney 1938-46.

Springdale, 1941 – Row one: Dean Donohue, Jeanette Noftsger, Lola Noftsger, and Marjorie Anthony. Row two: Vance Friday, Eva Biddle, Esther Anthony, and Dorothy Donohue. Row three: Betty Baysinger, Erma Biddle, Norma Anthony, Teacher Ella Kearney, Elnora Gehring, and Irma Anthony.

Sunnyside (2)

NESTLED IN THE valley of four hills, Sunnyside School stood on two acres about eight miles west of Knoxville. According to former students Irma Dop Williams and Charlotte Shivvers, in 1936 a new building replaced an earlier version that had been up the hill on what is now McKimber Street.

In November 2009, these two life-long friends who started primary together published a lovely tribute to Sunnyside in *The Knoxville Journal*. Here are a few excerpts from their story:

"Days at Sunnyside began with the Pledge of Allegiance and singing the national anthem; next came some kind of grooming inspection which could lead to stars up on the list in front. Then the teacher read aloud—Huckleberry Finn, Little Women, Robinson Crusoe—a favorite time. Yes, there were classes too."

"But noon and recesses were the high points."

"The best part had to be the coasting: A generous farmer allowed students and teachers to climb the nearby hill for incredible sledding from the top down across the flat almost to Hawk Run Creek. Toboggans were created by curling the end on a spare sheet of tin roofing. Then there were the coasting parties! Graduates, teachers, and parents sometimes joined the moonlit crowd as snow crunched beneath boots and sent sleds moving like lightning down the big hill."

"The teachers, of course, were the center of it all. Their accomplishments included not simply teaching nine grades of elementary school but all the housekeeping that was done; lighting the fire on cold mornings, providing emergency medical aid and monitoring library, music and art. Some even expanded on that to lead nature hikes, provide bird feeders, seine minnows on Hawk Run, and teach pole vaulting over creek and fence. They all deserve at least one gold crown—some should have two or three."

Teachers were Lizzie Leonard 1886; Miss Fannie Smith 1889; Miss Dora Heavener 1891; Miss Alice Lanham 1894; Eunice Fornerod 1895; Bertha Prichett 1896; Myrtle Spencer 1899; Lulu Crosby 1900; Thurman Ward 1901; Maud Plummer 1903; Beatrice Smith, Sylvia Woody, Ida Ash 1904; Ida B. Ash 1905; Gay Moose 1906; Sue Stone, Mary Caffrey 1908; Cora Van Zee, Ada Mae Riggs 1909; Fran Collins, Jo Mendenhall 1910; Nellie Bridges 1911; Louise Cox, Hattie Stoops 1912; Helen Cooper, Adah Frazier 1913; May Parker Davis, Cora Mathews 1914; Laura Mason, Liva Barrett 1915; Rose Eldridge 1916; Katherine Mott, Marie Shields, Rose Eldridge 1917; Mary Shivers, Edith Agan 1918; Albertine Ringrose, Grace Conrey 1919; Emma Butcher, W. Brewer 1920; Miriam Fletcher 1921; Mamie Slykhuis 1922; Grayce Juline, Eleanor Morgan, Mamie Slykhuis, Mrs. Dale Glover 1923; Eleanor Morgan, Grayce Juline Richards, Pauline Ward 1924; Pauline Ward 1925-28; Elizabeth Ritchie 1929-30; Myrtle Van Loon 1931; Edna Vinson, Madge Wilson, Ruth Hawk 1932; Esther Brown 1933; Maxine Hukill 1934; Elretta Barnett 1935; Mary Mae Sherwood 1936; Elizabeth Ritchie 1937-41; Grayce Richards 1942; Maxine Ball 1943-45; and Beulah Hildman 1947-48.

Sunnyside, 1929 – Sledding

Map of Indiana Township

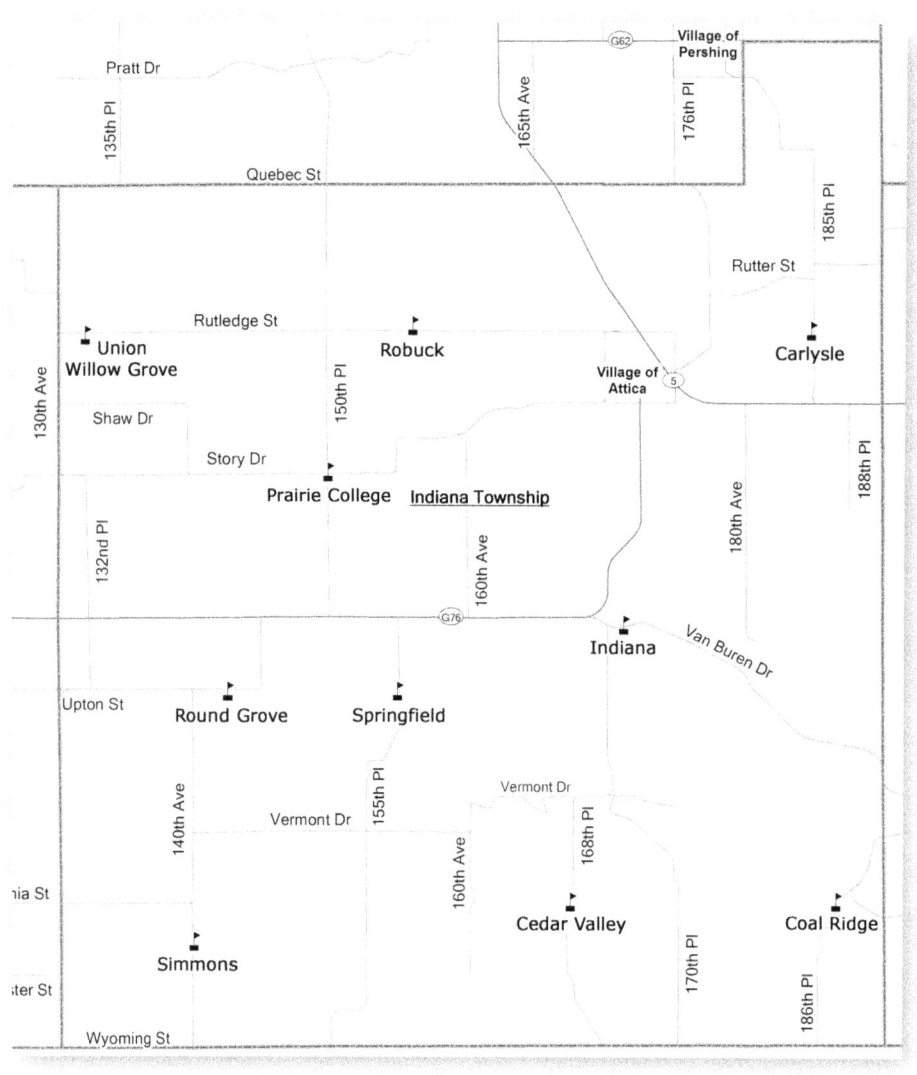

4

THE SCHOOLS OF
Indiana Township

Carlysle (1)

THIS SCHOOL WAS located east of Attica on what is now 185th Place. It was incorporated early into the Attica Consolidated District.

Records show the teachers were C. D. Applegate 1886; Emma Maddy 1891; S. M. Rogers, Aura Darnell 1895; Cora Lyman 1896; Cora Lyman, A. H. Crosby, H. G. Smith 1898; Mabel Reynolds, H. O. Smith 1899; Sarah Conn 1900; Eleanor Crosby, Mary Irma 1901; Eva L. Wilson, Ada Long 1903; S. M. Rogers 1904; S. M. Rogers, Mrs. Rosa Smith 1905; Mrs. Rosa Smith, Anna Ridenour 1906; Helen McConahey, S. M. Rogers, Clova Phelps 1907; Mrs. G. Dykstra, Eva B. Marshall 1908; Rosa Brubaker, Gladys Stephens, Cora Rankin 1909; Mae Davis, Hazel Rice 1910; Forest A. Moore 1911; J. P. Caffrey, Beulah Worstell 1912; Beulah Worstell, Cora Rankin 1913; and Adah Frazier 1914.

Cedar Valley (27)

CEDAR VALLEY SCHOOL was a few miles west of Marysville. The name Cedar Valley refers to its location near the North Cedar Creek. Old maps show it to be on the southern border of section 27 with Cedar Creek to the north, placing it somewhere along the present day road called 168th Place. This school was also known as the "frog pond school," although there was no pond nearby—maybe some puddles left after the creek flooded the valley. Enough for frogs.

A *Knoxville Journal* of 1891 reports that Lizzie Hall closed school with dinner, dialogues, declamations, etc.

In February 1894, *The Knoxville Journal* says that the school board had bought a flag which floated on a thirty-foot pole.

I talked with Halene King about this school, which she attended through 6th grade. Her brothers Howard and Harold also attended Cedar Valley. Their father farmed the creek bottom which was often flooded. Although he never had a crop failure, she recalls him wishing for a shower to wash the mud off the corn leaves after the water receded.

Sometimes Cedar Creek flooded the road and students would have to walk home through the fields. "We had school if the teacher could get there," she said. When the snow was deep, her father would walk through the pasture to make a path to school. Others attending this school in the late 30s and early 40s were children of the Ross, Pearson, and Bennett families. The Ross twins, Willa and Wilma, were in her class. Halene especially remembers teachers Echo Hukill because of her unusual name and Stanley Gullion because he was a very young man. Years later he would tell her it was his first teaching job and he didn't know anything about teaching school. (No one learns more in the classroom of a beginning teacher than the teacher!)

Teachers were John May 1883; Sarah Lyman 1885; Lizzie Hall, Elmer Van Winkle 1891; Miss Cora Batten 1893; Beulah Welch, James Hamilton 1894; Miss Eva Dailey, Chas. Kunkle 1895; Kate Brennen 1897; E. L. Metz 1898; Myrtle Eshom 1899; A. F. Conn, T. L. Vernon, Myrtle Eshom 1900; Myrtle Eshom, Nellie Rogers 1901; Noel D. Shinn 1903; Charles Brenna, Helen McConahey 1904; C. M. Brennan, Vera Witt 1905; Katherine Shinn 1907; W. J. Kincaid, Sue Stone 1908; Eva Marshall 1912; Kathryn Norris, Maude Hughes 1913; Vernon Van Loon, Blanche Meyers 1914; Patrick Kearney, Blanche Burdan 1915; Cora Bridges, Fern McMillen 1916; Agnes Reider 1917; Virgie Beedle 1918; Ferne Davis 1919; Mrs. Snow, Mrs. Rowland 1920; Ferne Davis 1921; Ruth Porter 1922; (no school) 1925; Margaret Kearney 1926; Jennie Evans 1928; (no school) 1930; Kenneth Baker 1936; Kathryn Beary 1937-38; Lora Cristy, Echo Hukill 1939; Stanley Gullion 1941; and Phyllis Laird 1942.

Cedar Valley – Postcard picture given by teacher around 1910. Row one: Blanche Nickell, (unknown), Grace Caulkins, Floyd Pearson, Mabel Nickell, Flossie Sanders, (unknown), Billie Booth, and Mary Ross. Row two: Clarice Schellinger, Beulah Caulkins, Thelma Booth, Ivan Nickell, Earl Booth, Glenn Ross, and Paul Pearson. Row three: Faye Ross, Desie Sanders, Bud Pearson, John Booth, Thlema Sanders, Gertie Booth, and Teacher Mary Roller.

Coal Ridge (25)

COAL RIDGE SCHOOL was in the southeastern corner of Indiana Township, south of Virginia Street on 186th Place. There was another school called Coal Ridge School near the Coal Ridge Church in Polk Township.

Teachers were Addie Rutherford, Clara Hamilton 1886; Elmer Van Winkle 1890; Aggie White 1891; Harry Smith 1892; Cora Lyman 1895; Alice M. Parker, Alicia Tucker 1898; Ethel W. Elder, Estella Reins 1899; Lulu Bevins 1900; Alice M. Parker, Elsie Manley 1901; Jas. D. French, Anna Monroe 1903; Betha Clingan 1904; Helen McCo-

nahey, Bertha Hughes 1905; Helen McConahey 1906; Myrtle McArthur 1908; Myrtle McArthur, Emmett Kincaid 1909; Anna Brouse, Mamie Jackson 1910; Mamie Jackson 1911-12; Adah Frazier, Beatrice Brennan 1913; Cora Terrell, Mrs. Chas Brennan 1914; Irene Thorpe 1915; Ruth Reeser, Mary Buchanan 1917; Irene Thrope 1918; (no school) 1919; Cora M. Durham 1925; Elizabeth Kearney 1926-29; Francis Allen, Mabel Palmquist 1930; Leah Baker 1931; Ferne Hetherington 1932-34; Leah Baker 1935-37; Lorea Christy 1938; Clarence Valliant 1939; June Lindly 1940; Mrs. Wilma Noah, Mrs. Evalyn Stevenson 1941; Mildred Lundy, Frances Whaley 1942; Mrs. Mary McCombs 1943; and Leah Davis 1944-45.

Top left: Coal Ridge – Schoolchildren from the late 1930s or early 1940s. Bottom left: Coal Ridge – Schoolhouse.

Indiana (23)

INDIANA WAS NEAR the juncture of 170th Place and Van Buren Drive. It was one of the country schools that was consolidated early into the Attica District.

Teachers were Lucy Booth, Chas. Hamilton 1895; Annie Monroe 1896; Anna Monroe, Alda Applegate 1800; Bernice Maddy 1900; A. C. Brennan 1901; Anna Monroe, Mary Rogers 1903; Anna Monroe, Kate Dinwiddie 1904; Mrs. Rosa E. Smith, Kate E. Dinwiddie 1905; Clova Phelps 1906; Dora Davis, Vera Witt 1907; Clova Phelps, Alice Parker 1908; Alice Parker, Ve Lola Blair 1910; Ve Lola Blair, Forest A. Moore 1911; John W. Pringle, Stella Brubaker 1912; Pearl Swayne, Mabelle Watkins 1913; Gertrude M. Way, Cora Rankin 1914.

Prairie College (9)

FROM THE OLD MAPS it appears that this school was in the northeast corner where 150th Place crosses Story Drive. By giving it the name Prairie College, its patrons must have had high hopes for a quality education for their children. It also was consolidated early into the Attica District.

Teachers were Clarence Smith 1892; Anna Monroe 1894; Anna Monroe, Mary Roller 1895; Mary Roller 1896; Owen Whitlatch, Alda Applegate 1898; Elsie Curtis, Anna Monroe 1899; Alda Applegate, Blanche Welch 1900; Ora Rutherford, Bernice Stickle, Anna Ridenour 1901; Rosa Smith, Anna Monroe, Conner Brennan 1903; Nora Welch, A. Wolfe 1904; Mae Moon, S. M. Rogers 1905; S. M. Rogers, Anna McMullen 1906; Richard Rice, Anna Monroe, Maud Welch 1907; Mary E. Flanders, Orrie A. Shinn 1908; Orrie Shinn, Mrs. Mary Whitney, Stella Harrington 1909; Myrta Hughes, Mrs. Albert Forgery, Norue Welch 1910; S. M. Rogers, Emmet Kincaid 1911; Pearle Swayne 1912; Eunice Kutz, Stella Brubaker 1913; and Cecil Way 1914.

Prairie College, 1897 – Front row: Cresco Applegate, Lois Applegate, Chas Coolley, Kerns Applegate, Teacher Elsie Curtis, Paul Applegate, Nellie Applegate, and Aura Brause. Back row: Loren Robuck, Park Robuck, Stanley Smith, Elma Coolley, Etta Applegate, Laura Robuck, Mary Coolley, Fannie Robuck, and Frank Robuck.

Robuck (7)

THIS SCHOOL was somewhere in section 7. The name Robuck is a familiar Marion County name, so it was probably named for the farmer on whose land it stood. Since Willow Grove was also in section 7, Robuck might have been an earlier name for that school.

A *Knoxville Journal* from the spring of 1892 reports that at Robuck there was a box supper which netted $3.00 to purchase a dictionary. The writer is "thankful to the girls from Attica and to the boys for their good behavior."

In December of that year an article states that Guy Etcher had only eight scholars. This could be the reason for its early closing. The only teachers mentioned in the records are Ella Coons 1878 and Guy Etcher and Kate Brennan in 1892.

Round Grove (20)

ROUND GROVE SCHOOL was on 140th Avenue. The cover of the 1905 souvenir booklet with its picture of the teacher and its list of pupils, along with some poetry, was typical of that given to students at the close of the school year. The Marion County Historical Society also has a copy of the 1906 school booklet. It lists many of the same students along with beginners from the Pack, Ridenouer, and Maddy families. Veda Ross, Ruth Holliday, and Roy Kennedy were new to the district.

There was plenty of room for them as the Hulgan and McCarty families were no longer listed. They were most likely farm renters who moved to a different area.

According to an 1894 *Knoxville Journal* article, "Voters are taking a vote for flying the flag, 5 are for and 7 against."

Teachers were F. M. Agan 1880; Miss Josie Smith 1891; Kate Brennen 1894-96; Mabel Taylor 1898; Blanche Welch 1899; Blanche Welch 1901; Alta Marsh 1903; Ethel Welcher 1904; Ada Houser 1905; Ethel Welcher, G. B. Houser 1906; Estella Brubaker, Maud De Raat 1907; Mabel Shook 1908; W. J. Kincaid, Della Ridenour 1909; Eunice Kertz 1910; L. May Miller 1911; J. Collins, Eva Agan 1912; Grace Stevenson 1913; Sadie K. Mullins, Hazel Chivers 1914; Stella Brubaker, A. R. Sanders, Pearl Gable, Fern Smith 1915; Fern Smith, Gladys Witt 1916; Ruby Cue 1917; Kathryn Norris 1918-19; Kathryn Norris Smith 1920-23; Mabel Fergison 1924; Naomi Kading 1925; Hollie Flanders 1926-27; Leona Whitlach 1928-30; Faye M. Wynn 1931-32; Alberta Nicholson, Ricky Moon 1933; Alberta Nicholson 1934; Helen L. Smith 1935; Lucille Moon 1936; Vera L. Kincaid 1937-38; Neva Loynachan 1939-40; Alberta Peter 1941; and Lois Agan 1942. An unidentified former student also contributed these additional names to the Marion County Historical Society: Tom Brennan, Roy Maddy, Emma Maddy, Ella Maddy, Mary Morrow, Lara Morrow, Will Hollowell, Coral Hollowell, George Morrison, Mary Simmons, Mabel Line, Anna Ridnour, Mary Parker, Nellie Rogers, Alberta Loynachan, Mary Pringle Chrismore, Josephine Smith, Wilma Nicholson Noah, and Marcia Gardner Reese.

Round Grove – Souvenir booklet typical of those given to students at the end of the year.

Simmons (32)

THE SIMMONS SCHOOL was blown away in a tornado. It was located not far from the Monroe County line along 140th Avenue just north of the North Cedar Creek. Its nickname was the Bluebird School. I visualize its location as being a place where there were once many of those beautiful little birds. And maybe there still are bluebirds there. In any case, it recalls another era when as part of our science, or perhaps art lessons, we were given the outlines of birds to color. We copied the descriptions of them and assembled all the sheets into a little booklet. Not all of us had a Gladys Black to take us on bird walks to observe the real thing.

I talked with Margaret Gee who started school in the Elm Grove District. During a period when Elm Grove was temporarily closed, she attended the Simmons School. She laughed about walking to school uphill both ways for two miles. (I believe this as I walked a mile and a quarter both uphill and downhill as the road dipped into a steep valley.) She said the school was sometimes so cold that the students had to keep overshoes on their feet to keep from being frost bitten. At that time one large family made up most of the students at Bluebird. To make it passable they threw the cinders from the stove onto the school driveway. This seems like a good idea unless you accidentally stumble and fall while running. Cinders are sharp as knives and I still have a scar on my knee from a fall on cinders. A memorable event for Margaret was the presidential Election Day when someone with a radio in his car came to the school house and told them who was elected.

Teachers were Miss Morrow, Charles Kunkle 1891; Mr. Stange 1892; Miss Riggs, Miss Lanham 1893; Owen Whitlatch 1895; Owen Whitlatch, Blanche Welch 1896; Blanche Welch 1898; Eleanor Crosby 1899; Blanche Welch 1900; S. M. Rogers 1901; F. E. Crawford 1903; D. J. Beary 1904-05; Anna Ridnouer 1906; D. J. Beary 1907-08; Florence Stanger 1909; W. J. Kincaid 1910; Frankie Carruthers 1911-12; Kathryn Shovelain 1913; Hazel Holland 1914; Emmett Kincaid, Katherine Shovelain, Edith Agan 1915; Ruby Bunting, Katherine Wise 1916; Lulu Pierson 1917; Tressa Kearney 1918-20; Maggie Agan 1922-23; Fern Welch 1924; Ruth Faye 1925; Rose Giles 1926; Ella Johnson 1928; Ella Kearney 1929; Florence Gibson 1930; Ruby Moon 1932; Ralph Robinson 1934-35; Eva Ford 1936; Velda Lucile Viers 1937; Wayne Exley 1938-39; Vera E. Stewart 1940; Edna M. Rankin 1941-42; Mrs. Lois Anderson 1943-44; Mrs. Mary Elizabeth Blackman 1945; Anna Bingaman 1947; Mrs. Chamberlain 1948; Mrs. Jean Cooper, Dorothy Carruthers 1950.

Simmons, 1897 – The students between five to twenty years of age were Nora, Bessie, Maude, Loren, Clement, and Fred Welch; Bertha, Dessie, Austin, and Frank Davis; Ann, Ada, Laura, Willie, George, Emmett, John, and Naomi Kincaid; Lulu, Jim, and Lawrence Mart; Lillie, Mary, Bernice, Lola, Fred, and Cecil Jeffers; Mary, Asberene, Robert, and Vint Allen; Lola, Arch, and Lewis Maddy; Loren and Curtis Guillion; Anna and George May; and Alice Sherwood.

Springfield (21)

SPRINGFIELD SCHOOL was south and west of Attica. Follow G76, turn off at 155th Place, and you will be on the road where the school once stood on what was then the farm of Clarence Klootwyk (probably about a mile from the turn off).

Former student Duane Jones e-mailed me about Springfield, which he attended for a short time when his parents moved to the neighborhood in March of 1947. He finished the 7th grade that spring and the next year graduated from 8th grade. He said he liked going to country school after moving from the huge Attica consolidated school. When he returned to Attica as a high school freshman the next year, the last teacher at Springfield,

Eloise Bucklew (Langstraat), boarded with his parents.

Duane did well in country school, as both he and classmate Richard Whitlatch earned the coveted honor " I " at 8th grade graduation. The third classmate, Mitchell Pearson, was also honored at graduation with an award in current events, sponsored by the Weekly Reader program. By today's standards, the Weekly Reader was far from current news, but it did keep us informed of a wider world than the information in our social studies books.

Duane recalls that when the school board talked his mother Fern Welch Jones into coming back to teach at this school in 1944, she hadn't done any teaching since 1928 and had to have additional training. The County Superintendent was Sylvia Plotts.

I visited by phone with Clarice Klootwyk Sams and Hugh and Richard Whitlach. I've interviewed many country school students, but I've never run across a group who were so unanimous in praising their excellent teachers and fellow schoolmates, whom they described as being like family. Hugh Whitlatch started to school in 1936 under the tutelage of his Uncle Merrill Whitlach. "Merrill," he said, "seemed more like a brother to me." Although country school boys were often mischievous, Hugh remembers getting into trouble only one time when the students built a log house in the corner of the schoolyard. This would have been a great engineering project except for the fact that they took fence posts from the neighbor's field without asking permission.

During the time Richard Whitlach was in school, there were fourteen or fewer students enrolled. Because there were several renters in the neighborhood, the school population changed frequently. Every day two students threaded a stick through the handle of the covered water can to carry water from a neighboring farm. The Whitlatch boys always walked to school unless the weather was really bad, and then their dad would take them in a wagon.

At this school there was no danger of the Halloween prank of toilet tipping, as the Springfield toilets had been constructed by WPA workers. The sturdy buildings were firmly bolted to a cement base. When I talked to Clarice Klootwyk Sams, who started school in 1940, I got the impression that the school building was not as carefully planned as the toilets. She said the south side had only one window while the north side had four, making the room very cold on blustery winter days.

Clarice reminisced about the fun they had at Halloween carving pumpkins, placing candles in them, and pulling the blinds to admire their work. She also enjoyed the Christmas program followed by a supper that always included pies. On winter evenings there were sleigh riding parties on her parents' farm. Her mother would invite the students into their home to play games and warm up with hot chocolate and popcorn. She still stays in contact with teacher Dorothy Lenzine Davis, who boarded with her parents.

Duane Jones had the final contact with this school, as one of his jobs in the late 1950s was to bury the residue of the remains of the schoolhouse.

Teachers who taught at this school included Miss Clara Maddy 1890; Mary Simmons 1891; Miss Fannie Young, Clara Maddy 1894; Miss Mollie Tucker, Jennie Keefer 1895; Belle Overton 1897; Alta Marsh 1898; Alta Marsh, Ida Hall 1899; Mary Rogers

1900-01; Frank Maddy 1903; Mattie Rankin 1904; Atha Wolfe 1905; Edna Sherwood 1907; Marjorie Cooper 1908; Norrie Welch, Norue Welch 1909; Miriam Rankin, Cora Goodwin 1911; Ve Lola Blair 1912; Helen Rankin 1913; Ina Marmon 1914; Fern Smith 1915; Gladys Taylor, Lillian V. Rales 1916; Rose Eldridge 1917; Helen Rankin 1918; Lula Pierson 1919; Sylvia Allen 1920; Lillian Neifert 1921; Mary Stone 1923; Fonda Monroe 1925-26; Fern Welch, Dorothy Foster 1928; Mable Lion 1930; Leona Cline 1931; Albertha Nicholson 1932; Bessie Robuck 1933-34; Merrill Whitlatch 1935-36; Lorraine Hamrick 1937; Adriana Kempkes 1938; Georgia Long 1939-41; Wilma Monroe 1942; Dorothy Lenzine 1943; Mrs. Fern Jones 1944; Cora Bridges 1945; Mrs. Bessie Kenney 1947; and Eloise Bucklew 1948.

Springfield, 1944 – Row one: Roberta Brubaker, Roberta Whitlatch, and Dolores Mathes. Row two: Clarice Klootwyk, Richard Mathes, and Martha Downs. Row three: Mitchell Pearson, Annabel Whitlatch, and Bethel Klootwyk.

Union (7)

UNION SCHOOL is listed in the official records as being in the northwest corner of section 7, making it very close to Willow Grove. Wherever it was, it closed early.

Teachers were Rachel L. Rogers, Julia Ruckman 1886; Julia Ruckman 1889; Miss Adda Young 1890; Mary Simmons 1894; Viola Goering 1895; Viola Goering, Blanche Welch, Effie Hamilton 1896; Nettie Stentz 1898; J. R. Hamilton, Jennie Kester 1899; Jennie Kester 1900; Alma Cloe Craig, Mammie Applegate 1901; and Nannie Hyatt 1905.

Willow Grove (7)

Willow Grove – Front row: Darlene Smith, Shirley Creech, Dean Smith, Betty Spaur, and Dwight Haug. Back row: Carl Haug, Elinor Haug, Norma Jean Spaur, Donald Haug, Bobby Spaur, and Beverly Haug.

WILLOW GROVE appears to have been near 130th Place just below Rutledge Drive.

Its teachers included Nannie Applegate 1901; A. C. Brennan, Effie McIntire 1903; Effie McIntire, Mary Irons 1904; Nellie C. Rogers, Lucinda Marshall 1905; Mary E. Flanders 1907; Anna Brouse, Arvilla Hayes 1908; Eunice Kertz 1909; L. May Miller 1910; Grace Metz 1911; Lottie McClymond, Clella Andrews 1912; Stella Brubaker 1913-14; Iva Houser, Pearl Gable 1915; Pearl Gable, Mrs. Rosa Smith 1916; Fern Smith 1917; Pearl Swayne 1918; Lucile How 1919; De Lana Barringer 1920; Iva Van Liew 1921; Mrs. Rhoda Culbertson, Ollie Evans 1922; Georgia Applegate 1925; Frances Clark 1927; Ruby Sarver 1928; Mildred Bybee 1929; Wilma Moon 1920-31; Kathryn Bybee 1932; Myrtle Smith 1933-34; Ruth Marie Smith 1935-37; Lois Agan 1940; Virginia Robuck 1942; Lida McMannis 1943; Lena Miller 1944-45; and Lena Miller 1947-54.

Map of Knoxville Township

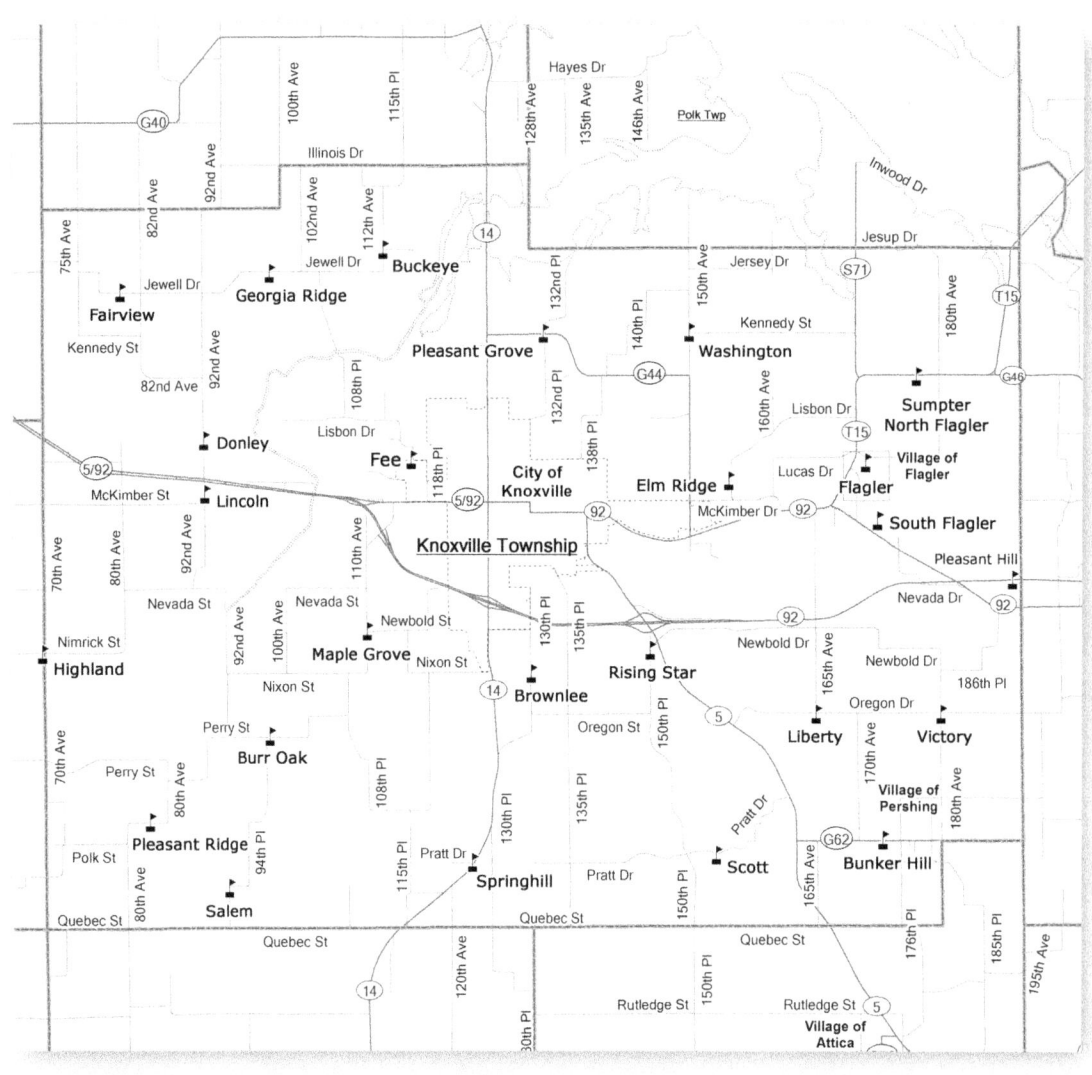

❦ 5 ❦

THE SCHOOLS OF
Knoxville Township

Brownlee (19)

Brownlee, 1953-54 – Top row: Johnny Haning, Shirley Wares, Janet Wares, and Gary Clingman. Row 3: Linda Caulkins, Dorothy Caulkins, Carla Caulkins, and Floyd Marshall. Row 2: Dennis Derringer, John Derringer, Donald and Margaret Derringer. Bottom row: Tommy Wilson, Dixie Wilson, Steven Lewis, and David Lewis

BROWNLEE SCHOOL stands on its original site two miles south of Knoxville near Highway 14 at approximately 1620 130th Place.

According to a story from Ruth Kenney, her aunt Emma Dennison was one of the first girls to teach a winter term. She writes that Uncle Steve Jenkins told of a schoolmaster who always hung his coat on a certain hook. Pupils thought he didn't have any switches in the schoolhouse but one day they tried his patience too far and he pulled out two switches from under the coat.

I talked with Linda Caulkins Mason, who attended this school through 6th grade, when it closed. She said she loved the school and the teachers and feels so privileged to have gone to a country school. Her father Harold Caulkins also attended Brownlee.

The school was down in a valley. She walked on a gravel road to school but sometimes the creek below the schoolhouse flooded and her father would have to drive the children into Knoxville and then take them back on another road to get to the school. Like students from many other country schools, Linda remembers fixing potatoes for lunch on a little wood stove, having to carry water from a neighboring farm, and playing games such as baseball and fox 'n geese.

One of Linda's treasures is the bookcase from the school which she refinished by stripping it of three coats of green paint. (At one time schools and other institutions seemed awfully fond of green paint. Was this a fad or simply a bargain purchased in quantity?)

Teachers were Lottie McClymond 1886; Lora Myers, Helen Herrick 1895; Helen Herrick 1896; Stella Winegardener 1898; Stella Winegardener, Bula Sniff 1899; Bula Sniff 1900; Bula Sniff, Victoria Noftsger 1901; Mabel Reynolds, Edith Dawson 1903; Alice Bittenbreder 1904; Beatrice Smith, Myrtle McArthur 1905; Walter E. Kester 1906-07; Genevia Nittel 1908; Jen Gardner, Carol Swayne 1909; Verna King 1910; Lottie McClymond 1911; Hilda L. Bowman 1912; Jo Mendenhall 1913; Mrs. Rosa Smith 1914-15; Grace Patterson 1916; Ethelle Bruce, Catherine Mott 1917; Grayce Rowland 1918; Lora Flanders 1919; Mrs. Geneva Morse 1920; Mrs. Geneva Morse, Ione Dotson 1921; Irene Chrismore 1924; Charlene Orr 1925; Lena Willets 1927; Kathryn Bybee 1930-31; Juanita Covey 1932-35; Atha Kincaid 1938; Velma Vanden Berg 1939; Martha Louise Whaley 1940-41; Violet McDonnell 1942-45; Miss Doris Burton 1947; Mrs. Mildred Lundy 1948-49; and Beulah E. Hayes 1951-53.

Buckeye (23)

Buckeye – School remodeled into a home.

BUCKEYE SCHOOL, located at 1242 Illinois about four miles north of Knoxville, has been remodeled into a house. It was moved two miles northeast of its original location on Jewell Drive. Unlike today's housing developments, which are named for trees where none exist, the country schools were frequently named for trees common to their neighborhood.

Buckeye teachers were R. C. Nace 1886; Altha Davenport 1889; Miss Grace Lanham 1893; Maggie Morrison, Flora Batten 1895; Myrtle More, Lizzie McKinney 1898; Thurman Ward, Julia Ruckman 1899; Cora Hon, Eleanor Sulllivan 1900; Fessie Palmer, Armanda Brown 1901; Pauline Sarver, Armanda Brown 1903; Art Betterton 1904; F. W. Parker, Berniece Stickle 1905; Blanche Fee, Charles Wren 1906; Ethel L. Barr 1907; Edna Neal, Florence Fee 1908; Laura Buckley, Bressa Welch 1910; Pearl Swayne 1911; Ruth Little, Aura Dickey 1012; Helen Towne 1913; Pearl Swayne 1914; Ethel Benson, Ruth Merris 1915; Mable Bush 1916; Margaret Cuthbertson, Rhea Clark 1917; Francis Conrey 1918-19; Dorothy Walker 1920; Gladys Harden 1921; Lela Watkins, Beulah Hawkins 1922; Mary Crouch 1925; Evelyn Knowles 1926; Ruth Smith 1929; Ruth Smith,

Beatrice Brown 1930; Almee Stroud 1931; Geneva Van Loon 1932-33; Ruth M. Smith 1934; Malvina Neely 1935; Marie Hegwood 1936; Eulalia McCormick 1937; Wilma Rinehart 1938; Hazel Worall 1939; Bette Adams, Pearle B. Poe, Virginia Robuck 1940; Miss Helen J. Rysdam 1941; Mildred Beary 1942; Mrs. Mary E. Blackman 1943; Miss Zelma Schroder 1944; Mrs. Ruth Hunt, Mrs. Wm. Lundy 1945.

Bunker Hill (26)

Bunker Hill, 1914 – Carrying a door to be used as a table board for a Thanksgiving dinner.

FAR FROM THE BATTLEFIELD site, the name Bunker Hill connotes a patriotic note.

The Knoxville Journal, April 1886, says the directors of Bunker Hill decided to move one-quarter mile east of the present site.

The June 1886 *Knoxville Journal* reported the Bunker Hill schoolhouse was moved and set on the foundation " when the carpenters do the necessary repairing it will make a fine place for the urchins to acquire a rudiment of education."

Teachers were Edith Ausberry, Rachel Rogers 1886; Rachel Rogers 1888; Clara Maddy 1891; Jennie Keefer 1893; Nellie Rogers 1895; Minnie Kendall, Lottie McClymond, Miss Ella Crosby 1896; Lottie McClymond, Ella Decker 1898; Nora Sullivan, Roscoe Rogers 1899; Rosco Rogers, O. K. Moore 1900; Fannie Eberhardt, Lulu Crosby, Jean Rogers 1901; Edythe Hartness 1903; Carrie Hunt 1904; Lizzie McKinney, Alta Marsh 1905; Alta Marsh, Caroline McClelland 1906; Caroline McClelland, D. W. Martin 1907; Junior McConahey, Bessie Cramer 1909; Bressa Welch 1910; Bessie Welch, Faye Cummings 1913; Edna S. Noe 1914; and Thelma Viers 1924.

Burr Oak (21)

BURR OAK WAS LOCATED about five miles southwest of Knoxville on Perry Street, which is part of the "crooked road to Melcher."

The first mention I've found of this school was in January 1, 1874, in the *Iowa Voter*, which states that Andy Kerr had a successful writing school in progress.

In 1877, *The Knoxville Journal* informs the public that C. F. Whitlatch will give a lecture at the school on Saturday, April 14, on prison life. On October 5, Governor Stone was coming to address citizens on issues of the day.

At the schoolhouse in the Marion County Park, one can kind find information about the school compiled by Janet (Agan) Ritchie. There is a copy of the September 19, 1898, Board of Directors meeting, the earliest one she could find. Among the expenses listed are three boxes of chalk for 45¢ and a teacher's daily record book for $1. There is also a listing of students with ages for each year from 1909 through the 1945 school year. A partial listing of surnames of students who once attended Burr Oak includes Agan, Betterton, Bonebrake, Caulkins, Chambers, Damon, De Vos, Harrington, Heemsbergen, Houser, Hughes, Hunt, London, Marshall, May, McMillan, Mihalovich, Miller, Newman, Pope, Roll, Scott, Skaggs, Smith, Shives, Ward, Weishaar, Whaley, and Wilson (see picture of Maycie Worthington's students for additional names). After the school closed, the schoolhouse was sold for $370, the coal house for $27, the swings for $32, and the pump for $6.

I visited in 2009 with former teacher Helen Ward Roberts, age 102, who resides at the Griffin Nursing Home in Knoxville. When Mrs. Roberts was hired to teach in the fall of 1926, she was warned that discipline was lacking. She solved that problem by "telling them who was boss." While she was teaching at Burr Oak, she boarded with her Uncle Ira and Aunt Elsie Ward and either rode a horse or pony to school. She remembers that she had to go to Treasurer Bill Bye to pick up her check of $70-80 per month. Schoolroom supplies were meager. With the money from pie suppers she bought curtains, a good teacher's desk, and a four-burner kerosene stove. The school, of course, had a coal-burning stove for warmth but she wanted the cook stove to prepare hot soup for the children, as some were bringing only a slice of bread for lunch.

She talked about many of her former students and was especially proud that one of them, Tony Maholovich, later became police chief of Des Moines.

Mrs. Roberts comes from a family who believed in the value of education. Her father T. E. Ward was also a school teacher. She said he was teaching at the Lincoln School the day she was born. Her youngest brother, Ira, who is still living, graduated from West Point and served in Korea and Vietnam. Following retirement he taught at Iowa State for sixteen years. Her great grandmother attended Central College when it was still a Baptist school.

After teaching at Burr Oak, Mrs. Roberts decided she would like to become a nurse and was accepted at Iowa Methodist for nurses training. However, instead of pursuing her dream of being a nurse, she got married. Years later, in 1948, she started working at the Collins Memorial Hospital. She served as administrator there for several years.

Burr Oak – Taken by Pearl Adams when Maycie Worthington was teacher from September 1, 1910, to February 24, 1911. Students were Pearl Adams; Clifton and John Cathcart; Esther and Marie Conner; Mamie Clark; Grace and Fred Houser; Selma, Beulah, and Mary Hawks; Roxie and Cleo Wright; Ruby, Esther, and Jessie Wilson.

She still has a keen mind and does as much reading as her eyes permit. None of those silly little romance novels for her. She reads quality fiction and asked me for recommendations of Civil War literature, her current interest. Although she said one of the boys at Burr Oak was bigger than she, I can just imagine she had no trouble letting him know who was boss.

Teachers at Burr Oak included Mary McClymond, Bettie Lyman 1886; Miss Letitia Keefer, Miss McClymond 1887; Mr. Wiliamson 1888; Miss Hannah Spencer 1889; Miss Hannah Spencer, Miss Essex 1890; Miss Essex 1891; Miss Maud Spicer, Laura Essex 1892; Laura Essex 1893; Katy Derry 1894; Lizzie Hightman, Sherman Wilson 1895; Lizzie McKinney, Alta Marsh 1898; Julia Ruchman, Flora Kester 1899; Flora Kester 1900; Nellie Morrow, Hettie Britton, Mary Kelly 1901; Walter Bone, Nellie Rogers 1903; Vella Karns, Mrs. Lillian Bennett 1904; Mrs. Lillian Bennett, Lizzie McKinney, Gertrude Mallory 1905; Floyd Putnam, Jennie R. McConoughey 1906; Cluna Karns, Cora Hill 1907; Katherine Sturgeon, Claudia Henry, Helen McConaughey 1908; Grace Foridell, Maude Shook 1909; Maycie Worthington, Mabel Bush 1910; Marjorie Stanger 1911; Beulah Jones 1912; Oletha West, Orba L Moore, Beulah Jones 1913; Beulah Jones 1914; Beulah Worstell, Laura Mason 1915; Laura Mason 1916; Nellie Gardner 1917; Lora Flanders 1918; Mabel Jenkins 1920; Olla Bennett 1920; Mabel Jenkins 1921; Beatrice Erb 1922; Beatrice Erb, Edith Mulby 1923; Edith Randall 1924; Edna Snow, Fern Orcutt Hughes 1925; Helen J. Ward 1926-28; Esther Bucklew 1929; Zelma Cain 1930-33; Ruby Penland 1934; Martina Agan 1935; Jessie Williams 1936-37; Rena Fee Welch 1938; Kathryn Nutt 1939; Maxine Adams 1940; Anna Ruth Beary 1941-42; Mary L. Turner 1943; Hazel E. Worrall 1944; and Miss Doris Burton 1945.

Donley (4)

DONLEY WAS ABOUT four miles west of Knoxville and about a quarter-mile north of the intersection of Highway 92 and 92nd Avenue. It was a shipping point on the railroad for the western part of Knoxville Township. It was named for Oliver Donley, who owned a large amount of land in the area. It had a store and at one time also had a school, as the following teachers are listed in the official records: Miss Dora Marsh, B. A. Hardin 1891; Dora Marsh 1892; Fred Smith 1894; and Mr. Elder 1896.

Elm Ridge (4)

ELM RIDGE SCHOOL, two miles east of Knoxville, stood on one-half acre of land leased from Joseph Frank for one cent in the spring of 1859. Elm Ridge was a natural name for this district, which at that time had many large elm trees.

According to a December 25, 1889, *Knoxville Journal* story, the first building was made of logs with a large old-fashioned fireplace. There were only two windows and no desks, only rough slab benches with no backs. The writer describes the modern conveniences of 1889 and the mottos on the wall: "God Bless Our School, Never Be Tardy, and No Idlers Wanted Here."

Elm Ridge was mentioned frequently in *The Journal*. February 1884: "There was a large crowd at the spelling match. Near 600 valentines distributed." (This would probably have been a match between Elm Ridge and two or three other nearby schools.)

January 1885: "There was a snow storm which blockaded the roads so that students and teachers couldn't get to school. The weather was so cold and bad that a woman who arrived with two small children by train broke the depot window. I hope that the railway will provide for the depot to be open at night."

January 19, 1887: The most unusual—and amusing—observation: "Elm Ridge neighborhood has 13 girls and 10 boys of marrying age and one widow and two widowers and still there has not been a marriage here in over a year."

In the spring of 1912, fire destroyed a relatively new building built twenty years earlier and the term was finished in the Flagler Chapel. All the books were lost including a set of encyclopedias and other items belonging to teacher Angie Stentz. The encyclopedias were valued at $21. By the fall term, a new school had been built.

On the last day of school in 1939, Othelia Freeman read a history of the school. Here are her comments on early lunches: "They consisted of bread, butter, sorghum, and molasses cookies brought in tin buckets. Often they would pour sorghum in meat fryings and they would have a fine spread for bread. Fresh fruits were unheard of. One teacher who came from the east was a little out of the ordinary, and he would bring an apple. He always peeled his apple before eating it and the boys stood around and fought over who would get the peelings to eat."

Elm Ridge – Ready for school. Dixie and Doris Adams and Robert Nichols.

Teachers included Florence Cunningham 1872; Miss Simpkins, Miss McClure 1884; Miss Barnes, Miss Jennie Keefer 1885; Miss Jennie Keefer 1886; Eva Hogue, Anna King 1887; Miss Laura Essex, Miss Nora White 1888; Miss Pace, Nora White 1889; Cora Wolf, Nora White, Birdie Pace 1890; Nora White, J. W. Millard, Letitia Keefer 1891; Miss Laura Essex, Miss Keefer 1892; Miss White, Laura Essex 1893; Letitia Keefer, Agnes White 1895; Ollie Gelderblom, Jennie K. Johnson, Marry Maddy 1896; Jennie Johnson, Fannie Eberhardt, Grace Stuenenberg 1898; Jennie K. Johnson 1899; Maggie Cooper, Stella Winegardener, Maude Lammere 1900; Maude Lammere 1901; Hettie Britton 1903; Irmagarde Braun, Josephine Teeter 1904; Velta Karns 1905; Sue Stone 1906-07; Estella Brubaker 1908; Maude De Raat 1909; Mabel Vierson 1910; Angie Reese, Angie Stenz 1911; Angie Stentz

1912-13; Blanche Cline, Mae Ida Davis 1914; Virgie Shinn, Mae Ida Davis 1915; Virgie Shinn 1916; Eva Rinehart, Francis Conrey 1917; W. H. Lucas 1918; Edna Neal Roberts 1919; Glenn Hollingshead 1920-21; Gladys Hardin 1922-23; Camille Leuty 1924; Mary Ghrist 1925-28; Clara Ridlen 1929; Ellen Fitzpatrick Ruth Ridlen 1931; Pauline Harsin 1932; Raymond White 1933; Helen Harsin 1934; Bessie Robuck 1935-37; Vera Welch 1938; Helen Louise Harsin 1939-41; Mary Esther Wilcox 1942-43; Mary Esther Walter 1944; Effie Heemstra 1945; Violet McDonnell 1947-48; Mrs. Joan East Hakes 1949; Mrs. Mildred Lundy 1950; Jean Cooper 1951; Mary L. Hindman 1952-54; and Mary L. Hindman 1956-57. Other early teachers mentioned by Othelia Freeman were Albert Reed, Lee Curtis, Aaron Yetter, L. Y. Atherton, Prof. Roberts, Wm. Banks, Van Horn, Arthur Leonard, Mary Momyer, Mary Roller, and Mary King.

Fairview (29)

Fairview, 1919 – Teacher Averile Stubbs. Row one: (unknown), (unknown), Agnes Carroll, Olive Price, and Pearl Price. Row two: (unknown), Otis Crozier, Tommy Murphy, Russell Crozier, and Carroll Price. Row three: Irene Price, Opal Crozier, Mary Jones, Charlie Carroll, Tommy Hughes, and (unknown).

THE FAIRVIEW SCHOOL was on the north side of Jewell Street between 75th and 82nd Avenue and was moved three-quarter of a mile west and remodeled into a home by Giles and Mary Judith Wadle. *The Knoxville Journal* of June 1877 reports that teacher Maggie Brown had forty-four students.

In December of 1881, the reporter comments that there will be two Christmas trees at Fairview. "The people of this district sure know how to decorate."

A January 1890 edition notes that teacher Agnes Manix treated her pupils to oranges and candy (most likely after the annual Christmas program).

Mary Judith Wadle writes that the school was located on a hill making it ideal for coasting in the wintertime. Because the snow usually drifted over the fence at the bottom of the hill, the students could fly right over the fence into the neighbor's field. She attended school there from kindergarten through 8th grade, while her brother Myles Murphy attended through 6th grade.

In a telephone conversation, Myles told me they lived two miles from the school and usually walked through the fields to get there. A call to Wayne "Doc" De Moss revealed that he too walked through the fields or rode one of his dad's horses to get there. Doc said that he acquired his nickname during his early school years when a teacher asked him what he wanted to be. His reply: "a doctor." He never became a doctor, he said, except a doctor for his horses.

Myles Murphy mentioned his appreciation for teacher Mrs. Beem, who took them on walks down the road to identify trees and other plants. She taught them a lot about nature. She was also very good at identifying the talents of each student and encouraged them to participate in appropriate activities. She entered him in a vocal contest at a Knoxville theater. He remembers being very nervous as he had never been on stage before. (She must have been an exceptional teacher to take the time to observe and encourage the special strengths of each student.)

In writing about her school days, Mary Judith Wadle says, "Our games included Annie-Annie Over, which has been enjoyed over the years by our children and their cousins as well as our grandkids throwing the ball over the same schoolhouse (our home)."

Teachers included Miss Maggie Brown 1877; Miss Edmonds 1878; R. A. Hardin 1879; Miss Boydston 1880; Miss Robinson 1882; Everet Murphy 1883; Leslie Vernon 1885; Cleumeria Derry, Edna Culver 1886; Miss Dena Kingery 1887; Miss Klienendorst, Miss White 1888; Annie Manix, May McCollum 1889; Miss Cora Snider, Miss Canon, Agnes Manix 1890; Eva Gardener 1891; Aura Darnell 1894; Etta Bivans 1895; Hattie Lemmon, Mrs. Conn 1898; Martha Ver Heul, Lora Myers 1899; Maggie Conway 1900; Maggie Conway, Anna Bush 1901; John P. Ward 1903-04; John P. Ward, Lloyd Putnam 1905; Lizzie McKinney, Martha Conway 1906; Martha Conway, Ethel Welsher 1907; Ethel Welsher, Virgie Shinn 1908; Mary Caffrey 1909; Edna Neal, Beulah Lever 1910; Beulah Lever, Kathryn Wren 1911; Kathryn Wren 1912; John P. Caffrey 1913-14; Mary Caffrey 1915; Blanche Pegram 1916; Brownie Gardner 1917; Averil Stubbs 1919; Mrs. Gail Horsman, John Pringle, Beatrice Erb 1921; Loretta Brown 1922; Minnie Hyatt, Loretta Brown 1923; Vera Covey 1924; Hazel Harkin 1925; Kate Ward 1927; Frances Kearney 1928; Frances Kearney 1930; Frances Kearney 1932-33; Madonna Beary 1934-38; Mildred Beary 1939-41; Mrs. Thelma Hilsabeck 1942; Catherine O'Brien 1943-45; Mrs. Helen Beem 1947-48; and Mrs. Mary Hester 1949.

Fee School (2)

FEE SCHOOL was about one mile north of the VA hospital. It can be found on its original site at 1349 118th Place, having been remodeled into a home in 1958.

The earliest mention I found of this school was in a March 1877 issue of *The Knoxville Journal*, which stated that teacher Mr. B. F. Woodcock has just completed a term from October 2 to March 23. Fifty-two pupils were enrolled with an average attendance of thirty-two. Myrtle Gamble and Frank Moose never missed a day. "The last day of school was the place to go for a square meal with fifty bringing enough food to satisfy the cravings of the inner man. Chicken, pies, and cakes prepared from the home larder."

One year later there is a letter to the editor commenting on the excellent teaching skills of Mr. Woodcock. In 1878, there were sixty pupils enrolled with an average attendance of forty-two. The ladies again prepared dinner for the last day of school. The activities consisted of class examinations, spelling contests, declamations, and music conducted by Mr. O. Barnes. "The A spelling class for nearly an hour contested for the honor of carrying off the prize, a Webster School Dictionary." The winner was Stewart Brown. Seven students recited the names of the Iowa counties by tiers eastward beginning at the northwest corner. (I'm not sure I could recite half the counties in any order.)

In 1889, *The Knoxville Journal* reports that Cora Workman was hired for a two-and-a-half-month term at $17 per month. In April of that year, "the ladies of the neighborhood met at the schoolhouse to white wash it and give it a good cleaning all over."

January of 1890 brought reports of trouble. On the 15th, the neighborhood correspondent reports, "we heard there was quite a number expelled for disturbance." On the 20th, there was a fire during the night when some coal rolled out and burned quite a hole in the floor which required $8 to repair. There was better news in January 1891: "Fee band boys gave an entertainment at the school. Program was well rendered but the audience was small."

1957 KHS graduate Marilyn Herman Miller talked with me about her experiences at Fee, which she attended from kindergarten through 8th grade. In February the year Marilyn was in the 3rd grade, the school burned down. The students were excited about this, imagining that they wouldn't have to go to school for the rest of the year. Unfortunately, her dad, Herman Miller, who was president of the school board, made provisions for them to attend the Knoxville schools for the remainder of the year.

Fee, 1947 – Teacher Mildred Lundy standing in back of classroom. Front row: Ardan Graves, Jerry Stone, Lew Arl Brent, and Jimmie Herman. Second row: Virginia Sams, Janice Fee, Dick Stone, and Roger Bryan. Third row: Twyla Little, Marilyn Herman, Ron Sherman, and Larry Little. Fourth row: Evelyn Shewmon, Carol Fee, Melvin Sams, and Lawrance Stone.

Marilyn and the other girls liked to play under a large lilac bush on the schoolyard. They also liked to swing high to try to flip the swing over the bar. Another student, Mark Hayes, recalls that one time when this swing flipped over, it injured his eye. Many country school students incurred minor injuries because of careless student behavior. However, Marilyn recalls that one time it was the teacher who created the problems when she asked the students to clear the fence row of weeds. Everyone but Marilyn developed a rash from poison ivy.

When teacher Miss Opal Caulkins became Mrs. Opal De Heer, the students had the fun of participating in a shivaree for the newlyweds. They "short sheeted" the bed and took the labels off their cans of food.

Melvin Sams also attended Fee for three years in the late 1940s. He recalls sleigh-riding parties on the hill north of the school. He also said the neighborhood gathered frequently for potluck suppers and wiener roasts in warm weather. Both Melvin and Marilyn loaned pictures, which have been copied and added to the school binders. One of the pictures shows all of the students sitting on top of a large cement-covered storm cellar. Storm cellars (food storage caves) were common on private property but not on schoolyards.

Those who taught at the Fee School included Miss Josie Parson, Mr. B. F. Woodcock 1872; Mr. B. F. Woodcock 1876; Mr. B. F. Woodcock 1877; Della Stewart, R. M. Morrrison 1886; Cora Workman, Miss Davis 1889; Miss Martin 1890; B. A. Hardin, Miss Grace Lanham 1891; Miss Flora Batten, Miss Agnes Mannix 1894; Agnes Mannix, W. H. Lucas 1895; W. H. Lucas 1896; W. H. Lucas 1898; W. H. Lucas, Lorence Putnam 1899; W. H. Lucas 1900; W. H. Lucas, Mrs. Gustin Nace 1901; Agusta Nace 1903-04; Berda Putnam 1905-06; Mary Greenaway 1908; Ida Sammons 1909; W. H. Lucas 1910; Angie Reese 1911; Virgie Shinn 1912-13; Eva Worstell 1914; Beulah Jones Hayes 1915; Katherine Shovelain 1916; Beulah Hayes 1917; Katherine Shovelain 1918; Helen Rankin 1919; Mrs. Beulah Hayes, Mrs. Bruce 1920; Grace Stanberry 1921-23; Mildred Covey 1925; Mrs. Fonda Fawcett 1927; Beulah Welch 1928; Cleta Stevens 1930; Mrs. Cleta Hall 1932; Beulah Welch 1933; Miss Beulah Wadell 1934; Mrs. Beulah Welch 1935; Beulah E. Hayes 1936-38; Rena Fee Welch 1939-41; Olive Shriner 1942; Opal I. Caulkins 1943; Opal I. Caulkins 1945; Mildred Lundy 1947; Dorothy Forgy 1948-52; Garneth Hill 1953-55; and Helen Beem 1956-57.

Flagler (2)

LOCATED ABOUT FIVE MILES east of Knoxville off Highway 15, Flagler was one of many small early settlements in Marion County. On May 27, 1872, Samuel Ridenour, superintendent of Marion County Schools, visited the Flagler School, where teacher Miss M. E. Livingston had thirty-seven pupils enrolled with an average attendance of twenty-six. (*Knoxville Journal*)

In 1875, the C. B. and Q. railroad line reached Flagler. This, combined with the abundance of coal deposits in the area, soon turned Flagler into a boom town. The town was platted in 1877. An 1884 atlas lists the population of Flagler's, an older name for the town, as forty.

In 1888, a larger three-room school building was built to accommodate the growing number of school-age children (defined as everyone age five to twenty-one). The number of children in the district grew from 249 in 1887 to 304 in 1888. The extra classroom space allowed for the employment of two teachers. Since different teachers were often employed for each of the three terms of fall, winter, spring, or summer, this made for a very long list of teachers before the school changed to one term per year.

On May 1, 1889, the Flagler correspondent reports that teacher "J. W. Elder has placed on the school grounds a telephone line. It affords great amusement to children during recess and leisure time." (He was certainly progressive, as our country school never acquired a telephone.)

In 1891, when the enrollment was 130, the school board put in shorter seats for the primary students. By 1894, enrollment had dropped to 81. The best source for information about the Flagler School comes from *Flagler Iowa Area History*, published in 1998. Several teachers and students have written personal accounts, giving much insight into the daily life of different decades. Find a copy in the genealogy room of the Knoxville Library.

In this book, teacher Johanna Rouwenhorst tells of her delight and surprise to be hired in 1934 to teach the three dozen students at Flagler. She had acquired a certificate at sixteen but wasn't allowed to teach until she reached eighteen. There was a large surplus of teachers and she had been turned down by thirty other school boards before getting the Flagler contract.

Beulah Kirkpatrick, who taught at Flagler from 1942 to 1952, recounts the fun activity of pyramid coasting. "We would put two sleds, side by side, and I would put one knee on one sled and one on the other sled, then someone would get on my back and someone on their back, sometimes as many as four high."

Student John Langford writes that teacher Edna Neal promoted all the 5th graders to 6th and 7th grade. At the request of their parents, they all had to take 5th grade over again with one of the best teachers, Helen Harsin.

Via e-mail, Sheryl Kersey shared fond memories of the Flagler School, which she attended in the 50s. "It was so sad when they tore the school down. I remember them loading up all the books in a dump truck to take to the dump. Our teacher Miss Mowrey gave each student a brand new pencil. It is so funny that in those days it didn't take much to make someone happy."

Flagler, 1914 – Row one: James Wignall, Frank Mitchell, Casey Zoutte, Bessie Barr, Rose DeCrotus, Elizabeth Dainty, Almeda Cooper, Francis Horton, Harry Nichols, and Thelma Wignall. Row two: Louis Dainty, William Horton, Rena Fortner, Germaine Zoutte, Louie Zoutte, Alfred Wignall, Irvin Pace, Frank Dainty, William Henderson, and Clabber Des Planges. Row three: Harvey Cecil, (unknown), Lois Dainty, Jess Nichols, Ronald Simpson, Marshall Des Planges, Henry Delpace, Arthur Chivers, and Henry Saville. Row four: Mary Murphy, Wilbert Dainty, Adolph Herduin, Robert Nichols, Fred Saville, Avis Chivers, Clara Fortner, Laura Murphy, Edith Simpson, and Zetella Herduin. Row five: Beulah Horton, Gladys Freeman, Blanche Fortner, Leona Pace, Ferne Dainty, Clarence Thompson, William Chivers, Cyprene Zoutte, Charles Nichols, and Walter Des Planges. Row six: Teachers Ruth Hill and Andy May.

Here is the list of teachers: Miss M. E. Livingston 1872; Mary Parks 1881; Mark Moore 1882; R. M. Manners 1886; J. W. Elder, Miss Cassie Tidball, Miss Pearl Simpkins 1888; Miss Dora Starr, J. W. Elder, Ms. J. W. Elder 1889; Miss Nora White, Zella McCollum 1891; Della Roberts, Ella Momyer, Nora White, May McCollerwin, F. M. Wright, W. J. Van Dyke 1892; Mr. J. W. Brillhart, Miss Grace Lanham, M. Harsin, Alice Cherrie, Nannie Stuart 1894; Mandelia Harsin, Alice Cherrie, Nora Sullivan, Maggie Momyer, R. E. McCollum 1895; W. J. Van Dyke, Agnes White, Nora Sullivan, Alice Cherrie 1896; William J. Van Dyke, Anna Sullivan, Sue Stone 1897; W. J. Van Dyke, Florence Wagoner 1898; W. J. Van Dyke, Florence Wagoner, Mattie McCollum, W. J. Van Dyke, Nora Sullivan, Vinnie Welch 1900; Mr. W. J. Van Dyke, Nora Sullivan 1901; Anna Sullivan, Eleanor Sullivan, Nora Sullivan 1903; Sue Stone, Nell McGowen, J. R. De Viny, Nell McGowen 1906; Lloyd Putnam, Nella McGowen, Mary King, Florence Fee, Gay Moore, Mabel Dickey 1907; Gay Moore, Mabel Dickey 1908; Gay Moore, Virgie Shinn, John Daily, Ruth Hill, Mrs. Susie Dolan, Mabel Dickey, Pearl Bonifield 1909; Virgie Shinn, Mable Dickey 1911; Alta Havley, Georgia Reichard 1912; A. J. May, Georgia Reichard 1913; A. J. May, Ruth Hill, Grace Rowland, Alice E. Murphy, Ruby Reese 1914; Ruth Hill, Grace B. Rowland 1915; Ruth Hill, Hazel Chivers 1916; Georgia Reichard, Hazel Chivers 1917; Ruth Hill, Hazel Chivers, Alice E. Murphy 1918; Grayce Rowland, Hazel Chivers 1919; Mrs. Lena Crouch, Helen Harrington 1920; Ellen Fitzpatrick, Virgie Shinn Anderson 1921; Virgie Anderson, Evelyn Bowman 1922; Johanna Paterson, Virgie Anderson 1923; Nannie Hyatt, Lillian Kissinger 1925-26; Ellen Fitzpatrick 1927-28; Helen Harsin 1930-33; Johanna Rouwenhorst 1934-36; Mary L. Beary 1937-40; Violet McDonnell 1941; Beulah Kirkpatrick 1942-51; Mrs. Tina K. Mowery 1952-55; Mrs. Minnie Davis, Tina K. Mowrey 1956; Marie Kingery 1957-58; and Maxine Adams 1959-60.

North Flagler (35)

ORIGINALLY CALLED SUMPTER, this school was located on the southeast corner of the intersection where 180th Drive crosses Highway T15. The name was probably changed to North Flagler around 1900 because the official records mention it only twice after that. Sometimes country schools were known locally by different names that referred to ghost towns or to prominent families in the neighborhood such as the Fairview (Kingery) School.

According to *The Knoxville Journal* of February 26, 1877, teacher Miss Alice Glen drew a large crowd to her school program. "The entertainment was well executed but owing to the house being so crowded it was impossible to be fully appreciated by the audience. Standing room with more outside the windows. We had a situation front and next to the stove. This afforded a fine view of the stage, but placed us as it were between two fires, however, by adroitly shifting positions as opportunity was afforded we came off well pleased, and with no serious tendency toward cremation."

On June 9, 1888, *The Knoxville Journal* writer comments, "As I passed the schoolhouse last Tuesday I found it vacated. The teacher and her scholars had taken up quarters under a large maple tree and had abandoned the schoolhouse for the time being."

In talking with Lawrence Van Zante, who graduated from the 8th grade in 1940, I found that he had been a rather shy student. He had a difficult time when one of the teachers required that he pick out a song and sing a solo accompanied by the Victrola before she promoted him to the next grade. For several years, he and brother Bill rode double to school on one pony. Stanton Metcalf also rode a pony and they built a pony shed on the side of the coal shed to accommodate these two ponies. Later they would all ride their bikes to school, carving a race track in the grass as they rode around and around the schoolhouse. Lawrence and Bill showed an early interest in creating things and with Stanton constructed a functional bridge across the road ditch from discarded fence posts.

I also talked with Darlene Monster Beyer, who graduated from 8th grade in 1954. Throughout her grade-school years, she was the only one in her class except for a brief period of six weeks when there was competition from another student. She didn't appreciate that. (In my opinion being the only one in a class was the major drawback of the country school.) She also stated that she always had to walk to school, except for the day after Halloween when her dad would take her to school because he would be called to set up a tipped over toilet. (I'm sure this yearly ritual may have been payback for many of the men who had done their share of toilet tipping a generation earlier.)

Teachers at Sumpter-North Flagler include: Miss Mary Parks 1870; R. W. Frey, Mary Auld 1872; Alice Glen 1877; R. M. Manners 1884; Nora Simpson, Miss Cora Armstrong 1885; R. M. Manners, Miss Charlotte Davis 1886; Miss Steele 1888; Mis Zella McCollum, Mis Letitia Keefer, Mary Momyer 1889; Zella McCollum 1890; Zella McCollum, Miss Welcher 1891; Agnes White, Mary Momyer, Nora White 1892; Letitia Keefer, Alice Cherrie 1893; Mary Stout, Jennie Keefer 1894; Jennie Keefer, Minnie Kendall, E. E. Denny 1895; Minnie Kendall, Agnes White, Lizzie Henry 1896; Miss Zella McCollum, Agnes White 1898; Vinnie Welch 1899-01; Nell McGovern 1903; Mary Greenaway 1904-05; Alice Phelps 1906; Mary King 1907; Grace Larew 1908-09; Alta Hanley 1910; Hazel Rice 1911; Izah Collins, Grace Dennison 1912; Ruby Reese 1913-14; Grace Larew 1915; Huldah Sherlock 1917; Ellen Fitzpatrick 1919-20; Margaret Curtis 1921; Bertha Augustine 1925; Mrs. Merle Amsberry, Opal Morgan 1927; Mildred Gregory 1928-29; Leila Hindman 1930; Helen Hindman 1931; Grace Toom 1932; Paulina Stittsworth 1933; Martha E. Sherwood 1934; Mrs. Woodrow Shives 1935; Mildred Harrington 1936-37; Helen Adair 1938; Inez Stittsworth 1939-40; Maxine Adams 1941; Marea Warder 1942; Mrs. Maxine Adams, Evelyn Stevenson Odom 1943; Maxine Adams 1944; Miss Betty Hollingshead 1945; Geraldine Biddle 1947-48; Helen Adair 1950-54; and Mildred Dooley 1955-57.

North Flagler, early 1930s – Front row: Marion De Zwarte, Bill Van Zante, and (unidentified). Middle row: Donald De Zwarte, Leroy Van Cleave, Lawrence Van Zante, and Stanton Metcalf. Back row: June De Zwarte, Katheryne Metcalf, and Leona Van Zee.

South Flagler (11)

South Flagler, little boys 1933-34 – Rex Barnhill, Abraham Nunnikhoven, Martin Nunnikhoven, and Lewis Henry Six.

BEFORE IT WAS RENAMED South Flagler, the little schoolhouse which stood near the English Creek was called the English Creek School. Over the years there has been a lot of flooding along this creek. Abe Nunnikhoven, who attended the school in the 1930s and 40s, recalls that at times the water would flood the schoolyard, forcing him and his brothers to walk the long way home.

Abe's most vivid memory was of his first day of school at South Flagler. One of the older boys picked him up and tossed him onto the roof of the coal shed and ran around to the other side in time to catch him as he slid down the other side. Abe thought he might have been singled out because he spoke only Dutch. He caught on quickly and in three weeks was speaking English.

Another memorable event for Abe was the elopement of teacher Betty Adams on March 1. He regretted that she never returned and a substitute finished the remainder of the term.

In my research of old newspapers, I found this reference from the December 18, 1895, issue of *The Knoxville Journal*. "The Flagler school board recently purchased an International Dictionary for the South Flagler School. This school board is awake to the interests of its schools. No school board can invest $10 in anything in the way of apparatus and other needed helps that will be of more real benefit both to the teacher and to the school than the purchase of an international dictionary. It would be used every hour of the day and every day in the week."

Doug Wilson provided some charming individual pictures of the South Flagler children in the 1923-24 school year. His mother was the only girl in the family of ten children born to John and Sara Barnett. Several of Doug's uncles are pictured. Tommy Barnett was killed at the age of twenty-one in the Lost City coal mine. Doug's grandfather and his great uncle Frank Barnett were coal miners who worked in Mahaska, Monroe, and Marion County. John's ten children were all born in various coal camps in the three counties. For many years, Marion County produced more coal than any other county in the state, and a number of the country schools got their start in the settlements that grew up around these early mines.

Fern Michaels Jarman says that when the South Flagler School closed, some of the parents did not want their children to attend the "rough" Flagler School, so she hauled ten of the students by station wagon to North Flagler. (This information was obtained from a *Flagler Iowa Area History*, compiled by Robert and Betty Clark and Tom and Donna Clarke in 1998. This book can be found in the genealogy room of the Knoxville Library.)

From the book comes this story written by Doug Wilson about his Uncle Howard "Babe" Barnett. He loved to fish, so before school started in the morning, he would put his fishing line into English Creek, behind the school, and would check it many times throughout the day (many restroom visits). He said he averaged twenty-three bullheads a day, which he took home, cleaned, and they all ate for supper. Friday afternoon at school was special game time—spelldowns, math contests, etc. Babe and John usually won all the contests, giving no one else a chance to be first, so the boys talked the teacher into letting them fish on Friday afternoons!

Teachers who taught at South Flagler include Miss Cassie Tidball, Miss Helen Lanham, Mattie Stenz 1892; Mary Sharib, Nannie Stuart 1894; Nannie Stuart, Grace Orenburg, Letitia Keefer 1895; Miss Jennie Keefer, Helen Lanham 1889; Letitia Keefer 1896; Sue Stone 1898-1903; Alta Poffenbarger, Irmaguarde Braun 1904; Irmaguarde Braun 1905; Norma Fee 1906; Florence Fee 1907; Hilda Bowman, Angie Stentz, Tugie S. 1910; Duinnie Gregory 1911; Laura Doolitte 1912; Alice Murphy 1913-14; Fern Dainty 1915; Gladys Abrams 1919-20; Evelyn Bowman 1921; Miss Johanna Peterson 1923; Margaret Wilene 1924; Pearl Robinson, Henry Slykhuis, Mary Frost, Pearle Clarke 1925; Iva Van Loon 1927; Letha Rushing 1929; Letha Rushing 1931-32; Jennie Shawver 1933; Nettie Belle Clark 1934; Vera Welch 1935-37; Melvina Neely 1938-40; Bette Adams 1941; Bette Adams, Bonnie Jean Nichols 1942; and Geraldine Biddle 1947.

Georgia Ridge (2)

Georgia Ridge – Inez Stittsworth and students from 1942-43 school year.

GEORGIA RIDGE was northwest of Knoxville, east of 92nd Avenue, and south of Jewel Drive.

From *The Knoxville Journal* of January 10, 1889, comes this bit of disturbing news: "As a school district Georgia Ridge is nearly depopulated. When we settled in it 30 years ago there were 60 scholars between the age of 5 and 21 now there are 5 or 6 and most of them will be past their school days in half a dozen years. The board of directors last fall decided to have no more school until the neighborhood is replenished." Parents with children must have moved into the district because the school continued until the spring of 1956.

Teachers were George Smith 1879; Miss Courtney 1880; Mollie Clark 1881; Mr. B. Manners 1882; Miss Agnes Manix 1883; Mary Clark, Aggie Manix 1886; Susie Stone, Cora Jacobs 1894; Agnes Manix 1896; Agnes Manix 1898-99; Agnes Manix, Amanda Brown 1900; Amanda Brown, Fannie Eberhardt, Maggie Conway 1901; Bernice Stickle, Margaret Conway 1903-04; Bernice Stickle, Lloyd D. Putnam, Martha Conway 1905; Martha Conway, Beatrice Smith 1906; Hazel Wilson, Beatrice Smith 1907; Charles Wren, Katheryn Wren 1908; Katheryn Wren 1909; Mae McMurphy, Mary Caffrey 1910; Beulah Worstell, John Caffrey 1911; Olive Breese 1912; Mary Caffrey 1913; Ruth Stittsworth 1914-15; Ruth Patton 1916; Bessie Williams 1917; Lee Goodenough, Forrest Bonifield, Margaret Leonard, Roman Reius 1918; Ruth Perry, Vida Davis Crabtree, Ruth Perry Greer 1919; Mrs. Chester Greer, Mary B. Mills Wagner 1920; Mrs. Mary Wagner 1921; Hazel Harkin 1922-23; Nellie Burt 1925; Mary Frost, Gladys Taggart 1926; Gladys Taggart 1927; Otis Crozier 1928-30; Agnes Wren 1934-35; Ivy Stittsworth 1936; Kate A. Mudgett 1938; Maxine Hukill 1939-40; Joy Morgan 1941; Inez Stittsworth 1942; Dorothy Cleair 1943; Miss Doris M. Turner 1944; Julia Simmons 1945; Marily E. Siefken 1947; Norma Eysink 1948-49; Lucille Morgan 1950-51; Marie Metcalf 1953; and Mrs. Ruth Kenney 1954-55.

Highland (13) - See Franklin Township

Liberty (22)

Liberty, 1935 - Students included Douglas, Bob, and Betty Barnett; Wilbur Tull; Wallace Thomas; Juanita and Harriet Hartshorn; Rose Ellen Welch; Oscar and Tommy Barnes; Hoyt, Glenna, Wilma, and Wanda Monroe; Bernice and Doris Waits; Betty Reeves; Ruby Gilchrist; and three Applegate children. Teacher Arlene Covey.

LIBERTY SCHOOL was located at the T-intersection of Oregon Drive and 165th Avenue on the south side of Oregon Drive. Former Student Doug Wilson writes that when you came to the T-intersection, you could have nearly driven through the front double doors.

According to a *Knoxville Journal* of May 1925, when Grace Robinson was the teacher, the Farm Bureau ladies gathered and surprised both pupils and teacher. "They brought well-filled baskets and helped with the weenie roast planned by the teacher at the noon hour. The men of the neighborhood, attracted, no doubt, by the delicious odor of the picnic dinner, came and an enjoyable time was had by all. The Board of Directors showed appreciation by reemploying Miss Robinson."

Doug Wilson wrote several pages of his personal memories of his school days, including the names of many students who attended from 1920 till the school closed in the spring of 1958. Readers can find his entire story as well as several pictures of the school and its students at the schoolhouse in the Marion County Historical Village.

Doug, who started school in 1947, says that rather than walking two miles down the road, he often cut "catty-corner" through the fields, shortening the distance to one mile. Although he was supposed to walk straight home, sometimes he stopped at the home of the Kelderman kids to listen to such radio shows as *The Sky King, Straight Arrow,* and *Sergeant Preston of the Yukon*. This got him in trouble with his dad.

He thinks the large two-room school was probably built around 1910, the time when the Anderson Coal Company opened the big mine and built forty to fifty houses in the area for coal miners' families. By the time Doug attended school, only one of the rooms was being used as a classroom and the other had become a "community room." It was filled with benches similar to church benches and was used for 4H meetings, the annual school play, and community potlucks.

When it was extremely cold outside the teacher would build a fire in the stove in the community room and push the benches aside to allow the children to play games at recess. "MY WORST MEMORY," he recalls, "was when the teacher brought her record player and we had to learn to dance the Virginia Reel—and we boys would have to hold a girl's hand during the dance!"

Like many other country schools, Liberty did not have a well on the schoolyard. During the morning hours, the teacher would ask a couple of the older students to go the Presley's farm and fetch a bucket of water for everyone to drink. The Presleys had two or three coon dogs who would howl and howl while the students were getting the water. Doug remembers one year they had caught a baby raccoon, which was chained to a tree. The students would play with it and sometimes bring it a piece of their peanut butter and jelly sandwiches. When the students returned with the water for the day everyone drank it from a common dipper. This practice changed in 7th grade when the teacher required everyone to bring their own cup or glass. (Remember those collapsible aluminum cups we all thought we just had to have?)

Teachers at Liberty included Abram Scott 1868; Sarah Lyman 1886; T. L. Conrey, Miss Julia Ruckman, Miss Carrie Burt 1890; Miss Carrie Burt, Miss Harvey, James Hamilton 1892; Ella Crosby 1894; Rena Snyder, Alice Crosby, Julia Ruckman 1895; M. V. Harsin, Jennie M. Kester, Mabel Reynolds 1896; Jennie M. Kester, Mable Reynolds 1898; Florence Inskeep, Mrs. Weyman, Eleanor Crosby 1899; Eleanor Crosby 1900; Grace Morris, B. D. Pope, Edythe Hartness 1901; Stella Jenkins, Nannie Hyatt 1903; Katherine Sturgeon 1904; Katherine Sturgeon, Rosa Brubaker 1905; Rosa Brubaker, Art Betterton 1906; June Burdick, Eva Nutter 1907; Anna B. Brouse, Cora Rankin 1908; Cora Rankin, Beulah Linn 1909; Edna Townsend 1910-11; Frank Palmer, Cora Rankin 1912; Cora Rankin, India B. Davis, Bettie Burkley 1913; John W. Pringle, Liva Barrett 1914; Mabel Leuty, Duinnie Gregory, Ada Alexander 1915; Gene Hollingshead 1923; Grace Robinson 1924-25; C. M. Hollingshead 1926; Mrs. Fern Etcher 1927; Opal Morgan 1929; Arlene Covey 1930-34; Ruby Penland 1935; Ruby Ver Steeg

1936-37; Betty Whaley 1938-42; Helen Adair 1943; Miss Mary E. Myers 1944; Maxine Adams 1945; Gladys Bowery 1946-47; Basal White 1948-49; Betty Mae Hollingshead 1950-51; Beulah Kirkpatrick 1952; Paulina Stittsworth 1953-54; and Virgie Feagins 1955-57.

Lincoln (4)

Lincoln – Students on an outing with Secretary of Agriculture Ezra Taft Benson and Teacher Mildred Lundy, who taught from 1955-57. Students included Christa Goad; Maribeth Mueller; Carol June Romick; Hazel Stanton; Mary Ann and Teddy Ward; Marzette and Katherine Perkey; Diana, Ronald, Donna, and Linda Jordan.

LINCOLN SCHOOL was about two miles west of Knoxville on what is now 92nd Avenue. An 1875 map shows it across the road from the Lincoln cemetery. The school building is still on its original location and has been converted into a home by Marvin and Alberta Miller.

A *Knoxville Journal* of June 1877 reports that C. C. Hardin had sixty-three students. C. C. Hardin was probably a man. In the early records, men teachers were often designated by their first and middle initials while the first names of women teachers were generally spelled out. School districts with large numbers of students often preferred to hire male teachers because they felt their strength was needed to maintain discipline.

In January of 1879, the writer tells us that the teacher was "whipping" some of the students with the words, "Miss Timmerman has been using the persuader on some of the boys."

In February of 1889, the school hosted a debate, probably at night or on a Saturday. "There was a debate at Lincoln School over women's suffrage. Four women and seven men were judges. There were eight for the affirmative and three for the negative, two of which were women." (That figures.)

Teachers were C. C. Hardin 1877; A. D. Clark 1878; Miss Timmerman 1879; L. Butterfield 1880; Mr. David Kennedy 1881; L. K. Butterfield 1882; Miss Stephens, James Clark 1883; Melle Boydston 1886; Mr. Butterfield 1887; Prof. Steele, L. K. Butterfield, Prof. Robert Nace 1888; Nellie Bishop, Candace Mach 1889; N. F. Muller, Dora Marsh, Mrs. S. M. Sherman, Dora Murphy, Byron Hardin 1891; Miss Dora Marsh, C. O. Williams 1892; Miss Eberhardt, Fred Smith 1893; Miss Ollie Crowdson, Miss Flora Kester 1894; Flora Kester, Miss Eleanor Cully, Leonard Bane 1895; Jennie Kiefer, Sue Stone, Miss Alice Crosby 1896; Miss Flora Kester, C. M. Wasson 1897; Sue Stone 1898; Julia Hocking, Jennie Keifer, Villa Parnel 1899; Loren Putnam 1900; Loren Putnam, Nellie Morrow 1901; Nellie Morrow, T. E. Ward, Blanche McTaggart 1903; Gerda

Putnam 1904; Maude Lamme, Mary Jones, Minnie Hyatt 1905; Minnie Hyatt, Bess Wright 1906; L. Bess Wright 1907; Lucy Ward, Hal Risse 1908; Thurman Ward 1909; Mary Greenaway, Louise Cox 1910; W. H. Lucas 1911; John Williams, Sue Stone 1912; John E. Williams, Nellie Johnson 1913; Nellie Johnson 1914; Murl McGuire 1915; Beulah Jones Hayes 1916; Olive Easter, Mary Shivers 1917; Mrs. Mary Suelson 1918; Pearl Wortham 1919; Ruth Flanders 1920-21; Mrs. Eugene Speed 1922-23; Mrs. Beulah Hayes 1925-28; Thelma Maddy 1929; Mildred Gregory 1930-31; Helen Emerson 1932-36; Helen Emerson 1938; Mrs. Helen Overton 1939-41; Mary Adair 1942; Mrs. Florence O' Melia 1944; Ruby Ver Steeg 1945; Ruby Ver Steeg 1947-54; and Mildred A. Lundy 1955-57.

Maple Grove (14)

Maple Grove, 1928 – "Time for learning," says Malvina Neely's school bell.

MAPLE GROVE SCHOOL was on the southwest corner of what was known for many years as the county "poor farm," now the Marion County Care Facility.

Robert J. Mulky refers to this school that he attended in an article written for the 1930 souvenir edition of *The Knoxville Journal*. He writes that the school was organized in 1860. A log building was erected and the students were taught that winter by Henry Sherman. Other early teachers were Mr. Vance, Miss Blair, Miss Esther Kelly, Mr. Abe Updegraff, and J. R. Young. This was Mr. Young's first school. He later became a teacher and principal in Knoxville. He also refers to Mr. Ben Kirk, "a most excellent teacher," who taught one term while the Civil War was in progress.

Textbooks used were McGuffy Readers and Spellers and Ray's Arithmetic. Some of the older pupils brought history or geography books from home, which often meant that no two were alike.

The Knoxville Journal of May 9, 1896, reports that Maple Grove was closed because the teacher had the measles. Such unscheduled vacations occurred often before vaccinations for common diseases were available. Substitutes were scarce and sometimes the teacher would ask a sibling or friend to fill in for them during an absence.

Teachers included Henry Sherman 1860; Nannie Harding 1877; Alice Williams 1886; Miss Ellie Taylor 1887; Miss Liza Croft 1889; Miss Hannah Spence 1892; Miss Cora Snyder 1893; Will Bye 1894; D. O. Bye, Alice Crosby 1895; Alice Crosby, Miss Mable Reynolds 1896; Miss Daisy McAtee 1897; Ella McKinney 1898; Ella McKinney, Katie Jones 1899; Estella Reins, Lulu Crosby 1900; Laura Ghrist 1901; Minnie Tysseling, L. Bess Wright, Mary Matthews 1903; Edna Black 1904; Florence Fee 1905; Velta D. Karns 1906; Alleta Cunningham 1907; Herman Browne 1908; Arvilla Hayes, Eunice Kutz

1909; Lizzie McKinney 1910-11; Eva Worstell 1912-13; Anna King 1914; Eva Worstell, Fern Collins 1915; Angeline Stentz 1916; Vida Davis 1917-18; Virgie Shinn 1919; Virgie Shinn Anderson 1920; Joye Black 1921-24; Blanche Borden 1925; Mary Crouch 1926; Malvina Neely 1928; Rena Fee 1929-30; Rena Fee Welch 1933-36; Maxine Moneysmith 1938; Frances Van Donselaar 1939-40; Frances Thompson 1941; Lorraine Roff 1942-43; Dorothy Cleair 1944; Mrs. Ruth Kenney 1945; Betty Hollingshead 1947; Jean Golfry 1948; and Mrs. Jean Cooper 1949.

Pleasant Grove (31)

Pleasant Grove, 1917 – Teacher Leulah Stuff Amos. Row one: Esther Jones, Agnes Wren, Edith Smith, Sarah Vander Linden, Fern Booth, Paul Jones, Thomas Wren, and Ted Sterling. Row two: Edith Bowery, Madeline Crozier, Agnes Jones, Glenn Booth, Worth Booth, and Everett Sterling. Row three: Edna Booth, Frances Smith, Mary Vander Linden, Matilda Barnes, and Lois Talbott.

PLEASANT GROVE SCHOOL was east of Highway 14 near G44. It was sometimes called the Crab Apple School.

An 1872 *Voter* (an early Knoxville newspaper) says that Miss Ruth A. Timmerman had forty-six enrolled with thirty-one present on the day the county superintendent paid a visit. He also reports that the House was frame and "poor."

The November 6, 1930, *Knoxville Express* comments on the school program when Elretta Smith was teacher. "A packed house bespoke the interest." Refreshments were served by the Pleasant Grove community club. Many country schools provided meeting places for 4H and other neighborhood clubs.

Teachers who served this school were Miss Ruth A. Timmerman 1872; Augusta Cronkhite 1886; R. A. Harp 1888; Ora Lake, Gusta Nace 1895; Gustie Nace 1896; Eunice Femorod, Esta Sweem 1898; Mary Roller, Katie Smith, Gustie Nace 1899; Eunice Cronkhite 1900; Anna Bush, Eleanor Crosby, Ella McKinny 1901; Mrs. A. Cronkhite, Flora Batten 1903; Nell McGovern, Iva B. Marsh 1904; Art Betterton 1905; Fay Tyrell, Bess Wright, Mary Greenaway 1906; Rosa Brubaker, Fessie M. Palmer 1907; Fessie M. Palmer, Mabel Shook 1908; Hazel Reiser, Mabel Vierson 1909; Arminda Ferguson 1910; Arminda Ferguson, Oletha Lemmon, Fern Stittsworth 1911; Rosa Smith, Maude Crowder, Faye Cummings 1912; Faye Cummings, Anna King 1913; Murl McGuire, Beulah Jones 1914; Mae Hamm, Eva Worstell 1915; Lula Cline 1916; Leulah Stuff Amos 1917; Merl Witt 1918; W. H. Lucas 1919; Camille Leuty 1920-21; Ellen Fitzpatrick 1922-23; Jennie Leuty 1924; Irene Bellamy 1925-26; Mrs. Abe Cronkhite 1927; Elretta Smith 1932-34; Miss Ruth Smith 1935-36; Eula Emerson 1938-40; Helen Adair 1941-42; and Paulina Stittsworth 1955.

Pleasant Hill

NOT TO BE CONFUSED with another Pleasant Hill in Perry Township, the official records do not tell its location other than Knoxville Township and list only three teachers: F. Coffman 1886; Miss Ella Momyer 1887; and Miss Lily French 1892.

Pleasant Ridge (29)

Pleasant Ridge, 1909 – Teacher Bessie Williams. Front row: Pearl Karns, May Ellison, Grace Ellison, Ward Colwell, and Johnie Sylvanus. Back row: Dale Woodle, Lloyd McConeghey, Wrex Colwell, Dick Sylvanus, and Van Merriman. Peeping out of the window: Hally Clark and Helen Sylvanus. Student Pearl Karns became the teacher at Pleasant Ridge in 1917 and 1918.

PLEASANT RIDGE SCHOOL was built in 1874 on land donated by John Merriman. The speculation is that he wanted his eight children to have a place to attend school. According to a *Knoxville Journal* article of June 28, 1872, Miss Mary E. Black was teaching twenty Pleasant Ridge students in a private home. On the day that the county superintendent visited, fifteen students were present and no grammar or history was taught.

The Knoxville Journal of April 27, 1874, reports that Pleasant Ridge was completing a new frame school house of twenty-four by thirty feet. "It will have iron seats and be otherwise eloquently furnished."

The neighborhood correspondent writes in December 1885: "School is settling down to practical work. It took several pretty severe applications of the birch system to convince some of the boys not to indulge their pugilistic propensities and practice the art of modern profanity. If application of hickory is needed we may lay it on Christopher. When a boy gets beyond moral persuasion we believe in corporal persuasion."

February 1, 1893: "Pleasant Ridge closed on account of scarlet fever."

According to Moe Wadle, the school was six miles from Dallas where the crooked road begins. When he started kindergarten in 1948 it was a ten-minute walk through the pasture. He remembers that his bologna sandwiches tasted like heating fuel because they absorbed fumes from the stove. One of the memorable events was the day teacher Mabel Gill, who had one of the early TV sets, arranged for the students to come to her house to view the inauguration of President Eisenhower in 1952.

John Barnett, an 8th grader in 1951, remembers running around a corner of the schoolhouse and colliding hard enough to give a girl a concussion. He also recalls being paddled by the teacher for not coming in after recess ended.

Several years after the school closed, Mrs. Jessie Adams purchased the school building and surprised the Marion County Historical Society by requesting that they pay to have it moved to the historical village and have a foundation put under it. The Historical Society gets many gifts but most do not require fundraising. After some discussion, it was decided that it would be a good addition and the funds were raised through many small donations of $1 to $5 as well as a few larger donations.

The little red schoolhouse was advertised as being authentically restored in 1964. However, the only red schoolhouses were those constructed of brick. Pleasant Ridge is a frame building and had always been white. Therefore when the historical society refurbished the building last year (2008), in order to obtain a $5,000 grant through the REAP foundation, one of the requirements was to restore the building to its original condition. This included replacing the rotting boards with new cedar siding painted white. In the school building is a book with a more complete history and pictures of the school.

Here is a list of many of the teachers who taught at the school. Note that there are no teachers listed for the years 1946 and 1947 because there were not enough students to attend and they were sent to another district: Miss Mary E. Black 1872; Miss Adda Rutherford 1882; Lydia Little 1895; Lizzie Leonard, B. S. Kirk, Augusta Cronkhite 1886; Miss Spence 1887; Miss Hannah Spence, Miss Laura Kirk 1889; Laura Kirk 1890; Herbert Curtis, Kate Derry 1892; Lou Bone 1894; Lillian Beaman, Flora D. Batten 1895; Lillian Beaman, Edith Fountain, Fred Stevenson 1896; Katie Derry, Len Bane 1897; R. N. Louster, Jennie Barrett 1898; Jennie Barrett, Thurman E. Ward 1899; W. S. Wilson 1900; Ella McKinney 1901; W. S. Wilson, Mrytle Snyder, Alice Burrows 1902; Ada Wilcutt, Orville Nye 1903; Doris Ervin, Ada Wilcutt, Ann Ridenour, Lizzie McKinney 1904; Lizzie McKinney, Anna Ridenour, Lucy Ward 1905; Mrs. Lillian Bennett 1906; W. G. Conrey 1907; Willie Conrey, Richard Rice, Conn Moose 1908; Rhea Cloe, Bessie Williams 1909; Eunice Kutz, Stella Brubaker, Edith Agan 1912; Maude Crowder, Ve Lola Blair, Vera C. Hardin 1913; Vera C. Hardin 1914; Vera Hardin, Walter Terrell, Gladys Witt 1915; Blanche McClary 1916; Pearl Karns 1917-18; Ethell Curtis 1919-20; Edith Mulley 1921; Maud Long 1922; Myrtle McArthur 1924; Miriam Fletcher 1925-26; Leona Cambrion 1928; Estelline Ownes 1929-30; Mable L. Dykstra 1931-32; Ruth Hawk 1933; Ruby C. Seaman 1934; Betty Whaley 1935; Jessie Shives 1936; Marjorie Litton 1938-39; Wilma Clark 1940; Margaret Mann, Joy Flanagan 1941; Miss Inez M. Blake 1944; Zelma E. Beebout 1945; Phyllis Nicholson 1948; Mabel Gill 1949-52; Iantha Bucklew 1953-54; Paulina Stittsworth 1955; Edna Johnson 1956; and Mrs. Ruth Kenney 1957.

Rising Star (17)

RISING STAR SCHOOL was about a mile south of the present Knoxville city limits on the west side of Highway 5. I didn't find anyone who could tell me the origin of the name with its poetic ring.

However, former student Sandra Brooks Chrisman commented that she always liked the name as it made the students feel like they were all rising stars. It was common for romances to begin in country school. Jack Sterling told me that his mother and dad started together at Rising Star about 1915. In 1976, a picture was taken of them standing beside the school. After the school was torn down, Jack made a frame for the picture from wainscoting used in the building. You can see a copy of the picture in one of the binders at the schoolhouse in the Marion County Historical Village.

The community made good use of the school building for after-school activities. The April 14, 1938 issue of *The Knoxville Journal* says, "At the community meeting at the schoolhouse a very interesting program was given by Miss Augustine and pupils. Mrs. Bess Momyer's name was drawn to receive the quilt given by the garden club." Later that year, *The Journal* reports that the Community Club met at the school house on September 9 for a program by the 4-H girls under the direction of Mrs. Jack Mark and Mrs. Roy Shilling.

I talked by phone with former teacher Imogene Ream Fee who has lived in California for the past twenty years. At eighty-four she is on Facebook! One of the things she mentioned was that country school teachers had to watch students for frostbite when they would come in soaking wet from playing in the snow. At Rising Star, she was grateful that the furnace was in the cloakroom. This meant she could close the door so no one had to endure the unpleasant odor of wet wool mittens drying near the heat.

She also shared a special memory of the day that World War II ended. She always parked her car in the driveway of a neighboring farm and when she left school that afternoon the little neighbor boy came running out to meet her to tell her that the war had ended.

Imogene suggested I contact Sandra Chrisman, who started kindergarten in 1945. Sandra remembers that she attended the wedding of Imogene and John Fee the summer after her primary year. She even remembers the wedding gift they picked out for them—a pair of pink Fenton hobnail vases. Sandra said Imogene was a very good teacher. She describes her next teacher, Ceola Liebhart, as a fun teacher who played the piano for them and pushed back the desks to clear a space so they could do the Virginia Reel. She also remembers that teacher Georgia Long invited her and her sister Connie Brooks, Betty Sue Pearson, and Lauretta, Dixie, and Sherrie Spaur to stay overnight in her home to watch the coronation of Queen Elizabeth on her black and white TV. Sandra has written a memoir of her days in school called "My Rising Star Journal." Find additional memories as well as the names of students who attended school with her in the copy at the schoolhouse museum.

Teachers included Mr. Graves 1883; R. G. Marlky, A. L. Steele 1886; Lettie Duncan, Lucia Jenkins, Abe Steele 1889; Miss Jenkins 1890; Miss Rogers 1891; Miss Mary Cox 1893; Miss Media Watkins 1894; Lottie McClymond, Miss Maggie Watson 1895; Lottie McClymond 1896; Mr. Schultz 1897; C. M. Gilson, Jennie M. Kester, Miss Gertie Pritchett 1898; Jennie M. Kester, Fannie Gelderblom 1899; Fannie Gelderblom, Anna Sullivan 1900; Lulu Crosby, Ollie Gelderblom, Alice Winters, Miss Roller 1901; Lucinda Marshall 1903; C. M. Wasson, Lulu Townsend 1904; Lulu Townsend 1905; C. B.

Howser 1906; Edna Tysseling 1907; Mabel Bush 1908; Lonice Cox 1909; Estella Brubaker 1910; Cora Rankin 1911; Emmett Kincaid 1912; Forest Moore, Sue Stone 1913; Sue Stone 1914; Edna S. Noe 1915-16; Alta M. Keane 1917-21; Jennie Leuty 1922; Alta Keene 1924; Iva Van Loon 1925-26; Thelma Maddy 1927-28; Nannie Hyatt 1929-30; Nannie Hyatt 1932; Bertha Augustine 1933-40; Malvina Neely 1941-43; Imogene Ream 1944-45; Imogene Fee 1946-48; Ceola Liebhart 1949-50; Mrs. Blackman 1951; Mrs. Blackman, Georgia Long 1952; Beulah Kirkpatrick 1953; Mrs. Ruth Goughnour 1954; Helen Adair 1955-56; and Tina K. Mowrey 1957.

Rising Star, early 40s – Malvina Neely's students gathering scrap iron for the war effort.

Salem (33)

Salem, 1935 - Row one: Clinton Hall, John Lenig, _____, Cornie Verwers, Glen Hall, ____ Hedrick, and Elmer Verwers. Row two: Dorothy Hall, Charlene Rinehart, Helen Rinehart, Jean Rickey, Cleo Verwers, Dana Bebout, Irene Hedrick, Jerry Rickey, and Betty Brees. Row three: Teacher Joye Black, Madonna Rickey, Forest Hedrick, Caraline Verwers, Vera Lening, Eva Mae Bebout, June Lenig, and May Hall.

SALEM WAS SOUTHWEST of Knoxville. In comparing a 1937 map with today's map, the school appears to have been on 94th Place west of English Creek. We associate the name Salem with that famous eastern seaport founded in 1626. It's an unusual name for a school. Was it chosen by locals who were descendants of those living in Salem or is it just a nod to a historic city?

From the February 1892 *Knoxville Journal*: "The patrons and scholars came with well filled baskets and about 40 partook of the gorgeous viands, which had been nicely prepared by the housewives."

Several years ago, Ruth Woodle Kenney, who attended Salem, contributed a photo and an article to *The Knoxville Journal* about the early days of rural schools. Ruth Kenney was a rural schoolteacher but she did not teach at Salem. She wrote that "learning the ABCs was the first thing required of the child. After he could distinguish most of the letters by sight, he was taught to spell simple words on the theory that no one could read properly until he had learned to spell well. More attention was given to orthography during the child's early school years than to any other branch of study. As a further encouragement to good spelling, contests were frequently held of evenings and in these spelling schools many of the parents participated. Two captains were selected to choose up sides."

Teachers were D. B. Bye 1886; Miss Minnie Smith 1887; Miss Scott 1888; Eva Scott, Charles McKern 1889; Miss Duncan 1890; Miss Keefer 1891; Mr. H. S. Bye, Miss Keefer 1892; Miss Kate Derry 1894; Kate Derry, Letitia Keefer 1895; Art Betterton 1898; Alda Applegate 1899; Art Betterton 1900; Mary Kelley 1901; Fannie Eberhardt, Nellie Rogers 1903; Nannie Hyatt, Mary E. Bruett 1904; Effie McIntire 1905; Mary Greenaway 1906; Maud De Raat, Della Ridenour 1907; Della Ridenour 1908; Idella Pearl Bonifield 1909; Cluna Karns 1910; Cluna Karns, Alta Havley, Jo Mendenhall 1911; Myrtle Lacken, Lucille Tysseling 1912; Vera C. Hardin 1913; Irene Tysseling 1914; Gail Cruyenberry, Fern Shults 1915; Electra West 1916; Vera Colwell, Lucille Tysseling 1917; Florence Willis, Mabel Bush 1918; Mabel Bush 1919; Ollie Evans 1921; Inez Grimes 1922; Susie Orcutt 1925; Helen Welsher 1928; Madge Wilson 1930; Edith Hamilton 1932; and Joye Black 1933-35.

Scott (33)

Scott, 1946-47 – Row one: Beverly Smith, Larry Moore, Gary Moore, and Raymond Smith. Row two: Maxine Kline and Richard Rowley. Row three: Jimmy Moore, Ruby McDonald, Zella Mae McDonald, Mary Hatch, Mary McDonald, and Alta Rowley.

THE SCOTT SCHOOL was near the Valley Chapel, the little church that has been moved to the Marion County Historical Site. Three former students who contacted me regarding this school all mentioned that it was often called the Valley School. The school was west of Highway 5 on Pratt Street.

Frances Brees Kain writes that her last four years were spent at this school. "I always thought it was such a pretty area, located about six miles southeast of Knoxville in a quiet valley with lots of singing birds and pheasants that would startle you as you walked down the dirt road and past the little country church."

Maxine Kline Bruinekool also mentions trudging down that road with boots caked with mud. She says that while playing baseball, some of the farm boys hit the ball so hard it could knock you over. One day a ball hit her nose, causing it to bleed for the rest of the afternoon. She also recalls that when it was her turn to take the wagon up the hill to get drinking water from a neighboring farm, she was afraid of the dog that always came running out to greet her.

Zella McDonald Brown also mentions having to carry water, which was used to fill a large crock with a push-button spigot. Zella came from a family of nine children, all of whom attended Scott School. Not all the children of Henry and Ethel McDonald were in school at the same time and some of them dropped out early to work. When Zella started school after Labor Day in 1936, there were five siblings in attendance. It was a very traumatic day for her because her pony had just been killed in a barn fire started by a lightning strike. Now she would have to walk to school. Zella went barefoot as soon as it was warm enough in the spring until it cooled off in the fall. One fall day, it snowed early and she walked home barefoot in the snow.

Many country schools were part of close communities where there was no controversy about which daily rituals should be followed; therefore, Zella was surprised that two new students who were Jehovah's Witnesses could not pledge allegiance to the flag. (I too was surprised to be called into the principal's office in Monroe in 1954 to be told I had offended half of the community by reading the Christmas story from the New Revised Standard version of the Bible rather than the King James version.)

Zella keeps a journal and writes many letters to friends and relatives. She still hears from some of her grade-school teachers, four of whom are still living (2009). Like many of us who attended country school, she credits her teachers with giving her a good start in life.

Here is the list of teachers known to have taught at Scott School: Julia Ruckman, Blanche Welch 1895; Katie Brennen, Katie Jones 1898; Nellie Roberts 1899; Estella Jenkins 1900; Lula Townsend, Connie Brennan 1901; Nannie Hyatt, Anna Ridenour, Walter Bone 1903; Doris Ervin, Edythe Hartness 1904; Edythe Hartness, Walter Kester 1905; Bessie Steen 1906; Irmagaarde Braun, Estella Brubaker 1907; Art Betterton 1908; Estella Brubaker 1909; Cora Rankin 1910; Stella Brubaker 1911; Lizzie McKinney, Ethel Jones 1912; Ethel Jones 1913-14; Nellie Johnson 1915; Ferne Rowland 1916-17; Charlene Scheele 1918; Ferne Rowland 1919; Hazel Chivers 1920-22; Avis Van Loon 1924; Fern Brause 1925; Mrytle Van Loon 1928-29; Clara Ridlen 1931-33; Geneva Van Loon 1934; Arlene Covey 1935; Betty Whaley 1936; Maxine Covey 1938-39; Marjorie Litton 1940-43; Betty Wing 1944; Mrs. Carolyn Sween 1945; Mrs. Arlene Stephenson 1946-47; Mrs. Helen Moore 1948-51; Mrs. Betty Catrenich 1952; Minnie McDonnell 1953; Minnie McDonnell Davis 1954-55; Paulina Stittsworth 1956-57; and Gertrude McCullough 1958.

Spring Hill (36)

THE SPRING HILL SCHOOL stands on its original location about three-and-one-half miles south of Knoxville. It is on the north side of Pratt Street and on the west side of Highway 14. When the school closed, the land on which it stands reverted back to the Finarty family and it was used as a shop. Near the old school, which could tumble down any day, is a grain bin. Both buildings are on land belonging to John Finarty.

The Knoxville Journal of November 26, 1884, says, "Spring Hill now boasts of the finest country school house in the county. It is an ornament in the community and speaks well for their interest in educational matters."

In the fall of 1888, the correspondent mentions the school had a new stove and that teacher Miss Davenport was paid $37.50 per month.

In November 1889, Spring Hill was having a three-week vacation, giving the "big boys" a chance to gather the corn.

On January 15, 1890, the correspondent says it was enough for people of the district to pay taxes to buy ground, build schoolhouses, etc., and those that get the benefit ought to rustle around and get their own books. (It seems there was never enough money to meet all school needs.)

Note the large number of students in the 1892 picture (next page). Several students were probably absent, as the following year the newspaper reports an enrollment of ninety-three school-age children, double the number in the photo, which was provided by one of the students, Lottie McConoughey, for a *Journal* story in 1932. She says these young men and women trudged through spring mud and winter snow in their copper-toed boots or shoes, carrying their lunch in a "poke" or a tin bucket, to master the intricacies of the three "R's."

I talked with Clarence Evans, who began his grade school education at Spring Hill and completed it at the Knoxville Middle School. He and two friends, who were in the same grade through high school graduation, are looking forward to their fifty-year high school reunion next year. His last teacher at Spring Hill was Freda Chamberlain, whom he described as a live wire, a real character. Sometimes Freda would take down an old mandolin that was stored at the school for an impromptu sing-a-long.

This summer (2010), Clarence visited Freda, now in her 90s. Although she has some memory problems, she recognized him. When he offered his arm as they walked down the steps she informed him that she was capable of going down the steps by herself.

Spring Hill was heated by a fuel oil furnace, which stood near the back of the classroom. Clarence said he always picked a seat at the back of the room as the wind blew through the sandstone foundation, making it pretty cold near the front. He sometimes spent an entire noon hour trying to toss a softball straight up to the chimney just so he could hear it clatter down the metal pipe. Teacher was not happy when he succeeded.

The Spring Hill students also played a version of Annie-Annie Over using a basketball rather than a smaller ball. "It made it easier for the younger students to catch it," he said. They devised a more dangerous game in which they would swing on the metal swing and someone would toss a football in their direction. Standing on one foot they would try to kick the ball as far as it would go. Once one of those flying footballs hit the neck of a farmer on his tractor. (I'd say they were lucky the farmer was able to be angry. He could have lost control of the tractor or even been killed by that ball.)

He also related an amusing incident involving one of his teachers and her boyfriend. The man sometimes stopped by the school and honked the car horn and she would step out the door to greet him. One day the teacher forgot that she had given a student permission to use the outhouse and when the student opened the door to return to the schoolroom he caught the two in an embrace. After that she always did a head count before she stepped out the door to greet her boyfriend.

Clarence expressed great admiration for country schoolteachers who had to teach every subject at every level and still carved out time each day to give extra assistance for the "slow learner."

Teachers at Spring Hill included Miss Lizzie Leonard, Ada Meek 1883; Dixie M. Cornell 1886; Della Smith, Miss Davenport 1888; Miss Adda Young 1889; Miss Lizzie Smith, Frank Wright 1890; Mrs. F. M. Wright, Sylvia Masteller, Miss Vincent 1891; Miss Crew, Mr. Denny, Miss Maggie Watkins 1892; H. J. Curtis 1893; Ada Meek 1894; Ada Meek, Laura Essex 1895; Kate Derry, Alma Cloe 1896; Julia Ruckman 1897; Alma Cloe, Flora Batten, Miss Julia Ruckman 1898; Flora D. Batten 1899-1900; Charles W. Conrey, Art Betterton 1901; Jean Rogers 1903; Iva B. Marsh 1904; Art Betterton 1905; Lucy Ward 1906-07; Carolyn Cooper 1908; Mary E. Flanders, Cora Rankin 1909; Maude Welch, Clara Mason 1910; Clara Mason 1911; Mary Greenaway 1912; Mrs. Rosa Smith, Edith Agan 1913; Virgie Shinn 1914; Mamie C. Smith, Bernice Phelps, Alletta Cunningham 1915; Mamie McKeigh 1916; Virgie Shinn 1917-18; Sylvia Allen 1919; Mrs. Maud Christiansen, Janie Black 1920; Sylvia Allen 1921; Marie Hand 1922; Mrs. Hon 1923; Ruth Woodle 1924; Beulah Welch 1925-27; Ruby Seaman 1928-30; Hollare Maddy 1931; Madge Crozier 1932-35; Evelyn Gurney 1936; Cleo Hill 1938-40; Inez Stittsworth 1941; Rena Fee Welch 1942; Bonnie Jean Nichols 1943; Luella Beebout 1944; Luella I. Beebout, Mary Myers Ely 1945; Kathryn Smith 1947-48; Rena Welch 1949; Violet McDonnell 1950-51; Mildred Dooley 1953-54; and Freda Chamberlain 1955-56.

Spring Hill, 1892 – Row one: Loren McKern, Carl McConaughey, Effie Shields, Lyman Masteller, Bert James, Howard Conrey, John Proudfoot, and Forest James. Row two: Cora Caulkins, E. Baty, Earl Brady, Pearl Proudfoot, Ella Moore, Cora Conrey, Cleo McKinney, Walter Caulkins, Isaac Brady, and Ed Harvey. Row three: Teacher Sylvia Masteller, E. Baty, Gertie Elder, Babe Fortner, Lewis Cloe, Earl Jones, Amos Ross, Delno Brady, May Brady, Charles Brady, Bert Conrey, and Caleb Moore. Row four: Earl Brees, Carre Brees, Florence Bowman, Belle McConaughey, Carrie McKern, Anna Hunt, Lillie Fortner, Eva Harvey, and Alta Conrey. Row five: Rinda Roff, Lottie McConaughey, Mary McConaughey, Mattie Harvey, Minnie Spicer, Jessie Young, Ann Harvey, Mossie Brady, and Nancy Conrey.

Sumpter (35)

NORTH FLAGLER was originally called Sumpter. From the official records, here are the teachers listed under the school name Sumpter: Miss Mary Auld 1872; Alice Glen 1877; Miss Mary Parks 1880; R. M. Manners 1884; Nora Simpson, Miss Cora Armstrong 1885; Miss Charlotte Davis, Miss Steele 1888; Mis Letitia Keefer, Zella McCollum, Mary Momyer 1889; Miss Zella McCollum 1890; Zella McCollum 1891; Mary Momyer, Miss Nora White 1892; Letitia Keefer 1893; Ruby Reese 1913-14; and Huldah Sherlock 1917.

Victory (24)

Victory, 1915 – Teacher Mariam Rankin with students: Leo Sims, Elmer Hammond, Otto Woolsey, Lee Hammond, Mae Woolsey, Creel Fortune, Orrie Gilchrist, Claude Fortune, Burdette Woolsey, Dale Hammond, Ralph Gilchrist, John Sims, Herbert Cline, Lorraine Jones, and Winifred Darnell.

VICTORY WAS ABOUT two miles northeast of Pershing at the southeast corner of Oregon Drive and 180th Avenue.

A souvenir booklet given by Ann Monroe in 1906 indicates the following students enrolled: Estell Cline, George Darnell, Ethel and Harold Fast, Lee Hollingshead, Ruth and Everett Perry, Zella and Fern Rowland, Beryl Cummings, and Mariam, Helen, and Richard Rankin.

Martha Sherwood Shivvers writes that this was her first school in 1933. She had twenty-four pupils in nine grades. At age eighteen, she had just received her certificate in August at Simpson. Martha stayed for one year at a salary of forty to forty-five dollars per month.

For several years this school was known as Victory Central.

Teachers were Miss Lizzie Nickeru 1872; Miss Hodges 1880; Wm. Jones 1883; Nora White 1886; Miss Kate Brennan, Miss Ella Maddy 1890-91; Miss Emma Maddy 1892; Anna Darnell, Aura Dickerson 1894; Julia Ruckman, Miss Kate Brennan, Miss Blanche Welch 1895; Nellie Rogers, Cora Lyman, Eunice T., Anna Hutchinson 1896; Cora Lyman, Katie Brennan 1898; Katie Brennan, Edith Stroud 1899; Edith Stroud 1900; Verna Gardener, Clara Banks, Lula Townsend 1901; Mary Rogers, Katherine Sturgeon 1903; Mary Rogers, Anna Monroe 1904; Anna Monroe 1905-06; Jennie B. McConnehy 1907; Arminda Ferguson 1908; Edna Townsend 1909; Martha Boylau, Margorie Worthington 1910; Lucille Tysseling 1911; Estelle

Claire 1912; Ina Cummings 1913; Maude W. Rankin, Miriam Rankin 1914; Maude Wilson, Edna Townsend Scott 1915; Fern Dainty 1916; June Hanna 1917; Opal Morgan 1918; Zella Maddy 1919; Mrs. Huff 1920; Miss Mabel Patrick 1921; Ruth Fast 1922; Lillian Rowland, Elizabeth Davis 1924; Lillian Rowland 1925; Mary Bridges 1926; Edna Neal 1927; Virgie Davis 1930; Irene F. Thompson 1932; Martha E. Sherwood 1933; A. Jeanne Harsin 1934-35; Jeanne Harsin Hollingshead 1936; Pauline Rankin 1937; Marie Ream 1939; and Genevieve Rankin 1940-41.

Washington (28)

Washington – End of the year school picnic, May, 1950. Row one: Alice Smith, Marlys Fee, Carol Tonda, Johnny Sharp, Donald Fast, Terry Keever, Ted Dykstra, Phillip Langstraat, and Dale Dixon. Row two: Keith Dixon, Floyd De Moss, Larry Smith, Patty Dykstra, Ronald Fast, John De Moss, and Jerry Sharp. Row three: Teacher Frances Thompson, Joyce Langstraat, Dorotha De Moss, Janice Dixon, Gloria Langstraat, Calvin Smith, and Tom De Moss.

WASHINGTON SCHOOL was on the north side of the intersection of Kennedy Street and 150th Avenue on the property now owned by Ted Dykstra II. After the school closed, the building was used as a hog house. While former student Joyce Langstraat Pearson was living there it was destroyed by fire when a heat lamp ignited some bedding. She said she felt worse about the loss of her school than she did about the loss of the hogs. Most students feel a sense of loss when their building, no matter how dilapidated, disappears from the landscape.

On Sunday, August 22, 2010, several former Washington School students gathered for their first reunion organized by Roberta Fast Dennison. Some wondered if they would recognize each other but found it easy as they jokingly said they now looked liked their parents. Former teacher Betty Wing Metcalf also attended. She was easily mistaken for one of the students, as the Washington School was her first teaching assignment after graduating from high school in 1943.

As I visited with various students, I found a common memory was the games they played. Annie-Annie Over was the most popular, followed by softball. Softball was not a favorite with Marlys Fee Gramley, who said it took her till 6th grade to hit the ball. And when she finally did, her schoolmates were yelling at her to run, run! "I knew what I was supposed to do," she said. She really liked to slide around in her boots as the many puddles on the schoolyard turned to slushy ice.

Bill Roff admitted to getting into a lot of trouble

with friend Kenny De Zwarte. Bill escaped punishment but Kenny did not and would be hit by the teacher, who also happened to be Kenny's sister.

Betty Roff Beal, now age eighty-two, told me she used to ride her pony to school. Riding remains a life-long hobby, as she still rides her mule. She also works in a real estate office in Albia. I don't believe she rides the mule to work, however.

Carol Tonda Black started school at age four with teacher Frances Thompson. She said that from the very first day of school she knew she wanted to become a teacher. And she did. Her friends laughed, recalling how she always wanted to play school and she was always THE teacher.

Many of us have an embarrassing memory from our country school days. Joyce Langstraat Pearson told us about the time she was swinging and her jumper caught on the swing. When she jumped off the swing the torn jumper stayed behind. Teacher Helen Adair provided an apron for her to wear for the rest of the day. Just another example of how country schoolteachers came up with creative solutions to all sorts of emergencies.

Teachers included: Miss Alice Barnes 1881; Miss Hege 1887; Miss Mary Parks 1888; Miss Laura Essex, Carrie Burt 1889; Miss Carrie Burt 1890; C. O. Williamson, Miss Jennie Keefer 1891; Rena Snyder 1892; Miss Dora Marsh 1893; Alice Crosby 1894; Mary Roller, C. E. Denny 1895; Katie C. Smith 1898; Katie Smith, Lulu Townsend 1899; Mrs. Don Smith, H.O. Smith, Fessie Palmer 1900; Fessie Palmer, Laura Ghrist 1901; Mary Groenenweg 1903; Fessie M. Palmer, Nell McGowen 1904; Mabel Bush, Mrs. J. C. Clark, Fessie M. Palmer 1905; Fessie M. Palmer, Estella Brubaker 1906; Tressa L. Fry, June Burdick 1907; Clina Karns, Luella Wright 1908; Pearl Bonifield, Mrs. Whitney 1909; Louise Cox, Ruby Miller 1910; Ruby M. Miller, Buelah Lever 1911; Merle Witte, Edna Townsend 1912; Edna Townsend, Mary Greenaway 1913; Luella Wright 1914; Pearl Swayne 1915-17; Laura Taggart 1918; Mrs. Jennie Patton 1919-20; Miss Ruth Fast 1921; Jennie Patton 1922-24; Mabel B. Powers 1925; Mrs. Faye Douglas 1926; Mildred Covey 1927-28; Alice Vinson 1929; Helen Emerson 1930; Josephine Crouch 1932; Josephine Crouch, Loyt Martin 1933; Loyt Martin 1934; Pluma Martin 1935; Loyt Martin 1936; Lorene De Zwarte 1938-39; Mary L. Turner 1940; Eula Hodgson 1941; Marie Filliman 1942; Betty Wing 1943; Norma Jeanne Emerson 1944-45; Helen Adair 1947-48; Frances Thompson 1949-51; Mrs. Minnie McDonnell 1952; Basal White 1953-54; Basal White 1956-58; Alice Vander Zyl 1959; Sarah Harvey 1960; Maxine Adams 1961; and Blanche Templeton 1962-64.

Map of Lake Prairie Township

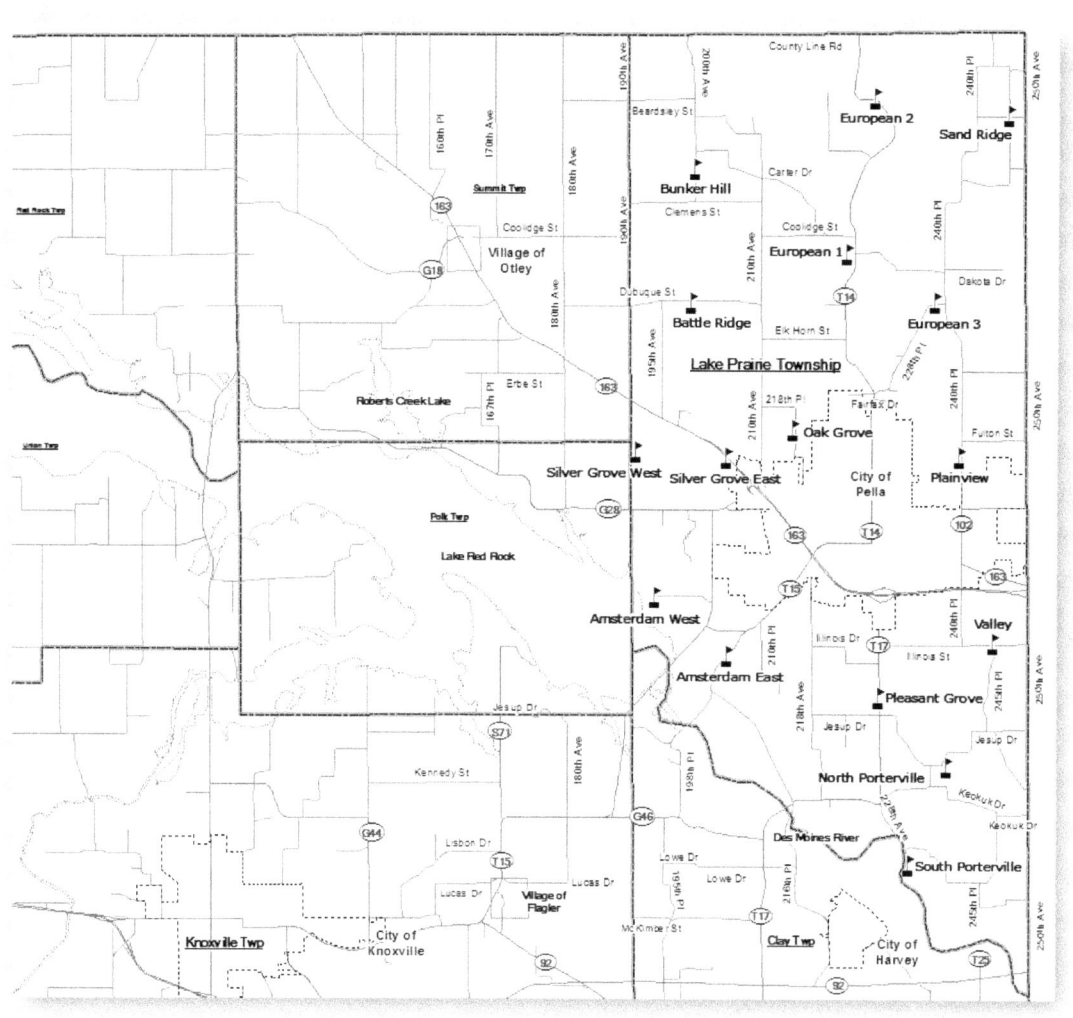

~6~

THE SCHOOLS OF
Lake Prairie Township

East Amsterdam (20)

East Amsterdam, 1929 – Front row: Bob Dingeman, Walter Kamerick, Tenes Kamerick, Willie Ter Louw, Gilbert Kamerick, Floyd Kamerick, Paul Ter Louw, Marie Vander Veer, and Marie Kamerick. Back row: Teacher Fern Rietveld, James Kamerick, Bertha Kamerick, Effie Kamerick, Thelma Miedema, and Wilma Kamerick.

THE EAST AMSTERDAM SCHOOL building, now located at 198th Place, was constructed in 1882, replacing an earlier building, a little red brick schoolhouse. The brick school stood just south of the large basement barn on the Toom farm near where the Wabash Railroad was built in 1882. The reason for changing the location was that the Wabash company had sent a letter to the Board informing them that the school would be in the way of the construction of the necessary side tracks.

The Board decided to build the East Amsterdam School further up the hill because the deep water filling ditches along the tracks could be hazardous to the children. At the same time, to accommodate the growing number of children in the district, the Board decided to add another identical building further west called West Amsterdam. Both buildings were erected for a total cost of $1,010.

Amsterdam School takes its name from the proposed town of Amsterdam in section 20 between the banks of the Des Moines River and Lake Prairie. The "port of Amsterdam" was planned to be a river outlet downstream to St. Louis, Missouri. The town had been platted, a few lots sold, and a few businesses started. However, the devastating flood of 1851 put an end to the plans for the town and the area reverted to farm ground.

Several former students and teachers have written their memories of East Amsterdam. Twins Apollos and Paul Ter Louw attended this school during the late 20s and early 30s. Their father Henry, who had lost "everything" in the Depression, made his living selling Bibles, books, and other items. When it was time for the two to graduate from "the University of Amsterdam," there was no money for a pair of new shoes. One of the neighbors loaned them the money in exchange for helping with corn picking in the fall. Paul says his father was a very religious man who taught Bible School at five rural schools.

Vera Baughman Horman remembers the sound of coal trucks from across the river going up the long hill toward the Pella Light Plant. "When the miners went in with the last load I knew our school day would soon be over also." Her mother and children also attended this school.

Wilma Mathes Brouwer recalls her family using the building as a home during the summer of 1947 after the June flood. Her parents slept on the elevated platform at the front of the room and she slept in a little corner in the back area. She thought camping out was a lot of fun. The Mathes home was cleaned and readied for the family to move into in time for school to resume.

In the summer of 2011 I visited Grace Bertha Kamerick Mathes, who moved to the neighborhood from Holland when she was eight. She was the third oldest of nine siblings, none of whom spoke English. She remembers walking along the railroad tracks in her black shoes and stockings and that some mice got into the pump organ. She said some of the older boys were very naughty and would grab the teacher and hold her down when she tried to discipline them.

The Amsterdam School District was organized in 1875 and functioned as a one-room school until 1960. After the school closed, it continued to be the site of monthly neighborhood gatherings. Neighbors Tunis and Clara Schakel mowed the schoolyard and kept the school clean on the inside until 1990 when the Pella Historical Society took over its care. In 1968, the Pella Historical Society had purchased the building and began converting it into a school museum. It is one of the few museum schools still on its original site. Several teachers have held classes at the school to enable their students to experience a day in a country school.

Teachers who taught at East Amsterdam include Flora Hopson, Tunnie Coffman 1885; May McCollum, Alice Vander Zyl, Mary E. Durham 1886; Hattie Harmsen, Mary E. Durham, Alice Vander Zyl 1887; Hester Ver Steeg, Josie Viersen 1891; Anna De Haan, Bessie Vander Linden 1895; Minnie Veenstra 1898; Grace Dickey 1899; Grace Dickey, Lydia Varenkamp 1900; Lydia Varenkamp, Orissa Veenstra 1901; Hattie Harmsen, Minerva Pugh 1902; Minerva Pugh, Delia Rietveld 1903; Delia Rietveld 1904-05; Bertha Hughes, Margaret Fennema 1906; Cornelia Hospers 1907; Helene Bookman, Jennie Huff 1908; Alta M. Vander Linden 1909; Helene Bootsma, Gertrude Renaud 1910; Clarence Renaud, Mrs. A. A. De Bruyn 1911; Mrs. A. A. De Bruyn 1912-15; Nannie McDillon 1916-17; Hattie Neyenesch 1917-18; Sara McCallister 1919; Wilma Vande Kieft 1920; Irma Visser 1922; Minnie Colyn 1924; Harriet Toom 1925-26; Fern Rietveld 1929-31; Leona Arens 1935-36; Anna Mae Vande Noord 1936; Anna Mae Vande Noord Gosselink 1937; Frances Van Donselaar 1938; Kathryn Herny 1939; Dorothy Synhorst 1940-41; Dorothy Witzenburg 1942; Olive Palmquist 1944-45; Mrs. Nadine Wood 1946; Rena Marie Klein 1947; Joyce Snyder 1948; Marie S. Vander Hart 1950-52; Mrs. Ruth Vande Kieft 1954-56; and Helen Adair 1957.

West Amsterdam (18)

West Amsterdam, 1922 – Front row: Gertrude Bogaards, Margaret Van Veen, Wilbur Vander Kieft, and Nellie Van Veen. Back row: Florence Bogaards, Clara Van Veen, Leslie Bogaards, Teacher Marie Roorda, Dena Van Veen, and Bessie Bogaards.

WEST AMSTERDAM sat on a bluff overlooking the Des Moines River southwest of Pella. There is a site marker for the school on Hemstead Drive, the road that leads to the T'Lam Cemetery. Built in 1882, the eighteen by twenty-six foot building was identical to the East Amsterdam building, which has been preserved as a museum. When the school population dwindled in the 1940s, West Amsterdam closed and the remaining children attended East Amsterdam. The school building was purchased by George Wassenaar and moved to the corner of University and West Second Street in Pella and remodeled into a two-story home. The last owners of the house were the David Ways, who had four small children. Tammy described it as a doll's house, which she decorated in whimsical colors. They sold the property to Central College, which razed the house. According to the 1934 School Board report, there were thirty-five trees growing on the schoolyard.

The report also states there was no well, more seats and a phonograph were needed, and the blackboard needed to be lowered.

When former student Dick Schippers was interviewed in a 1936 *Chronicle* article, he said that most students wore wooden shoes. That was not so surprising, as Amsterdam was an early Dutch settlement. The Tooms, Van Lints, Rietvelds, and Kleins were among the Dutch who opted to live there rather than stay in Pella. Before the school district was divided into East and West Amsterdam, the children of the area attended a little red brick school house on the Toom farm near Howell Station. The record of teachers at this school shows Rufus H. Snavely, winter term of 1874; C. A. Vander Linden 1875; J. W. McDonald 1876; and A. Jennie Fosdick 1878.

Velma De Prenger Rempe phoned me to talk about her first year of teaching at West Amsterdam in the 1939-40 school year. Velma was a graduate of the class of 1938 but had to postpone teaching for a year because she was only seventeen. That fall, instead of being in the classroom, she found herself helping her dad with the corn husking. While teaching at West Amsterdam she boarded at the Art Van Haaften home. The roads in the area were poor. She always hoped it would not be raining on a Monday morning when her parents dropped her off at Howell Station to walk up the railroad tracks to the school.

Velma said the Valster boys sometimes interspersed Dutch with English and she wondered what one meant when he said, "And the mouse ran up the naaimachine [sewing machine]." Her seven students (one girl and six boys) were natural actors and put on a good Christmas program. It seems this school provided a good start for Velma, who taught six more years in schools closer to her home near Leighton.

Marilyn De Hamer De Jong also called to tell me about her days at the West Amsterdam School. She too mentioned the bad roads when her dad would drive her to school in his jeep. She attended primary through 3rd grade and made the transition to East Amsterdam after the school closed in the spring of 1944. There used to be a slogan about neither rain nor snow keeping the mailman from his rounds. This was certainly true of both students and teachers in the rural schools, which were seldom closed because of bad weather.

Here are the names of teachers known to have taught at West Amsterdam: Minnie Veenstra 1899; Katherine Boland 1900-01; Alice Veenscholer 1902; Delia Rietveld, E. Van Nimwegen 1903; Cora Hoogenakker 1904; Cora Hoogenakker, Sylvia Woody 1905; Tillie De Wit 1906; (?) Adams, M. Vander Linden 1907; Alta Vander Linden 1908; Lottie Koopman, Hattie Harmsen, Marie Vander Burce 1909; Ethel Truer, Oletha Lemmon 1910; K. L. Byran 1912; Edna Patterson, Grace Toom, Jennie Huff Patten 1913; Besse Vande Garde 1914-16; Ethel Rovaart 1917-18; Hattie Van Veen 1919; Ethel Rovaart 1920; Gertrude Sels, Marie Roorda 1922; Nellie Brack 1924; Margret LeCocq 1929; Ila Van Ness 1929-32; Ida Kuper, Margaret Keuning 1933; Margaret Keuning 1935-38; Velma De Prenger 1939; Birdy Beintema 1940-41; Dorothy Synhorst 1942; and Norma Schakel 1943.

Battle Ridge (19)

Battle Ridge, 1943 – Left to right: Donna Walraven, Ralph Eugene Van Gorp, LaVelma Walraven, Verlan Van Gorp, Vernon Weilard, Raymond Den Adel, Dorothy Van Gorp, Marjorie Van Zante, and Arvin Menninga.

BATTLE RIDGE SCHOOL, located about five miles northwest of Pella at 1998 Dubuque Street, was built in 1870 on three-quarters of an acre of ground purchased from Mr. and Mrs. A.P. Hasselman and J. Schippers. It closed in the spring of 1960.

A January 1891 newspaper says the scholars of Battle Ridge made their teacher a present of a fine rubber inkstand and a box of fancy stationery, which was greatly appreciated.

On Arbor Day in 1891, students set out 120 trees and many flowers. The yard was cleared off and paths made with the cinders.

The original school building was destroyed by fire on December 12, 1933. In preparation for a rehearsal for a Christmas program to be given the following week, a fire was lit in the stove early in the evening. The fire was discovered at 7 p.m. and was thought to have been ignited by a stove explosion. Fortunately, the school had purchased insurance the year before. The next day, neighbors met to make plans to use the $1,200 they would collect to build a new school.

In the meantime, teacher Janet Steenhoek invited students Wilma Faye Van Zante, Ada Blanche Van Steenis, and Arthur Van Zee to her home for lessons so they would be able to pass their 8th grade exams. The younger children had a short vacation until the basement of the new building was completed.

Following school reunions in 1976 and 1981, Mrs. Virgil Klein, Raymond Den Adel, and Vernon Wielard put together a two-volume history of the school. It contains many pictures of students with their teachers, newspaper clippings, programs, and personal memories of students. A copy is available for reading in the Pella Historical Village.

Vernon Wielard recalls a visit from County Superintendent Sylvia F. Plotts (country schoolteachers were always a bit nervous about these unannounced visits.) Mrs. Plotts drove onto the schoolyard the last period of the day and was not happy to find a Halloween party in progress with everyone in costume enjoying special treats.

In her memoir, Cora Jonker Hayes also mentions a visit from the county superintendent. Her teacher, Rosetta Walraven, actually invited the county superintendent to hear one of the spelling bee contests. Smart teacher. The invited visit probably meant there would be no unannounced visit that year!

In "Fond Memories of Battle Ridge 1922-28," Mrs. Hayes gives a detailed account of how lessons were taught and how special holidays such as Christmas were observed, and gives us insight into why she was obviously a good student who enjoyed school and appreciated her teachers. She says that her parents, who liked to read, encouraged their seven children to read books from the Pella library. When all their school work was done, they were allowed to read one hour before going to bed. At school Miss Walraven also allowed the students to choose reading materials from the bookshelf when lessons were done. Mrs. Hayes stated she worked hard to finish early.

In the early days, the school year was divided into three semesters—fall, winter, and spring. Sometimes three different teachers would be employed for the year, making for a very long list of teachers. Here is the list of known teachers: Nettie Ross, J. W. Elder 1886; Maude Todd 1898; Gertrude Ver Steeg Kamerick, G L. Hackert 1899; G. L. Hackert 1900; Garrett Bos, Minerva Pugh 1901; Lynn Platt, Minerva Pugh 1902; George P. Niemeyer, Margaret Vander Linden 1903; Margaret Vander Linden 1904; Bert Kersbergen 1905; Cora Hoogenakker 1906; Minerva Pugh 1907; Minerva Pugh, James Verhey 1908; Mons S. Quam 1909; Gertrude Renaud, Gradus Vriezelaar 1910; William Onstine 1911; Hattie Neyenesch Van Wyk 1912; Gertrude Den Hartog Hoskbergen 1913; Anthony Hospers 1914; Laura Verrips 1915; Lorna Lewis 1916-17; Cornelia Brummel 1918; Caroline Brummel, Margaret Burns 1919; Pearl Steinkamp, Lucy Hoskbergen 1920; Lucy Hoksbergen Bennick, Jennie Van Osstrum Van Zante 1921; Arthur Sels 1922; Rosetta Walraven Kolenbrander 1923-25; Avis Van Houweling Van Zomeren 1926-28; Alma Rietveld Ver Ploeg March-May 1929; Olive Schakel 1929; Leona Arens Van Rees 1930; Antoinette Rietveld Vander Wal, Gertrude Hoksbergen Renaud 1931; Janet Grootveld Steenhoek 1933; Mae M. Vogelaaar 1934; Mrs. Henrietta L. Van Roekel Van Zante 1935; Jeanette Vander

Wal Ver Meer 1937; Anna Slocum Koons 1939; Alice Postma Kaldenberg 1940; Eleanor Ver Ploeg Gaass 1942; Marjorie Boot Vos 1946; Agnes Vander Hart 1949-54; Lena Hoskbergen Van Rheenen 1955; Florence Hackert Van Gorp spring 1956; Anna Mae Vande Noord Gosselink 1956-59. Other teachers known to have taught there were first teacher Nora Hayes; George Kimmell; Frank Wright; Laura Fisk Dykstra; Bessie Vander Linden; Mary Howell; and George Carnahan.

Bunker Hill (17)

Bunker Hill, early 50s – Seven students in the same grade. Left to right: Sharon Tuinstra, Dorothy Poortinga, Edith Nollen, Jerry Bogaards, Phyllis Ver Ploeg, Eileen Dieleman, and Kay Slycord.

THE BUNKER HILL SCHOOL was on 200th Avenue near Clemens Street. The north side of the district bordered Jasper County.

On September 11, 1858, Johannes Hendrikus Schyff and wife Gertrui sold one acre for one dollar for the school. This was from the northwest corner of the 160-acre farm, which he had purchased three years earlier from the government, the purchase being signed by President Franklin Pierce. At first the school was known as District 68, referring to the fact that this was the 68th school district established in the state of Iowa. It was given the name Bunker Hill by Mr. Gerrit Klyn. The name seemed fitting because of its historical significance and because the school stood on a hill with a view of the surrounding countryside. There were two other country schools named Bunker Hill in Knoxville and Swan Townships.

The Pella Historical Society has the original handwritten copy of a three-month contract with teacher L. A. Garrison, who was to begin teaching on April 7, 1890. Among the stipulations were that he "agrees to the exercise of due diligence in the preservation of school buildings, grounds, shade trees, furniture, apparatus, and other school property; agrees to keep the scholars on the school grounds at noon and recess; agrees to have the English language used as much as practicable, in and about the school house."

When the school held its first reunion in 1966, they obtained much information from Mr. A. B. Van Houweling, who attended school in the 1890s. He related the incident of a sand rock, which was used as a pencil sharpener, but which also made a dent in the blackboard! This incident was followed by the culprit being sent from the building to get a hickory stick, which was intended to further his education. The offender returned after carving notches in the stick so that when it was applied it broke. The children burst into laughter at the wit of the culprit, and the rising temper of the victimized teacher, Mr. Crosby. A copy of the events during different decades may be found in the Bunker Hill scrapbook at the Pella Historical Society.

Antoinette Rietveld Vander Wal, who taught during the years 1935-37, writes about the need for conserving water, which had to be carried from a neighboring farm. She confesses to letting the water get pretty dirty from the noon hand washing before throwing it out. Each child, however, had a personal towel and bar of soap. She says she usually drove to school, but if the roads were muddy, she would stay with one of the families overnight.

Marie Hol Beekhuizen, who taught during the war years, was particularly impressed by the cooperation of the parents in the Bunker Hill neighborhood. In a conversation with Edie Buwalda, I learned that there were seven students in her grade. This was quite unusual in the early 50s, as it was common to have only one or two in a grade. And often there would be no students in some of the grades. Edie began her education with Joyce Schippers, whom she described as a good teacher with good discipline. She remembers that one of her teachers taught the students knitting during recess (a good way to keep them occupied on bad weather days). She also recalls an unfortunate incident when she and Pat Rietveld rolled down the hill into a patch of poison ivy. Edie was unaffected but Pat got very sick.

Here are the teachers from the official Marion County Records and two teacher contracts: Allen Wagaman, Jeanie Rhynsbergen, Allen Hopaman 1886; John Van Pelt 1889; L. A. Garrison 1890; Albert Crosby 1893; D. W. Langerak 1894; A. H. Crosby 1895; A. H. Crosby, Lena Braam 1896; Laura Fisk, Fred Voorhees 1897; Laura Fisk 1898; Jennie De Haan 1899; Hattie Harmsen 1900-01; Mae Marshall, Hattie Harmsen 1902; G. L. Hackert 1903; G. Hackert, Lola E. Tade, Bess Van Gorp 1904; Leona Reuvers 1905; Leona Reuvers, Cora Hoogenakker 1906; Olivia Hollester, Hattie Harmsen, Cattolina Fennema 1907; Cornelia Hospers 1908-10; Caroline McIntire 1911; Margaret Den Burger 1912; Leulah Stuff 1913; Caroline McIntire 1914; Edith Cummings Burggraaf, Verna Talbot, Virginia Acklin 1915; Winifred Marshall 1916; Ruth Grundman 1917-18; Sam Ver Steeg 1920; Artie Van Zee 1921; Celia Keuning 1922-23; Celia Keuning, Minnie Van Gorp 1924; Alma K. Rietveld 1926; Dorothy Van Ommen 1927; G. W. Hollingshead 1928-29; Agnes Van Zante 1930; Margaret M. Hiemstra 1931-33; Mrs. Elmer Vogelaar 1934; Antoinette Rietveld 1935-36; Antoinette Rietveld Vander Wal 1937; Florence Hackert 1938-39; Thressa Van Heukelom 1940; Miss Marie Hol 1941; Rena Marie Klein 1942; Marie Hol 1943-45; Ruth Vander Linden 1946; Mrs. Ed Kooi 1947; Vada Jane Hughes 1948; Joyce Schippers 1949-53; Mrs. Opal De Heer 1954-55; Johnita Van Wyk, Mrs. Opal De Heer 1956; and Mrs. Johnita Van Wyk 1957.

European #1 (22)

EUROPEAN #1, KNOWN as the Bell School, was located on the Galesburg Road (T14). Students who attended the school describe it as anywhere from three to four miles from Pella, depending on how far the city limits extended during their school years.

A 1927 *Chronicle* reporter interviewed several individuals who had connections with the Bell

School. Tunis H. Klein said that his grandfather Jan Akkerman settled there in 1854, which is thought to be about the time the school district was first organized. At first it was called the Vos School—the name was changed in 1874 to European #1. It appears that the board of directors wanted to recognize that there were pupils of German, French, and English descent as well as Dutch. The popular name was the Bell School, as it was the only school in Lake Prairie Township with a bell on the roof.

Mr. Nick Gesman related that his father, N. J. Gesman, taught at the Bell School during the Civil War period, receiving a salary of $15 a month. Mrs. A.T. Klein, mother of Tunis H. Klein, mentioned having a photograph of the Bell School taken on Feb., 27, 1897. Miss Sylvia Platt was the teacher with thirty-five pupils enrolled.

Mr. Henry Beyer said he and his siblings all attended school at Bell after their parents moved there in the early 1850s. The Beyer children were Henry, Edward, John, Sam, Mrs. Hubert Versteeg, and Mrs. Ira Elscot. Henry recalled a cruel punishment administered by one teacher, who would make the offending pupil stand on a seat holding a book in each uplifted hand. If the pupil showed signs of weakening, the teacher would tap him on the elbow with a ruler. "A tall girl wore a hoop skirt. When she went through the standing exercise, the wide skirt afforded ample protection for the boys behind her who used the opportunity to get rid of their surplus energy."

In his memoir, Harold Van Zee, who was born in 1915, mentions attending the Bell School. Harold and classmates Edgar Roorda, Mrs. Ardelia (Bensink) Steenhoek, and Arie Beyer attended all eight grades together.

He recalls one rainy day when the boys decided to pierce one of the De Kock boys' ears to see how much it hurt. Harold said, "Well, that don't amount to nothing. You don't have no feeling in your ear there anyhow." After going to the teacher to obtain a darning needle Walt De Kock said to his brother, "Why don't you let me try that once, see whether I can drive a hole through your ear?"

Bill says, "I'd rather not do that."

"You old coward," Walt says, "If you don't dare, why let me do it. You drive it through." So they laid Walt on the desktop and got his head shaped right down to where his ear hit the desktop and took a backside of a book and drove it in. And boy, you could have heard Walt for three, four, five blocks away. He thought somebody had shot him.

"Then we had that darning needle in there and we had to pull it back out and boy, we didn't have no recess time for three days because that happened. Finally got it out—never hurt him a bit. So that was my first experience with putting in earrings. Had him pinned right down to the desk."

Another time that Harold got in trouble was when he checked his trap lines on the way to school and found a live skunk. Fearing it might get out, he killed it and arrived at school with a strong odor. The teacher sent him home and his father ordered him to only check the trap lines on the way home from school.

The Bell School, built in 1870 by Charles and Richard Lautenbach, local Pella residents, stood until it was torn down in 1960. The bell hangs in the belfry of the replica of the Scholte Church at the Pella Historical Village. In 1954, when the school district closed, the younger children were sent to European #3 and the 7th and 8th graders went to town school.

Teachers who taught at European #1 were Pearl Simpkins, Ora King, Kate Cookley 1886; Permelia Compton 1894; Gertrude Ver Steeg 1895; Sylvia Platt 1896; Josie Thomassen, Bessie Brooks 1898; Dirkie Wormhoudt 1899; Dorothy Wormhoudt 1900; Bessie Brooks 1901; Martha Ver Huel 1902; Edith Cummings 1906-07; Edith Cummings, Pearl Van Zee 1908; Gertrude Renaud 1909; Marjorie Cooper 1910; Sarah Maasdam, Ruth Grundman, Anna Grant 1911; Hazel Held, Antionette Neels, Anna Grant 1912; Ida May Adams, Christina Ter Louw 1913; Edward Den Adel, Jacob Van Wyk 1914; Edith Cummings 1915; Mrs. Edith Burggraff 1916; Laura Taggart 1917; Sylvia Platt 1918; Kate Hudson 1919; Dora Roorda 1920; Sylvia Platt, Janet Den Hartog 1921; Christine Ver Steeg 1922-23; Camille Leuty 1924; Dena Ver Steeg 1925; Esther Kaldenberg 1927; Louise Grandia 1928; Ruth Vander Linden 1929; Alma Ver Ploeg 1930; Helen Grootveld 1931; Lavina Klein, Antionette Rietveld 1932; Antionette Rietveld 1933-34; Lena De Nooy 1935; Jeanette Vander Wal 1936; Agnes Bensink 1937; Marie S. Vander Hart 1938-40; Johanna M. Van Roekel 1941; Bertha Rouwenhorst 1942-43; Agnes C. Vander Hart 1944-47; Marjorie Vos 1949; and Mabel Bogaard 1950.

European #1, 1907 – Front row: Dick Vander Wilt, John Den Adel, Pauline Ver Ploeg, Lonnie Ver Ploeg, Bill Den Adel, Henry Ver Ploeg, Sunny Van Baale, Dick Ver Ploeg, Mamie Boat, Nettie Van Helton, and Dave Van Haaften. Back row: Johnie De Kock, Lewis Vander Wilt, Dean Van Helten, Betha Den Burger, Nelis Bensink, Grace Vos, John Boat, Gertie Bensink, and Deila Van Zee.

European # 2 (10)

WHILE MOST COUNTRY SCHOOLS stayed in the same spot, European #2 seems to have moved around a bit. Its last location as a school when it closed in 1945 was about six miles north of Pella on the Galesburg Road (T15). According to a 1976 interview with Arie Klyn, then age ninety-three, when he attended the school it was located near a covered bridge in an area which was called Stump Town. This school was closed in 1890 and a new schoolhouse called European #2 was built on the Herman Swank farm for $256 in Section 3. In 1922, the school was moved about a mile further south. Since the district never had a deed to the building or the land on which it stood, it never became the property of the Pella Community School. The final move was to a farm field owned by Ed Keuning, where it is now surrounded by grazing sheep instead of playing schoolchildren.

In 1936, Sara Klyn and her pupils won a bit of publicity and a merry-go-round for the school when they placed first in a contest sponsored by the *Pella Chronicle*. The contest started in the fall and ended in January. Each week, teachers brought in all the sales slips the students had collected from participating merchants and the points standings were published in the *Chronicle*.

Like many rural teachers, Sara Klyn did not make teaching a life-long career. Older Pella residents may remember her as a clerk at Black's Style Shoppe. A 1942 article in the *Pella Chronicle* speaks to the problems of finding teachers for rural schools, as many found good paying jobs elsewhere, especially during the war years. While teachers were becoming harder to find, the number of students was also declining. In the year 1931-32, the enrollment for Marion County country schools was 1,943, but by 1941-42 it had fallen to 1,565. The article attributes this to a decreasing number of family farms and the fact that some parents were sending their children to town school. (I suspect that a significant drop in the birth rate was also a major factor.)

Recently two former students, Dee Swank Wassenaar and Betty Heyveld Ver Meer, toured the schoolhouse and found it to be in a decrepit condition. The only evidence that it was once their familiar classroom was the potbellied stove and a blackboard with ABCs. Dee recalls that sometimes in the winter the teacher would not arrive early enough to fire up the stove so that the first two or three classes in the morning were pretty chilly. Like many other schoolchildren, she helped the teacher with such tasks as cleaning the blackboard or using sweeping compound on the floor at the end of the day. She also tutored the younger students.

Annie-Annie-Over seemed to be a universally loved game. Most schools tossed the ball back and forth over the schoolhouse but at European #2 students tossed the ball over a shed. Too bad we didn't do that at North Porterville because it would have saved my parents the cost of replacing a window pane when I lobbed the ball through the schoolhouse window. After all the teasing from the other students, Annie-Annie-Over was no longer one of my favorite outdoor games.

European #2, December 15, 1916 – "to Emma Swank from your teacher Lizzie Woods."

Records for teachers who taught at this school show Etta Viersen 1894; Sylvia Platt, Minnie Dickey 1895; Lynn Platt 1896; Josie Thomassen, Simon Douwstra 1899; Lydia Varenkamp 1900; Dorothy Wormhoudt, Winifred Fowler 1901; Lizzie Snyder, G. B. Niemeyer 1902; Maggie Van Zee 1903-04; A. H. Crosby 1905-07; Elizabeth Cox 1908; Marjorie Cooper 1909; Sara Maasdam 1910; Anna Grant 1911; Antionette Neels 1912; Jessie Warner 1913; Ruth Grundman 1914; Helen Brooks 1915; Lizzie Woods, Cunera Van Emmerik 1916; Cunera Van Emmerick 1917; Lynn Platt 1918; Dora Roorda 1919; Janet Den Hartog 1921; Georgia Roorda 1922; Marie Beyer 1924; Cornelia Gosselink 1925; Dorothy

Van Duren 1928; Mabel De Jong 1930; Mrs. Alma Ver Ploeg 1931-32; Mrs. Margaret Klyn 1935; Sara Klyn 1936-38; Agnes Vander Hart 1939-40; James Brass 1941; Johanna Rouwenhorst 1942-43; and Leona De Vries 1944.

European # 3 (23)

European #3 – Pupils of Lois Eysink on a field trip. She taught from 1948-51.

EUROPEAN #3 WAS LOCATED three and one-half miles north of Pella on the Pella to Sully Road. Much of the information for this article was taken from a booklet compiled by Valentine Mathes in 1977-78. Mr. Mathes, who is now 101 years old (2008), is currently a resident in the Pella Community Nursing Home. He was named for his grandfather Valentine Mathes, who with his wife Aggie in 1878 deeded for the sum of ten dollars the one-quarter acre on which the school stood. The other one-quarter acre for the school ground was deeded by Frederick C. and Mary Mathes.

The first building was a small structure only sixteen by twenty feet. In 1925, the school district voted to replace it with a new building: the total cost for the building with furnishings (furnace, desks, etc.) was $4,509.73. When the school closed in 1958, Gary Vogelaar purchased and remodeled it into a house, which stands south of Pella on the elevator road (228th Avenue).

In looking at a list of surnames of pupils who attended European # 3 between 1908 and 1937, we can see why it was known as the Mathes School. After 1937, the predominant names were Vander Kraats, Kuiper, Blom, Rus, Van Wyk, Van Zee, Waits, Stursma, and Nollen.

Teachers who taught at this school were Sylvia Platt 1894; Sylvia Platt, Jacquelin Platt 1895; Sarah Lautenbach 1896; Dirkie Wormhoudt, Mable Cook, Agnes De Vries 1898; Bessie Brooks, Laveda Van Doren 1899; Marie Stegeman 1900; Minerva Pugh, Mae Fisk 1901; Fern Young, Lizzie Snyder 1902; Edna Ver Heul 1903-07; Martha Brimmer 1908; Martha Brimmer, Agnes Ballenger 1908; Elizabeth Ver Huel 1909-10; Bertha Grundman 1911; Anna Grant, Antoinette Neels 1912; Antoinette Neels 1913-14; Antionetta Neels, Etta Vander Hart 1915; Helen Brooks 1916-18; Pearl Steinkamp 1919; Dora Roorda 1920; Janet Den Hartog 1921; Georgia Roorda 1923; Irene Vander Linden 1924; Irene Vander Linden, Margaret Le Cocq 1925; Mae Meppelink 1926; Janet Grootveld 1927; Anna Verhey 1928; Malvina Neely, Ruth Vander Linden 1929; Ruth Vander Linden 1930-31; Artie Hasselman 1932-34; Gretchen Fennema 1935-36; Henrietta Van Roekel 1937-41; Johanna Van Roekel 1942-43; Dorothy Witzenburg 1944; Mrs. Dorothy Witzenburg Monsma 1945-46; Ruth Vander Linden 1947; Lois Jean Eysink 1948-51; Louise Van Zee 1953; Mrs. Gladys Nieuwsma 1954; Mrs. Janet Steenhoek 1955; and Mrs. Darlene Bevan 1956-57.

During the school years 1951-1953, pupils were transported to Pella Community Schools or the Sandridge School.

Additional teachers who taught at European # 3 were Luella Shaw, Nettie Lankelma Geelhoed, Dora Bremmer, and Gideon Beyers. These names were found in a *Chronicle* article, which pictured the students from 1929-30. The reporter interviewed Mr. Henry Renaud, who stated his parents Mr. and Mrs. L.L. Renaud moved to the neighborhood December 10, 1854. Mr. Renaud had a vivid recollection of teacher Gideon Beyers, whom he described as "long-headed and an expert in figures. When asked if the boys played any foolish pranks he said they did nothing else when they were not occupied with their studies but he does not remember any of them."

John Stursma, who attended school there through the 4th grade in the early 30s, remembers that his dad would not permit his brother to play the role of Santa Claus in the Christmas program. The teacher was disappointed but found someone else whose parents didn't think Santa Claus was too worldly for the religious holiday of Christmas.

Another student told me that one day all the children decided to extend their lunch hour by continuing to play in a large culvert near the schoolhouse. Gradually everyone trickled in for afternoon classes and all found themselves making up time after school. I'm sure nearly every country teacher has had a similar experience with students who decided it was just too nice a day to return to the building. I recall one sunny winter day when all of us decided to continue sledding in the pasture behind the schoolhouse. Instead of detention, our teacher joined us for a half hour more of sledding. Even teachers sometimes knew it was simpler, and more fun, to break the rules rather than enforce them.

Oak Grove (33)

AS HIDDEN AS ITS HISTORY, the Oak Grove School building still stands on the outskirts of Pella. It comprises part of the home of Alan and Cindy Roorda at 689 218th Place. One can see the outline of the school on the right hand side of the picture of their house. The front door to the schoolhouse has been replaced by three windows. The inside of the school has become a living room and a bedroom.

I was first alerted to the existence of this school by Alan's Uncle Robert Walter Roorda. He told me that he was born in the schoolhouse and that he and his father Wigert Roorda were both taught by the same teacher, Dora Bootsma. Miss Bootsma, who graduated from Pella High School in 1894, was a teacher in the Pella school system for forty-seven years.

Although I have found no records of teachers for the little one-room school, Cindy Roorda shared a souvenir booklet from the Oak Grove School District given by Dora Bootsma to her students. Usually these booklets are dated; this one is not. The pupils listed (spelled as they were in the booklet) are John Bauman, Willie Maasdam, Abram Rooda, Esther Maasdam, Dina van de Zyl, Wigert Roorda, Andrew

Langerak, Laura Hiatt, John Blanke, Edith Hiatt, Sarah Maasdam, Anna Hiatt, and Lorence Blanke. After the school closed, the pupils in this district then attended one of the schools in the town of Pella. According to the Pella School Board minutes of November 11, 1901, a problem developed when a Mrs. Beerends had offered to take two of her own children and two of the Buwalda family to the city schools for .75 per day but she would not carry the children of Laurens Blanke nor in any way permit her children to be taken with them.

The school building, which was sold in 1905, is on land that has been owned by the Roorda family since 1869. The original farm owners were Anne and Doertje (Buwalda) Roorda, who sold eggs, molasses, butter, and dressed chickens, in town. After the school closed they used the building as a barn. In 1912, it was moved closer to the road and converted into a home for newlyweds, son Wigert and Reino (Borgman) Roorda. In 1938, one of Wigert and Reino's sons, Paul, and his bride Eva Mae (De Kock) Roorda moved into the house. Later another son, Robert Walter, and Wilma (De Haan) Roorda lived in the house. Over the years there were many changes and additions to this house.

Then in 1973 one of Paul's sons, Alan, and his wife Cindy (Butler) Roorda purchased the home along with three acres. In 1977, they began a total renovation and addition to the house. One of their interesting discoveries was the original slate boards still attached to the schoolhouse wall. Cindy is hoping that a fourth generation of the Roorda family may someday want to occupy the schoolhouse turned family home.

Oak Grove – Original schoolhouse is on the right side of the present-day house.

Plainview (1)

THE FIRST PLAINVIEW SCHOOL was built in 1875 on a farm owned by J. Markel, one mile east of Pella on the Vermeer Road where Vermeer Manufacturing corporate offices are now located. Plainview is appropriately named because it was built on flat land offering a clear view of the surrounding plain. The first teacher hired was paid twenty-five dollars per month.

By 1880, farmer Markel no longer wanted the building on his land and it was moved three-quarters of a mile north. In 1883, a new schoolhouse was built at a cost of $460.26. This figure comes from the carefully kept school board records which also show that the first teacher's salary was $25 per month while the last one was hired in 1955 for $255 per month. After the school closed, it was sold to Harold Ver Meer in 1959.

The first reunion of former students and teachers was held in 1972. For this occasion, Mr. T.T. Verros, then eighty-seven years old, wrote about his memories of school days at Plainview. On his first day in 1890, two neighbor girls, Marie Schakel and Sara Schippers, took him to school. A few days later, when they stopped by he decided he didn't want to go to school. His father, who happened to be in the yard, picked up of a piece of harness strap and gave him one good lick. He changed his mind about not going to school.

Mr. Verros said that in the fall of the year, the students often left the schoolyard to gather hickory nuts in the nearby Vermeer timber. One noon hour, Henry H. Ver Meer, John Vande Lune, and Mr. Verros lingered too long picking up nuts under an especially good tree and returned a half hour late. As punishment the teacher told them they would not be allowed to leave the schoolyard for the rest of the year. However, by the next week the boys followed the other students into the timber and the teacher said nothing. (Probably most of us have taken a privilege away from a child and later changed his/her mind, as did this teacher.)

John P. Vermeer, who attended school in the 30s, recalls that the well water was poor and students were sent across the road to his parents farm (the Paul Vermeers') for drinking water. In the winter, the students often enjoyed ice skating on their farm pond. This is the pond that many will remember as the site of the annual tug of war between the Central College freshmen and the upper classmen.

During World War II, the school children of Plainview conducted a scrap drive using their ponies and a cart to carry scrap from neighboring farms to the schoolhouse. A *Chronicle* picture shows Arie Boot on his pony Goldie and Vernon De Vries on his pony Foxy along with eleven other students and their teacher Emily Hiemstra. They expected to sell two tons of metal to purchase a globe and other supplies for their school.

Plainview – Parents and children gather for the last day of school celebration in 1907.

Teachers at Plainview were Miss Doolittle 1875; Maria Davenport 1876; Miss A.M. Dana 1878; Ida Dunn, Miss Wilson 1880; J.J. Stoddart, C.S. Pruit, E. Vingari, G. W. Kimmel 1882; Sallie Martin, Sadie Lacy 1883; Frank Vande Ven 1884; Minnie Edmand 1885; Frank Vande Ven, F. Wright 1886; Aletha Davenport 1887; Anna De Haan 1888; Minnie Forsythe 1889; Nora Boswell, Kate De Haan 1890; Anna Dunnink 1894; Jennie Kuyper 1898; Dora Thomassen, Sylvia Platt 1899; Nellie Van Der Sluis 1900; Katie Boland 1902; Avis Veenschoten 1903; Katie

Boland 1904; Katie Boland, Cora Hoogenaker, Cornelia De Cook 1905; Cornelia De Cook 1906; Tille De Wit 1907; Bertha Dykstra 1909-10; Bertha Dykstra, Elizabeth Ver Heul 1911; Elizabeth Ver Heul 1912-16; Edna Ver Heul 1917; Meda Heki, Agnes Vander Hart, Alice Tysseling 1919; Cornelia Gosselink Van Donselaar 1927; Janet Grootveld, Elva Brummel 1936; Esther Grootveld 1937; Ardella Grandia 1938; Beulah Grandia 1939; Emily Hiemstra 1941; Betty Vriezelaar 1943; Mildred Gosselink 1944; Betty Vander Beek 1950; Thelma Grandia 1952; Joyce Leydens 1953; Mrs. William De Bruin 1954; and Gloria Daggey 1955.

Pleasant Grove (22)

Pleasant Grove, 1939 – Row one: Verlan De Zwarte, Gladys Hoekman, Ida Jane Hoekman, Mary Ann Sels, and Teacher Alda Mae Van Heukelom. Row two: Marvin Hoekman, Gene Rietveld, Margaret De Zwarte, and John Hoekman. Row three: Josephine Hoekman, Marvin Smith, Ralph Hackert, and Dale Hoskbergen.

THE FACT THAT THERE WERE three schools and a township named Pleasant Grove in Marion County is testament to the pioneers' appreciation of trees. In the early days, land with trees had a greater value than the prairie, as wood was needed for fuel and building material.

Pleasant Grove School (the Van Zee School) was located approximately two miles south of Pella on the east side of the "Elevator Road" (T17). The first of three schoolhouses was a log cabin built in 1855. The second was a brick building erected in 1871 and the last, a frame structure built in the 1920s, is still standing on a high hill. It has been converted into a comfortable home.

In talking with former student Lenora De Jong Van Weelden, I learned that teacher Darlene Bevan made the school comfortable for Monday morning classes by banking the furnace on Sunday night. She attended school at the time when schools could obtain government commodities and remembers walnuts, grapefruit, and kidney beans. Mrs. Bevan would ask different students to bring pickles and boiled eggs from home so they could have kidney bean salad. The De Jong children, who lived on the "washboard road," had to walk a mile and a quarter to get to school. They were happy whenever they could catch a ride in a neighbor's spring wagon when the weather was especially bad. She also mentioned that Norman and Shirley Vanden Baard used to perform tap dances for the school program accompanied by their grandmother Agnes Weyerse.

Both Lenora and Shirley Ward mentioned that the girls' toilet was made of bricks (that was pretty rare). Halloween pranksters might tip over the boys' toilet but the girls' toilet always remained standing.

Shirley said she always envied the Van Houwelingen boys, who had only to walk across the road to get to school. She recalls a unique swing from a tree near the ditch. A student could take a run for it and swing out over the high road embankment in a half circle.

She remembers that whenever the teacher would go down to the basement to fire the furnace the students would leave their seats and run around the classroom, imagining that the teacher couldn't hear them. (I suspect the teacher found their running around a harmless way for them to let off some steam when bad weather kept them indoors.)

Teachers who taught at this school include Jennie Harmsen 1886; Jacquelin Platt, Marie Lautenbach, Hattie Harmsen 1898; Hattie Harmsen, Bessie Brooks 1899; Bessie Brooks 1900; Winifred Fowler, Theo H. Kaldenberg 1901; Sylvia Platt 1902; Sylvia Platt, Eleanor Cully 1903; Edith Cornelius 1904; Gove Hackert 1905; Margaret Vander Linden 1906; Henry W. Pietenpol 1907; Joe Fassen 1908; Helene Bootsma 1900; Kamp Wormhoudt 1910; Yella Menninga 1912-13; Ruth Aschenbrenner 1913; Mrs. Alta Pope 1914-17; Lois Brooks 1918-22; Martha Adrian 1924-25; Bertha Van Zante 1926; Myrtle De Haai, Lynn Platt 1927; Myrtle De Haai 1928; Emma L. Kaldenberg 1930-32; Gladys Fennema 1933; Emma Kaldenberg 1934; Frances Van Donselaar 1936; Alda Van Heukelom 1939; Florence Hackert 1940; Darlene Bevan 1941-43; Betty M. Crum 1944; Ada Marie De Haan 1945; Dorothy Witzenberg Monsma 1947; Darlene Bevan 1948-54; and Mrs. Alice Vander Zyl 1955-57.

In 1929, a *Chronicle* reporter interviewed Mr. L. Hackert and Gove Van Zee, who recalled these additional teachers: W.W. Simpkins and daughters Lyda and Dale, Dr. W.W. Allen, Lois Brooks, George Kimmell, Newt Wilson, Lee Curtis, Mattie Pierce, Cynthia Fisk, and Cyrenus Cole. Mr. Cole later became an Iowa congressman.

Both men especially remembered Mr. Simpkins, who wrote a book on the Book of Revelation, and was very interested in astronomy and "was often seen focusing on the firmament with a spyglass." He wore a stove pipe hat and shawl which was pinned together with horse blanket pins. He separated the boys from the girls and made his students learn the alphabet backwards as well as forwards.

North Porterville (25)

NORTH PORTERVILLE, a little white schoolhouse, stood on a slight rise with land sloping off to the east toward Sand Creek and to the south and west toward the Des Moines River. To the north a neighbor's pasture hill was just right for sledding in the winter. When I started school in 1938, a dirt road wound past the school connecting what is now Keokuk Drive and Jessup Drive. The road has been absorbed by farm fields, and the school building, now converted to a farm building and covered with sheet metal, has been moved to the Murray Kamerick property. Purchase price was $335. As one drives along 228th Avenue one can spot it on the river bluff overlooking the flood plain.

The building plan was typical of country schools of that era. From the south entry the boys' cloak room branched to the left and the girls' to the right. Each had identical shelves for storing lunch pails and other items and a row of hooks for hanging coats. In the main classroom, the north wall was dominated by a large chalkboard with a heating stove in the northwest corner. It was thought that students benefited from light coming over their left shoulders, hence the west wall contained six large windows while the east wall had two smaller windows located high on the wall. Just as well or they would have been covered up by the pump organ, victrola, and the cupboard on which the water bucket sat. Even though there wasn't a lot of bare wall space there was room for a flag, a bulletin board, pull-down wall maps, and the requisite pictures of George Washington and Abraham Lincoln.

The south side of the classroom was most intriguing to me because it had a high cubby hole called the library. During my first few years, I had to stand on a chair and boost myself into this little nook. There I would spend my happiest times curled up, surrounded on three sides by books. Of course, I could never stay too long as at least once each hour I would be called to the recitation bench for questioning over some lesson or other.

The Porterville School has a long history, as the neighborhood was one of the first settlements in Marion County. When the territory was opened for settlement in May of 1843 William and Levi Nossaman with their wives Sarah and Caroline, daughters of William Welch, staked a claimed here. Both families came to this wilderness with three-month-old babies. Soon they were joined by other families with surnames of Hamilton, Clark, Miller, and Gillaspy. At first the children of the neighborhood were taught in a log cabin and then in a small brick structure sixteen by twenty-four feet known as the Hamilton School.

When Mrs. Mary Nossaman Todd taught in the neighborhood, she received eight dollars per month and boarded in the homes of pupils.

According to a 1931 *Chronicle* interview with John P. De Cook, Herman Van Zante, P.G. Van Zante, John Steinkamp, and Abe Ver Ploeg, all of whom had attended this school more than sixty years before, in 1868-69 the Hamilton School was renamed the Porterville School. Both Robert G. Hamilton and Joseph Porter had donated land for the school and the Portergrove Cemetery (formerly the Hamilton Cemetery). Eventually the Porterville School became four schools: North Porterville, South Porterville, Union Corner, and Rock Island. This was necessary, as there were too many students enrolled and many of them had to walk too far to reach North Porterville.

D.G. Van Zante recalled that some of the "boys" were as old as twenty-five, the teachers used harsh discipline, and there were many fights during and after school. One day the bitter arguments over the Civil War became so fierce that the teacher had to dismiss school for the day. Sometime after 1910, the original brick building burned down and was replaced with the present building.

When the Dutch came to Pella in 1847, "the Americans" in the Porterville neighborhood helped them to get acclimated to life in an unfamiliar country and also began selling off their land to them. By the early 1900s, the student roster was dominated by Dutch names like Ver Ploeg, Van Zante, Vander Werff, Langerak, Snellers, De Cook, Blom, and Van Steenis.

In the fall of 1943, there were so few students attending North and South Porterville that the schools merged and all students in the Porterville neighborhood attended North Porterville. The school was closed at the end of the school year in 1958. It is quite fitting that one of the last teachers, Mrs. Billy E. Brown, the former Wilma Nossaman, was a direct descendent of the first families to move into the neighborhood in 1843.

Teachers were Sally Miller, George W. Kimmel 1874; Jennie Simpkins, M. B. Liter 1875; Alice Burns, Adda Monahan 1877; M. M. Goldsmith, Flora Hopson, Mary Durham 1879; Ricka M. Holst, Miss Florence Durham 1880; C. Beers, C. Spruit 1881; H. Shaw 1882; Lily Schurbring 1884; Ella Brager 1885; Allen Nossaman, Mary L. Hamilton 1886; Mrs. Mary E. Todd 1888; Lulu Webb 1889; Lou MacLaughlin 1890; Clara Redding 1891-92; Millard W. Wise, Mrs. Todd 1894; Mary E. Todd, E. T. Hollingshead 1895; Maud Todd 1896; Eleanor Cully 1898; Martha Ver Heul 1900-01; Katie Rietveld 1902; Elizabeth Gezel, Marinus Vander Linden 1903; Marinus Vander Linden 1904; Anna McMillen 1905; G. L. Hackert 1906; Henrietta Ver Heul 1907; Geraldine Ashenbrenner 1909; Mary Clark 1910; Mary Parker, MaBelle Lemmon, Leona Berg 1911; Jessie Warner, Hollis Byram, Mabelle Lemmon 1912; Hollis L. Byram, Florence Marsch, Nellie Bennink 1913; Edward Den Adel 1914; Kenneth L. Byram 1915; Hattie Van Veen, Manford Moore 1916; Manford Moore 1917; Lorna Lewis, Louise Wright 1918; Helen Brooks 1919; Allen De Long 1920; Jennie Harmsen 1922-23; Hattie Harmsen 1924; Jennie Harmsen 1925; Reda Martin 1926-27; Marvel Meekma 1930-31; Edna Hackert 1935; Janet M. De Jong 1936-37; Eva Mae Van Wyngarden 1938-39; Clara Gosselink 1940-41; Junella Grandia 1942-44; Beulah Hayes 1945-47; Thelma Grandia 1948; Joyce Roorda 1949; Mrs. R. G. McClelland 1951; Miss Wilma Nossaman 1952; Mrs. Wilma Brown 1953-57; and Mrs. Lillian De Prenger 1958.

North Porterville, 1909 – Row one: Tone Blom, (unknown), and Dave Van Steenis. Row two: (unknown), (unknown), ____De Vries, (unknown), Will Van Zante, Sarah Van Steenis De Haan, and (unknown). Row 3: Lester Lankerak, (unknown), (unknown), Clara Van Steenis Van Zee, Teacher Geraldine Ashenbrenner, Gertie Van Zante Huyser, (unknown), Martha Ver Ploeg Dykstra, Josie Ver Ploeg Blom, Tryne Ver Ploeg Bloem, and Gradus Van Zante.

South Porterville (2)

South Porterville, 1929 – Front row: Arnold Kamerick, Maxine Rebertus, Frances Daughterty, Cornelia Van Oenen, Pearl Verrips, and Elsie Van Oenen. Back row: Donald Kamerick, Marion Monster, Rosie Verrips, Anna Van Oenen, Antoinette Monster, Darlene Rebertus, and Teacher Clara Gosselink.

LOCATED JUST A FEW hundred yards from the banks of the Des Moines River, South Porterville School stood just beyond what is now the home of Howard De Jong. According to J. J. Vander Werff, long-time record keeper for the Porterville District, South Porterville split off from North Porterville in 1887. Students met in a home for three or four years, then in a log cabin, and finally in the school building erected in 1892. In 1943, there were so few students that South Porterville merged with North Porterville. The building was dismantled by Neil Kuiken, who used the boards to build a house in Pella.

Over the years, various enterprises thrived in this basically farm neighborhood. First there were the mills and a pottery works, and later the Porterville coal mine (located on the Kamerick property) and a rock quarry. For many years, John Rebertus grew tons of watermelons just up the sandy hill from the school.

Nearly every country school of my era had a weekly event called "Question School," in which a pastor or a Bible scholar taught a Bible lesson (followed by questions). Question School was a part of the school curriculum at South Porterville and on Sundays all the residents of the neighborhood were invited to Sunday School, which was taught by a missionary Sunday School teacher. Here is an account of the annual Sunday School picnic held in William Monster's pasture in the summer of 1936. "It was a help yourself dinner with plenty of chicken, pie, cake, etc. In the afternoon Rev. Van Dellen gave a fine talk. There were recitations and singing and the Porterville orchestra (all girls) rendered some fine music. Races and other amusements were held. It is estimated that 200 persons were present and all greatly enjoyed the event, the writer especially."

For many years, Ruth Vanden Baard was the weekly *Chronicle* correspondent for the Porterville neighborhood, faithfully recording the school programs, which child was "entertaining the measles," details of the Porterville ball teams, and, most importantly, who was visiting who. But then on December 24, 1936, her readers found this apology instead of her usual column: "We regret that we couldn't have the Porterville news in last week as it was burned in Cornie Vanden Baard's truck last Tuesday morning while he was on his way back from taking a load of coal to his father John Vanden Baard. The cab was destroyed but they saved the box."

Murray Kamerick, a descendent of John Armstrong Nossaman, one of the early settlers, still lives in the neighborhood (2008) where he attended school. He recalls the time a teacher sent him and Gerald Monster into the timber for a Christmas tree for the school. When they came upon a raccoon in a hollow tree, Murray went to get land owner, Bastian Goemaat, while Gerald guarded the coon in the tree. Mr. Goemaat shot the coon and divided the bounty with the boys. Murray said that playing ball was a favorite activity and the students were often able to coax the teacher into letting them play a half hour longer before returning to classes. Since country schoolteachers did not have to adhere to as strict a schedule as did town teachers, on a nice spring day they might go to the timber to pick wild flowers or study the returning birds. This flexibility was one of the many perks of being a country school student.

Teacher included Sylvia Platt, K. Van Zante 1894; K. Van Zante, Maud Todd 1895; Julia Van Zante, Maude Todd 1896; Sarah Todd 1898; Bertha Van Zee 1899; Bertha Van Zee, Arie De Cook, G.L. Hackert 1900; Gerrit Hackert 1901; Sara Todd, A.H. Crosby, Minnie H. Gaass 1902; Minnie Gaass 1903; Nina Norris, Maggie Van Zee 1904; Maggie Van Zee, Stella B. Clark 1905; Mrs. Susie Dolan 1906; Virgie Shinn, G.L. Hackert 1907; Pearl Van Zee, Gertrude Anderson, Mabel Lemmon 1908; Nellie Snyder, Edith Haines 1909; Edith Haines 1910; Ethel Tandy, Beulah Worstell, Myrtle Laske 1912; Alta Vander Linden, Lizzie Morris 1913; Nellie Cain, Gladys Barnwell 1915; Edith Anthony 1916; Edith Anthony, Lois Brooks 1917; Mrs. Alta Pope 1918; Lola Comer 1919; Mrs. W.A. Jansen 1920; Mrs. W.A. Jansen 1921; Hattie Harmsen 1922-23; Elizabeth Van Zante 1925; Elizabeth Van Zante 1927; Clara Gosselink 1928-29; Mabel Van Zante 1930-32; Leona Ahrens 1933; Leona Hiemstra 1936; Geraldine Gosselink 1937-38; Johanna M. Van Roekel 1939-40; Cleo Hill, Margery Van Heukelom 1941; and Dorothy Ver Dught 1942.

This list was also identified as teaching at Porterville (N? or S?): Lou McLaughlin, Hester Ver Ploeg 1889; Nora Cully, Mrs. J. Tood 1890; Clara Webb 1892; Permelia Compton, Hattie M. Tice 1893; Mary E. Howell 1897; Faye Tyrell 1907; Nellie Snyder 1910; Margaret Wren 1912; and Etta Vander Hart, L. Goodenough 1919.

Rock Island

ROCK ISLAND SCHOOL was on the county line road about six miles southeast of Pella. Just to the north was the Rock Island Line and nearby was what the children called School Creek. In suitable weather, the children ate their lunches there and caught minnows and bullfrogs. The closeness of the railroad track was a distraction to students and teachers as trains rattled by. The school was built about 1883 on an acre of land donated by William Vander Kraan. Although it was always on the east side of the county line road, it was under the supervision of Marion County until 1926 when it was transferred to Scott Township, section 6, in Mahaska County.

In her *History of Rock Island School* Bertha

Van Zante, a student and later a teacher there, mentions that in 1909 the school board bought six steel guards costing $26.14 to protect the windows from stray balls as well as to keep tramps from getting into the school building at night. In her description of the interior, she mentions that mice could often be seen playing around the shelves that held the lunch pails. These pails were recycled tobacco and syrup buckets. She records there was a good well on the schoolyard. Sometimes the boys would carry water from the well or the creek to drown ground squirrels in Joe McCombs' pasture.

The original building burned down the last day of school in 1939. Eleanor Ver Ploeg was the teacher that year. A new building was erected on the same site in time for the fall opening.

Abe Vanden Berg, who attended school there in the 20s, told his daughter Delores Van Rees about riding the railroad repair car home; workers would say, "You big kids hop on and hold tight. We'll hold the little ones."

In the spring of 1932, Delores' mother, Miss Edna Hackert, sent a letter of application to the school board for the teaching position at Rock Island. The letter states "I am eighteen years of age, in perfect health, and a member of the Third Reformed Church of Pella... I will be willing to teach for whatever you think you should pay a teacher of my ability."

The letter of acceptance from the school board president, D. G. De Jong, offered $65 (the minimum wage for a beginning teacher with a high school normal training certificate). He writes, "If you accept our offer, call 616 on 39 at 8 pm and say 'yes or no' and don't say anymore over the telephone on account of other applicants on this line applying."

In 1958, the school was closed and the grade school children were sent to Leighton. In 1961, the school was sold at auction to Lee Nossaman and remodeled into a home.

The official records of Marion County show these teachers: Fannie Gelderblom 1898; T. H. Kaldenberg 1899; T. H. Kaldenberg, Bertha Van Zee 1900; Jessie Inskeep, Lela Coster, Ollie Gelderblom 1902; Maude Inskeep, M. E. Gelderblom, Ethel Ghrist 1905; Margaret Dulen 1908; Bernice Phelps 1909; Eva Corey 1909-11; Bertha Harvey 1911-13; Cora Mathes, (?)Mathews, Byron Bush, Mamie Jackson 1914; Mary Wilson, Katherine Shovelain 1915; Gladys Barnwell 1916; Amy (Elma?) Chapman, Christine Ter Louw 1917; Mrs. Ethel Hawk 1918; Reefa Wilson 1919; Hattie Van Veen 1920; Eva Dixon 1922-23; and Margaret Wynia 1924.

From the lack of any further information about the school, it appears it was transferred to Mahaska County in the fall of 1925.

Other teachers who are known to have taught at this school are Minnie Redding, Bertha Van Zante, Beulah Steinkamp, Marcia Garden, Sarah Klyn, Edna Hackert, Ethel Van Zante, Irene Van Haaften, Esther Brummel, Wilma Den Hartog, Eleanor Ver Ploeg, Lousie Dillinger, Mattie Olivier, Freida Reed, Esther Kooi, and Ruth Rempe.

Rock Island – Rock Island school fire.

Sand Ridge (12)

Sand Ridge, 1909 – Row one: Vernie De Briun, Herman Westerkamp, Gerrit Van Gorp, Arie M. Van Haaften, Edgar Vander Hart, Neal Ver Steegt, Lester Van Gorp, Nellie Westerkamp, Sara Ter Louw Van Hemert, Marie Eeling Dykstra, Walter Vander Hart, Roy Van Haaften, Clarence Sheehy, Herman Zwank, Marion Klyn, Arie Klyn, and John Eysink. Row two: Josie Van Haaften Groenendyk, Sophia Vos Geurts, Maggie Eysink Vander Pol, Jennie Vos Zwank, John S. Ter Louw, Minnie Eeling Ostrum, Tryna Eeling Beyer, Teacher Nelle Hahn, Anna Ter Louw, Bennie Zwank, Jacob Eeling, Ed Vos, John Boertje, Arie H. Van Haaften, Louis Van Haaften, and Lydia Ter Louw.

SAND RIDGE SCHOOL, which takes its name from the condition of the soil in the surrounding area, was located about six miles north of Pella in the northeast corner of the intersection of Blue Street and 248th Avenue.

There are no records of when the first schoolhouse was built, but in 1888 it was sold to Walter Van Der Hart for $41.50 and a new one was built which stood until the fire of 1944, at which time a third school was built. In February 1961, that building was auctioned for $1,130 and moved to Beacon.

Two students, Mrs. Anna Ter Louw Roorda and Annette Vander Hart Ter Louw, have left detailed descriptions of the school as it was when they attended in the first decade of the 1900s. (The large, gray one-room schoolhouse with attached coal house sat on the north end of a one-acre playground. On the south end was a small barn which housed a burro, and later a pony, whose owner, Harry Awtry, rode them to school.

The entry door was on the south side. A blackboard stretched the length of the north wall. There were three large windows on the east and west walls and between them were hooks where students hung their coats. A large coal-burning pot-bellied stove stood in the center of the room. In the winter time the area around it was often crowded with wet mittens, coats, and their owners trying to keep warm. Most days students remained at their assigned place in one of four rows of double desks.

In the southeast corner was a raised platform on which was the teacher's desk and an organ. In front of the platform was the recitation bench. When the teacher called pupils for class, she would say, "First grade reading, turn, rise, and pass." Turn meant turn in your seat so feet were in the aisle, rise meant stand up, pass meant walk to the bench.

A few open shelves along the west wall held a small library of books and the lunch pails. On the front seat was a pail with drinking water. At times, water from the school well was "questionable" and children were sent to get a pail of water from a nearby farm. At first they all drank from a common dipper but later they were required to provide their own cups. They continued, however, to wash their hands in a common basin and dry their hands on a common towel.)

This school burned down March 8, 1944, and on March 13 the board contracted for use of the Pete Slycord farmhouse for three months for eighty dollars. Donna Zwank Gosselink remarked on the big improvements in the new school, which had an oil furnace, running water, a library, Rolscreen windows, and a cement-floored basement. She also tells how her dad, Peter J. Zwank, who was not allergic to poison ivy, would avoid being "tagged" by running into a patch of it when students played tag. Other popular games of that era were Blackman, fox and geese, drop the handkerchief, and shinny which Cornelius Schakel describes as hockey on the grass with a tin can—very dangerous. In the winter time they also enjoyed skating on a pond which was near the school.

Mollie Brom recalls helping one little girl in school who always cried because she had a "headache in her legs" (probably from walking a long distance).

Several students from different decades mentioned the pastors and lay persons who came to school to teach Bible classes once a week. Sometimes these pastors also held services on Sunday and brought three or four schools together for vacation Bible School. Rev. H. L Van Dellen, long-time missionary for the American Sunday School Union, walked from Pella to the school when C.C. Ver Dught, father of Arie Ver Dught, was a student there. He told Arie that since his family didn't have opportunity to attend church services regularly he really appreciated the early training he received through these classes.

Teachers and the dates in which they taught include Minnie Dickey 1897; Sylvia Platt, Julia Van Zante 1898; Jennie Vander Zyl, Julia Van Zante 1900; Elizabeth Van Nimwegen 1900; Florence Hammer, Minerva Pugh, Hattie Harmson 1901; Julia Van Zante 1902-03; Jas D. Frank, Orville Ney 1904; Henrietta Gaass 1905; Kate Flannegan 1907; Elizabeth Clifford 1908; Nellie Hahn, Ella Ashton 1909; Nelle Hahn 1910-11; Gesiena Van Pilsum, Clair Mattox 1913; Henrietta Gaass 1915; Cassa Clark 1916-18; Lena Hoksbergen 1919; Marie Vander Hart 1920-24; Jeanette De Jong 1925-26; Marie Vander Hart 1927; Perry Smith 1928-30; Rhoda Culbertson 1931; Otis Crozier 1932-33; Irene Roose 1934-35; Johanna Rouwenhorst 1937-1940; Lena Nugteren 1942-43; Marjorie Litten 1944-46; Darlene Bevan fall 1947; Johanna Rouwenhorst spring 1948; Gladys Leusink Nieuwsma 1948-50; Mrs. Dale Gosselink, Mrs. Jeanne Walstra 1951; Mrs. Margaret De Ronde 1952-53; Elizabeth Tuinstra 1954-55; and Olive Palmquist 1956.

East Silver Grove (5)

THE EAST SILVER GROVE schoolhouse was a few miles west of Pella on old Highway 163 on the hill east of the farm owned by Larry and Lillian Terpstra. According to official county statistics in 1878, there were two buildings in the district, one brick and one frame (wood). Two schools were certainly needed that year as there were 101 student enrolled with an average daily attendance of 46.

However, Carl Nollen has found a deed dated August 30, 1888, establishing the East Silver Grove School site on one acre of land owned by Cornelis and Zwaantje Welle. Was the 1878 school on a different site or was it on the land the Welles deeded ten years later? We do know that the school was closed at the end of the 1921-22 school year. Myron Nollen recalls that he and his brother Elmer were the last two students who attended East Silver Grove before it closed in 1921. They wrote, he says, with slate and chalk.

Dr. Anthony Hospers, in a memoir written before 1974, recalls walking over a mile on a dirt road to reach the schoolhouse. He wore shoes with buttons that were fastened with a shoe buttoner, long black stockings, shorts pants that were several inches above the knees, and a blue shirt with large flaring collar. He graduated from high school in 1913, attended Central College, and taught at the Battle Ridge School for one year before he got the wanderlust and decided to go to Chicago.

Miss Cornelia Hospers was a teacher at East Silver Grove in the school years 1911 and 1912. Student Dorothy (Nollen) Van Gorp says about her: "It was through Cornelia's efforts that I have learned to enjoy poetry and what they called 'penmanship' or writing. She always had one line of a good poem or gospel hymn to write on a page. We used notebooks in which we wrote one line of poetry on each page for one class period in writing. We had poems by Longfellow, gospel hymns 'From Greenland's Icy Mountains,' 'Rock of Ages,' 'Faith of our Fathers,' and many others. And following through the poem in succeeding pages. I could quote many of them from memory and have never forgotten them."

Gertrude Gezel was the teacher in the 1905 school year. Miss Gezel's life ended tragically on August 28, 1913, when she, Cornelia De Geus, and Delia King drowned in Lake Geneva, Wisconsin. They were at a Y.W.C.A. camp representing Central College. Their bodies were recovered from 120 feet of water in early December of 1913.

Teachers who taught at East Silver Grove included Mary (Marie) Vander Zyl; Delia Rietveld 1894; Delia Rietveld 1895; Henrietta F. W. Gaass 1896; Gertie A. Gaass 1897; Anna Barendregt 1898; Sarah Lautenback 1899-1900; Marie Lautenback 1901; Elizabeth Van Nimwegen 1902-1903; Elizabeth Gezel 1903-04; Elizabeth Gezel, Gertrude Gezel 1905; Bertha Dykstra 1906-08; Lydia Grundman, Jeannette Hospers 1909; Gertrude Bennink 1910; Cornelia Hospers 1911-12; Hattie Neyenesch 1913-14; Helen Neyenesch 1915; and Mrs. A. A. De Bruyn 1916-1920.

Silver Grove East, spring 1912 – Left to right: Peter De Haan, Marion Nollen, Willie Klein, Harold Klein, Teacher Cornelia Hospers, Nellie Van Houweling, Marie De Haan, Dorothy Nollen, Helen De Haan, and Florence De Haan.

Silver Grove West (6)

Silver Grove West, 1901 – Row one: Freda Marinus, Hattie Klein, Margaret Vander Garde, Jennie Klein, Jeanette Onstine, Bessie Vander Garde, Bessie Van Houten, Emma Van Houten, Reka Van Houten, and Henry Martinus. Row two: James Van Loon, Art Klein, Gerrit Dykstra, John Van Peursem, Tunis Witzenberg, and John Slot. Row three: Jennie Van Peursem, Luedna Witzenberg, Blanche Witzenberg, Lois Van Loon, Sarah Vander Leest, Tone Klein, Gradus Vander Linden, Gradus Dykstra, Andrew Van Houten, and Andrew Mersbergen. Row four: Anna Marinus, Gerrit Klein, Richard Klein, Yella Witzenberg, Gertie Van Peursem, Lucy Witzenberg, Jennie Mersbergen, Maggie Slot, and Mille Van Peursem. Row five: John Vander Leest, Dora Van Loon, Gertie Dykstra, Teacher Bessie Vander Linden, Martin Vander Linden, Richard Vander Leest, and Ed Kooinegor.

LIKE MANY OTHER SCHOOLS, Silver Grove started as a single school splitting into two districts, East and West Silver Grove, when the school population increased in the late 1800s. (The records are unclear as to when this occurred.) In 1921, East Silver Grove closed and all the school children in the area again attended West Silver Grove until it too was closed at the end of 1960-61 school year. The records show a district population of 160 aged 5 to 21 in 1877, 83 in 1901, and 25 in 1942.

In his detailed history of Silver Grove, author Carl Nollen says that Silver Grove was four different school houses in three different locations at different times three or four miles west of Pella. The name, he says, might have been suggested by a grove of silver poplars (European in origin) or the native silver maples.

The first teacher known to have taught at Silver Grove was Louisa Adele Boekenoogen, who most likely taught during the years 1858-1861. The August 6, 1860, federal census lists Louisa Bokenoogen, seventeen, as a school teacher. The family name is Dutch for "eyes in a book." Her other occupations included being a Civil War correspondent in Europe, field agent (recruiter) for Central College, and an officer with the State Training School for girls at Mitchelville.

Carl Nollen's book on Silver Grove contains detailed information about many of the teachers at Silver Grove, a list of teachers for several area schools, photos of the remaining schoolhouses in Marion County and those of the Pella School District in Mahaska County, plus lots of memories from those who attended or taught at Silver Grove. He has also published a smaller updated book of this school.

Memories: Dorothy Klein Reed recalls the story her dad told her of her older brothers. Gerrit, age four, followed Jake, age five, to school. Dad found Gerrit sitting on the teacher's lap with his night cap still on. Teacher thought he was so cute that he was allowed to stay and soon learned to speak "American" as well as Dutch.

Bill Dieleman remembers pounding a broom handle on the concrete basement floor so hard that it broke driving a splinter in one side of his finger and out the other. It was bleeding profusely so the teacher bandaged it and sent him home (a mile's walk). His mother washed it and his dad pulled it out with the pliers. His mother poured iodine on it, re-bandaged it, and sent him back to school. (Kids had to be tough back then.)

Marion Witzenberg attributes a change in attitude to Bernice Wagner, whom he says transformed him from a rowdy urchin into a good student.

Lucille Dykstra Groenendyke and Lee Van Hemert both wrote fond accounts of getting ready for the Christmas program. Lucille mentions that there was a name drawing and gifts of twenty-five to fifty cents were given to the person whose name was drawn. The teacher gave a gift to everyone. For the evening program a gas lantern was hung from the ceiling. Lee mentions that one of the dads would bring in a fresh tree which was anchored in a bucket of sand. Students made their own decorations to add to the few commercial ones.

Several students mentioned riding to school in Eva Mae Van Wyngarden's 1938 Chevy Coup.

Teachers at the Silver Grove school were Louisa Boekenoogen 1858-60; Peter Lankelma 1879; Kate Keables 1880; Emily Vinyard 1881; George W. Kimmell 1883-84; Minnie Clutter, Franklin Milton Write, Minnie Keran 1885; Minnie Keran 1886-89; Hester Ver Ploeg early 1890s; Mary (Marie) Vander Zyl, Jennie Rietveld 1894; Jennie Rietveld, Bessie Bootsma 1895; Bessie Bootsma 1896-1898; Bessie Vander Linden 1899-1902; Bessie Vander Linden, Minera Pugh 1903; Minerva Pugh 1904-05; Anne Hospers 1906-09; Nelle Neels 1910-11; Luedna Witzenburg 1912-1914; Hattie Neyenesch, Luedna Witzenburg 1915; Sam Ver Steeg 1916-17; Hattie Van Veen 1918; Daisy Black 1919; Allie Van Polen 1920-21; Henrietta Plette 1922-1924; Jeannette Dekker 1925; Georgia Roorda 1926; Elizabeth Hesselink 1927; Gladys Fennema 1928-1931; Lawrence Fennema 1932; Ruth Langerak 1933-34; Helen Huyser 1935; Geraldine Gosselink 1936; Bernice Wagner 1938-39; Eva Mae Van Wyngaarden 1940-46; Alma Sims 1947; Ruth Vander Linden 1948-51; Marcile Van Zee, Janet Steenhoek 1952; Thelma Grandia 1953; Greta Van Hemert 1954-55; Greta Van Hemert, Ceola Liebhart 1956; Joyce Schippers 1957; and Ruth Vander Linden 1958-60.

Valley (13)

VALLEY SCHOOL was on the north side of the "T" where 245th Place abuts Illinois Street (an east/west road). Longtime residents will identify it as the school about one half mile north of the old airport. The school was established in 1869 as Lake Prairie District #9 and was closed in the spring of 1961. The building was destroyed by fire in 1965, reportedly by five Pella High boys in a Halloween prank. (*Pella Chronicle*)

One of the unusual things about this school

is that it was closed for five years from the fall of 1946 to the fall of 1951 because there were too few pupils to attend the school. In the fall of 1950, newlyweds Henry and Pauline (Steenhook) De Cook made their home in the school for about four months. During the time the Valley School was closed students attended Pleasant View (Mahaska County) or one of the grade schools in Pella. Several of the students who were at first apprehensive about attending town school felt that they were well prepared by their educational experience in a country school.

I remember this time well, as Marjorie Van Donselaar's mother asked me to keep her safe from the time she was dropped off at the high school until the bus arrived to take us home about an hour later. The reason for the wait was that the school had just purchased its first bus which ran two routes, one north of town and the other south of town; ours was the last route. Little Marjorie was the youngest child on the route and my having to keep my eye on her kept us both out of mischief during that unsupervised hour after school.

Carl Nollen has compiled a "scrapbook" of information about Valley teachers and students. A copy may be viewed at the Pella Historical Village. Several of the students mention the Halloween prank of tipping toilets and sometimes finding a toilet in the middle of the road the following morning. One year men of the neighborhood took turns guarding the toilets through the night. They finally solved the annual problem by setting posts in the ground and bolting the four corners of the toilets to them. Helen De Briun De Lawter has a different toilet memory about a snake skin she found on the toilet seat. She didn't think it was the snake that left it there. Others remembered the time shy kindergartner Wanda K.

Furcht hid in the toilet and would not come out until her little friend Ronald Liter coaxed her out.

In 1926, the old school building was torn down and replaced with a "modern school" with basement and furnace. The basement provided a great space to play during rainy or winter weather. Shirley Van Donselaar De Bruin's favorite indoor game was Fruit Basket Upset; Howard Vroom's was the card game Rook. Elmer Van Steenis said popular outdoor games were Simon Says, Geen Light - Red Light, and Annie-Annie-Over.

Dale Van Donselaar recorded detailed memories of his school days at Valley, including field trips to the State Capitol, State Historical Museum, the Des Moines Police Department, the Amana Colonies, the Sac and Fox Indian Reservation, and several factories. Because of limited budgets, most grade school students today do not get to take these kinds of trips.

Valley, 1938-39 – Balanced on the teeter-totter. Left to right: Ralph Vander Linden, Ray Van Dusseldorp, Junior Naaktgeboren, Nancy Van Maanen, Naomi Vroom, Lucille Van Zee, Beverly Den Hartog, Duane Vander Linden, Ralph Van Dusseldorp, and Teacher Almira Klein.

When she was ninety-five, Dale interviewed his aunt Leona Ver Meer about her experiences at the school. One of the questions asked was, "Did you study home economics (cooking, sewing) in school?" Her reply, "No, we learned that at home. We didn't have to go to school to learn how to work."

Carl Nollen's book has pictures and information about fifty of the Valley teachers. (Even if you don't know any of them, you'll enjoy looking at the changes in hair and clothing styles for almost a century.) Here is the list and the years (starting with the fall term) they taught: Cynthia Fisk, Henry Morgan 1869; (from the 1870s—Mariah Erp, Mary Belle Liter, Gordon Clark), Lula Viersen, Nora Davenport 1886; Annie Vander Ploeg, Anna De Haan 1895; Cornelia Lubberden 1896; Gerret Bos, Cornelia Lubberden 1897; Gertrude Vroom 1898; Cornelia Lubberden 1899 (others from the 80s or 90s were George Kimmell, George Lacey, John P. De Cook, Samuel F. Cole, Mary Hamilton, Alice Vander Zyl, Jennie Rietveld, Maggie Cooper, Leona Gillespie), Anna De Haan 1900; Kate Ver Heul 1900; Mae Fisk 1902; Katie Boland 1903; Leona Vander Linden 1904; Johanna Vande Kieft 1906; Maggie Van Zee, Leona Reuvers 1905; Bert Kersbergen, Caroline Gezel, Dena Verhey 1907; Dena Verhey 1908; Mrs. Mamie Smith 1909; G. L. Hackert, Anna Hospers 1910; Anna Hospers 1911-12; Mrs. Edith Burggraaf 1913; Nellie Bennink 1914; Joe Vandenberg 1915; Helen Neyenesch 1916-18; Ethel Roovaart 1919; Helen Brooks 1920; Ethel Roovaart 1921-22; Lois Brooks 1923-28; Cornelia Gosselink 1929-31; Sara Klyn 1932-35; Eva Mae Van Wyngarden 1936-37; Almira Klein 1938-39; Edna De Jong 1941-42; Beulah Roorda, Edgar Van Arkel 1943; Effie Heemstra 1944; Esther Kooi 1945; Mrs. Thelma Van Hemert 1951-55; Mrs. Ruth Ver Hoef 1956-57; Mrs. Alice Vander Zyl 1958; and Mrs. Naomi Koob 1959-60. He also included the information that teacher Helen Brooks died in 1929 of typhoid fever.

Map of Liberty Township

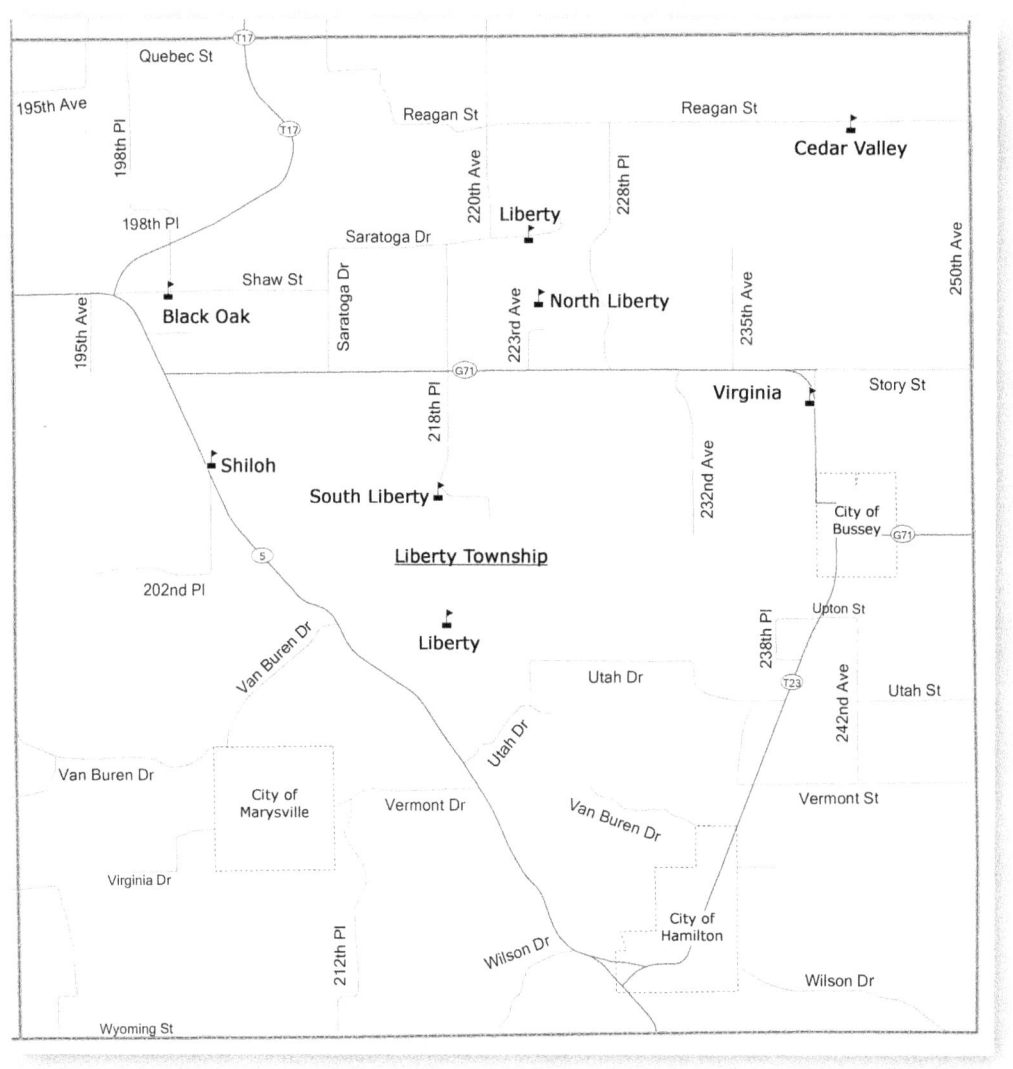

~7~

THE SCHOOLS OF
Liberty Township

Black Oak (6)

Black Oak, 1909 – Front row: Clark King, Everett King, Toney Butterfield, Grace Hauenstein, and Arminta Rose. Back row: Glen Rose, Ward Hauenstein, Elva King, Teacher Cora Davis, Nora King, Areta Rose, and Irma Rose.

ACCORDING TO THE official teacher records, Black Oak was located in the southeast corner of sec. 6 of Liberty Township. It was consolidated into the Attica School District before 1920.

The Marion County Historical Society has the souvenir booklet, which a very young-looking J. W. Van Benthuysen distributed to his pupils on March 14, 1902. This would have been at the close of the second or winter term of that year. His pupils included Abraham, Gustavis, and Edward Allen; Lynford Cade; Anna, Nora, Cora, May, Carroll, and Horace Davis; Jessi and John Ellis; Lottie, Mary, and Ralph Hart; and Lena, Beth, and Dwite Rose.

MCHS has another souvenir booklet given by Mrs. Rosa Smith to her pupils who attended during the third term (spring term) from April 10 to June 2, 1905. Many of the same surnames appear and added to the list are those of Butterfield, Coop, Carter, King, Marshall, McGruder, Rhodes, and Simmons.

In the picture to the left, we find teacher Cora B. Davis, who was listed as a student in the souvenir booklets of 1902 and 1905 and has now become the teacher. Note that the little girls' legs are well covered with black stockings and high top shoes while the two little boys in the front row are casually barefoot.

Teachers were Clara Davidson 1886; C. D. Applegate 1895; P. Edgar Adams 1896; C. W. Conrey, T. L. Conrey 1898; L. D. Bane, Art Betterton 1899; W. H. Leamime 1900; J. W. Van Benthuysen, Nina Pringle 1902; Lizzie Snyder, S. M. Rogers, Rosa Smith 1903; Rosa Smith 1904; Merle Brownfield,

Helen McConahey 1905; Mrs. Rosa Smith 1906; Myrtle L. McArthur, Anna Ridnouer 1907; Anna Ridnouer, Dora Rice 1908; Cora B. Davis 1909; Ve Lola Blair, Eva Marshall 1910; Bertha Brenniman, Bessie Williams, Eva B. Marshall 1911; Alice Holden, Eva Hutchings 1912; Christina Moffatt, Cora Rankin, Maude Martin 1913; and Marjorie Cooper 1914.

Cedar Valley (1)

THIS SCHOOL located north of Bussey was on the east side of the railroad tracks. The eastern edge of the district bordered Mahaska County. Cedar Valley was once called Egypt School.

Teachers were Ella Sanders 1886; Jim Hamilton 1894; Eva Daily, E. E. Larson 1895; C. D. Applegate 1898; Mary Roller, H. O. Smith 1900; Clara Mather, H. O. Smith 1902; ? Smith, Jean Rogers 1903; Katherine Shinn, Emma Gilchrist 1904; Mary Roller 1905; Beatrice Smith 1906; Ruby B. Miller 1907; Myrtle M. McArthur, Berlita Sarver 1908; Thos. Cooper 1909; Beulah Stuff 1910; Nora Westner 1911; Georgia Totten 1912; Nellie Cain 1913; Blanche Myers, W. H. Lucas 1914; and Fern Davis 1921.

Liberty North (10)

LIBERTY NORTH was northwest of Bussey and was consolidated into that district.

Teachers were Miss Julia Ruckman 1890; James Hamilton 1891; Miss Ella Maddy 1892; Cora Lyman, Alice Quillen 1895; Addie Rutherford 1896; Nellie Wilson, Mary Roller, Cora Lyman 1899; Nellie Cooper 1900-01; Bertha Totten, Fern Young 1902; Stella Brubaker 1903; Mary Roller, Leta Banifield 1904; Nora E. Davis, Stella Brubaker 1905; Mary Roller 1906; and Arie Shinn 1907.

Liberty South (16)

LIBERTY SOUTH was southwest of Bussey. It also was consolidated into the Bussey District.

Teachers were Ola Wright 1895; Pearl Bussey, Nellie Wilson, Ida Hall 1898; Mary F. Parker, Bertha Totten 1899; Loveda Van Doren, Bertha Totten 1900; Eva M. Walker, Mrs. Maude Cloe, Ethelle Sullivan 1902; Ethelle Sullivan 1903; P. Van Benthuysen 1904; Mary Irons, Minnie Runnels 1905; Minnie Runnels 1906; and Myrtle McArthur 1907.

Without being designated as serving the North or South Liberty Schools, these additional teachers are listed: Ella Dodd 1894; Charlie Conrey 1897; Pearl Bussey, Nellia Wilson, Ida Hall, Lida Young 1901; Alice Parker, Bertha Hughes 1908; Luisa Van Benthuysen 1909; Virgie Shinn 1910; Maude Martin 1912; Alythe Darnell 1913; Nellie Bridges 1914; Mamie McKeigh 1917; and Mary Simms, Hazel Kendrick 1918.

Shiloh (17)

Shiloh, school year 1946 – Mrs. Thomas, teacher. Row one: Carolyn Cline, Joan Beaver, Joyce Beaver, David Bailey, and Tommy Parker. Row two: Paul Feagins, Harry Hart, Keith Bailey, Sally Parker, and Richard Bailey. Row three: Russell Kephart, Charles Feagins, Alice Feagins, Beth Bailey, Dolores Bailey, and Mary Parker.

SHILOH SCHOOL WAS NAMED after one of the bloodiest battles of the Civil War, fought on April 6 and 7 in 1862. Shiloh School stood on a little hill off Highway 5, not far from North Cedar Creek. The school sat on the present north edge of the property of Robert and Judy Bailey, who have lived there since 1970. Also on this farm was the village of Everist, one of the county's ghost towns that brought in a temporary influx of miners. The two-story Shiloh building, one of the largest country schools in Marion County, was built to accommodate the children of these workers as well as the children of area farmers.

Judy Bailey has provided information from Mr. W. A. Young, who wrote letters about his memories of the school for the third annual Marysville reunion. Mr. Young started school just before he was five in the spring of 1876 with teacher Rolla Hoyt. Another one of his teachers was R. C. Davidson, a Civil War veteran with a college education. This teacher spent thirty minutes a day after school teaching algebra to him. Mr. Young was still in school at age eighteen, the same age as his teacher Hiram Curtis. Farm boys often attended school only during the winter term so it was not unusual for them to be the same age or even older than their teachers.

Mr. Young named other early teachers: J. W. Kitch, Charles Harlow, Willie Runyan, Lon and Wilson Rice, Kate and Sadie Rose, Bettie and Tabitha Lyman, Eva Scott, Cora Rowland, Della Ruchman, Nancy Cross, Nettie Mosier, and Addie Bailey, whom he described as gentle and kind, a very capable teacher.

He also noted that although most directors were men, two women, Melissa Joliffe and Vashti Demy Bailey, served as very capable directors. This was many years before women were allowed to vote.

Judy's grandmother, Dessie Bailey Robuck, has fond memories of attending Shiloh around 1910-12. She remembers seeing her younger brother Frank spelling aloud for the class the word "Mississippi" as follows: M, I, crooked letter, crooked letter, I, crooked letter, crooked letter, I, humpback, humpback, I. "Grandmother was an excellent speller and in a pinch you could use her instead of a dictionary," commented Judy.

Former student Harry Hart started school in 1941, attending primary through 8th grade. He compliments teacher Bessie Robuck Kenney, stating his freshman year at Albia seemed like a review of what he was taught at Shiloh.

Judy's husband David Bailey also attended Shiloh in the 1940s when there were fifteen or fewer students in this once large school. He says the first floor was about three-quarters classrooms and the rest a small gym with eight-foot high ceilings and a walk-in closet with hooks to hang coats, hats, and slingshots. You could, if you wanted to, keep your slingshot in your back pocket.

The second floor had church-like wooden pews and a three-foot high stage. He tried to avoid the plays and programs given there, stating some teachers didn't care if you didn't participate. (None of my teachers offered that option. We all participated—never even thought to object!)

Corporal punishment was allowed. In fact, his father Charlie Bailey made willow switches for the teacher to use. Switching was not an everyday occurrence and if a student needed to be punished the teacher took him into the hallway and he could not come back into the room crying.

Former student Alice Feagins Woerpel writes from Hutchinson, Kansas, that she was the only student in her grade, and many days the teacher didn't have time for a class for her. She felt left out. The teacher did, however, include her in spelling tests with the other grades. She always got an A in spelling. This helped her as she worked thirty-five years as a medical transcriptionist. Both she and David Bailey commented on the appearance of the school, which looks like brick in the black and white photos. It was actually some kind of gray metal, most likely tin.

These teachers taught at Shiloh: Rolla Hoyt 1876; Cora A. Hollowell 1886; Jennie Ghrist, Miss Tillie Hamilton 1891; Miss Ella Maddy, Miss Rose Shannon 1892; Myrtle Eshom, Anna Young 1895; Nellie Wilson 1898; Laveda Van Doren, Elsie Manley 1899; Elsie Manley 1900; Lucina Marshall, T. L. Conrey, Anna Ridenour 1902; T. L. Conrey, Ollie Gelderblom 1903; Mrs. Della Castor, Lulu M. Jones 1904; Mrs. Della Castor, Maude Inskeep, Effie Harmes 1905; Conner Brennan, Nora E. Davis, Mary Rogers, Sara Hart, Effie Haines 1906; W. J. Kincaid, Mrs. C. Maulry 1913; Isa E. Houser 1921; Edna Mae Stone 1923; Beulah Hawkins 1924-25; Eulice Davis 1926-27; Mrs. Eulice Sims 1928; Leona Bogaard 1929; Leona Baker 1931; Edna M. Stone 1932; Leah Baker 1933-34; Wilma Nicholson 1935-36; Mary Carrington 1937; Alice Edna Smith 1938-39; Bessie Robuck 1940-42; Mrs. Bessie Robuck Kenney 1943-45; Mrs. Thomas 1946; Miss Nicholson 1947; Bessie Kenney 1948-49; Wilma Noah 1950; Wilma Noah, Mrs. Georgia Long 1951; and Mrs. Eulice Sims 1952.

Sometimes the Shiloh School was listed in the records as Everist. Here are the teachers listed under that name: J. J. Roue, Mae Davis, Myrtle McArthur, Blanche McClary 1910; J. J. Roue, Mae Davis, Laura Gibbons, Evelyn Slayman 1911; J. J. Roue 1912; Wm. J. Kincaid, Myrtle Sharon, May Long, Hazel Chivers, Christina Moffatt 1913; H. C. Maulry 1914; Kathleen Norris 1915; and Isa Houser 1920.

Virginia (11)

VIRGINIA WAS PROBABLY named in recognition of the state of Virginia. Many of the early settlers in Marion County were part of that great wave from the New England states that was steadily moving westward as new territories opened up. It was a short distance northwest of Bussey and was consolidated early into the Bussey District.

When Cora Lyman taught during the school year of 1899-1900, the following were listed as her students: Alf, Dwight, Harry, Mamie, and Royce Ayers; Belle, Ethel, Johnie, and John Chambers; Bernard, Everett, Jennie, Kelley, and Minnie Johnson; Charley and Mattie Ross; Earney, Ira, Ollie, and Ray Tandy; Elmer and Fred Mick; Earnest, Grace, and Roy McCombs; George, Lloyd, and Mary Anspach; Grace Bonnett; and John Wade and Vera Attwaters.

Teachers were Meria Sharon, Miss Anna Behnock 1886; Clara Barton 1889; Miss Ella Pace 1892; Anna Jemison, Mrs. C. W. Mather 1895; Mary Johnson, Mary Anspach 1896; Ethel E. Burton 1898; Cora Lyman 1899; Bertha Totten, Maude Inskeep 1900; Esta Swem, Lillie Mick, Maude Inskeep 1902; Bernice Rolfe, Lulu Gibbons 1903; Lillie Mick, J. O. Angel 1904; Lucie Gray 1905; Lillie Mick, Clara Phelps 1906; Bertha Hughes 1909; Burch Doughman 1910-11; Bessie L. Fall 1912; Dora Rice 1913; and Nellie Cain 1914.

Weir City

THIS SCHOOL was south of Bussey. When the new building was constructed, half of the old one went for the school at Weir City.

Teachers listed were Miss Mary Roller 1901; Rosa Rice 1905; Atha Wolfe 1906; and Nellie Wilson 1909.

Map of Perry Township

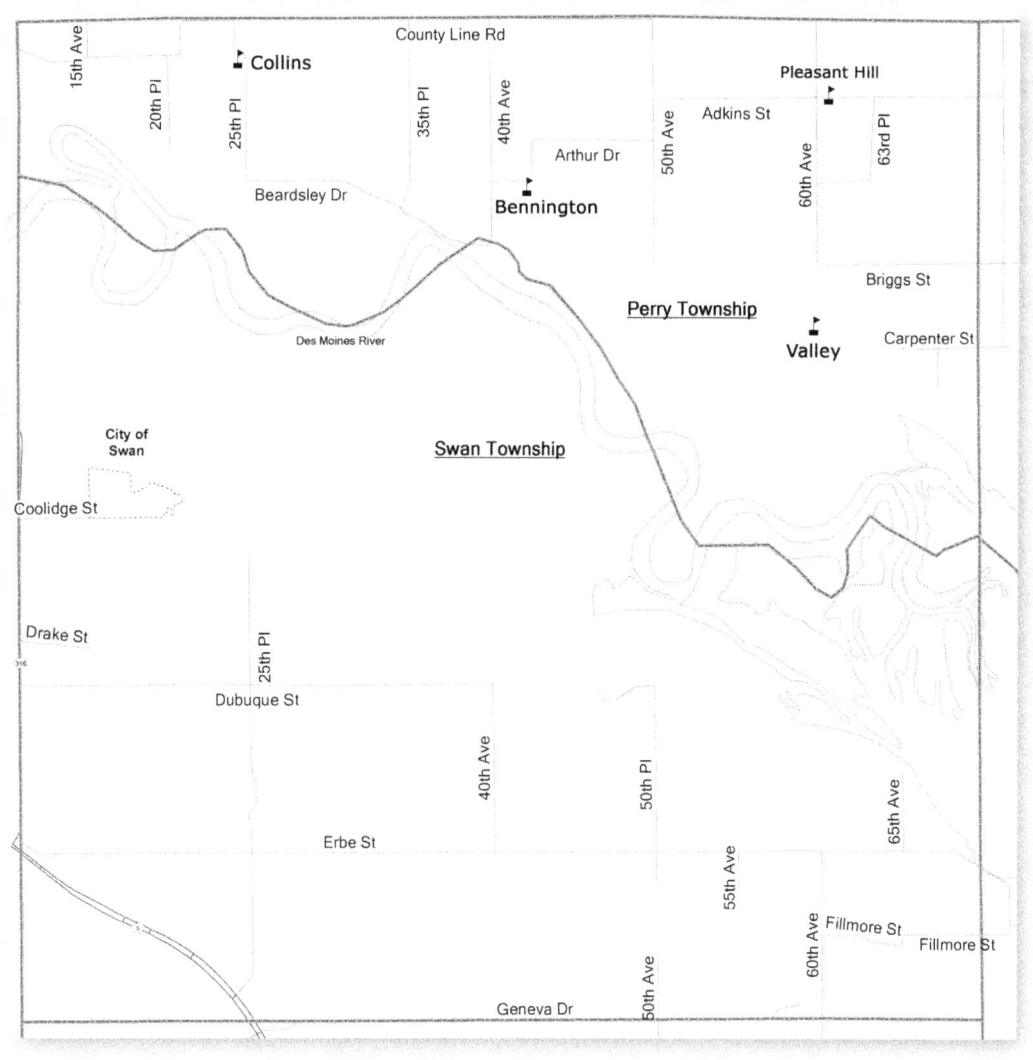

8

THE SCHOOLS OF
Perry Township

Bennington (10)

BENNINGTON WAS LOCATED on the north side of the Des Moines River in the east half of Section 9. It was platted in 1848 by William Gregory and Wm. Baker, but never contained more than a few houses. It was near the site of the Bennington Ferry, which later became the Bennington Bridge.

Teachers were H. M. Matheney 1886; Gertie Wassenaar, Nellie M. Bride 1895; J. L. Cochrane 1898; J. L. Cochrane, Maggie Cooper 1900; Maggie Cooper 1901; Mary C. Clark 1902; Mary Clark, Stella De Vany, Alpha Reeves 1903; Lizzie M. McKinney, Jessie Clark, Mary Clark 1904; Marion Wilson, Marjorie Leuvin, Jessie Clark 1905; Minnie Hyatt, Marlon Wilson, Maymie Lewin 1906; Nannie Hyatt, Mary E. Clark, Jessie Clark 1907; Mary J. Clark, Mae Davis 1908; Mae Davis, J. L. Cochran 1909; Mae Davis, Hazel Rice, Beryl O'Dell 1910; Ida Freeman, Laura Buckley, Nellie Bridges 1911; Nellie Bridges 1912-13; Elizabeth Herschauer, Nellie Bridges 1914-16; Nellie Bridges, Jennie Johnson 1917; Jennie Johnson, Ola Bennett 1918; Gladys Ray 1919; D. W. Martin 1920; Ruth Morgan 1921-23; Ina L. Honold 1924; Jessie Hunter 1925-26; Mrs. Mamie Walker 1927; Evelyn Colyn 1930; (no school) 1931; Mrs. Leo Headlee 1937; and Pauline Heaberline 1938.

Collins (6)

THE COLLINS SCHOOL was on 25th Place in the northwest corner of Marion County. The district was bordered on the west by Polk County and on the north by Jasper County. A log cabin served as the school for first teacher, Ida Brous. This was replaced by a frame structure, which burned down. A third building was erected southeast of the one that burned down. It was also a frame building with a bell tower. That building was sold after the school closed.

In the list of teachers, you will note the name Nannie Hyatt, a long-term teacher who began her career by teaching in country schools. She taught in Marion and Guthrie Counties for a total of fifty-one years, retiring from teaching in 1935. She was born September 6, 1864, and died July 25, 1935. Oh, what stories she could tell us!

A picture of the West and Clark children and their mothers appeared in the June 14, 1937, edition of *The Knoxville Journal*. Both families were at the doctor's office at the same time for a general exam. At that time, the West family had eleven children while the Clark family had eight. The catchy header above the picture read "An Entire School—Just Two Families."

The reporter entirely missed the fact that there were also students from other families who were attending the school. These two families do illustrate why there was a need for so many country schools in an earlier era.

Teachers included Molly McCoy 1886; Mary E. Clark, Ola Fairley 1898; Maude Inskeep, Hattie Huckaby 1899-1900; Clara Langebartels, Elsie Daly, Hattie Huckaby 1901; Clara Langebartels, Mary C. Clark 1902; Lizzie Snyder, Mattie Rankin, Alpha Reeves 1903; Lizzie McKinney, Jessie Clark, Mary Clark 1904; Lizzie Snyder, Bess Van Gorp 1905; Katherine Finnessy 1906; Nannie Hyatt, Katherine Finnessy 1907; Nannie Hyatt, Edna L. Lusk, Eunice Kutz 1908; Mable Bush, Edna Spires, Edna Lusk 1909; Mary C. Clark, Edna Spires 1910; Mary C. Clark, Jessie Warner 1911; Mary Clark, Olivia Hollister, Mary Entler 1912; Lois Richards 1913; Lois Richards, Walter P. Heisel, Forest Moore, Jessie B. Kinsell 1914; Mrs. Hazel Cooper, Ida Fenningkeit 1915; Bernice Ramsey, Hazel Cooper 1916; Bernice Ramsey, Lydia Hughes 1917; Lydia Hughes, Olive Freeman, Evelyn Ash 1918; Lola White 1919; Alice Conner 1920; Elsie Daly, Jessie Rogers 1924; Mary Hunt 1925; Elsie Daly 1926; Frankie Carter 1928; Thelma McCoy 1929; Stella Danks 1930; Geneva Young 1931; Adeline Herweh 1933-34; Miss Pauline Ingle 1935; Ernest Klinker 1936; Bethine Wilson 1937; Gretchen Robinson 1938; Mollie P. O'Berg 1939; Pauline Heaberlin 1940; Mary L. Turner 1941; and Mrs. Frances Freeman 1943-45.

Collins, spring 1899 – Left to right: Teacher Maude Inskeep, Louella Spencer, Roxy West, Frank Morrison, Georgia Spencer, Alfred Spencer, Mable Ball, Sadie West, Cordis West, Flossie Morrison, Henry West, Benjamin West, and Grace West.

Pleasant Hill (1)

PLEASANT HILL SCHOOL is now Pleasant Hill Community Center, 615 Adkins Street, Prairie City. It is on the original site six and one-half miles straight south of Prairie City, two miles northeast of the former town of Percy, and one-half mile south of the Jasper County line. The school is shown in this location in an 1875 plat book.

In 1995, the annual Percy Fair published a book called *Country School Reunion Memories*. The following comments about the Pleasant Hill School are excerpts from that book:

"The day I was supposed to start kindergarten (1937) I had pinkeye and had to sit in the car in front of the house and watch the kids walk by. Rainy days

Pleasant Hill, spring term 1915 – Teacher Sadie Coulson. Row one: Leo Wilson, Cleo Cowman, Maude Kain, and Coral Kain. Row two: Keith Cowman, Clarence Cowman, Lorene Cowman, Roy Schrader, Paul Tidball, Fay Wilson, Mildred English, Oleta Rinehart, and Dorothy Cowman. Row three: Gladys Kain, Margaret Umble, Letha Cowman, Floyd Wilson, Marie Rinehart, Harry Schrader, and Vernie Umble. Row four: Robert Schrader, Harold Wilson, Tommy Schrader, and Ransom Rinehart. (Ivan Hughes was absent.)

Fonda (Fawcett) threw things from her desk and we scrambled for them. She took kids home with her, usually in two's. Lola West went down the clothes chute. She (Fonda) always filled our lunch boxes with lots of good things." – Shirley Walker Funk

"The boys built what they called the high-dive by packing snow several feet high. We would go down hill on the sled and over this. Once I hit my chin and damaged my lower front teeth." – Oleta "Peg" Rinehart Clymer.

"On passing the school house from the west on one long ago evening in the family car we noticed an improvised 'white flag' being waved frantically out the small west window of the coal room. Somehow Fonda had locked herself in that room in the process of banking the fire for the evening." – Edward L. Cowman

"Teacher Florence Templeton Miller had a 1929-30 Ford Coupe and all of the children were told not to touch that car. There were 9 Schrader brothers and they formed a ball team called the Schrader 9 and were all good players." – Henry Erskin

"One of the best childhood memories I have is every year about 2 weeks before school started, our whole family would make a trip to Knoxville. First, we'd go to the County School Superintendent's office in the Court House and get registered for school. Then we'd be given a list of textbooks and work books we needed for the term. We'd take the list across the street to the book store and get our new books. Sometimes if the same text book was to be used as the year before, you could trade in last year's books or buy someone's used book. But then the best best part was the new crayons, pencils, paste, erasers, tablets, maybe a new pencil box and ruler or even a note book. Then we would get some new school clothes and shoes! It was better than Christmas!" – Sandra Kain Harsin

"Teaching at Pleasant Hill 2 years and Collins 3 years was the highlight of my life. My pupils were all such good children and I loved each and everyone so much. I recall one time I asked Wayne Erskin and Hollis Kain to break up some coal for the furnace as I couldn't lift it, so they did and they really had fun." (She goes on to say she regrets not apologizing to their parents for sending them home covered in coal dust.) – Teacher Adeline Herweh Jenkins. The students gave her a surprise shower just before she got married and moved to California.

"I am glad I attended country school. Four generations of us attended Pleasant Hill. My grandmother Lizzie Johnson Wilson, my mother Leo Wilson Walker, me, Coleen Walker Keuning, and two of my sons Donald and Danny Keuning started school there." – Coleen Walker Keuning

"One of the nicest things about Pleasant Hill School was the support I received from director Elmer Walker and the other parents of the community. Another thing I remember well is the heavy population of mice. Actually, there maybe wasn't that many but two or three were way too many for me. Max Kain kindly cleaned out my desk each day until I got screen wire on the bottom of it." – Teacher Eileen Taylor

Teachers included Mattie Richards 1881; A. J. Swain 1886; Lizzie Henry, Emma Kain 1895; Emma Kain, P. Edgar Adams 1896; Ona Harp 1898; Robert L. Swearingen 1900; R. L. Swearingen, Maggie Cooper 1901; Maggie Cooper, Pearl Beeman, Maggie Cowman 1902-03; M. L. Wilson 1904; Mable Bush 1905; Mabel Bush, Katherine Finnesy 1906; Nora M. Alexander, Faye Cummings 1908; Viola Oster, Hazel Rice 1909; Frankie Brown, Gladys Webb 1910; Gladys G. Webb, Cora Rankin 1911; Gladys Webb 1912; Marie Webb 1913; Ernest Dowden, Sadie A. Coulson 1914; Leota Godfrey, Maude Martin, Virginia Biggs 1915; Virginia Biggs, Beulah Beckwith 1916; J. J. Hammond 1917; Blanche Perry, Karl Kemper 1918; Jennie Leuty 1919; Kate Erskine 1920; Blanche Van Gorp 1921; Jeanette Schultz 1922; Mollie Passmore 1925; Frances Clark 1926; Ellie Morgan 1927; Abigail Pardee 1928; Florence Templeton 1929; Marjorie Kingery 1930; Merle Taylor 1931-32; Ruth Young 1933-34; Adeline Herweh 1936; Bernice De Graff 1937; Norma Carter 1938; Fonda Fawcett 1939-41; Mrs. Eileen A. Charles 1943-44; Fonda Fawcett 1945; and Fonda Fawcett 1947-56.

Valley (11)

THE VALLEY SCHOOL (Perry #1) was located near the town of Percy. An 1875 map shows it in the same location as it was when the school closed. Marjorie Kane Fee, who began teaching there in 1934, contributed a story to the Percy Fair book, *Country School Reunion Memories*, of 1995. She said Bennington was closed that year and the children were sent to Valley. She had thirty pupils and was paid fifty dollars per month with a five dollar a month raise for two years. Her certificate was a first grade certificate, which meant she had good grades plus one year of experience. Some country schools, she wrote, hired those with 3rd grade certificates to save on costs.

The building stood on one-half acre of land. Skinned knees were common because of the cinder paths leading to the "necessary little buildings." On muddy spring days she sometimes used the coal shovel to get the mud out of the cloakrooms.

The school was usually warm but in the winter of 1936 when the roads drifted and the temperature was below zero for many days, the directors closed the school for three weeks. She had chilblains and her feet itched terribly. She took off her shoes and stockings and stood in the snow to cool off.

Teachers included: Ida Putnam 1882; Mede B. Brous 1886; Miss Dora Ruckman, Miss Mary Vaughn 1889; Miss Gertrude Reed 1892; L. H. McKinney, Cora Henry, Hiram Curtis 1893; Nellie McBride, Nellie Brockett 1895; J. L. Cochrane, Nellie Wassenaar 1896; Emma K. Hughes, J. L. Cochrane, R. N. London, L. H. McKenny 1898; J. L. Cochrane, Mary C. Clark, Nellie Rogers 1899; Emma K. Hughes, J. L. Cochrane 1900; J. L. Cochrane, Pearl Beeman 1902; Lizzie Gifford 1903; Walter E. Wellons, Lizzie Clifford, Maggie Cowman 1904; Walter E. Wellons, M. L. Wilson 1905; Emma Smith 1906; Claudia Henry, Elva Helm, Emma Hughes 1907; J. L. Cochrane, Mabel Fouts, Alice McRae 1908; Olivia Hollester, Cecil Way, Fay Cummings 1909; Cecil Way, Maude Wilson, Bertha Harvey 1910; D. Butcher, Alta Rowland 1911; Dean Butcher, Viola Hamilton 1912; Hazel Nell Failor, Peter Danks 1913; Peter B. Danks, Mamie Chambers 1914; Dora Rice, W. D. Campbell, Mabel Leuty 1915; Florence Jones, Eva James, Flossie Hamilton 1917; Mrs. Mabel Johnson, Lee Goodenough 1918; Jennie Leuty 1919; W. D. Campbell 1920; Lena Park 1923; Betty Jean Colyn, Lena Park 1924; Gertrude Taylor 1925; Miss Fern Brause 1926; Mrs. Fonda Fawcett 1928-32; Clifford A. Holt 1933; Marjorie Kane 1934-36; Ernest Klinker 1937-38; Miss Wald 1939; Lavonne Walker 1940; Betty Louise Kool 1943; Mrs. Norma McDaniel 1944; Mrs. Norma McDaniel, Wanda Recktenwald 1945; Gertrude Thornton 1947; Ina L. Umble 1948; Mrs. Lavonne Walker 1949; Mrs. Russell De Haai 1951; and Hazel De Haai 1953-56.

Valley – Front row: Ray Mikesell, Pearl Manning, Loren Owens, Jennie Bullington, Free Walker, Jennie Leuty, Camille Leuty, Bertha Keller, Zuella Walker, and Pearl Mikesell. Back row: Rachel Mikesell, Henry Wagner, Lorenzo Bullington, Minta Brown, Hazel Flory, Emma Keller, Della Bullington, Chase Keller, Martha Leuty, Ethel Walker, Lizzie Keller, and Izora Manning. The date is probably early 1900s. The teacher is listed as Effie Hanes, but she is not in the official list. MCHS has a souvenir booklet from Walter E. Wellons, who taught the first term of 1905. Many of the same students are listed in that booklet along with others named Holmes, Schafer, Robinson, Carter, and Colyn.

Map of Pleasant Grove Township

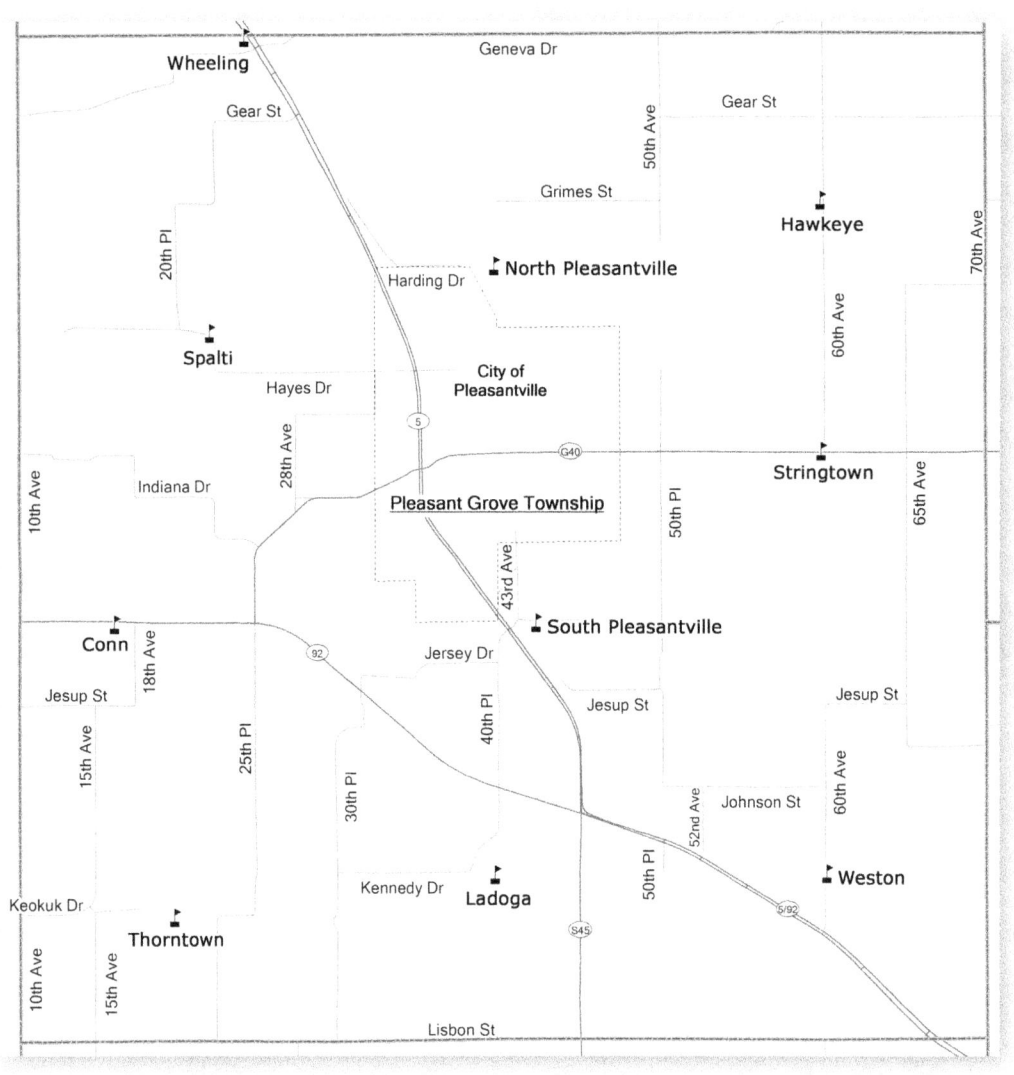

9

THE SCHOOLS OF
Pleasant Grove Township

Pleasant Grove Township

MANY OF THE EARLY SCHOOLS were subscription schools where a school was held in the teacher's home and the parents paid a small fee for each child to attend. In Pleasant Grove Township, Daniel Shea taught the first school in 1847 in a cabin a little southwest of Pleasantville. His sixteen students paid two dollars each for a three-month term. He is described as a warm-hearted, visionary Irishman, once a flourishing merchant in Montreal, Canada; a fine scholar, a good mathematician, and an honest man (*History of Marion County*).

On February 2, 1915, Pleasantville voted to consolidate its remaining eight country schools in Pleasant Grove Township. The voters in the town of Pleasantville cast 165 votes for consolidation and 37 against. The country folk in the township voted 68 to 65 against sending the children to town school. A newspaper account says the school was very proud of the fact that every teacher had a first-class certificate. Before a teacher was certified, that person had to take certain tests and the grade point average determined whether the teacher was given a first, second, or third-class certificate.

It took several months for the completion of the new building. In the meantime, two additional rooms were added to the old building, the 4th grade was taught in a nearby home, and the 5th grade in a business building. Nine rural school wagons (Studebakers) were purchased to transport the country school children to town. The drivers' salaries ranged from forty-five to sixty dollars per month. After the school year of 1917, there are no more records for Conn, Hawkeye, Ladoga, Spalti, Stringtown, Thorntown, Weston, and Wheeling. It appears that two other country schools, Pleasantville North and Pleasantville South, whose records date to 1874, closed several years earlier.

Conn (19)

CONN WAS WEST of 50th Avenue and south of Gear Street.

Teachers were Effie Hamilton, Nora Danihy 1895; Edna Summy 1898; Iva Summy 1899; Nora Harding, Iva Marsh, Grace Gillaspie 1900; Nora Harding, Iva Marsh, Grace Gillaspie 1901; Elsie

Clark, Esta Sweem 1902; Flossie Hollowell, Belle Shawner 1903; Belle Shawner 1904; Tomie De Witt, Ida B. Ash 1905; Flossie Hollowell 1907; Grayce M. Freel 1908; Georgia Jane Jesse 1909; Joanna Reed, Georgia Jesse 1910; Maude Spalti, Beulah Worstell, Estella Stockholm 1912; Pansy Thornberg, Jessie Warner 1912; and Pansy Thornberg 1914.

Hawkeye (2)

HAWKEYE DISTRICT bordered Warren County. It was between Highway 92 and Jessup Street.

Teachers were Miss Almira Mohler 1885; May Bishop, Gertrude Prichett 1895; Ola Fairley, Grace Gillaspie 1898; Grace Gillaspie, Maude Spalti 1899; Bertha Hayes 1900-01; A. I. Reed 1902; Ross De Veny, Blanche Litchfield 1903; Maude Spalti, Blanche Litchfield, Daisy Richards 1904; Maude Spalti, Mary A. Jones, Daisy Richards 1905; Daisy M. Richards 1906; Vivian Inlow 1907; Vivian Inlow, Edna Neal 1908; Julia Smith, Grace Freel 1909; D. S. Reed, Bessie Williams 1910; Bessie Williams 1911; Ina LaFayette, Fay Johnson, Cornelia Smith 1912; Cornelia Smth, Fae Schuack 1913; Mabel Lyman Spalti 1914; Edna Buckner 1916; Hallie Black, Mertie Battles 1917; and Mamie Lucile Watson 1918.

Ladoga (33)

LADOGA WAS LOCATED south of Highway 92 on 40th Place.

Bob Banes of Pleasantville writes, "Ladoga was named for a town in Indiana where early settlers came from. My grandmother, Myrtle Brown Bane, was one of its early teachers. The Iddings family was among her students."

The January 5, 1885, *Knoxville Journal* says there was a spelling bee and sack lunch at Ladoga Thursday evening.

Teachers were C. A. Hanson 1891; Ollie Drake, Sara Conn 1895; Sadie Cline, Emma Prentice 1898; Roxy De Witt 1899; Elsie Clark 1900; Grace Gillaspie, Nora Prewett 1901; Paul Dale, Gertrude Almach 1902; Amanda Brown, Tomie De Witt 1903; Bertha H. Marsh, Maude Abernathy 1904; Maude Abernathy, Ada Profitt 1905; Birdie Reynolds 1908; Birdie Reynolds, Ida Simmons 1909; Georgia Jesse 1910; Mrs. Bertha Marsh 1911; Catherine Benge 1912; Joanna Reed 1913; and Everett Walker 1914.

Ladoga – Mr. Robert Bane sent the photo of the Ladoga School where his grandmother Myrtle Brown was a teacher. She graduated in the spring of 1892 and married his grandfather Bane in the fall of 1895, so the picture can be dated to the 1892, 93, or 94 school year. She is 4th from the left in the back row.

Pleasantville North (9)

THIS SCHOOL WAS NORTH of the town of Pleasantville and east of Highway 5 on 40th Place.

Teachers were Miss West 1874; G. A. Fike 1876; F. M. Compton 1814; Miss E. Wilson 1885; Nora Spalti 1895; Maud Plummer 1899; Ione Printz 1900; Emma Prentice 1901; and Joanna Reed 1911.

Pleasantville South (22)

THIS SCHOOL WAS south of Pleasantville near where Highway 5 intersects with 40th Place.

Robert Banes of Pleasantville writes that his father attended this school. It was also called Eureka. *The Knoxville Journal* of 1879 reported that Miss M. J. Howard of Pleasantville South had been disposed, replaced by Mrs. Brady. Correspondent thought the district a little unjust.

Teachers were Miss Shadle 1874; Miss Ruth Cheetham 1876; Miss M. J. Howard 1878; Mrs. Brady 1879; John Shadle 1884; Dora Painter 1885; Anna Sunny 1895; Ethel Hayes 1899; Ruth Hayes 1900; Iva Summy 1901; and Georgia Jesse 1911.

Pleasantville South, 1899 – Ethel Hayes, teacher.

Spalti (8)

SPALTI WAS NEAR 20th Place and Hayes Drive. Spalti is a very familiar local name so I think we can assume the land for the school was donated by a family named Spalti.

Teachers were Ada Jordan 1885; May Spalti 1886; Emma Prentice 1895; Maud Plummer 1898; Maude Spalti 1899; Nora Harding 1900; Maude Spalti 1901; Nora Hardin, Roxy De Witt 1902; Nora Harding, Maud Plummer 1903; Marie Marsh, Nora Hillabolt 1904; Nora Hillabot 1905; Meryl Sterling, Maybel De Witt 1906; Grace M. Freel 1907; Roxie Burch, Laura B. Buckley, Birdie Reynolds 1908; Oletha Lemmon, Eva Worstell 1910; Marcie Gardner 1911; Blanche Summy 1912; and Maude Spalti 1913.

Stringtown (14)

THIS SCHOOL was on the Stringtown Road, now G40. There was never a town, just a series of farmsteads strung along the road. The school was on property owned by Marc Worthington, whose address is 573 G40. It was moved an eighth of a mile from the corner and used as a granary and machine shop.

Teachers: Sara Rose 1886; Ada Terwilleger 1895; Maude Spalti, Maude Plummer 1898; Nora Spalti, Ione Prentz 1899; Nora B. Spalti, Bertha Hayes 1900; Roxy De Witt 1901; Bertha Hayes 1902; Maude Spalti, Maude Abernathy 1903; Tomie De Witt, Margaret Conway 1904; Thirza Dyer, Maude Spalti, Minnie Powell 1905; Roxy De Witt, Iva B. Marsh 1906; Maude Spalti 1907; Ruby Iddings 1908; Bessie Summy 1909; Mary Caffrey, Jeanie Iddings 1910; Jessie Iddings 1911; Mrs. Maude Marsh 1912; Maycie Worthington 1913; and Sadie Billingsley 1914.

Thorntown (31)

THORNTOWN was the southwestern-most district in Pleasant Grove Township. The school was near 20th Place, south of Kennedy Street.

Teachers were Stella Kuhn 1895; Flavia Williams, Nora Hardin 1898; Nora Hardin 1899; Florence Batten 1900; Florence Batten, Bertha Hayes 1901; Ina Hook, Belle Shawner 1902; Belle Shawner, Bertha Stevens 1903; James W. Brady 1904; Emma Smith, Mary Irons 1905; Nellie M. McEdrea 1906; Agnes Patterson 1907; Bessie Summy 1908; Beulah Stuff, Ethlyn Nelson 1909; Bessie Summy 1910; Mabel M. Woodcock, Ethel Kennedy 1911; Mrs. Bertha Marsh 1912; Jessie Warner, Laura Buckley, Rhonda Eddy 1913; and Rhonda Eddy 1914.

Weston (36)

WESTON WAS PLOTTED as a town in 1856 but was never built up. This district was in the southeastern corner of the township south of Kennedy Street and north of Highway 92.

Teachers were Miss Maggie Brown 1878; Emma Rowley 1886; Miss Cora Snider 1891; Musa De Witt 1895; Flavia Williams 1899; Ernest Norman 1901; Roxy De Witt, Ima Jordan 1902; Blanche Litchfield, Roxy De Witt 1903; Roxy De Witt, Blanche Litchfield 1904; Beatrice Smith 1905; Adah Profitt, Mrs. Bertha Marsh 1906; Mayme Murphy, Edna Tysseling 1907; Edna Tysseling 1908; Adah Profitt, Ida Sammons 1909; May Parker 1910; Olive Brees, Jeanie McRae 1911; Lucile Tysseling, Carrie Long 1912; Carrie Long 1913; and Bessie Williams 1914.

Wheeling (5)

THE TOWN OF WHEELING, two and a half miles northwest of Pleasantville, was laid out in 1851 and had a post office from 1852-84. The town was on the northern border of the township along Highway 5.

The Knoxville Journal of October 5, 1875, said Wheeling was a villa of 150 with 85 to 100 children, and they would be open for the winter term next month.

By 1884 the population had declined to 69.

Teachers were Miss Chadwick, Miss Slack 1875; J. L. Radcliff 1886; Miss Carrie Watkins 1891; D. W. Martin, Maud Plummer 1895; D. W. Martin, Maud Plummer 1898; Edna Summy 1899; Maud Plummer, Maude Spalti 1900; Elsa M. Clark 1901; Maude Spalti, Edith Reeves, Nora Hardin 1902; Nora Hardin, Roxy De Witt, Maude Spalti 1903; Mrs. Bertha Marsh 1904; Bertha Marsh, Maude Spalti 1905; Iva B. Marsh, Ida B. Ash 1906; Helen T. Hyatt, Bessie Steen 1907; Jonia Greenwood 1908; D. W. Martin, Wilma Cart 1909; Wilma Cart 1910; Nellie Kirkpatrick, Maude Spalti 1911; Ruby Moon 1912; Everett Walker 1913; and Maude Marsh, Maude Moore 1914.

Map of Polk Township

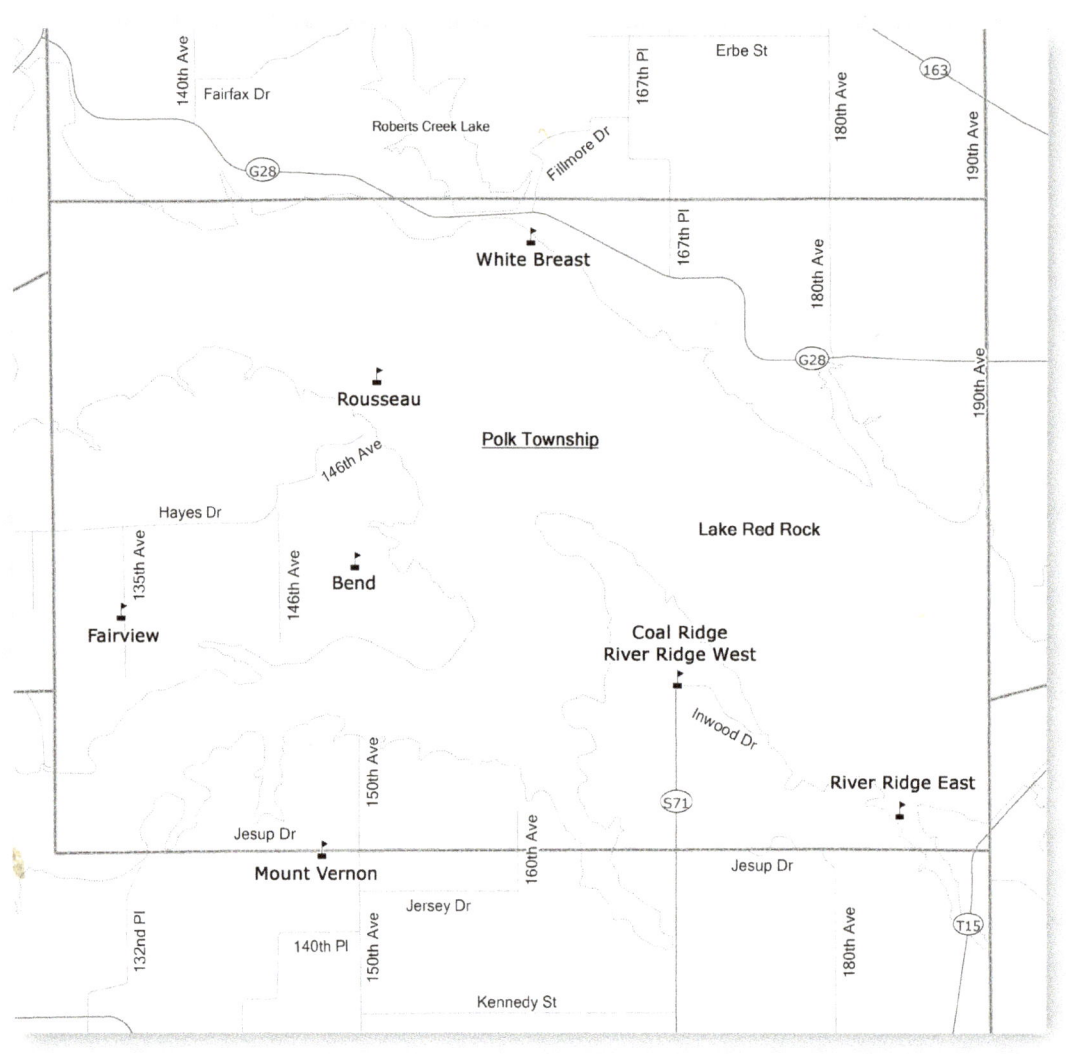

10

THE SCHOOLS OF
Polk Township

Bend (17)

Bend, 1930 – Madge Crozier, teacher.

BEND SCHOOL was located just inside the eastern border of sec. 17 on a road which no longer exists. It was south of the Des Moines River and north of White Breast Creek. If the building were still there today it would be nestled in the curve where Lake Red Rock backs up into White Breast Creek.

The earliest mention of this school is from the January 18, 1884, *Knoxville Journal*. The correspondent for the Rousseau neighborhood news wrote that there would be a spelling match at Bend that night.

Spelling contests were an important part of early education. In February 2, 1884, the Rousseau reporter said that there had been two matches between Bend and Fairview and a third was scheduled.

The Marion County Historical Society has some of the record books from this school. Teacher Lois Wright, in 1914, commented that she "used supplementary readers for all grades and this should be kept up as the school is behind in reading. Also writing has been neglected."

In the fall of 1942, teacher Mary L. Turner reported these receipts: $6.17 for scrap iron, $1.50 for fortune telling and popcorn sales, $12.60 for scrap iron, and $1.00 for Christmas cards. Teacher Madge Crozier received $0.40 for milkweed pods and spent $1.98 for water colors, $0.36 for state tests, $0.45 for toilet tissue, $0.80 paint for art, and $0.80 for clay. (During World War II, many country schools collected scrap iron and milkweed pods as part of the war effort.) The record book also included a report on communicable diseases, giving the ages when children had the disease and if they had had vaccinations.

A 1938 article said that prior to the erection

of a log house in 1854, Peggy Topping taught school in 1854.

Teachers included: Jimmy Nichols 1854-56; Joel T. Walton, Jimmy Nichols 1857-58; Elizabeth Crozier 1865; Elizabeth Snowden 1866; Elizabeth Crozier 1867; D. I. Phillips 1878; Lillie Workerman 1886; D. I. Phillips 1887; Ora Rutherford 1895; Ella Decker, Alma Cloe 1898; Alma Cloe, Martha Ver Heul 1899; Maggie Toom, Jennie K. Johnson 1900; Eva L. Wilson, Mabel Reynolds 1901; Lottie McClymond, Fessie M. Palmer 1902; Kellie Morrow, Fessie M. Palmer 1903; Bertha Clingan, Elsie Mason 1904; Bertha Clingan 1905; Mabel De Witt, Cluna Karns 1906; Fessie M. Palmer, Virgie Shinn 1907; Hazel Risser 1908; Anna B. Brause, Tressa Faye Woody, Grace Toom 1909; Tressa Faye Woody 1910; Helen Cooper 1911; Velta Jones 1912; Grace Toom 1913; Marguerite Moffat, Lois Wright 1914; Evelyn Slayman, Leota Godfrey 1915; Tressa L. Fry 1916; Margaret Moffit, Frances Conrey, Grace Conrey 1917; Jane Ann Robinson 1918; no school in 1919; Grace Toom 1923-25; Mildred Shoemaker 1926; Mrs. Ella Crozier, Rose Giles 1927; Estalene Owens 1928; Lucille Crozier 1929; Lucille Crozier, Madge Crozier, Meryle Staley 1930; Madge Crozier 1931; Mabel Palmquist 1932-33; Mrs. Clarence Mohler 1934; Betty Heaberlin 1935; Evelyn Lyon 1936; Loveda Kamp 1937; Inez Stittsworth 1938; Elretta Burnett 1939; Leah Hegwood 1940; Dorothy Alley 1941; Mary L. Turner 1942; Mary L. Turner, Marjorie Blom 1943; Madge Crozier 1944-45; Joy Flanagan 1946; and Madge Crozier 1947-51.

Four additional early teachers mentioned in the 1938 article were Susanna Nichols, Wm. McPheter, Lydia Davenport, and Mary Davenport.

Coal Ridge (14)

THE COAL RIDGE SCHOOL was north of the present Coal Ridge Church, which is on Highway S71. Church services were held at the schoolhouse from the time it was founded in May 1852 until the first church building was erected south of the school in 1860. Below the crest was Coalport Village, which consisted of one store, a saw mill, a grist mill, a potter's shop, a blacksmith shop, and a bank. B. McCowan, in his book *Down on the Ridge*, writes, "there was no post office because Washington had heard there were still Indians and that an occasional white man was burned at the stake. There were about a half dozen families which boasted a large number of children for those good old days there was little else to do."

Here is his description of the Coal Ridge School:

"Coal Ridge was a seat of learning. It was a little frame building about eighteen by twenty feet. It was made of native lumber. In the center of the room stood a wood stove which at that time was up-to-date. On cold days the boys were kept busy chopping wood. The writing desks were wide boards attached to the wall by hinges and, when the hour for writing had arrived, these boards were elevated to their proper positions where they were supported by sticks, leg fashion. For seats we had slabs, flat sides up. These slabs were held up with legs, a la bench. For backs we employed the ones God gave us when we came into this forest. These seats and benches were made of the same height for both large and small. We little fellows climbed up on our benches where we sat humped up like Texas steers in a blizzard, our feet swinging in space. I venture to assert that that old schoolhouse sent out more curved spines into the world than any seat of learning in Marion County."

The schoolhouse remained on the ridge for a long time until it reached such a deteriorated condition that it was destroyed.

Coal Ridge, 1887 – Row one: Bill Neely, Wessie Poffenbarger, ___Vander Werf, ___Vander Werf, Joe Pifer, and Clyde Davis. Row two: Cora Dickey, Ollie Poffenbarger, Emily Blackman, Grace Davis, Georgia Poffenbarger, ____ Vander Werf, Lucy Woodyard, Lida Woodyard, Edith Smith, and Dick Smith. Row three: Will Dickey, Roy Dickey, Emma Armstrong, Warren Woodyard, Vick Obrian, Teacher Laura Essex, Orve Reynolds, Brade Davis, Della Wheeler, Annie Robinson, Addie Smith, Alma Poffenbarger, Alta Poffenbarger, and Sarah Franklin in back.

One of the teachers was Squire Martin, who tended his vegetable garden and raised sheep from which his wife carded wool. He taught in the winter time and used a birch rod. The author didn't think he needed to use it.

In typical childhood fashion they dallied in getting water for the school and also in going to and from school. "We stopped on our way both coming and going to make strict search in every hazel bush for a stray bird's nest, stopping the while to make our naked toes the appearance of a snake track in the dust."

As punishment for putting ink on his forehead, cheeks, and chin, "the teacher put an old splint Sunbonnet on me and set me down between two big girls, where for a full hour or two nothing was more fascinating to me than a small knot-hole in the school house floor; and then you devilish boys called me sissy for a week."

They played "black man, rollie-bole, leapfrog and blind man and then we would gather up a bunch of girls and play ring around the rosy, frog in the meadow, and then it was game mumble peg, and to wind up we would 'crack the whip', big boys at the head the little lads on the tail end, you know what happened."

He quotes the first recitation for the school program:

You'd scarce expect one of my age
To speak in public on the stage;
But if I could chance to fall below
Demosthenes or Cicero
Don't review me with a critic's eye
But pass my imperfections by

At which point he either forgot his lines or developed so much stage fright he says, "I couldn't go any farther and ran outside."

The official list of teachers includes Alex Whaley 1885; Nora White, Della Roberts 1889; Miss Essex 1890; Miss Ollie Gelderbloom 1895; and Miss Alice Crosby 1897. Squire Martin is not mentioned nor is his first teacher Mary Davenport, who ran a subscription school, possibly out of her home rather than the Coal Ridge building.

Fairview (8)

Fairview, 1948 – Bonnie Nichols, teacher. Front row: Harold De Vos, Myrna Vander Linden, Don De Vos, Larry Rowley, and Donna Slocum. Back row: Dorothy De Vos, Richard De Vos, Avis Vander Linden, Kenneth Onstank, Myrle Rowley, Anna Louise Rowley, and Melvin Vander Linden.

ON ITS ORIGINAL SITE at approximately 901 135th Avenue, now in Knoxville Township, a picture of the school building was taken by Carol Nollen for his book of Marion County schoolhouses published in 2004.

According to a 1923 *Knoxville Journal* article, there were fifty-five trees on the schoolyard, quite a contrast to its last days surrounded by farm machinery in a bare farm field.

According to the school record books during the years 1926-29, each teacher commented about how easy this school was to teach, yet none stayed more than one year.

Teachers were Miss Ruckman 1883; Mable Ayres, May Jones 1895; Flora Jarman 1896; Ella Decker 1898; Mary Rogers, Minnie Dickey 1899; Minnie Dickey 1900; Jacquetta Wright, Lula Crosby 1901; Mary Greenaway, Lucinda Marshall 1902; Myrtle Stentz, Alta Poffinburger 1903; Josephine Tucker, Ada Houser 1904; Meryl Sterling, Bessie Stine 1905; Eva Nutter, Tressa L. Fry 1907; Tressa L. Fry 1908; Arminda Ferguson 1909; Mabel Dickey, Grace Metz 1910; Edith Hughes 1911; Rena Reese, Frank Crawford 1912; Lucile Tysseling, Helen Cooper 1913; Robert McGraw 1914; Grace Toom 1915-18; Mrs. Anna Slattery 1919; Mrs. Anna Slattery, Mrs. Ruby Davis 1920; Hazel Harkins 1921; Nannie Hyatt 1922; Virgie Anderson 1923-24; Suzanne Shinlow, Curtelia E. Ridpath 1925; Grace Toom 1926; Marie Beebout 1927; Mrs. Etha C. Moon 1928; Mrs. Anna Anderson 1929; Malvina Neely 1930; Ruby Penland 1931-32; Mabel Dykstra 1933; Erma Slocum 1934; Erma Rowley 1935; Vione Hendrix 1936-38; Ellen Robinson, Anna Ruth Beary 1939; Anna Ruth Beary 1940; Ruby Ver Steeg 1942-44; Marilyn Crozier 1945; Bonnie Jean Nichols 1947; and Mrs. Garneth Hill 1948-51.

Mt. Vernon (21)

Mt. Vernon, 1931 – Elreta Smith, teacher.

MT. VERNON SCHOOL was located on the east side of 150th Avenue near the area of the South Shore Heights development.

From an 1895 entry in a *Knoxville Journal*, we learn that Miss Jennie Johnson gave a good program on Flag Day February 22. Exercise opened by saluting the flag. After several exercises, they marched around the room carrying flags and singing "three cheers for the red, white, and blue." The house was decorated with flags and the picture of George Washington hung on the wall.

The late Jerry Graham started school at Mr. Vernon in the fall of 1942. The school, he writes, was on a grassy hillside of land donated years earlier by the Holmes family. He and his brother Larry, who was in 7th grade, walked a mile and a quarter to school. Along the way they were joined by others, including playmates Donna and Glenna Anderson.

Like most of his schoolmates, he carried his lunch in an old lard or tobacco pail. "Lunch would be a sandwich made with thick slices of homemade bread sometimes with home-canned chicken, pork, or beef or maybe a slice of cheese or a fried egg. More often the sandwich would be just butter—we didn't have sliced lunch meat and peanut butter was too expensive." There would also be a sweet treat such as a cookie, cake, or pie. Also, fresh fruit in season and a jar of milk if the weather was cool enough.

His first teacher Grace Toom drove a Model A Ford from her home near Elk Rock. Grace was a strict disciplinarian and maintained order by punishing naughty students in front of the entire school. They bent over hanging onto the desk while she paddled them on the butt with a two-foot-long paddle. Jerry's greatest fear was a whack across the fingers with a lead pencil if caught whispering or not paying attention. There was no nap or resting period for five year olds, who continued studying like the older students.

In November, there was a school program, and as the youngest he was the first to perform. He recited perfectly: "Turkey, turkey, gobbling up your corn, turkey, turkey, soon will be Thanksgiving morn." After he was finished he got to sit with his parents to watch the rest of the program.

In his story, Jerry gives a detailed account of the school building, the grounds, and a couple of memorable accidents. Although the family moved in February of 1943 and he then attended the Pleasant Grove School, he concludes with the words, "Mount Vernon will always have a special place with me." His five-page account of his first year is included in one of the binders in the schoolhouse at the Marion County Historical Village.

Teachers were Mary Elliot, T. L. Conny 1886; Robert McCollum, Lettie Keefer 1891; Miss Cooper 1892; Rev. J. E. Van Winkle 1893; Miss Marsh, Miss Johnson 1894; Eunice Fornerod, Miss Jennie Johnson 1895; Jennie Johnson 1896; Nora Hegwood, Lillian Bernette, Mrytle Spencer 1898; Nora Hegwood, Lulu Crosby 1899; Martha Reynolds, Mable Reynolds 1900; Mable Reynolds, Nora Hegwood 1901; Bernice Rolfe, Nora Hegwood 1902; Nora Hegwood 1903; Lela Banifield 1906; Izah Collins, Anna Brouse 1907; Beatrice Smith, Jen Gardner 1908; Mary Greenaway 1909; Pearl Swayne 1910; Ferne Stittsworth, Maude Caswell 1911; Jessie Warner, Beryl O'Dell 1912; Velta M. Jones, Grace Patterson 1913; Grace Patterson 1914; Lois Wright 1915-16; Lois Wright, Marie Tucker 1917; Ruby Garnett 1918; Marie Tucker 1919; Opal Morgan 1920; Dorothy Clark 1921; Anistacia Ridlen 1922; Carroll N. Hollingshead 1925; Grace Toom 1928; Grace E. Toom 1930; Elretta Smith 1931; Velma Brubaker 1932; Grace Toom 1933-35; Grace E. Toom 1937-42; Nadine Reed 1943; Jessie Hunter 1944-45; Jessie Hunter 1947-49; and Helen Adair 1949.

East River Ridge (24)

East River Ridge, 1939 – Phillip Bishop, Donald Visser, Martin Visser, John Coster, Mary Belle Coster, Loretta Visser, and Catherine Visser.

EAST RIVER RIDGE SCHOOL was on the Gerrit Visser farm. Some students crossed the ridge on nearby Honey Creek to get to school while others cut through the pasture. Once a beautiful area covered with trees, the land now lies under the waters of Lake Red Rock. Former students Maxine Slykhuis Prichard and Mary Visser Mattson shared their memories of school days at East River Ridge, one of the smallest country school buildings in the county. While they were students, a small lean-to was added for a place to hang coats and to store water. Like many country schools, there was no well on the property, which meant a half-mile walk to the John Durham farm to obtain water for drinking and washing up before lunch.

The ball diamond, which was located in the pasture behind the school, slanted uphill giving new meaning to the saying "an uneven playing field." On the last day of school, students and their families enjoyed a picnic. In the fall they picked up buckeyes to string. Maxine and Mary laughed about the year one of their teachers often held classes in the morning only and let them ride horses in the afternoon.

Mary was also amused about the time her brother Don got a "D" in deportment and wondered why because he insisted he was never bad.

Although her brother Buck was too young to start school at age four, the teacher allowed him to stay, as he kept running from his grandparents' home to the schoolhouse.

Maxine's brothers also attended this school and remember that they always tried to get a seat near the window so that when it was hot they could get the most air. They also recall that Mrs. Beem would tape their mouths shut with scotch tape when they were talking when they were supposed to be quiet. Ouch!

Here is the list of known teachers: Alice Crosby 1896; Alice Winters, Nora Hegwood 1898; Katie Jones 1899; Mary Sarver 1900; Lula Bivans, Orpha Woody, Florence Hammer 1901; Orpha Woody 1902; Orpha Woody, Martha Shepherd 1903; Anna Cornelius, Alta Marsh 1904; Mary Woody 1905; Mary E. Woody, Blanche A. Fee 1906; Susky Woody 1908-09; Jessie Schmidt, Mary Woody 1910; Mary Connaway, Beulah Stuff 1912; Alice Templeton 1913; Mabel Nye 1914; Mamie McKeigh 1915; Olive Easter 1916; Grace Toom 1917; Inez Watkins 1918; Henry Slykhuis 1919; William Brunia 1920; Harold Van Maaren 1921; Camille Leuty 1922; Marjorie Avery 1925; Mabel Palmquist 1926-27; Helen Hindman 1929-41; Katheryne Ann Metcalf 1942; Neola June Owens, Betty Vriezelaar Den Beston, Johanna Mathes 1945; Pauline Beem, Mrs. Janet Steenhoek 1947; Anna Bingaman 1948; Jessie Hunter 1949-50; Mrs. Katheryne Visser 1951-54; and Mrs. Leah Kerr 1956. Sometime in the 1940s, the school was closed for a couple of years and the students attended Iola.

West River Ridge (14)

West River Ridge, 1913 – Lloyd Rouze, teacher. Note clothing styles and everyone frowning into the sun.

WEST RIVER RIDGE was about an eighth of a mile north of the Coal Ridge Church on S71. Sometimes this school was known as the Coal Ridge School, but in the official records it is always called West River Ridge. The building is gone but some of its trees are still visible on what is now government ground.

Bonnie Jean Nichols Gruenhopt taught several terms here as well as in other Marion County schools. She graduated from high school at age sixteen and began her teaching career at age seventeen. She was hired at West River Ridge shortly after her dad became a director. Discipline had become lax. For example, kids were jumping out windows instead of using the door, and he wanted order restored. Bonnie did restore order and also had the unusual experience of being the teacher for her younger siblings.

I interviewed three of Bonnie's former students. Dixie Simmons Feagins said that all Bonnie had to do was snap her fingers at you and you knew you were in trouble. She remembers Bonnie taking them to the Sadie Hawkins Day parade in Knoxville where they all dressed as characters from the Lil' Abner comic strip.

Both Dixie and Bonnie mention the fun of winter sledding. They would skip recess times to allow for a longer noon hour for sledding. In the afternoon the smell of wool mittens drying on the stove would fill the air.

Because there was so much poison ivy on the schoolyard the students liked to play in the dirt of the steep banks that led to the school, sometimes sneaking down the road to hide under the buck brush. During the war, Dixie remembers walking the roads to gather milkweed pods and a pot of government commodity beans heating on the coal stove.

Jim Bailey also mentioned the fun of sledding, especially when one of his teachers allowed them to stay out until 3 p.m. A memorable incident occurred the afternoon he was walking home from school and was teasing one of the Laird girls as usual. She took him down and literally rubbed his nose in horse manure. The five Bailey siblings all attended this school.

Colleen Kingery Haug walked through the fields to get to school. She remembers the boxes of raisins that were part of the commodities they received during the war and pie sales that were held to raise money. Born in the early 30s, Colleen and I share the common experience of having to wear long stockings to school. Both of us rolled them down after we got to school and rolled them back up before going home.

Now in her 80s, teacher Bonnie Nichols Gruenhopt, a Grinnell resident, remains active with volunteer work and belongs to three quilting groups. She has hand quilted twenty-eight large-size quilts. It's hard for a once-busy teacher to sit back and do nothing.

Here are the teachers from the official records: J. S. McCown 1878; Ella Moreyes, J. M. Karrbeding 1886; Ollie Gelderbloom 1895; Maude Stuart 1898; Lulu Crosby, Belle Henby 1899; Eleanor Sullivan, Lizzie McKinney 1900; Leta Coster, Ada Wilcutt, W. J. Van Dyke 1902; Earl Duvey, Kate Dinwiddie 1903; Alma Poffenbarger, Mary Woody 1904; Lenora Hegwood, Walter Kester, Nellie Rogers 1905; Mrs. Mamie C. Smith, Kate Dinwiddie 1906; James Funk 1907; G. L. Hackert, Beatrice Johnson 1908; Tessie Everett, Angie Reese 1909; Angie Reese 1912; Clarence Jennison, Ruby Reese 1912; Lloyd Rouze 1913; Grace Toom 1914; Ethel Logan 1915-16; Gladys Garnett 1917; Winfred Reese 1918; Opal Morgan 1919; Edna Neal 1920; Ruby Davis 1921; Clarence Rietveld 1922; Ruth Linscott 1925; Mrs. Ruth Chivers 1926; Mrs. Cleo Anderson 1927; Mabel Bush 1928; Inez Neely 1929; Opal Morgan 1930; Frances Allen 1931-32; Frances Van Donselaar 1933; Otis A. Crozier 1934-35; Eula Emerson 1936-37; Mildred Ray 1938-39; Wanda Main, Beulah Hays 1940; Leah Hegwood 1941; Leah Karr 1942; Katheryne A. Metcalf 1943; Bonnie Jean Nichols 1944-45; Garneth Hill 1947; Bonnie Jean Nichols 1948-50; Bonnie Jean Nichols, Mrs. Leah Karr 1951; Mrs. Inez Dumville 1952; Gertrude McCoullough 1953; and Ferol Chamberlain 1954-56.

Rousseau (9)

ROUSSEAU WAS LAID OUT in 1850 in the western part of Section 9 on the south side of the Des Moines River. Evidently the river changed its course, as later maps show it on the north side of the river. It had a post office from 1873-1903. It derives its name from Dr. James Rousseau, surveyor, who laid out a number of early Marion County towns. An atlas of 1884 lists the town as having a population of 200.

Teachers listed in the official records are Mr. E. Crozier 1884; Miss Maggie Watkins 1894; and Miss Maggie Watkins 1896.

White Breast (3)

White Breast, 1954 – Row one: (surrounding project) James Garrett, Julian Garrett, Philip Vanden Berg, Gary Welshons, and Jack Welshons. Row two: Johnnie Garrett, Lee Klyn, Chuck Welshons, Arlyn Perkey, and Teacher Mrs. Wanda Jones. Row three: Kenneth Robus, Duane Robus, Carol Koopman, Joyce Garrett, and (unknown). Row four: Dale Klyn, Gene Welshons, Janice Robus, Arlene Klyn, Mary Ann Klyn, and Charlotte Perkey. Kayanne Welshons standing behind Charlotte.

AS SOON AS THE TERRITORY opened in 1843, Richard Watts, Alexander Caton, Mordecia Yearns, and Andrew Stortes established a settlement in the White Breast area. John Baback; Warren, Frank, and John Everett; Andrew, George, and William Karr; and Robert Ethrington settled there between 1845 and 1847. A log school building was built sometime between 1845 and 1849 (from research by Mrs. Ralph Kuiper).

The flood of 1851 swept the log school building away. It was replaced by a frame building located above the water line on a half acre of ground transferred from James Karr to Polk Township for $12.50. This school remained until it was replaced by a newer building in 1920. In 1924, when a few feet of land were added to the school ground, the price was $150 (from research by Jennie Breen).

White Breast was located about eight miles west of Pella. Because of its proximity to the town of Fifield, it was sometimes called the Fifield School. Today the site of this former town may be located by looking west over the Lake from the Fifield recreation picnicking area to the point where Roberts

Creek and Red Rock Lake join.

John Van Hemert, who attended this school in the 19th century, said that the Dutch and English did not mix very well in the days when he attended school. "There was peace and harmony on the school ground because the rule was there was to be no fighting. The fur began to fly as soon as the premises were vacated (*Pella School History*).

White Breast also served the spiritual needs of the community thanks to the leadership of American Sunday School missionary Rev. H. L. Van Dellen. For many years, Gerrit Vander Kieft served as the Sunday School superintendent, making sure that each Sunday there were classes for all ages.

The picture (previous page) comes from a *Chronicle* story, which featured the work of the entire school in constructing a papier mache model showing the best use of the land on a 160-acre farm. Duane Robus, one of the students, has no memory of that particular project but he does have a lot of fond memories of attending this school, especially of the hikes to the Painted Rocks area, hunting for mushrooms, and learning to identify rocks, birds, and wild flowers.

During the noon hours, students from Red Rock, Liberty Corner, and White Breast sometimes traveled back and forth to eat lunch and engage in competitive ball games.

The school also toured the Amana Colonies and traveled to Des Moines to the State Capitol and historical building, as well as places like the Hiland potato chip and Colonial bread factories.

Nearly every school has a skunk story in which the teacher has had to send a strong-smelling student home for the day. On the way to school, Duane and his brother Kenneth came upon a skunk with its head in a bottle. They attempted to free the skunk and found that although the skunk couldn't use its head, the other end was still operational. Since there was no way to help this particular skunk their father shot it.

Teachers known to have taught at this school include Anna Barber, Nellie Karr 1886; Florence Hammer, Ella Sullivan, Marie Van Gorp 1898; Marie Van Gorp, Delia Rietveld 1899; Delia J. Rietveld, Mae Cooper 1900; Delia Rietveld 1901; Delia Rietveld, John W. Ward, Mary Greenaway 1902; Ida Marsh, Lizzie Snyder 1903; Albert Crosby, Lucie Van Gorp 1904; Lucie Van Gorp, Lizzie Synder 1905; Margaret Fennema, Delia Rietveld 1906; Katherne Finnesay, Minnie Hyatt 1907; Helen Bootsma, Nannie Hyatt 1908; A. H. Crosby, Mrs.Mamie C. Smith 1909; Mamie C. Smith 1910; Melvina Saville, Mamie Smith 1911; Mamie Smith 1912-14; John W. Pringle 1915-16; Nannie Hyatt 1917-18; Gertrude Vos 1919; Vera Lucille Beck Gray 1920; Cornelia Mol 1921; Helen Brooks 1922-23; Helen Brooks, Hazel Chivers 1924; Gertrude Vos 1925; Opal Morgan 1927-28; Ellen Murdy 1928-31; Blanche Karr 1932-34; Irma Mae Verwers 1935; Henrietta Hoksbergen 1936-37; Bonnie L. McCaulley, Kathryn Nutt 1938; Marie Hegwood Metcalf 1939; Loveda Kamp 1940; June Ramage 1941; Helen Hindman 1942-43; Miss Louise Rupalo 1944-47; Wanda Jones 1948; Minnie McDonald 1949; Rena Welch 1950; Mrs. Wanda Howard Jones 1952-53; Mary E. Blackman 1954-55; and Thelma Van Hemert 1956-57.

In her research, Jennie Breen has found Sara Lewis and Sara Masteller as two of the very earliest teachers and the following additional teachers who taught sometime between 1895 and 1902: Flora Jarman, Agnes De Vries, W. S. Stevenson, and Minnie Dickey.

Map of Red Rock Township

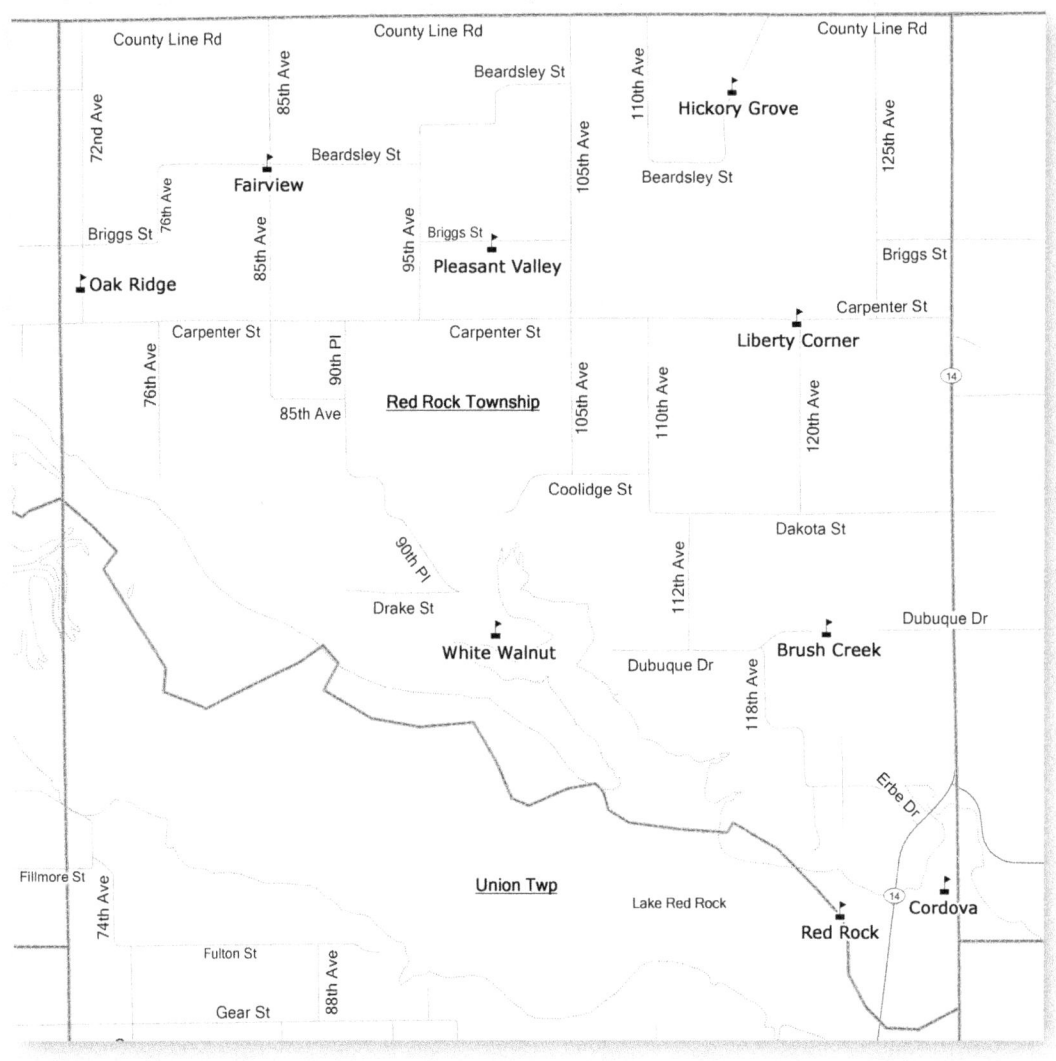

11

THE SCHOOLS OF
Red Rock Township

Brush Creek (24)

Peggy Terpstra, daughter of Henderson Reese, who was a teacher and later on the school board for Brush Creek, gleaned these bits of information from the directors' record books.

The first school board minutes available were March 8, 1880. Taxes levied were $100 for the Teachers Fund and $100 for the Contingency Fund.

In 1887, there were thirty-five pupils.

In 1910, taxes levied were $302.25 for the Teachers Fund and $105.65 for the Contingency Fund.

In July 1939, the board determined they could operate Brush Creek School cheaper with five students than to pay tuition and transportation costs. In July 1940, the board sent four students to Monroe High School and had five grade school students. At a later meeting they agreed to close the school.

With nine pupils in July of 1941 the board reopened Brush School.

The school population increased in July 1942 to 13.

There was a fire at the schoolhouse on December 12, 1944, and classes were moved to Joe Stevenson's home.

By July 1945, Brush Creek was down to six and Superintendent Sylvia Plotts would not give permission to run the school.

In July of 1946, students were sent to Monroe and White Walnut. The board continued to tuition students out through 1951.

In 1951, the board voted to sell the schoolhouse due to increasing vandalism. It was sold to W. N. LeGrand for $325 in September.

Teachers were J. H. Browning, Joshua Collins 1874; Miss Shellady 1875; S. Ridenour 1885; Eva Hoge 1886; Robert Shannon 1887; Zerilda McCleary 1888; Ella Crue 1889; Alice Templeton, W. S. Snyder 1895; Nellie LeGrand, Florence Hammer, Mrs. Solder 1896; Florence Hammer, Nellie LeGrand 1898; Maggie Leeper 1899; Victoria Noftsger, Alice Templeton 1900; John LeGrand Jr., Mattie Lemmon 1901; John P. Ward, Florence Hammer 1902; C. M. Wasson 1903; Edith Dawson, Alice Templeton 1904; Elizabeth Templeton 1905; Ulric Clevenger 1906; Elizabeth Templeton, Mabel Dickey 1907; Jennie Huff 1908; Alice Templeton 1909-11; Ethel Jones 1912; Emma Armstrong, Nellie Newman 1913; Rhea E. Wilson, Alice Templeton, Ona Acklin 1914; Pearl Goble, Blanche Davis 1915; Blanche Davis 1916; Irene Ragan, Ruth Cline 1917; Ruth Cline 1918; (no school) 1919; Henry Slykhuis 1920; Avis Van Loon

1921; Janet Den Hartog 1922; Ruby Riherd 1925; Mrs. Grace Karr 1926; Helen McConeghey 1928-29; Cleta Simbro 1930; Velma Roff 1931; Ruth Templeton 1932-22; Catherine Tonda 1934; Henderson Reese 1935; Nita Johnson 1936; Mrs. Catherine Black 1937; Miss Ruth Perkey 1938; Wilma Marie Clark 1939; Mrs. Clark Carnanahan 1941; Eileen McConeghey 1942; Mrs. Lucille Mullins 1943; and Betty Jones 1944.

Cordova (31)

THIS LITTLE COMMUNITY made famous by Grace Karr in her column "the Cordova News" evidently had a school for a short while as I found these teachers in the official records: Miss Nellie Karr 1890; Harry Moomaw 1892; and Orville Nye 1901. Cordova was east of Red Rock.

Fairview (5)

Fairview, 1907 – Row one: Clifford Waddle, Margurite Nimmo, Hugh Templeton, Junior Nimmo, and Sarah Jane Templeton. Row two: David Nimmo, Ruth Templeton, Dorothy Kool, Vera Kingrey, Gladys Clevenger, Catherine Kingrey, and Josephine Templeton. Row three: Earnest Kingrey, James Templeton, Cleta Simbro, Marie Kingrey, Ora Kingrey, and Teacher Sadie Mullins.

ONE OF SIX SCHOOLS in the county named Fairview, this one was so far north it had a Monroe address. It appears to have stood in about the middle of sec. 5 along what is now 85th Place, a road running north to the county line road.

A picture inside the school was taken when Sadie Mullins was teacher. She taught at different times beginning in 1906 and ending in 1922. From the bobbed hair of the girls, I would guess this picture comes from the 1920s.

Teachers were Miss Mary A. Reed 1881; Miss Connie Patchen 1885; Alice Elrod 1889; J. T. Curtis 1893; Ada Jordan 1895; Nellie Van Maaren 1896; Vada Roush, Dora Waddle 1898; Mary Kain 1899; Mary Templeton 1900; Ed Templeton, Mary Templeton 1901; Mary Templeton, Laura Bahaner 1902; Sadie K. Mullins 1903; Claudia Henry, Mabel Bush, Lola Mullins 1904; Lola Mullins, Alice Ferrurne 1905; Sarah K. Mullins 1906; Jessie Clark, Sadie K. Mullins 1907; Sadie K. Mullins, Nora Alexander 1908; Nora M. Alexander 1909; Nora Alexander, Lois Kutz 1910; Lois Kutz, Sadie A. Coulson 1911; Dorothy Erb, Francis Coulson, Sadie Coulson 1912;

Hazel Nell F., Avis Ham 1913; Vela M. Moore, Sadie K. Mullins 1914; Ruth Hamilton, Lucile G. Murphy 1915; Eva James, Hazel Sweeny 1917; Kate Erskin Smith 1918; Laura Taggart 1919-20; Velta Brock, Sadie Mullins 1921; Sadie Mullins 1922; Hazel Neff 1924-25; Elizabeth Kane 1926; Florence Templeton 1927-28; Mrs. Bessie R. Headlee 1929; Josephine Templeton 1930; Dorothy Kool 1931; Marjorie Kane 1932; Genevieve Rees 1933; Hazel Timmins 1934; Miss Catherine Tonda 1936; Ruth Hart Perkey 1935; Marie Kingery 1937-38; Ellen Robinson 1939-40; Mrs. Helen Shaffer De Haai 1941; Florence O'Melia 1942-43; Gladys Bowens 1944; Mrs. Florence O'Melia 1945-46; and Arthur Coding 1947.

Hickory Grove (2)

HICKORY GROVE was near the middle of section 2 in East Red Rock Township. Its name is an indication that at one time hickory trees were quite prevalent in the county or that it was a favorite tree of the board of directors.

Its teachers were Jacob Bennett 1875; Miss Sadie Smith 1885; Jennie Worth 1886; Jennie Worth, Sara S. Smith 1887; Miss Maggie Foot 1893; Clara Fry, May Marshall 1895; Bertha Sellers, May Marshall 1898; Bertha Sellers, May Marshall 1898; May Marshall 1899-1900; May Marshall, Hattie Huckaby 1901; John McDonald, Victoria Tool 1902; Victoria Tool, Mae Carney 1903; Jean Rogers, Jeanette Warner 1904; Margaret Fennema, S. S. Templeton, Lizzie Clifford 1905; Bess Cowles 1906; Sadie K. Mullins 1907; H. F. Ammer 1908; Ruth Culver, Kate Finessay 1909; Peter Danks, Merle Worth 1910; and May Rhinehart 1911. From the records it is not clear when the school closed, as "no school" is listed for the years 1919, 1925, and 1931.

Liberty Corner (11)

IN THE OFFICIAL RECORDS, this school is listed as Liberty Corner and is often confused with another school in Summit Township, which is listed as Liberty but was popularly called Liberty Corner. It was located on what is now Carpenter Street.

Teachers were Miss Ballard 1875; Miss Kate Bicklehaupt 1885; Miss Scarborough 1887; Corney Patchin 1889; Amelia McMichael, Alice Templeton 1895; Fred Crew, Mrs. Ed Larson 1896; Clare Evans 1898; Amelia McMichael 1899; Eleanor Cully 1900; Eleanor Cully, A. H. Crosby, Miss Ruby Cook 1901; Sadie K. Mullins, Albert Crosby 1902; Ira Honnold 1903; Lucie Van Gorp, M. G. Gelderbloom 1904; Peter Danks, Lola Mullins 1905; Lola Mullins 1906-07; Georgia Roach 1908; Gradus Vriezelaar, Gladys Karr 1909; Mary Charles, Grace Schakel 1910; Georgia Roach, Aura Dickey 1911; Laura Taggart 1912-13; Olga Wright, Bertha Postma 1914; Laura Taggart 1915; Yella C. Young 1916; Clelia Anderson 1917; Ruth Reser 1918; Ruth McConeghey 1927-28; Bernice Mohler, Cleta Simbro 1929; Beatrice Brown 1930; Irene Vriezelaar 1931; Ada Van Dusseldorp 1932-33; Mabel Hiemstra 1934-35; Kathryn Vriezelaar 1936; and Eva Mae De Kock 1937.

Oak Ridge (18)

Oak Ridge, 1922 – Teacher Eleanor Morgan. Row one: Doyle Carter, Dea Owens, Lester Miller, Delbert Kain, Garry Vander Mann, and Paul Brown. Row two: Janette De Haai, Olive Kain, Marie Owen, and Herbert Carter. Row three: Janette Vander Mann, Merle Owens, Ona Owens, and Carl Miller.

THE LAST LOCATION for this school would have been off Carpenter Street on what is now property owned by the De Haai family. From a book of minutes concerning the schools in the Red Rock Township, I found a copy of a contract stating that one-half an acre of land had been purchased for twenty dollars from Wm. H. Cadwalder for building Oak Ridge School. The book covers the time period from 1859 to 1864 but does not give the date on the contract.

In an undated newspaper article which I found in a scrapbook at the Marion County Historical Museum, Ed De Haai details the history of the school building and describes the oak ridge from which it derives its name.

Mr. De Haai begins his story in 1881 when the Red Rock Coal and Mining Company purchased 4,000 acres of land in Marion County, mostly in Red Rock Township. At this same time, what was to become the Wabash railroad was being built. Many farmers then sold their land, leaving more in the north portion of the district than in the south. He says, "We were told that the folks of the north moved the schoolhouse (1 and 3/4 miles) about the year 1891 without permission of anyone and it was claimed to be stolen from the ones that were living in the south part of the district."

In the fall of 1904, the school burned during the night time. In the morning he recalls gathering with parents and other students at the school. Teacher Mabel Bush wept because she thought it might have been her fault. In 1905, a new school was built at a different location at a cost of $500 with concrete foundation and two coats of white paint.

No well was dug so water had to be carried by the older students.

Around 1913 the schoolhouse was moved again. Teacher Jennie Hamilton, who later became his wife, was the teacher at the time. Drinking water was carried to the school from the McDaniels' farm where Jennie boarded.

After the 1945-46 term, there were not enough students to continue school. The children of the neighborhood then attended the Pleasant Hill School until consolidation with Monroe. In 1952, Mr. Fred Mohler purchased the building at auction for $512.50 to be razed for its lumber.

The four different locations for this school were all on the Oak Ridge, a section of land that ran from southeast of Dunreath in a northwesterly direction to one and one-half miles west of the Prairie

City park, connecting to the divide of the Des Moines and Skunk Rivers. In earlier times the first five miles were mostly white oak timber, the next two miles mostly red oak, then four miles of burr oak, with the last five or six miles of open prairie.

Teachers were J. Savool 1875; B. F. Hines 1885-86; Miss S. S. Smith 1887; Mrs. Leo Pomeroy 1889; Emma K. Hughes, Ona Harp 1899; Laura Balmer 1900; Emma K. Hughes, Pearl Beeman, Paul Brennan 1901; Laura Behner, Alpha Reeves 1902; Maggie Cooper, Maggie Cowman, Lizzie McKinney 1903; Maggie Cooper 1904; Mabel Bush, Elizabeth Templeton, Bess Van Gorp, Hattie Leach 1905; Hattie Leach, Lizzie Snyder 1906; Lizzie Snyder, Minnie Runnels 1907; Virgie L. Shinn, Mammie Buckingham 1908; Kate Alexander 1909; Kate Alexander, Arvilla Hayes 1910; Arvilla Hays, Gertrude Quiener 1911; Mary Entler, Gertrude Quiener 1912; Mabel Watkins, Jennie Hamilton 1913; Nellie van Rheenan, Mamie Chambers, Jennie Hamilton 1914; Jennie Hamilton, Rhea Clark 1915; Rhea Clark 1916; Violet Bishop, Irma Lemmon 1917; Irma Lemmon 1918; Marie Snider 1919; Mrs. Olive Freeman 1920; Mary Butcher 1921; Eleanor Morgan 1922; Elizabeth Kane 1925; Bessie B. Reeves 1927-28; Margaret Danks 1929; Verona Lawther 1930; Mary Taylor 1931; Ruth Young 1932; Dorothy Waddle 1933-34; Nina Wicker 1935; Pauline Berkenbosch 1937; Freda Stewart 1938; Matilda Jabaai 1939; Kathryn McGreery 1940; Kathryn McGreery Wessels 1941-42; Miss Betty Jones 1943; Mrs. Boyd Perkey 1944; and Miss Hazel Simmers 1945.

Pleasant Valley (9)

PLEASANT VALLEY (Frog Pond) appears to have been located on the west side of Calhoun Creek in section 9, although the official records place it in the west central part of section 10. In any case, it has gone from the landscape.

The October 2, 1886, *Knoxville Journal* reports, "the school board have put on a new roof, sealed it and put in a slate blackboard."

From the *Pella Blade* of February 25, 1897, the White Walnut, Red Rock Township correspondent says "At a meeting of the literary society at Pleasant Valley School House (White Walnut school was 3 miles northwest of Red rock at the town of Dunreath. Pleasant Valley School was 2½ miles north of White Walnut) a most shameful riot occurred in which a number participated, some of which were badly cut up, others seriously bruised and quite a number hugely scared.

"Revolvers were drawn, stones were thrown, and false knuckles freely plied. A warrant was issued and several arrests have been made; but others of the guilty gave bail and, of course, will be unwhipped of justice. Several of the participants are undergoing legal proceedings before Esquire West of Red Rock township. This affair has stirred up a strife in its immediate vicinity that may reach far into the future."

Bernie (Guy) Reeves started school there and walked two and one-half miles, the last one-half mile down a dirt road. The school was called Frog Pond because of a swampy area in a corner of the schoolyard. He said there were more snakes than frogs there. His teacher, Wilma Sargeant, whose home was in Indianola, boarded with the Walt Wheatcraft family during the week and walked

Pleasant Valley, 1953-54 school year – Top row: Mrs. Wilma Sargeant, Bill Carter, Janice Walker, Roger Walker, Henrietta Breen, Larry Walker, and Kay Carter. Row two: Vic Carter, Shirley Faidley, Linda Faidley, and Larry Snook. Row three: Karen Carter, Keith Templeton, Bill Templeton, and Shirley Templeton. Bottom row: Jim Walker, Dale Faidley, Becky Carter, Ronald Faidley, and Gary Williams.

through the field to get to the school. Her son later became a principal at Monroe.

Guy remembers looking up from his studies one day and wondering who the woman all dressed in black strolling down the aisle was. It was Sylvia Plotts, the county superintendent. (Who of us can forget Sylvia Plotts?)

One time while they were playing hide 'n seek, Gene Waddle fell through a window and broke his arm. With no phone or car, the teacher walked him to his parents' home, leaving the older children in charge.

At this school, they had a play date in which another school was invited for a day of competitive games. They also had a day in which they were to bring a favorite pet to school. Gene brought a pigeon (not a favorite pet) with a ribbon tied to its foot. The pigeon escaped and was later found caught in the hay track of a neighbor's barn. (Death by ribbon.)

Keith Templeton tells the story of the morning the wind chill factor was minus twenty-seven. His father went to the barn, got some twine, and tied his dinner pail to his neck so he could put his hands in his pockets while walking to school.

Teachers included Sarah K. Mullins 1881; E. Beardon 1885; S. Ridenour, Sadie L. Smith 1886; Miss Dora Hughes 1887; M. E. Beardon, Della Harp 1889; Miss Ella Crew 1890; Miss Minnie Houck 1891; Miss Myrtle Judd 1892; Sadie Mullins 1895; Jno. Stevens 1896; C.A. Shultis, Mary Kain 1898; S. S. Templeton, Gertrude Wassenaar 1899; Lizzie Carter 1900; Mary Templeton, Ernest Norman 1901; S. S. Templeton, Mary Roller 1902; Mary Roller 1903; Armanda Brown, Pauline Sarver, Gertrude Almach, Beatrice Smith 1904; Marjorie Levin, Julia Fennema 1905; S.S. Templeton, Mrs. Mamie B. Smith 1906; Frances Nemer, Ethel L. Bush 1907; Martha Taggart 1908; Ethel L. Barr 1909; Jno. Caffrey, Alice Templeton 1910; Catherine Bruce, Olive Brees 1911; Thayne Gheist, Frances Coulson 1912; Beatrice Fennema, Frances B. Coulson 1913; Agnes C. Belson, Helene Beem, Frances Coulson 1914; Frances Coulson, Mary L. Charles, Mrs. S. S. Templeton 1915; Margaret Carr 1916; Selma Hawkins 1917-18; W. D. Campbell 1919; Marie Snider Kingery 1920; Lora Jennings 1921; Gertude Dykstra 1922; Gertrude Dykstra, Florence Vander Kraan 1923; Violet Smith 1925; Letha Nimmo 1926; Merle Taylor 1927; Gertrude Thornton 1929; Ruby McReynolds 1931; Marie Kingery 1932-33; Sarah Jane Templeton 1934; Gretchen Robinson 1935; Marie Kingery 1936; Gretchen Robinson 1937;

Betty Robinson 1938; Darlene Rebertus 1939; Darlene Rebertus, Arlene McConeghey 1940; Inez Schroder Thomson 1941; Dorothy Alley Ellis 1942; Hazel E. Worrall, Mrs. Leo Mullins 1943; Mrs. Lucile Mullins 1945; Lucile Mullins 1947-51; and Wilma Sargeant 1952-54.

Red Rock (36)

Red Rock, 1925 – Reda Martin's primary students (she also taught thirty-nine other students in the other eight grades.)

ALTHOUGH IT WAS LOCATED in what could be considered a frontier boom town, the school was always classified as a country school. Red Rock was laid out just east of the Red Rock line, the line that from 1843 to 1845 divided the area open for "white" settlement from the territory held by the Indians. Because of its location, it attracted both those who wished to trade with the Indians, those who provided services for fellow settlers, and criminals who were moving as far west as possible.

Before it was covered by the lake, old Highway 14 ran through Red Rock, which was on the north side of the Des Moines River. Much of the information about the Red Rock School comes from the book *Red Rock, Iowa (annals of a frontier community 1843-1969)*, written by the late Harriet Heusinkveld.

In 1845, a tiny log cabin served as schoolhouse for the twenty pupils taught by teacher David Hickey. He was almost drowned in the Des Moines River because he refused to serve liquor at the schoolhouse in observance of New Year's Day.

By the school year 1848-49, there were enough students to hire husband and wife John and Isabelle McCollum. While leaving school one evening, her foot got caught in a stirrup and she was dragged to her death. She was the first person buried in the Red Rock Cemetery.

The first "real" schoolhouse was built in 1854 to accommodate eighty-seven, with lower grades on one floor and upper grades on another. It burned to the ground shortly after. This was the first of three buildings destroyed by fire. The last building that served as a school was moved to Monroe and converted into a home.

By the time my mother Reda Martin taught there in the year 1925-26, school enrollment was down to fifty. She found the year difficult because eleven of the students were beginners, requiring much of her time. Every day she sent them home at eleven to eat lunch and take a nap before returning at two. During that period she concentrated on teaching the other eight grades. Added to her standard contract were the instructions to vacate the school in case of flood water. Over the years this school was flooded numerous times.

Mary Beary, who taught during the year 1941-42, recalls that the government provided commodities of apples, oranges, canned beans, and soup to supplement the children's lunches. She was asked to prepare one hot dish each day using the materials consisting of a large kettle, a can opener, and Reynolds aluminum wrap. Periodically the school would be dismissed for a day so the people of the community could come and get ration cards for flour, sugar, shoes, etc.

The school board made the schoolyard into a playground and picnic area for the entire community. A social group called the double R-C's (Red Rock-Cordova Club) held its meetings in the schoolhouse.

The last teacher who served the school was Mr. Edgar Van Arkel, who started teaching there in the fall of 1952. He had been hired for the 1958-59 school year with an anticipated nineteen pupils. However, during the summer several families moved away leaving only six pupils (the state required seven), and the remaining students were transferred to other schools. The closing of the school ended the strong social ties that held the community together and soon the rising waters of Lake Red Rock would leave only memories of the town of Red Rock.

Teachers who taught at Red Rock include: David Hickey 1845; Isabell Hayes McCollum, John McCollum 1848; Hattie Starr, E. A. Conrey 1854; Camela M. Patchin, E. G. Bearden, Dora Stan 1886; J. B. Weed, Florence Hammer 1898; Florence Hammer 1898; Orville T. Nye 1900; F. M. Wright 1901; Florence Hammer, Percie Sarver 1902; Florence Hammer, Pauline Sarver 1903; Pauline Sarver 1904; Pauline Sarver, Lillie M. Mick 1905; Bess Van Gorp, Alta Marsh 1906; J. M. McGrew, Elizabeth Templeton 1907; Jesse Couch 1908; Dora Rice, Nannie Hyatt 1909; Myrtle McArthur, Nannie Hyatt 1910; Kate Dinwiddie, Ethel Jones 1911; Nannie Hyatt 1912; Faye McConnell, Nellie Smith, Maycie Worthington 1913; Nannie Hyatt 1915-16; Florence Ellison 1917; Lora Townsend 1918; Nannie Hyatt 1919; Edith Sharpe 1920; Laura Taggart 1921; Ruby Riherd 1923-24; Reda Martin 1925; Mrs. Zella M. Rowland 1927; Mildred Covey 1929-30; Jessie Williams 1931-32; Ellen Karr 1933; Arthur Richard 1934; Sara Jane Templeton 1936; Mrs. Dwight Harvey 1937; Alberta Core 1938; Mrs. Ruth Perkey 1939-40; Mary Beary 1941; Jessie Bruce 1942-43; Sara Jane Harvey 1944-45; Mrs. Mary Perkey 1947-48; Mrs. Ruth Perkey 1949; Basal White 1950-51; and Edgar Van Arkel 1952-57.

White Walnut (21)

ITS FORMER LOCATION now underwater, this school is also known as the school at Dunreath. The first mention I found of this school was in an 1870 *Iowa Voter* under reports from the County Superintendent following visits to the schools. It said, "George H. Smith has been hired for a four month term at $40/month. House is good" (referring to the physical condition of the school building).

The Knoxville Journal, March 28, 1877: A "writer" comments, "Sam Ridenour has completed a 6 months term. Patrons of school and visitors present. Exercises reviewed in arithmetic, geography, grammar, and U. S. history. Good discipline and teaching. Several addresses delivered, rewards of merit distributed, and a unanimous vote of thanks tendered by school to the teacher."

Another visitor said, "I think I never visited another school where teacher and pupils appeared so interested." Average attendance was over thirty-two. "One of the pupils, a young lady, did not miss a day of school in the six months, and part of the time walked three miles. We have hitherto been hiring cheap teachers—some as low as $25 /month. For this term we paid $45, and this school was really the cheapest we ever had in the district."

In 1889, Mr. S. Ridenour returned to finish out a term and died at age sixty-nine on May 6 after teaching only one month. The correspondent reported there were no applicants for the job.

By 1890, a teacher had been found as the reporter noted: "Our school is progressing nicely under the efficient management of Mr. P. S. Harris. Never has a teacher labored so faithfully as he is laboring. He is only a young teacher, not yet a voter, but conducts the school better than some teachers with years of experience and we are sorry that we cannot keep him more than one term, but I guess it cannot be. His skill, management, and labor will never be forgotten by his pupils. Mr. Harris bade farewell with candy, gum, and a short talk." (He left because the board wanted to close the school.)

The Knoxville Journal of March 14, 1892, says at Dunreath there were five or six stores, a barbershop, a blacksmith shop, coal industry, and a good school, which was used as a church building. Dunreath was on the Wabash railroad line.

In May 1892 there were 112 enrolled (*Knoxville Journal*).

In 1895 the school at Dunreath closed because of scarlet fever.

Myrle Timmons attended Dunreath in 1903. He was four years old and kept following his twelve-year-old sister Pauline to school. His mom would have to go after him and bring him home. Finally the teacher let him stay because he liked school so well (*Country School Reunion Memories*—the Percy Fair book of 1995).

Paul Clark, one of the students pictured, felt that country school students had more fun than town students. He was glad that he had had the experience of attending country school where there was a closeness among the students and the entire neighborhood. He recalls that when teacher Helen White got married to Paul Coulson everyone was invited.

I talked with Guy Reeves, former Pella High teacher, who attended 7th grade at this school, the last year it was open. He said it was a big double building with one half used as a school and the other as a community center where church services were held. When the dam for Red Rock Lake was being built, the building went to the Clark family and was being lived in by Seth Clark. Guy had to walk quite a ways to the school and would begin walking to school before the Monroe bus driver stopped to give his older sister a ride to school. The driver would stop along the road and offer Guy a ride the rest of the way to school. (He supposed this would be illegal today.) Evenings he walked home from school. Lucille Mullins was his teacher there and also in his previous school, Pleasant Valley. He was impressed by her unusual mode of transportation. Lucille drove an old 8N Ford tractor to school. The tractor had a cab with a windscreen and a canvas door.

Teachers included George H. Smith 1870; Lucy Bell 1871; Samuel Ridenour 1875-76; Miss Dora Starr 1885-86; Miss Churchill 1888; Ida Pomroy, Sam Ridenour 1889; Mr. John Jennings, Mr. J. P. Harris 1890; Mr. Meek 1891; Elmer Van Winkle, Mr. and Mrs. Meek 1892; Alice Dearth, L. H. McKinney 1895; J. L. Cochrane, Eva L. Wilson 1898; E. A. Leighton 1899; Ona Harp, Stephen Templeton 1900; S.S. Templeton, Eva L. Wilson 1901; Nellie Rogers 1902; Nellie Rogers, Jas. D. Frank 1903; Claudia Henry 1904; Claudia Henry, Lucie Van Gorp 1905; Lucie Van Gorp, Claudia Henry 1906; Sadie D. Mullins 1909; A. H. Crosby, Mary Greenaway 1910; Ethel Jones, Mabel Bush 1911; Mabel Bush 1912-13; Mabel Bush, Mrs. Gertrude Way 1914; Helen Fox 1915; Olive L. Ryan, Margaret Cuthbertson 1916; Ona Acklin 1917; Ona Acklin, Amy Norris 1918; Nannie Hyatt 1920-21; Mrs. Velta Hunt 1923; Charlene Scheele 1925-26; Mrs. H. C. Bingaman 1927-28; Bernice Mohler 1929-30; Opal Morgan 1931; Beatrice Staley 1932; Jessie Williams 1933-35; Roberta Lewis 1936; F. V. Elliot 1937; Eleanor F. Wilkin 1938; Eleanor Mohler, Ernest Klinker 1939; Edith Wheatcraft 1940; Mary Jenkins 1941-42; Betty Whaley 1943-44; Mrs. Mary V. Perkey 1945; Helen White 1947-48; Violet Lucille Powell 1949-51; and Mrs. Lucille Mullins 1952-54.

White Walnut – The individual pictures were taken when Helen White was teacher at White Walnut during the school years 1947 or 1948. Top row: Wayne Barr, Connie Bumgardener, Earl Clark, Daisy Clark, and David Clark. Row two: Ila Clark, Milo Clark, Paul Clark, Seth Clark, and Violet Clark. Row three: Caroline Large, Mary Ann Large, John Leonard, Dorothy Pietersma, and Mary Pietersma. Row four: Eilen Pinkerton, Jerry Sellers, (unidentified), and (unidentified).

Map of Summit Township

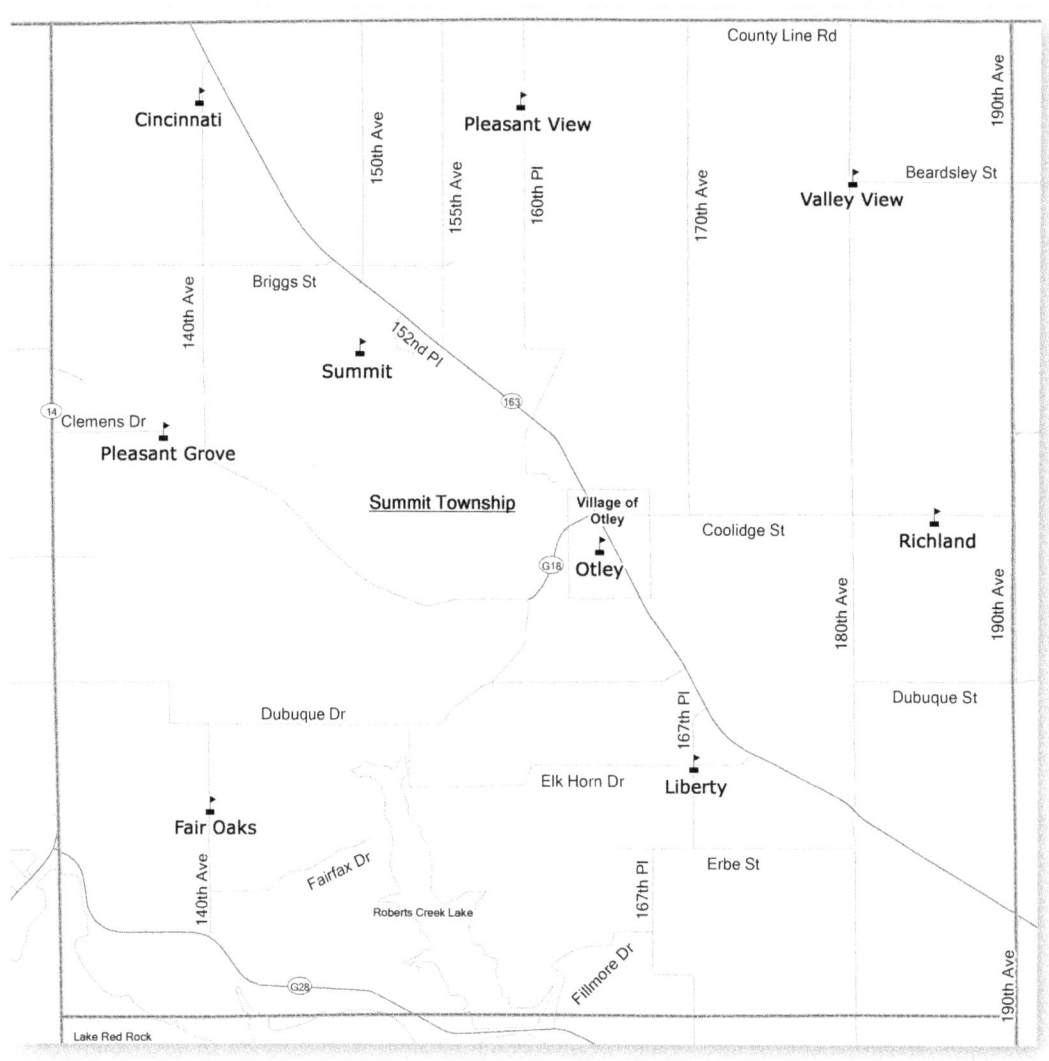

12

THE SCHOOLS OF
Summit Township

Cincinnati (6)

THE CINCINNATI SCHOOL DISTRICT, located northwest of Otley, bordered on the Jasper County line. A couple of record books from the Pella Historical Archives provide records of students and teachers from 1917 to 1933. In comparison to other county schools, there was a small number of students, which is probably the reason it closed earlier than most. In her end-of-year comments, Mrs. Mable Mathias (1918) bid farewell to the district with the words, "This is a beautiful country school and also a good district to teach in, have enjoyed my teaching here very much. The pupils are very nice." Her successor Ruth Balmer, whose monthly salary was seventy dollars, commented on the lack of a school library. In 1926, Miss Helen Dykstra alerted the next teacher to the fact that one of the students was "Rather slow and needs to be pushed" while another was "Very eager to learn but skims too much."

Eighth grade graduates were: 1924 – Carrie Hulleman, Peter Meindertsma, Deda Monsma; 1925 – Arthur Vander Ploeg, Jozena Meinderstma; 1927 – Marion Hulleman; 1929 – Kathryn Vriezelaar, James Vriezelaar; 1931 – Roy Vander Ploeg, Rick Hulleman, Arnold Meindertsma.

In the 1945-46 school year, the school building was moved to the Liberty Corner (Summit Township) school yard where it currently stands. Carl Nollen believes the building was constructed in 1918.

Teachers included Miss Nannie Eyerly 1879; Emma Schalk 1886; Paul Scarbro 1895; Amelia McMichael, Leo Coffey 1898; Leo Coffey 1899; Gail Smith 1900; Will H. Romans 1901; Maye Shroder 1903; Lizzie Clifford 1904-06; Martha Taggart 1907; Hal Cowles 1908; Bess Cowles 1909; Myrtle Coakley 1910-12; Marie Jarnagin 1913; Grace Schakel 1914; Bessie Williams 1915; Vera M. Graves 1916; Elizabeth Clifford 1917; Mrs. Mabel Mathias 1918; Ruth Balmer 1919; Irene Hodgson 1920; Marie Brummel 1921-22; Edna Jack, Catherine M. Charles 1924; Edna Jack 1925; Helen Dykstra 1926; Faye Dykstra 1927-28; Margaret Hiemstra 1930; and Margaret Warren 1931-33.

Fair Oaks (29)

Fair Oaks, school year 1949-50 – Back row: Karen Ball (behind her sister), Joann Ball, Twyla Van Hemert, Teacher Anna Macbeth, John Vanden Berg, Ronald Van Englenhoven, Bill Van Waardhuizen, and Marvin Van Englenhoven. Front row: Mary Ann Vander Peut and Melba Van Hemert.

THE FAIR OAKS school was located on 140th Ave. which is a short stretch of road between G28 (the perimeter road) and Dubuque Ave. Several years after it was closed in 1956 the school building was torn down by the land owner Delos Vanden Berg. There is no clear record about when this school district was actually formed. Early county records indicate that Sarah Lewis was teaching there in 1886. Also a 1936 *Chronicle* article refers to a Mr. Henry Van Ginkel as having moved to that school district in 1886.

In one of his Buck Saw columns the late C.C. Beurkens paid tribute to Fair Oaks teacher Grace Cronkhite Karr. He says that after graduating from Knoxville High School in 1919 she began teaching at Fair Oaks for $70 per month. Because there were only three students in the district for the 1920-21 school year the school was closed and the three were sent to Liberty Corner or Brush Creek schools. In 1921-22 Grace again taught at Fair Oaks. She then taught at Bussey for three years returning as Mrs. Roy Karr to teach at Fair Oaks for the 1925-26 school year. Mrs. Karr was a very popular teacher. Older readers will remember her as the writer of the folksy Cordova News.

Mary Ann Vander Peut Klyn De Boef has written a memoir and provided a picture of her first day at school at Fair Oaks in the fall of 1949. About the picture she says ,"I'm stiff and my eyes are peeled to my left, hands straight down at my sides. What is going to happen to me today?" Although she was obviously apprehensive that first day turned out to be a fun time even though there were a lot of rules to learn. Her transition to school was certainly eased by the fact that Anna Macbeth boarded at the Vander Peut's and would be there for supper every night and would sleep in the bedroom next to Mary Ann's. Mary Ann also described the experience of making Plaster of Paris ware under the direction of teacher Ellen Karr. She showed them how to make molds using wall paper cleaner. Wall paper cleaner was a dough like substance that one rubbed over the surface of wallpaper and it would magically pick up the year's accumulation of grime. Sort of.

The students kneaded the dough to make it more pliable, applied a powder of some kind, and pressed the object into the dough. They then mixed up the plaster and carefully poured it into the mold so as not to form air bubbles. After it stood for 12 to 24 hours, they could break away the mold, and let the object cure for a few days before painting. Some of the creations the students made were Indian head girls with hooks to be used for pot holders, praying hands, and various animals.

When school closed at the end of the first term in 1956, the directors allowed the parents to decide which school they wanted their children to attend. This meant that buses from Otley and Monroe would pass the same house going in different directions. Mary Ann describes her ride on the "short bus." It was like a prison inmate carrier with no windows except for the front and back. It was a crowded, dark, and bumpy ride on the padded wooden benches along the side. Clarence Bricker was the driver of this bus to Otley.

Teachers known to have taught at Fair Oaks were Sarah Lewis 1886; Minnie Dickey 1894; Florence Hammer 1895; Marie Van Gorp, Martha Stuart 1897; Bertha Rietveld, Gertrude Ver Steeg 1898; Bertha Rietveld, Florence Hammer 1899; Florence Hammer, Nellie Childers, Loveda Van Doren 1900; Minnie Dickey, Bessie Sarver 1901; Percie Sarver, Earl Dewey 1902; Katie Rietveld, Earl Dewey 1903; Mella Rankin, J. B. Weed, Pauline Sarver 1904; Bertha Sarver 1905; J. Roscoe McGrow, Mabel Bush 1906; Fay Tyrrell, Marie Jones, Mary Jones 1908; Jessie Templeton, Ida Freeman, Jennie Lemmon 1909; Jennie Lemmon 1910; Marjorie Cooper, Kate Dinwiddie 1911; Bertha R. Sutton, Cecilia McLaughlan, Nannie Hyatt, Lucile G. Murphy 1913; Florence Ellison 1914-15; Josa Pruitt, Fanny Eide 1916; Florence Williams, Carolina Vos 1917; Ethel Curtis 1918; Grace Cronkhite 1919; (school closed) 1920; Grace Cronkhite 1921; Marie Muilenberg 1922; Gertrude Hoksbergen 1923; Mrs. Roy Karr 1925; Doris Lee 1927; Blanche Karr 1929; Doris Lee 1931-32; Geraldine Gosselink 1933-34; Anna Slocum 1935-36; Florence Ruckman 1937; Bernice De Graff 1939; Hazel E. Worrall 1940-41; Opal J. Caulkins 1942; Miss Mary E. Myers 1943; Marjorie Blom 1944; Dorothy Alyce Ver Dught, Freda Ballard 1945; Anna Macbeth 1947-49; Wanda C. Clark 1950; Wanda C. Deitrick 1951; Mrs. Ellen Karr 1952; Mrs. Ina L. Umble 1954; Hazel Reeves 1955; and Hazel Reeves, first semester and then merged with Otley 1956.

Liberty Corner (26)

LIBERTY CORNER SCHOOL stands on its original location about two miles southeast of Otley. If you look to the south as you drive along Highway 163, you will be able to see it. The school is in good condition, having been restored in the fall of 2000 by members of the County Line 4-H club as a meeting place. This school is sometimes confused with another Liberty School, which is not too far away in sec. 11 of Red Rock Township. Both of these schools have been called Liberty or Liberty Corner at different times in history. Liberty was a popular name. Other Liberty Schools in Marion County were located in Knoxville, Washington, and Liberty Townships. The latter had three schools named Liberty, Liberty North, and Liberty South.

According to the *Pella School History 1847-1980*, the board minutes describe what was to be done for a particular year. For example: "scrub and oil the floors, wash windows and desks, wash and iron the curtains, clean the stove pipes and scrape the peeling calcimine off the walls then replace it with a fresh coat."

The minutes note that in March 1920, the board voted to require all children to speak only the English language during school hours. (My school, North Porterville, could have used such a ruling. Although all of my schoolmates spoke English, one of our teachers frequently got mad at me because I was the only one who didn't understand the Dutch phrases she mixed in with English instructions.)

After reading a letter in the *Chronicle* pleading for help after World War II, the students packed and sent twenty-five eleven-pound relief parcels of clothing, towels, and blankets to Holland.

Carl Nollen, who is gathering information for a book (2009) to be published about Liberty Corner, shared some reminiscences of former students. Here are a few excerpts:

"Recess was an unhappy time according to Luella Menninga Warnshuis, who describes herself as an unathletic girl. "We had enough kids to make two baseball teams. I was always the last one chosen because I always struck out."

Albert Van Zee recalls his experiences with a bee tree on the schoolyard. The older boys would lift him up to get the bees riled up. When the bees came out they would drop him and run. He would get stung because he couldn't run fast enough.

When Clara Gosselink, was the teacher there were three boys in school named Gerald, says Gerald Bogaard. She distinguished them by calling Gerald Van Andel "Axhandle," Gerald De Jong "Gerald," and Gerald Bogaard "Bogie."

Gweneth Mathes Krueger mentions many field trips. Especially memorable was the time Ruth Vander Linden had the students walk to the nearest coal mine. While there Ruth Vander Linden sprained her ankle and the oldest student was given permission to drive her car in order to get her back to school.

Lorraine Portinga Verros describes a lunch treat. "My mother would boil a hot dog before I went to school and then she would pour the water along with the hot dog in a thermos. When it was time to eat I would drain off the water and slide the hot dog on a bun—hot lunch!"

Marvin Hiemstra gives credit for a success as a poet to teacher Johanna Rouwenhorst. He says, "I think the first two or three years of school is the most important for anyone and I am fortunate to have spent mine at Liberty Corner."

Phil Schreiner states that teacher Ruth Vander Linden was an excellent teacher who ruled with an iron hand. Liberty Corner was a great foundation for high school and college. Today he works for Lockheed Martin helping design satellite systems for the government. In 1959, Phil and his six brothers, sons of Mr. and Mrs. Warren Schreiner, all attended Liberty Corner. See them pictured on the following page. (She may have ruled with an iron hand but note her happy face.)

Teachers who taught at Liberty Corner include Auria Berns, Nellie Karr 1886; N. Hackert 1895; Garret Bos 1898; Garrett Bos, Mae Fisk 1899; Ruby Cook, Loveda Van Doren 1900; Winifred Fowler, Beulah Stuff 1902; Winifred Fowler 1903; Katherine Rietveld 1904-05; Minnie H. B. Gaass 1906; Katherine Rietveld 1907; Queene Adams 1908-09; Marie Vander Busse, Beulah Stuff 1910; Leulah Stuff 1912; Beulah Stuff 1913; Nannie M. Dillon, John W. Pringle 1914; Nannie M. Dillon 1915; Leulah Stienman 1916; Hattie Harmsen 1917; Henrietta Gaass 1918-24; Mabel Morris 1925; Margaret Wynia 1926; Dena Ver Steeg 1927; Marie Vander Hart 1928; Lois Grandia 1929-30; Agnes Van Zante 1931-32; Clara Gosselink 1933-38; Gretchen Dunnick 1939-40; Irene Van Haaften 1941; Margery Van Heukelom 1942; Edna De Jong 1943; Betty Kool 1944; Johanna Rouwenhorst 1945-46; Mrs. Cornie Tromp 1947; Rena Marie Klein 1948-49; Mrs. Ellen Karr 1950-51; and Ruth Vander Linden 1952-58.

Liberty Corner, 1959 – The seven Schreiner brothers with teacher Ruth Vander Linden. Left to right: Rex, five; Mike, six; Tom, eight; Bob, nine; Terry, ten; Philip, twelve; and Jay, thirteen.

Otley (22)

THE OTLEY SCHOOL was classified as a country school until it was consolidated into the Pella School District in 1958. The unincorporated town of Otley takes its name from Colonel Otley, an engineer of the Des Moines Valley Railroad Company, who was instrumental in choosing the town as a shipping point for the railroad.

The Otley School is thought to have been organized in 1868 or 1869. The first building was a one-room frame structure, but by the summer of 1876 according to *The Knoxville Journal*, the board was calling for a new building to accommodate the growing number of pupils. The October 13, 1876, issue of *The Journal* says that a two-room building was ready for use. The newspaper also reports the town had a population of 200 with two churches and no saloons. In 1927, a third new school was built with a full basement under its two rooms. Later a wing was added to this building. The Pella School District continued to hold classes in the building until 1992. Its ownership then passed to Marion and Marge Van Haaften.

In a story in the *Pella School History*, long-time teacher Doris Lee writes that in 1876 there were 146 pupils ranging in age from five to twenty-one years. In 1887, there was an enrollment of 125. As coal mining in the community decreased from the 1920s until the time of reorganization, there were seldom more than sixty-five enrolled. When the surrounding country schools began to close, more students again began attending the Otley School.

The picture of the end-of-the-year picnic on May 27, 1945, shows forty-two pupils with two teachers, who taught the upper and lower grades. The accompanying story reported eleven primary students (a large number for the school) while there was only one 8th grade graduate, Howard Buwalda. Two upper grade students, Ruth Kaldenberg and Louisa Longdin, had perfect attendance and Raymond Van Hemert had a perfect spelling record for the year.

Both the primary and upper grades had been faithfully buying Defense Stamps and Bonds. The upper grades had been engaged in several projects such as the Milk Weed Floss Drive and Waste Paper Salvage and had held a carnival with the proceeds going to Defense Stamps.

After teaching six years in other country schools, Doris Lee began teaching at Otley in 1933 and taught there for twenty-seven years. She then moved to the Pella Middle School and continued as a teacher there for another thirteen years. She also taught the children of U. S. servicemen in Munich, Germany, in the 1960-61 school year. After her official retirement, she continued teaching by assisting with the ESL program and teaching GED courses at Pella High and for prisoners at the Riverview Release Center in Newton.

During its long history, the Otley School no doubt served more students than any other country school in Marion County. There were several long-term country schoolteachers who later taught in town schools, so I'm not sure Doris Lee holds the record for touching the lives of the most students but she has to be near the top.

From the official records comes this list of teachers: Miss Dunlap, Irene McCleary, Miss Flora Baker 1876; E. M. Reynolds 1877; Prof. Andrews 1879; Grace Orcutt, Mary Edwards 1883; Aura Dickey, Minnie Davis 1886; J. A. Sloan, Eva Jones, Amelia McMichael, Maggie Cooper 1895; Amelia McMichael, Carolyn Mae Harris, Minnie Forsythe 1896; Forsythe and Jankia 1898; E. F. Pierce, Laura Fisk 1899; Laura Fisk, Mrs. C. P. Cook 1900; Albert Vander Ploeg, Alma Rambo 1901; Albert Vander Ploeg, Annie Vander Ploeg 1902-03; Sylvia Platt, Sadie K. Mullins 1904; Nellie L. Gaass, Lula M. Carr 1905; Albert Vander Ploeg, Ethel M. Welch 1906; Albert Vander Ploeg, Mary Clark 1907; Albert Vander Ploeg, Katherine Rietveld 1908; Elsie McReynolds, Edna Ver Heul 1909; Edna Ver Heul, Lillian McReynolds 1911; Leulah Stuff, Edna May Ver Heul, Marie McDonald 1912; Marie McDonald, Hollis Byram 1913; Katherine Rietveld, Marie McDonald, Bessie Williams 1914; Bessie L. Fall, Beatrice Fennema 1915; Bessie Fall, Hazel Rice, Nellie Van Rheenen 1916; Ada Alexander, Hazel Rice 1917; Cornelia Kleinendorst, Anita Ford 1918; Sylvia Rankin, Lynn Platt 1919-20; Elsie Charles 1924; Cornelia Kleinendorst, Marie Muilenberg 1925; Cornelia Kleinendorst 1926-28; Marie Vander Hart, Bertha Van Zante 1929; Carl Hoefker, Bertha Van Zante 1930-31; Florence Van Sittert, Mae Vogelaar 1932; Doris Lee, Dick W. Miller 1933-35; Frances Spratt, Doris Lee 1936; Minnie Rozeboom, Doris Lee 1937-39; Doris Lee, Irene M. Vriezelaar 1940; Doris H. Lee, Loren D. Wing 1941-42; Doris Lee, Rena Marie Klein 1943-44; Doris Lee, Rena Marie Klein, Anna Koons 1945; Doris Lee, Marie McDonnell 1947-48; Doris Lee, Florence Van Steenis 1949-52; Doris Helen Lee, Bertha M. Wittmer 1953-55; and Doris Lee, Hazel Reeves, Bertha Wittmer 1956. Other early teachers were Minnie Fall, Miss Alexander, Miss Taylor, Miss Rankin, Nellie Graves, Mr. Blakely, Mr. Haines, Mr. Pearson, Mae Edmonds, Miss Anderson, and Mr. Davenport.

Otley, November 8, 1935 - Row one: Ivan Kaldenberg, Wilma Pol, Darlene Postma, Robert Schuring. Row two: Harold Pothoven, Lawrence Dykstra, Henrietta Schuring, Evelyn Kool, Eva Van Baale. Row three: Gerald Veenendal, Gene McKeever, Edward Van Ee, Marion Pol, Ralph Poortinga. Row four: Billy Vriezelaar, Jake Schuring, Leonard Pol, Luella Vos, Norma Dykstra, Betty Longdin. Row five: Ralph Van Vliet, Nedra Neely, Webb Neely, Hubert Postma, Raymond Robus, Betty McKeever. Row six: Clarence Van Buren, Bernie Van Ee, Cora Heeren, Lois Van Vliet, Geraldine Van Wyk. Teachers: Dick Miller and Doris Lee.

Pleasant Grove (18)

Pleasant Grove, 1938 – Front row: Wilbur Birkenholtz, Gerald Verros, Ralph Birkenholtz. Back row: Elizabeth Tukker, Teacher Catherine Berkenbosch, and Doris Verros.

PLEASANT GROVE SCHOOL was about three miles west of Otley on the right hand side of Clemens Drive. If you drive down that road you can pinpoint its location by the flagpole, which is still standing. According to Gerald Verros, who started school there in 1932, the school was indeed surrounded by a pleasant grove of trees.

Gerald speaks with fondness of his first teacher, Miriam Huigen. The first book he learned to read was the now politically incorrect *Little Black Sambo*. For the Christmas program, he was to read from the book. Ms. Huigen took him aside and explained that there would be a lot of people there that he didn't know and if he got scared he was just to look at the stove pipe and read to it. That worked for him. (I've noticed that Gerald, a well known storyteller, no longer has stage fright and looks directly at his audience rather than at a stove pipe.)

When Gerald attended school, the playground was not very well equipped. One day a road crew from Otley was working nearby and noticed the students were using a stick as a ball bat. John Steinman (spelling?) from the crew went to the coal shed and found an ax and piece of wood that he whittled into a bat for them. The next day Mr. Steinman died and one of the children carved his initials into that special bat.

Gerald mentioned that it was a hard walk going up the hill past the Vander Ploeg farm. When the roads were muddy they would stop periodically, cross the ditch, and scrape the mud from their boots on the wire fencing. Mrs. Ed Vander Ploeg was often in the yard and when it was hot would invite them in for a drink of water or give them a bouquet of her flowers.

On cold mornings, sometimes a teacher would open the door to find the room was unexpectedly warm. The assumption was a hobo had entered through a window and spent the night in the school room.

According to an undated *Chronicle* article, Mrs. Gertrude Hoksbergen and her pupils had given a Christmas program followed by pie and coffee supper. This event had netted fourteen dollars, which she was going to use to purchase an organ and other useful things. This would have been Christmas of 1926 or 1927.

Lasting bonds were often formed between the country school students and their teachers. In the *Pella School History* book I found a letter dated June 13, 1943, from U. S. Marine Sgt. J. J. Rozenberg to Mrs. Hoksbergen thanking her for writing and sending some "swell" reading material. He says of his school days, "I was afraid to say boo at the time. I've changed a little since that, certainly wished I had spent a few more years in school, but no need to cry now, it was only my own fault."

Pleasant Grove School closed in the late 1940s and the students in the district were sent to Monroe, Otley, or another country school.

Teachers at this school included Mary Le Grand 1886; Albert Van Der Ploeg 1897; Mae Marshall, Maggie Smith 1898; Laura Balmer 1899; Albert Van Der Ploeg, Lulu Marshall 1900; Blanche McGaggart, Mary Marshall 1901; Bertha Rietveld, Eva L. Wilson 1902; Lulu Marshall, Edith Irwin 1903; Minnie H. B. Gaass 1904-05; Pearl Monroe, Caroline Gezel 1906; Minnie H. B. Gaass, Pearl Mooman 1907; Jennie Lemmon 1908; Jennie Lemmon, Evelyn Slayman 1909; Grace Schakel, May Parker 1910; A. H. Crosby, Marjorie Cooper 1911; Marjorie Cooper, Maude E. Crowder 1912; Christina Ter Louw, John W. Pringle, Govert Hackert, Laura Taggart 1913; Nellie Van Rheenen 1914; Bess Fennema 1915; Elizabeth Meade 1916; Phyllis Gillogly 1917; Lena Steele 1919; Mary Beall 1920; Evelyn Vaught 1921; Vera K. Bruce 1922-24; Gertrude Hoksbergen 1926-27; Harriet Van Roekel 1928; Henrietta Van Roekel 1929; Irene Durham 1930; Miriam Huigen 1932-33; Pauline Warren 1934; Agnes Bensink 1935-36; Catherine Berkenbosch 1937-38; Helen Robison 1940; Mary Shutts 1941-42; Dorothy Alyce Ver Dught 1943; E. Darlene McDonnell 1944-45; and Lulu Zerley 1947.

Pleasant View (4)

THIS SCHOOL DISTRICT bordered the Jasper County line. The building sat on what is now 160th Place Road. The students in the picture do present a pleasant view evidently dressed for the photographer with most of the boys in their suits rather than overalls.

The teachers included Nora Simpson, Ellen Woody, Mary Le Grande 1886; Elva Allfree 1895; Delia M. Gray, Laura Balmer, S. S. Templeton 1898; Della Hammer 1899; Bertha Rietveld 1900; Bertha Rietveld, Pearl Romansis 1901-02; Carrie Starrett 1903; Ira Honnold 1904; Ira Honnold, Cora Hill 1905; Lena Fern Taggart, Bessie Steen 1906; Bessie Steen 1907; Winifred Marshall 1908; Elvin M. Nolin, Luedna Witzenbeg 1909; Gradus Vriezelaar, Nettie Danks 1910; Nettie Danks, Elvin M. Nolan, Sue Stone 1911; Georgia Roach, Bessie. L. Fall 1912; John W. Pringle, Laura Taggart 1913; Frances Marshall 1915; Frances Marshall, Marie Henderson 1916; Mabel Quick 1917; Francis Marshall 1919; Celia Keuning 1920; Cecil McConeghey 1921; Mabel McConeghey 1922; Frances Marshall 1925-27; Kathryn Tuinstra 1929-30; Henrietta Van Roekel 1931; Margaret L. Hiemstra 1932-33; Jennie Keuning 1934-36; Edna Ver Dught 1937-38; Mary Jane Van Hemert 1939; Bernice Wagner 1940; and Johnita Vos 1941.

Pleasant View, 1908 – Winfred Marshall, teacher.

Richland (24)

Richland, 1925 – Teacher Harriet Toom. Eight girls in one class.

RICHLAND WAS LOCATED two miles east of Otley on Coolidge Street near the intersection with 190th Avenue. Built on land owned by Geert Dykstra, it probably derives its name from the rich land surrounding the school. In 1959, the building was auctioned off and purchased by Mrs. Ralph (Marie) Dykstra. According to a story in the *Pella School History* book the only vandalism suffered by the little school was having the outhouses turned over nearly every year at Halloween.

Teacher Marjorie Boot Vos, a long-time teacher who taught in both country and Pella schools, told me that the only unusual memory she has of this school is that a skunk took up residence under the building. Among her students were the Pol children. I talked with Jeanette Pol Van Hal, who told me there is just one year age difference between each of the four siblings. Her mother, she said, was very busy but still managed to make the girls' clothes, including their underwear from feed sacks. Sometimes they wore their brothers' overalls. Her two brothers got up early to help with chores and went home right after school to help with the farm work. They had only one bicycle, which the boys usually rode while the girls walked the mile to the school.

She recalls that every morning someone put out the flag, but if a rain came up they brought it back in as it was very important to keep the flag dry. They often skipped recess to allow for a longer noon hour when conditions for sledding were good. One year their teacher became pregnant and two or three others finished the year. "That wasn't a very good year," she said. (Imagine how difficult it must have been for the students in the late 19th century who routinely had a different teacher for each of the three terms.)

Teachers included Algie Kelsey 1891; Gertie Prickett, George Douwstra 1895; Katie Ver Heul 1898; Elizabeth Gosselink 1899; Mae Fisk, Grace Hawthorne 1900; Elizabeth Van Nimwegen 1901; Lula Marshall 1902; Hattie Harmsen 1903-04; Marinus Vander Linden, Maggie Van Zee 1905; Caroline Gezel 1906; Hattie Harmsen 1907-08; Marie Vander Busse, Hattie Harmson 1909; Hattie Harmsen 1910-16; Anna Brummel 1917; Hattie Harmsen, Lola Comer 1918; Raymond Vos, Miriam Fetcher 1919; Grace Pannekoek 1920-21; Rosetta Walraven 1922; Harriet A. Toom 1924; Leona Bogaard 1925; Jeanette Kentz 1926; Jeanette Rouwenhorst 1927-28; Leona Arends 1929; Mrs. Lena Schippers 1930-31; Henrietta Van Roekel 1932-33; Ada Van Dusseldorp 1934; Mae M. Vogelaar 1935-37; Irene M. Vriezelaar 1938-39; Emily Hiemstra 1940; Alta Beyer 1941; Mrs. Vyola M. Tuttle, Ruth Van Essen 1942; Marjorie Boot 1943-45; Beulahdean Bos 1946; Darlene Bevan 1947; Ellen Karr 1948-49; Jo Ann Crawford 1950; Mrs. Mabel Bogaard 1951-56; and Mrs. John H. Rozendaal 1957.

Summit (9)

Summit, 1940 – Front row: Arla Jane Van Doornick, Robinette Ross, Sally Van Doornick, Mary Vriezelaar, Coralee Vriezelaar, and ___ Van Wyk. Back row: Dale Ross, Ralph Poortinga, Ralph Van Wyk, Etta Bell Ross, Willa Mae Van Doornick, and Velma Vriezelaar.

SUMMIT SCHOOL was located about two miles northwest of Otley just off Highway 163 on that little dead-end jog now officially called 152nd Place. (I prefer the names that actually identified roads by their characteristics like "the Airport Road" or the "Washboard Road.")

According to a 1936 *Chronicle* article, the school was thought to have been organized in the 1860s. The school burned down in the fall of 1921 when Hattie Van Veen Vos was the teacher. Ada Van Dusseldorp Van Wyk recalls that for the rest of the term she and her fellow schoolmates attended school in a small shop on the Bart Van Dusseldorp farm. "Since nearly everything was destroyed in the fire we had a minimum of supplies to work with the first few years."

One of the early teachers was Dick C. Van Zante, who became a prominent Pella lawyer. Mr. Van Zante, who was born in 1890 and died in 1981, wrote in his personal history, "I taught country school for one year in 1909-10 at Summit School. I boarded and roomed with Mr. and Mrs. William Jelsma for $2.00 per week."

Another early teacher who taught several terms was Annie Vander Ploeg Van Spankeren. She was the daughter of the founder of the Vander Ploeg Bakery. Annie was also one of the founders of the Farmers and Merchants Bank, which later became the Farmers National Bank.

When Matilda Jabaai began teaching at Summit in September of 1940, she was paid only fifty-five dollars per month. The following year her salary was increased to sixty dollars per month. In 1945, she returned to teach at Summit under a one year "special war emergency certificate." This time Matilda, now Mrs. Albert Van Zee, received $140 per month.

Teachers who taught at Summit included Julia Welch 1886; Annie Vander Ploeg 1896; Annie Vander Ploeg 1898; R. L. Swearingen 1899; Annie Vander Ploeg 1900; Jacqueline Platt, Bertha Reitveld 1901; Mrs. O. P. Cook, Lucie Van Gorp, May Marshall 1902; Rosa Brubaker, Edith Cummings 1903; Edith Cummings 1904; Mrs. Mamie G. Smith 1905; Laura Vickers 1906; Georgia Roach 1907; Elsie McReynolds 1908; Dick C. Van Zante 1909; Sarah Mullins 1910-11; Hazel McFarland, John Pringle 1912; Hazel Holland 1913; Leulah Stierneman 1914-15; Ruth Cash 1916; Lena Hoksbergen 1917-18; Mrs. Nellie Klein, Estelle Pinnick 1919; Lena Steele 1920; Hattie Van Veen, Sadie Mullins 1921; Grayce Pannekoek 1922-25; Marie Vander Hart 1926; Letha Nimmo 1927; Doris Lee 1930; Mae Vogelaar 1931-33; Margaret Warren 1934; Mattie Belle Clark 1936; Helen Van Den Berg 1937; Anna Keuning 1938-39; Matilda Jabaai 1940-41; Mildred Gosselink 1942-43; Miss Lois Denotter 1944; Mrs. Matilda Van Zee 1945; Mrs. Jeanette Perrin, Marilyn Nadine Kool 1947; Evelyn Vander Hart 1948; Mrs. W. Lubberden 1949; Mrs. Evelyn Van Dusseldorp 1950; Rena Marie Klein 1951; Miss Joan Van Zomeren 1952; and Margaret M. Vogelaar 1953-58.

Valley View (1)

VALLEY WAS STARTED in 1872 and used the same building until it was closed in 1958. The building was located north of the Van Zante Creek at the T intersection of 180th Avenue and Beardsly Street, northeast of Otley. The enclosed porch and coal shed were later additions. Sometimes this school was called Valley while at other times it was called Valley View, perhaps to distinguish it from another school in Lake Prairie Township, also called Valley.

The Pella Historical Society has quite a nice collection of school souvenirs, certificates of attendance, reports cards, etc. from Mary Hiemstra, who stared school there at age four in March of 1913. There are some original compositions and a few pages from her spelling book. In the speller, the left-hand column was used to write the words dictated by the teacher and the right hand column was for writing any misspelled word five times.

Valley View, 1935 – Row one: Clarence Menninga, Leroy Blom, Albert Rouw, Bernie Menninga, and Robert Blom. Row two: Leona Blom, Margery Blom, Cathryn Menninga, Arie Van Weelden, Gys Van Weelden, Art Van Weelden, and Elizabeth Menninga. Row three: Helen Van Ryswyk, Alta Marie Van Zante, and Bob Beyer. Teacher was Irene Vriezelaar.

Mary Hiemstra was one of the eleven children of John F. and Maggie Hiemstra, all of whom attended the Valley School. Maxine Hiemstra Verros and her brother Don also attended the school for a while as did their father John C. Hiemstra (Mary's brother). Maxine mentioned that her grandmother Maggie was a school board member for a few years during the 1920s. At that time most school boards consisted of men only.

Maxine recalls the time she was part way to school when she noticed her pet lamb following her. Not wishing to be late she continued on to school and the teacher helped her put the lamb in the coal shed for the day. Of course, the students teased her about the nursery rhyme "Mary Had a Little Lamb." Fellow student Albert Rouw mentioned that one year Maxine was the only girl in school. I'm sure the boys teased her about a good deal more than a lamb.

Albert Rouw also remembers that when they first got their merry-go-round, they rode it so much that everyone got sick. For several years one of the teachers, Miss Bertha Rouwenhorst, boarded at his parents' home. Boarding at a home in the district was a common practice; often the teacher would live at several different homes during the school year.

Teachers known to have taught at this school are Emma McQurney, Ed. T. Fisher 1886; Henrietta Gaass 1898-99; Minnie H. B. Gaass 1900-01; Minnie Gaass, Lucie Van Gorp 1902; Lucie Van Gorp 1903; Annette Gilbert 1904; Annette Gilbert, Louis Barnett 1905; Elsie McReynolds 1907; Elvin M. Nolin 1908; Lena Fennerma 1909; Luedna Witzenberg 1910-11; Robert McGraw, Hallie Swain 1912; Hallie Swain, Christina Ter Louw, Anna Ter Louw 1913; Anna Ter Louw 1914; Nellie Van Rheenen 1915; Mamie Chambers 1916; Anna Ter Louw, Pearl Steinkamp 1917; Pearl Steinkamp, Mrs. A. D. Van Zante 1918; Grayce Pannekoek 1919; Caroline Brummel 1921-11; Caroline Brummel 1924; Caroline Brummel 1926; Opal Lust 1928; Frances Marshall 1929-31; Jennie Keuning 1932-33; Henrietta L. Van Roekel 1934; Irene Vriezelaar 1936; Bertha Rouwenhorst 1937-41; Johnita Vos 1942-44; Johnita Vos Van Wyk 1945; Effie Kathryn Hiemstra 1947; Mrs. Wayne Lubberden 1948; Mrs. R. G. McClelland 1949; Gwyneth Bump 1950; Miss Christina Vander Voort 1952; Mrs. Cornie Vander Zyl 1953; Arlene Ver Ploeg 1955; and Wanda Jones 1956.

For many years all schools participated in the county spelling bee. In 1941, the *Pella Chronicle* showed a picture of Valley student Clarence Menninga, the county spelling champion, along with his proud teacher Bertha Rouwenhost. For the final round the three words he spelled correctly were annihilation, nonchalant, and phenomenon. Winning the county spelling was an honor for the student and his or her school. Now we are content to let "spell check" do the memory work for us.

Map of Swan Township

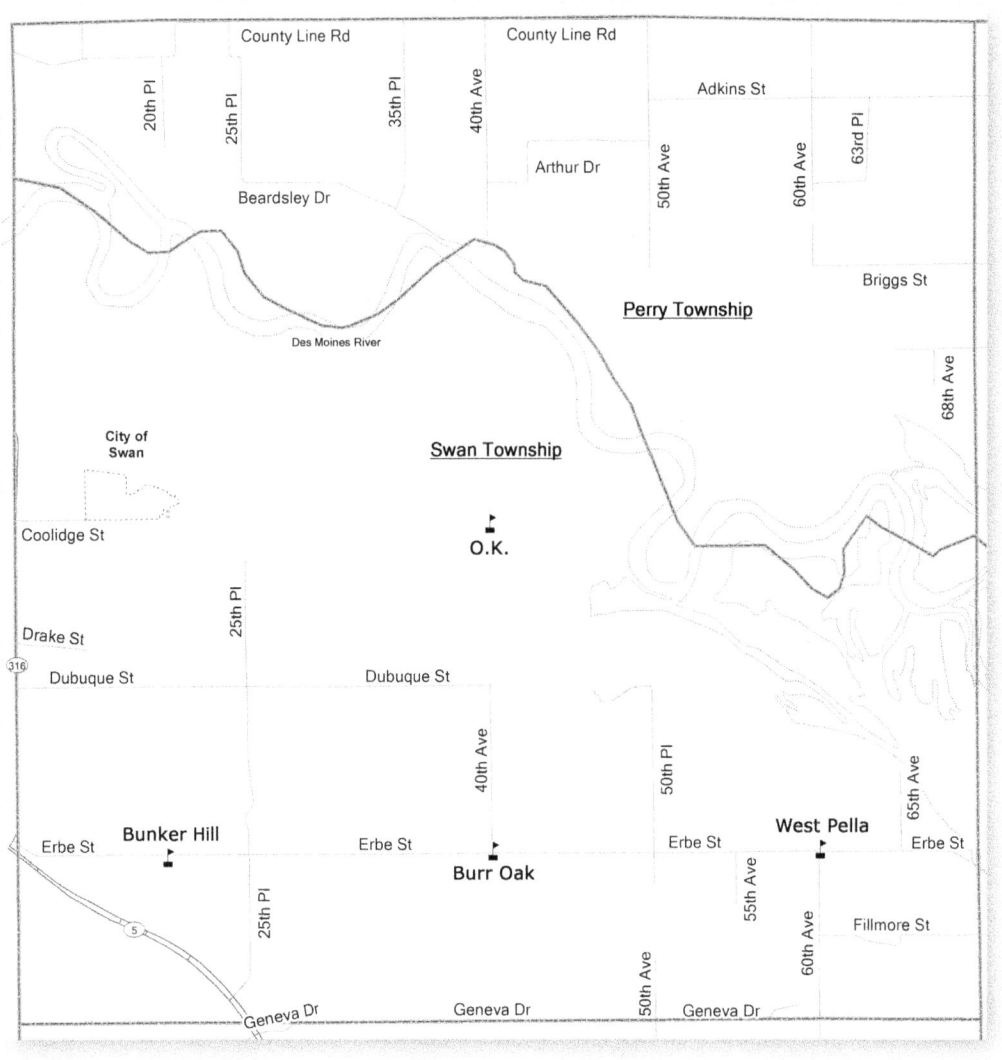

13

THE SCHOOLS OF
Swan Township

Burr Oak (27)

From an old map it appears the Burr Oak School was in the northeast corner of the intersection of Erbe Street and 40th Avenue. This area of the county was once a part of Swan Township but is now part of Pleasant Grove. It was consolidated into the Swan school system before 1920.

Here is the list of teachers: A. W. Rouze 1872; Ola Fairley 1895; Clara Coffey, Lena Gillaspie 1898; Clara Coffey, Nannie Taylor, Charles W. Conrey, Maude Plummer 1899; Nannie Taylor, Charles W. Conrey, Maude Plummer, Mary C. Clark 1900; Mary Clark, Marye Shroder 1901; D. W. Martin, Myrtle Stradley 1902-03; Myrtle Stradley 1904-05; Lizzie Snyder, Orah Monroe 1906; Wilma Cart, Gerry Reed 1909; Myrtle Stadley 1910; Helen Oliver 1912; J. R. De Viny, D. W. Martin 1913; Florence Beckworth, Bess L. Kingman 1914; Dean Butcher, Marie Shoemaker 1915; Marie Shoemaker 1916; and Josa Prewitt 1917.

Bunker Hill (31)

Bunker Hill School was in the southwest corner of Swan Township, north of present Highway 5. Many school districts chose names that were associated with American history, thus there are three school districts in Marion County named for the famous battle of Bunker Hill.

The official school records for 1917 list no teacher and instead say the school burned down. We can assume the students either stayed home or were sent to another district.

Teachers were Mrs. Rutherford 1874; Fannie Smith 1886; Miss Mae Henderson 1892; Florence Thornburg 1895-96; Miss Kendall, Cora Hamilton 1898; D. W. Martin 1899; Alta McRae 1900; Maude Plummer 1901; Myrtle Stradley, Elsie McClark, Rosa Blodgett Viers 1902; Roy Hunt 1903; Olive Nutter, Ross De Viny 1904; Nellie Fleming 1905; Belle Shawver, Mrs. AInez Kise 1906; D. W. Martin 1907; Myrtle Stradley 1908; Edna Spires, D. W. Martin, Ida Freeman 1909; Nellie Kirkpatrick 1910; Wilma Cart 1912; Edna Wilson 1913; J. R. De Viny 1914; Mary Mix 1915-16; Dorothy Jones, Frank Baldridge, Ona

Acklin 1918; Loyt Martin 1919; Ethel Couch 1920-33; Berneice Visser 1924; Clarence Rietveld 1925-28; Clarence Rietveld 1930-34; Daisy A. Mohler 1935-36; Opal I. Caulkins 1937; and Loveda Kamp 1938-39.

O.K. (15)

O. K., 1920

THE O. K. SCHOOL was about a mile south of the old Bennington Bridge. When we first started copying the names of teachers from this school, my helpers and I wondered what the initials stood for. I am still wondering.

I have located three pictures of students from this school. Only the one above was of printable quality; unfortunately no names are given. Note that the school building is quite small to accommodate so many students.

In 1921, a picture was taken on the last day of school. It shows the O.K. and Bennington students together with parents but gives no names. It does indicate that the bridge allowed easy accessibility between the two districts for spelling bees and parties.

The third picture, taken in 1916, lists the names of the following students: Lawrence, Bion, and Marie Hunt; Marion, Harley, and Orval Kain; Johnny, Marie, Golda, and Lulu Rodda; Bernice, Merle, and Gertrude Taylor; Paul, Clyde, Ruth, Eleanor, and Allie Morgan; Cecil, Jessie, and Fay Hunter; Roy and Lois Nutter; and Harold Miller. The pictures can be found in a binder at the schoolhouse museum in the Marion County Historical Village.

Teachers were Alice Gaass 1886; Kate Beltzell 1895; Mabel Taylor, Alta McRae, A. L. Miner, Ola Fairley 1898; A. L. Miner, Ola Fairley, D. W. Martin, Alta McRae 1899; D. W. Martin, Alta McRae, Nellie Fleming 1900; D. W. Martin, Nellie Fleming 1901; D. W. Martin, Pearl Monroe 1902; J. M. Kice, Nellie Fleming 1903; Nellie Fleming 1904; D. W. Martin, Bess Hunt 1905; Mabel Vierson 1909; Grace Metz 1910; D. W. Martin 1912; D. W. Martin 1914; Loyt Martin 1915-21; Myrtle Printz 1923; Marie Williams 1924; Mrs. Myrta Miller 1925; Merle Taylor 1926; Viola Beem 1927; W. E. Wellons 1929; Mrs. Edna Wilson 1930-31; Rena Reeves 1931-34; Laverda McIntyre 1936; Daisy Wohler 1937; Beulah Blake 1938-41; W. E. Wellons 1942; and Marie Metcalf 1943.

West Pella (25)

WEST PELLA seems a surprising name for a school located so far from the town of Pella. School historian Carl Nollen believes the name originated with the nearby settlement in the 1850s of three

Dutch families from Pella: Koen Van Iperen, Arie Kamp, and John Scholten. The school was about five miles southeast of Swan at the intersection of Erbe Street and 60th Avenue.

The first mention that I find of this school is a report by County Superintendent Samuel Ridenour, who visited this school on March 19, 1872. Teacher Jno. Alexander was employed for a four-month term at $37.50 per month. "There are 49 scholars enrolled with an average of attendance of 30. All the branches taught except history. Order good. This is last day of school; all were interested. The teacher works with great zeal. Quite a number of visitors present" (*Iowa Voter*).

When Lena Nugteren Vanden Berg taught there during the school year of 1941-42, she had only seven pupils, six boys and one little girl, all of whom were in a different grade. From time to time the school received government commodities. She remembers heating cans of beans on the oil burner to supplement the children's lunches.

Lena is well known for her musical talent, which she used to engage her students in music appreciation. She writes, "The school had a piano so usually on Friday afternoons after recess we would have music. No instruments but mainly things to keep rhythm with such as drum, cymbals, triangles, wristlets with bells, etc. These all belonged to me. The kids really enjoyed this." She enclosed the picture which shows the students with their instruments.

Susan Hodgson Tinder e-mailed me about her days at West Pella. Susan attended kindergarten the last year the school was open. Siblings Leo and Janice attended West Pella through 8th grade while she and brother Jim attended Pleasantville after the school closed. She recalls the Christmas programs as the highlight of her early childhood. Emma Carr, Pleasantville piano teacher, would accompany them as they sang many Christmas carols. She says the roots of her education were solid, thanks to a one-room schoolhouse and her parents. Her life gives credence to her words as she closes with, "This is my 30th year of teaching, the rewards are unmeasurable" (2009).

West Pella – Lena Nugteren's students with musical instruments: Eddie West, Lyle Hodgson, Norman Proffit, Donald Prichett, Jack Proffit, Richie Cooper, and Norma Cooper.

Teachers included Jno Alexander 1872; H.C. Williamson 1892; F. E. Wells, Henry Johnson 1895; Ione Printz, Ola Fairley, Nora Spalti 1800; D. M. Martin, Amanda Brown, Nellie Morrow 1900; Ethel Hays, Maude Inskeep, A. J. Reed 1901; Pearl Monroe, A. J. Reed 1902; A. J. Reed, Ross De Viny, Pearl Monroe 1903; Ross De Viny, Meryl Sterling 1904; Minnie Powell 1905; Grace Freel 1906; Adah Proffit 1907-08; Mayme Murphy 1909; Edna Spires 1910; Loyd S. Rouze 1912; Helen Beem, Lloyd Rouze 1914; Marie Shoemaker, Everett Walker 1915; Sadie Billingsley 1916; D. W. Martin 1917; Florence Beckwith,

D. W. Martin 1918; Gladys Abram, Florence Crone 1919; Iva Profitt 1920; Nadina Freel 1921-22; Velma Rhinehart 1924; Lela Galvin Morgensen 1925; Blanche Borden 1927-29; Clara Savage, Evelyn Gurney 1932; Evelyn Gurney 1933; Genevieve Reese 1934-36; Marie Hegwood 1937-38; Miss Ruth Harrison 1939; Evalyn A Long 1940; Lena Nugteren 1941; Martha Louise Whaley 1944-45; Miss Jennie Johnson 1948; Opal De Heer 1950; and Mrs. Velda L. Dunn 1951-54.

Map of Union Township

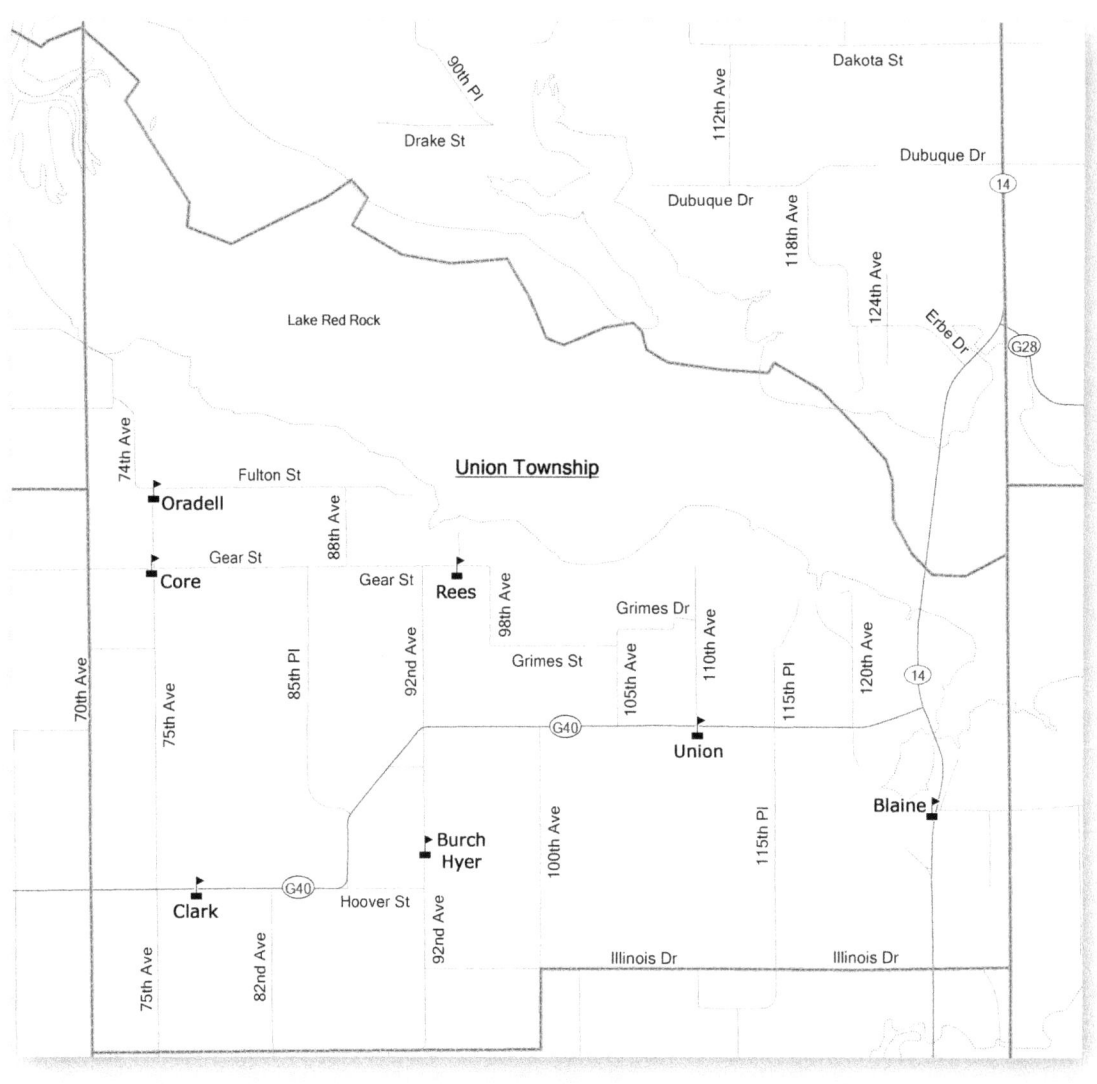

14

THE SCHOOLS OF
Union Township

Blaine (12)

Blaine, 1917-18 – Teacher Martha Leuty. Row one: Mable Williams, Cecil Karr, Lois Teter, Velma Fry, Lois Karr, and Jimmy Noftsger. Row two: Berneice Fry, William Noftsger, Lester Karr, and Kate Williams. Row three: Tommy White, Pearl Noftsger, Elizabeth Noftsger, and Ione Noftsger.

THE BLAINE SCHOOL was about five miles north of Knoxville on Highway 14. After closing, it was moved about a mile south and remodeled into a two-story house located at 1238 Illinois Drive.

The school was named for Captain Blaine, farmer and Civil War veteran. Every Monday he checked to see if hands were clean. If not, he dipped a corn cob in water and then in ashes and rubbed them clean. After such treatment, a child was not likely to come to school with dirty hands. He constructed a comb from a cow's horn by boiling it in water to soften it and then sawing teeth into it. He used this comb if children neglected to comb their hair.

On Saturday evenings there was a singing school and on Sundays a Baptist Church used the building for services and the 7th Day Adventists used it for classes.

From *The Knoxville Journal* of February 1888, we learn that the first division was studying natural philosophy, civil government, physiology, history, grammar, higher arithmetic, and algebra. The top student was Florence Teter. Nellie Amos was the top student in the second division, which was studying arithmetic, physiology, history, geography, reading, and spelling. The third division top student was Robert Blain. This group was studying mental arithmetic, primary geography, primary grammar, reading, and spelling. The article also named John Swalm and Con Amos as the top primary students but does not say what they were studying.

The Knoxville Express reported that on February 13, 1930, there was a birthday party for Reese

Rinehart, son of Mr. and Mrs. E. B. Rinehart. The party given by his mother at home from 3 to 5 p.m. featured games and a two-course lunch. Teacher Etha Moon and schoolmates Helen Martin, Floyd Teter, Chas. Pool, Maxine Monroe, G. W. Heaberlin, Billy and Wilma Rinehart, and Neva Teter attended. They had place cards bearing pictures of Tarzan and funny paper caps.

One day while I was working at the Marion County Historical Museum, the Knowles sisters, Claudia and Jane, came in to see if we had any pictures of the Blaine School which we would copy and send to them. We did. They had attended Blaine School in the 50s and had many fond memories to share. They liked the fact that teacher Wanda Jones wore pants to school and let them jump on her back when they were sledding. A discarded hood of a car was one of their improvised sleds. They remembered kids standing on the roofs of the outhouses and hurling corn cobs at each other. Some of the boys wore capes as they attempted to fly off the outhouse. The most unusual outhouse story concerned the time that the younger of the two girls left the classroom to use the outhouse. When she did not return in a reasonable amount of time the teacher sent her older sister to bring her back. However, she was not in the outhouse. Soon the teacher sent everyone out to look in the surrounding fields for the little girl, and fearing the worst, she took a long pole and probed the toilet to make sure she hadn't fallen in. The story ended happily when the girl was discovered safe at home. She hadn't made it to the outhouse on time and wet her pants so she walked home without telling anyone.

Donna Betterton sent an e-mail telling of the older students, during the time of consolidation, being sent from Blaine School in the middle of the year to Knoxville. "Very traumatic for a country girl to be uprooted in the middle of the year and sent to a foreign place! But we survived. Blaine School," she said, "sat at the top of Daubenspeck Hill, which was quite steep and great for winter sledding. Also in the winter time we'd take a hot dog for our lunch wrapped in aluminum foil and put it on top of the oil stove so it was hot for lunch (usually quite over cooked!). Occasionally we'd hear a loud BANG when one of the hot dogs exploded." Donna's father, Lloyd Karr, and his siblings also attended Blaine.

Teachers at the Blaine School included: J. A. Steves 1872; T. W. Teter 1888-89; Miss Lettie Duncan, Ava Nace 1892; Myrtle Moore 1898; Mable Reynolds 1899; Fannie G. Eberhardt, Ida Staggs 1900; Ida Stags, Pearl Monroe 1901; Mattie Lemmon, Jessie Inskeep, Mrs. John Swaim 1902; Edith Dawson, Bernice Rolfe, Myrtle Snyder 1903; Walter Bone, F. W. Parker, Bertha Clingan 1904; Bertha Clingan, Amanda Brown 1905; Charles M. Wren, Bertha Clingan 1906; Maude Welch 1907; Mayme Murphy 1908; Ida Freeman, Mrs. Nellie D. Ruckman 1909; Eva Worstell, Beulah Stuff 1910; Alta Hanley, Anna King, Georgia Totten 1911; Anna King 1912; Anna King, Georgia Totten 1913; Beulah Worstell 1914; Adah Frazier 1915; Beulah Worstell, Eva Rinehart 1916; Martha Leuty 1917; Ethel Jones 1919; Ethel Jones, Jennie Leuty 1920; Beatrice White 1922; Virgie Anderson 1925; Mrs. Abe Cronkite 1926; Mrs. Hyatt 1928; Etha Moon 1930; Ruby Seaman 1933; Alberta Core 1937; Mildred Maddy 1938; Miss Wilma Rinehart 1939-42; Inez Stittsworth, Hallie Shera 1945; Florence O'Melia 1947; Betty M. Hollingshead 1948-49; Paulina Stittsworth 1950-52; Dorothy Forgy 1953; Wanda Jones 1954; and Gertrude McCullough 1956.

Burch (16)

Burch (Heyer), September 1926 – On the way to school. Left to right: Lloyd Vroegh, Paul Maddy, Thelma Vroegh, Bud Vroegh, and James Vroegh.

BURCH SCHOOL was northwest of Knoxville. If it were still standing it would be on 92nd Avenue about midway between G40 and Illinois Drive. In the official records it is listed as Hyer with the alternate name Burch. There were seven country schools in Union Township, and, like Burch, four of them closed in the 1940s. The two that remained open until the late 50s were Union and Blaine.

My sole source of information about this school comes from Cheryl Thompson, who lives in Montgomery, Texas. She interviewed her 90-year-old mother Thelma Vroegh Pickering, who started school there in 1925 and graduated from 8th grade in the spring of 1934. In the picture, Thelma is the little girl in the bonnet seated in the buggy. In the back is her brother Bud Vroegh, the driver. The other three are brothers Lloyd and Jim and a neighbor, Paul Maddy. She remembers that day that it was a little slick and their one-horse buggy tipped over.

At the beginning of each day they pledged allegiance to the flag and did simple warm-up exercises. Students took turns putting up and taking down the flag. The older students also took turns walking a quarter mile each morning to get a bucket of water for drinking and hand washing.

They carried their lunch from home in tin dinner buckets. Sandwiches were homemade bread with dried beef or peanut butter. They purchased the peanut butter in smaller containers dipped out of a big barrel of peanut butter. There might also be an apple and a cookie. Thelma also remembers fig bars. The Vroegh family were dairy farmers. In the winter they would set jars of milk outside to freeze. These jars were sent to school to be eaten as a "spoon-a-treat." (That was a pretty creative way to ensure the children had a nutritious lunch.)

After lunch the teacher would read a few pages each day from a book. Many teachers did this and I think we all enjoyed this quiet down time after playing during the noon hour. Thelma remembers listening to the stories about Tom Swift.

Like many country schools, this one could be cold enough in the winter that they sometimes huddled around the center coal-burning stove to keep warm. The county, she said, kept the coal house filled with coal. The other important use for the coal house was to throw the ball across the roof to play that favorite game, "Annie-Annie Over."

Here is the list of teachers: Emma McQuerry 1886; Mr. M. V. Harsin, Miss Madge Davenport 1880; Bertha Prichett 1895; Kate Cotter, Nora Summy 1898; Loren Putnam 1899; Grace Barr, Anna Bush, Minnie Gaston 1900; F. I. McGraw, Belle Shawver 1901; Blanche Litchfield, J. R. McGraw,

Margaret Conway 1902; Margaret Conway, Belle Shawver, Flossie Hollowell 1903; Maude Abernathy 1904; J. R. McGraw, Lila Taylor 1905; Adelaide Hollister 1906; Adelaide Hollister, Mary Caffrey 1907; Ada Terwilleger 1908; Beulah Lerr, John P. Caffrey, Alice Templeton, Anna Brause, Tressa E. Woody 1909; Adelaide Hollister 1910; Thayne Ghrist 1911; Oletha Lemmon, Grace Marsh, Callie Clark 1912; Callie Clark 1913-16; Callie Clark, Florence Cooper 1917; Jane Ann Robinson, Callie Clark 1918; Grace Stanberry 1919; Grace Juline 1920; Hazel Harken 1921; Mary Morrrissey 1922; Mildred Shephard 1923; Vane Rees 1925; Loveda Caffrey 1928; Tomie Smith 1929; Elizabeth Core 1932; Vione Hendrix 1933; Evelyn Gurney 1934-35; Agnes Wren 1936-38; Dorothy E. Dixon 1939; Marie Metcalf 1941; and Hazel E. Worrall 1942.

Clark (18)

Clark – Clark schoolhouse

CLARK SCHOOL was east of Pleasantville on G14 near the intersection of 75th Avenue. After its closing, the school was remodeled into a home by Henry Arthur and Betty Bensink and has since been torn down.

Helen Louise Batten Severns was one of the students who attended Clark. She recalls that one large family made up most of the students. She felt that some of the boys were too big to be in school. The oldest boys helped with such tasks as starting the fire. The smell of baking potatoes always makes her think of country school. Another food that was heated on the school stove was canned pork 'n beans, one of the government commodities distributed to country schools. Her mother often sent boiled eggs for lunch. Although not part of the lunch menu, she remembers many of the students chewed weeds to simulate chewing tobacco. (It's a wonder more kids didn't die of accidental poisoning.)

The teachers usually boarded with Helen's family. She stated that Mary Jenkins Perkey, who started teaching at Clark right after completing normal training, seemed like an older sister to her.

Teachers included Miss Mollie Clark 1883; E. S. Hardin, Ella Cornell 1886; Charles Clark 1889; Lina Barnes, Alta Marsh 1895; Blanche Litchfield, Emma Prentice 1898; Elsie Clark, Grace Gillaspie 1899; Grace Gillaspie, Effie Allsup 1900; C.C. Hardin, Martha Conway, Blanche Litchfield, Emma Prentice 1901; Martha Conway, Blanche Litchfield 1902; Martha Conway 1903-04; Amanda Brown, Margaret Conway 1905; Amanda Brown 1906; Mary Jones, Ada Terwilliger 1907; M. A. Foster, Bessie Summy 1908; Grace Draper, Joanna Reed 1909; Grayce McFreel 1910; Mayne Murphy, Willard Shannon, Laura Buckley 1911; Laura Buckley, Maude Crowder 1912; Elizabeth Wren 1913; Flossie Rinehart 1914;

Elizabeth Wren 1915; Grace Donway 1916; Sadie Billingsley 1917; Sadie Billingsley, Vida Davis 1918; Emma Butcher 1919; Hazel Harkin 1920; Orin Stubbs 1921; Emma Butcher 1922-23; Ella Kearney 1925-26; Ella Kearney 1928; Ruth Williams 1930; Ruth Smith 1931; Ruth Williams 1932; Malvina Neeley 1933-34; Geneva Van Loon 1935-36; Marie Maddy 1937-38; Mary Jenkins 1939-40; Maxine Hukill 1941; Rose Ellen Welch 1942; and Mrs. Rose Ellen Exline 1943.

Core (6)

THE CORE SCHOOL BUILDING appears to have been about a mile south of Oradell near where Gear Street crosses 75th Avenue. Because Core is a familiar Marion County name, we can assume it may have been on Core property.

Teachers were Miss D. Blain 1872; Ella Crosby, Linda Barnes 1895; W. S. Stevenson 1896; Beatrice Nye 1898-99; C. C. Harding, Estella Reins 1900; A. H. Crosby, Iva Marsh, Beatrice Nye 1901; Mont. E. Case, Jennie Lemmon 1907; G. T. Randolph, Mary Roller 1908; Mary Roller, Ethel Kennedy 1909; Velma Jordan 1910; Jennie Lemmon, Aletha Lemmon 1911; Alice Fennema, Rhonda Eddy 1912; Liva Barrett, Ethel Ditto 1913; W. Campbell, Ethel Ditto 1914; Ethel Jones 1915; Ruth Stittsworth, Josa Prewett 1916; Ethel Jones 1917; Martha Leuty, Ethel Jones 1918; Edith Sharpe 1919; Grace Cronkhite 1920; and Gladys Scheele 1923.

Oradell (31)

Oradell – 8th grade graduates of 1934. Row one: Dean Hodgson and Sadie Billingsley. Row two: Irene Galvin and Bertine Slykhuis. Row three: Garold Galvin and Irma Roff.

ORADELL WAS ONE of the early hamlets that developed along the Des Moines River during its steamboat days. Today you can find the former location of the school by turning north off G40 onto 75th Avenue until it curves west onto Fillmore Street. In recalling its early history, one writer describes Oradell as being located near the largest bend known along the Des Moines River. The town had a doctor, a blacksmith, a school, a church, a general store, and Isaac Bodgerson's mill, which supplied settlers with lumber, flour, and corn meal. The general store had a huckster wagon that weekly covered a large area selling groceries in exchange for eggs or produce. Early maps show the outline of this bend before the river changed course. Sometime after the river flowed further north, a writer says, the town was situated on Wild Cat Creek two miles from where it empties into the Des Moines River. Earlier, this writer says, it was called "Hell's Half Acre" and later Pinchey. The population in 1885 was 123, clearly enough to support a school.

The Oradell School is also sometimes called the Pinchey School. Popular legend has it that this name arose because the owner of the general store was so stingy that he would pinch a bean in two to make the exact weight. Whatever the reason, 75th Avenue was called the Pinchey Road while a few miles upstream is an area called the Pinchey Bottoms. Its mudflats are reputed to be the best shorebird viewing area in the state of Iowa. The official name Oradell is all but forgotten, but Pinchey lingers on.

Teachers were Miss Lena Graham 1885; Miss Litchfield 1889; Miss Emma Snyder 1890; Miss Carrie Watkins, Ira Miner 1891; Miss Emma Prentice 1894; Bertha Pickett, Florence Hammer, A. D. Worthington 1895; Jack Galain 1896; Nora Spalti, Flavia Williams 1898; Billie Henby, Flavia Williams 1899; Blanche Litchfield, Rae Coffrey 1900; Rae Coffrey, Carrie B. Watkins, Nora Spalti, Flavia Williams 1901; Rae Coffrey, Maude Spalti 1902; Myrtle Stradley, Rae Coffrey 1903; Blanche Litchfield, Tracie Scott 1904; Ross De Viny, Mrytle Stradley 1905; Flossie Hollowell, Daisy M. Richards 1906; Bressa Welch 1907; Mary Caffrey 1908; Edna Neal, Mayme Murphy 1909; Rae Caffrey, Olivia Hollister 1910; Sadie Billingsley 1911-13; Catherine Benge, M. J. O'Brien, Sadie Billingsley 1914; Mabel Nye 1915; Dean Butcher, Sara Thondale, Electra West 1916; Electra West 1917; Zora Kamp 1918; Sadie Billingsley 1919; Bernice Core 1920-21; Ruth Summy 1922; Marie Hardin 1925-26; Mrs. Tomi Smith 1928; Dorothy Reed 1929-30; Malvina Neely 1932; Sadie Billingsley 1933-35; Bernice Patch 1936; Myrtle L. McArthur 1937; and Wilma Anderson 1938.

Rees (4)

Rees – After the October 1923 snowstorm. Teacher Reda Martin. Front row: Alberta Slykhuis, Grace Slykhuis, John Able Dickenson, Waldo Dickenson, and Gracie De Moss. Back row: Donald Rees, Cynthia De Moss, Tommy De Moss, and James Rees.

REES SCHOOL was northeast of Pleasantville. Today you would follow G40 out of Pleasantville, turn north on 92nd until you come to Gear Street, then turn right. The schoolhouse stood on the south side of Gear Street, a short distance from the T intersection. Sometimes it's difficult to figure out why certain Marion County schools acquired such names as Electra, O. K., or Rising Star, but the name Rees is no mystery. Rees is the surname of several families who had lived in that neighborhood for a very long time.

When I attended North Porterville School (southeast of Pella), I didn't have much awareness of other country schools, but I did know about the

Rees School because my mother Reda Martin taught there for two years after she graduated from Knoxville High School with the class of 1923. She always spoke with great fondness of the Rees students and kept in contact with several of them for many years. As a fundraiser, she organized a pie supper. Much to her dismay, her pie was purchased by a young man in whom she had no interest for the enormous sum of seventeen dollars. The money did allow her to purchase much-needed supplies for the schoolroom. She took the picture on the facing page with her camera and years ago removed all of the pictures of this school from her photograph album and gave them to the Marion County Historical Society. Unfortunately, she didn't identify most of them by name, but the souvenir booklet which she gave to each student does list their names. Hers are the only photographs I have found for this school.

I talked with Nancy Rees Naaktegeboren, who attended primary and first grade with Miss Beary the last year the school was in session. After that, the neighborhood students rode the bus to Pleasantville. Classmate Kathy Flockhart was Nancy's best friend throughout her school years and until Kathy died of cancer in her 50s. As a souvenir of the Rees School, Nancy's dad Harvey Rees framed a section of the blackboard for each of the girls. Nancy had to walk about a mile to school and was often accompanied by Clyde Fouch, an older boy, who would sometimes pull her up the hill on a sled. Others who lived in the neighborhood were the Cores, the Van Ecks, the Van Ryswyks, and the Worthingtons.

Teachers were Altha Davenport 1886; Nannie Danthy, Rena Snyder 1895; Bessie Hatfield, Beatrice Nye 1896; Beatrice Nye, Orville T. Nye 1898; Leona Gillaspie, Maggie Cooper 1899; Leona Gillaspie, Nora Spalti, Blanche Litchfield 1900; Blanche Litchfield, Beatrice Nye, Orville Nye 1901; A. H. Crosby, Earl Dewey, Amanda Brown 1902; Berda Putnam 1903; Mrs. Bessie Loomis, Minnie Powell 1904; Myrtle Umpleby, Elvira E. Hollister 1905; Mary Jones 1906; Charles M. Wren 1907; M. A. Foster, Idella Graves, Bessie Wiliams 1908; Ethel Truer, Gay Moore 1909; Agnes C. Smith 1910; Fay Worthington, Ethel Beckworth, Margaret Wren 1911; Margaret Wren, Grace B. Fee 1912; Flossie Rinehart 1913; Elizabeth Wren 1914; Hazel Chivers, Ruth Hill 1915; Bertha Alexander 1916; Bertha Alexander, Ruth Hill 1917; Helen Dunlap 1918; Adda Dickensen 1919; Grace Stanberry 1920; Ruth Summey 1921; Bernice Core 1922; Reda Martin 1923-24; Henry J. Slykhuis 1925; Vane Rees 1926; Iva Thornburg 1928; Lee Thornburg 1929; Iva Thornburg 1930; Eleanor Gerling 1932; Sarah Jane Templeton 1933; Maude Maddy 1934; Marie Maddy 1935; Lillian Flockhart, Wanda Jones 1936; Ruth Ruckman 1937; Loren D. Wing 1938-40; and Cecilia M. Beary 1941-45.

Union School (11)

UNION SCHOOL was about seven miles northwest of Knoxville. For many years after it closed it stood on its original location at 1100 G40 at the intersection of 110 Avenue on the property owned by Clarence Van Waardhuizen. In August 2009, while former student Donna Karr Betterton was on vacation, her husband Dwayne noticed an ad in the paper for the building to be given free for its removal.

When the Bettertons returned this familiar landmark had been burned down.

This schoolhouse had eight windows on the west, an unusually large number for a school of its size. Just inside the entry door there was a cloak room for hanging coats and storing lunch pails. While in kindergarten, Donna and a fellow student had a big tub of sand to play in and would get in trouble for throwing sand. Donna says she can still smell the sweeping compound. On the schoolyard was a large lilac bush that the smaller children like to play under.

Every spring, the students would hike to the sandstone bluffs for a picnic. Someone had built steps into the face of the cliff—rather steep steps for a small child—and Donna was always afraid there might be a snake lying on top of the next step.

Donna attended school there from 1950 to around 1955 when the school was reorganized and she and her sisters were sent to Blaine while others in the district went to Pleasantville.

Verna Presley Mecham also attended Union School. Her most vivid memory was that their teacher had a boyfriend who flew planes. Just before he was being shipped overseas he flew over the school and dropped her a letter tied to a rock. Later the students learned he had been shot down and killed. (A fellow student says Verna must be thinking of another teacher at another school. It makes a good story though.) One of the things they did to support the war effort was to collect leftover grease "to be used for what ever they used it for."

One day, Verna and her sisters, who usually carried their lunch to school in Karo syrup pails, forgot to take them to school. The teacher drove them home to let their mom fix lunch for them.

"Betty," she said, "was a good teacher but could be stern as Verna found out a few times, being held in after school to finish her tasks. At recess they usually played tag, hop scotch, or dodge ball as there weren't enough students for baseball. In the winter, there was sledding and one snowy night Betty invited them to bring lanterns and sleds to her house for a sledding party."

Verna took four grades in two years and graduated from 8th grade at the same time as her older sister Norma. The teacher gave them each a compact, which Verna still has.

Teachers included Granville Teter, Miss Rena Snyder 1889; Edgar Fee, Ava Marsh 1902; Leta Banifield 1903; J. O. Angel, Adelaide Hollister 1904; Beulah French, Lillie A. Hays, Mary Jones 1905; Howard B. Stone, Fern Mason 1906; Gladys Scheele 1922; Grace Stanberry 1924; Joye Black 1925-26; Mabel Bush 1929-30; Wanda H. Jones 1932; Joseph C. Ruckman 1933-34; Rose Ellen Welch 1939-40; Miss Betty Jones 1945; Wanda Jones 1947; Rena Fee Welch 1948; Wanda Jones 1949; Mrs. Betty Ver Dught 1950; Opal De Heer 1951-53; and Marie Metcalf 1954.

Union, mid 40s – Left to right: Billy Shoup, Jim Karr, Paul Karr, Norma Presley, Verna Presley, Doris Shoup, and Leona Presley.

Map of Washington Township

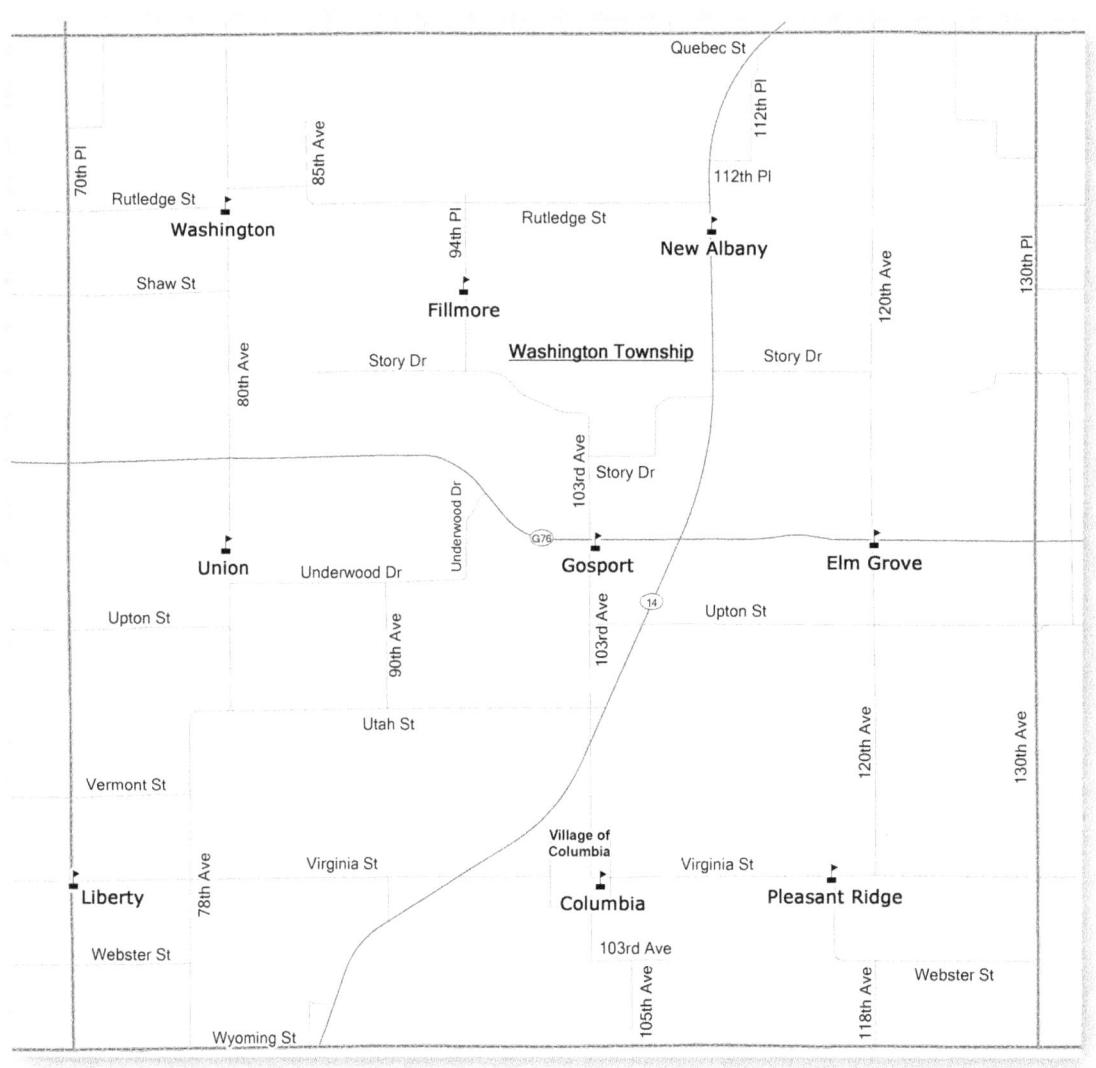

15

THE SCHOOLS OF
Washington Township

Columbia (34)

Columbia, April 1928 – Teacher Mrs. Carl Beebout.

COLUMBIA, LOCATED OFF Highway 14, was named for the oldest settlers who came from Columbia, Kentucky. It was surveyed in March 1857. An 1884 atlas lists its population as 111. Looking a little shabby, the school building is still standing and being used for storage by McCorkle's.

The June 22, 1871, *Knoxville Journal* reported that a new schoolhouse was being built at Columbia. The two-story building was to be twenty-four by thirty-six feet with the upper story being used for a literary hall. Mr. N. Mitchell sold the ground for seventy-five dollars.

All was not well in the neighborhood as the July 9, 1874, *Journal* correspondent wrote: "A school house three miles west of Columbia was entirely destroyed by some vicious person for some evil purposes." (The writer refers to the Liberty School which was burned and not replaced for several years.)

An 1895 *Journal* said, "There will be a Pink Tea supper at the school house on Sat., Oct. 19 for the purpose of raising money for a school library. Supper .25 per couple."

In May, 1896, we read that "Quite a few teachers have been studying two new branches, economics and civics, which have been lately suggested by the school law."

By 1898, Columbia felt they had enough students to have a "graded school."

In October 1900, school was closed due to scarlet fever.

Teacher Edna I. Burton in January 1901 reported thirty-three students enrolled with an average attendance of twenty-nine. There were seventy cases of tardies. Neither absent nor tardy: Merle Witt, May Dawson, Verne Brown, Cleo May, and Bonnie Bingeman.

The school was burned in 1933 and replaced with a one-story structure. Lori Jahner told me that she attended kindergarten there the last year before students were sent to Knoxville. Both her mother and grandmother also attended this school. Her teacher, Gemaine Whitlatch, told me how much she enjoyed teaching the approximately eighteen students in kindergarten through 4th grade. For a few weeks in the spring, the students who would be entering kindergarten in the fall would also attend. Although these teachers were expected to teach everything, she admitted that she depended on the record player for the music lessons. I too remember music lessons centered around the record player. The legacy of teaching continues with some of Germaine's children and grandchildren. "They have some good years and some bad years just like always," she said.

I received a call from Brenda Van Loon Rollison who noticed I had mentioned County School Superintendent Sylvia Plotts in one of my articles. She related the story of what happened to her when she was in kindergarten in 1947. Brenda was nearly finished with her lunch when Mrs. Plotts arrived at the door of the Columbia School for a visit. Having been thoroughly frightened by tales about the formidable Mrs. Plotts from the older students, Brenda immediately became sick. Mrs. Plotts offered to take her home and soon she found herself in the car with the dreaded Mrs. Plotts. Mrs. Plotts was very kind to her parents and said she couldn't understand what made Brenda so sick as she had examined her lunch and it was lovely. Her parents were just as gracious to Mrs. Plotts, pretending ignorance of her illness, although they suspected it was because the older students had been telling tales of how mean the superintendent was.

She was recently reminded of this story when one of her grandchildren had said to her, "Grandma, you are never afraid." Brenda, who retired in 2007 from working in several overseas embassies, said she never was afraid except the day Mrs. Plotts stepped in the schoolroom door. A Knoxville High School graduate, she lives in Chadron, Nebraska.

Teachers included Kate Tinkey 1882; Miss Etta Steele 1885; Liza Croft 1886; Miss Emma Johnson 1888; Sherman Wilson 1892; Albert Tracy, Lizzie Witt 1895; Lizzie Witt, Owen Whitlatch, Edna I. Burton 1896; Maggie Smith, Orlan Whitlatch 1898; Edna I. Burton, Annie F. McGrew, Mary Stotts, Orlan Whitlatch 1899; Edna Whitlatch, Mary Stotts, Miss Burton, Anna McGrew 1900; Maggie Smith, Edna Whitlatch, Mary Stotts 1901; Floyd Stotts, Mary Stotts 1902; Floyd Stotts, Mary Stotts, Lois Mobswarth 1903; Alice B. Bearden, Minnie Vannoy 1904; Arilla McDowell, Victoria Swanson 1905; Sevilla McDowell 1906; Benita May, Martha B. Long 1907; Ida E. McMannis 1908; Mattie Hyatt, Benita May 1909; M. A. Foster, Mary Roller 1910; W. J. Kincaid, Berneice Kuty 1911; W. J. Kincaid, Gretta Noftsger 1912; Sue Stone, Gretta Noftsger 1913; Helen Cooper, Edith Agan 1914; Edith Agan, Minnie Stanger 1915; Edith Agan, Minnie S. Noftsger 1917; Hazel McClure, Helen McClure 1918; Bessie Fall, Louise Johnston 1919; Edith Agan 1924; Lulu B. Pierson, Ruby Miller 1925; Lulu B. Pierson 1926; Mrs. Carl Beebout 1927; Marie Beebout 1928; Lulu Vierson 1929; Faye Stuart, Ina Bingaman 1930; Duane Bingaman 1931; Thelma Agan 1932; Cleo Black, Thelma Paulding 1933; Cleo Black, Duane Bingaman 1934; Rachel Beebout, Duane Bingaman 1935; Donald Murr, Rachel Beebout 1936; Miss Elwood, Duane Bingeman 1937; Mrs. Grace States, Duane Bingaman 1938; Grace I. States, Duane Bingaman 1939; Grace I. States, Raymond E. Shore

1940; Grace I. States, Kathleen Roberts 1941; Grace I. States, Cleo Hill 1942; Doris Heston, Virginia Taylor 1943; Susie M. Relph, Clinna Beebout 1944; Susie M. Relph, Anna Bingaman 1945; Marjorie Agan, Dorothy Foster 1947; Eunice Jane Nelson, Bertha Johnston 1948; Bertha Johnston, Imogene Fee 1949-51; Mrs. Thelma Stroup, Mrs. Donna Coffman 1952; Mrs. Selma Miller 1953; Thelma Straup, Selma Miller 1954; Mrs. Hazel M. Wood, Mrs. Geraldine Young 1955-62; Germaine Whitlach, Georgia Hubler 1963-64; and Germaine Whitlach, Florence Whitlach 1965.

Elm Grove (13)

Elm Grove, May 1941 – Front row: Eileen Butrum, Florence McCormick, Mary Ann Butrum, and Mildred Flaugh. Back row: Geraldine Agan, Marjorie Agan, Halbert Laird, Mary Flaugh, and Teacher Georgia Hubler.

ELM GROVE SCHOOL was about two miles east of Gosport on the corner of 120th Avenue and Highway G76. Its present day address would be 1201 Highway G76.

The *Iowa Voter* of July 7, 1870, reported that the concert conducted by Miss Ida Marshall was a success with the proceeds of seventeen dollars to go to the Sabbath School at Elm Grove.

In 1879, the reporter said that "the old Elm Grove School is being moved to Columbia and fitted up for a dwelling."

In February of 1886, *The Knoxville Journal* announced that there will be a Valentine's spelling at Elm Grove, Saturday, February 13. The exercises after recess will consist of selected readings, declamations, essays, and distributing Valentines.

On April 26, 1886, the Gosport reporter for *The Knoxville Journal* slammed the Elm Grove school board directors with the comment that the district paid only eighteen dollars and probably expected the teacher to board the pupils and do the washing for the district.

The school was flourishing in 1897 when eight scholars received diplomas (*Knoxville Journal*).

The November 17, 1900, *Journal* reported that S. B. Wolfe was about ready to begin the winter term. He has just dug 500 bushels of potatoes.

Former teacher Lois McCormick Akins telephoned to share her experiences at the school. On December 15, 1942, she took over for teacher Mary L. Hindman, who was pregnant. She continued teaching the following school year and after that spent two and a half years in the navy. "I enjoyed my years in the navy better than any other job," she said. In addition to teaching country school, she taught nearly thirty years in the upper elementary grades at Knoxville.

Lois remembers Elm Grove as being fairly

new and well equipped. She taught music using records that were played on a little portable "suitcase" record player. As a war time teacher, she was responsible for registering the district families so they could obtain rationing books. Raising the flag was a daily ritual. One day someone accidentally hoisted it upside down and it got caught at the top of the pole. She had to ask her married brother who lived north of the school to come and help her get it down.

Lois feels that country schools provided a better educational experience than town schools. Students had the opportunity to hear a lesson more than one time, students helped each other, and they learned respect for students of all ages. Country schools fostered a community spirit.

Margaret Beebe Gee started school in 1946. She recalls fun times playing marbles, jumping rope, and the games of Annie-Annie Over, Hide and Seek, and Red Rover. Even though there were windows along the south and west sides, without electricity the schoolroom could be pretty dreary on dark cloudy days.

Mary Lou Miller Bingham started school when she was only four years old. On the first day, teacher Frieda Chamberlain spanked her because she refused to take a nap. Mary Lou told her she didn't take naps. However, that day the teacher sat with her until she did fall asleep. She didn't wake up until it was time to go home. She said that Frieda Chamberlain, who was her teacher through 5th grade, was an outstanding teacher and probably saw the need to take control on day one. She and her brother usually rode home with the teacher. One day they were wrestling and the car took off and they landed in the ditch. She also remembers that the older boys dismantled an old hand-cranked telephone, which they took to the coal shed. Schoolmates were invited in to be shocked until the teacher put an end to this unauthorized scientific experiment.

Teachers included Kate Black 1872; Miss Maggie De Moss 1879; Miss Ellen Beebout, G. E. Bonebrake 1880; Miss Etta Steele 1883; Dave McKinnis 1885; Ida Whitlach 1886; Lillie McCreary 1889; Miss Freddie Eberhart, Mr. Fassett 1891; W. H. Fassett 1892; Miss Emma Maddy 1894; Corda Venable, Rena Snyder, Lillie Parker 1895; Lillie Parker Cordye Venable 1896; Miss Ollie Maddy 1897; Corda Venable, Cordye Venable 1898; Flora Kester 1899; Gertrude Prickett, D. B. Wolfe 1900; Maude Inskeep, Cordye Hunt, S. B. Wolfe 1901; Ida C. Hall 1902; Bert Bingaman 1903; Anna Ridenour, W. H. Conrey 1904; Frank Crawford 1905; Art Betterton 1906; Cora Hill, Floyd Hedrick 1907; Eva M. Cory 1908; Arvilla Hayes, Frank Crawford 1909; Frank Crawford 1910; Eva Marshall, May Miller, Frank Crawford 1911; Frank Crawford, Emmett Kincaid 1912; Mary Greenaway 1913; Mary Caffrey 1914; Fern Collins, Vernon Van Loon 1915; Agnes Render 1916; Nellie Braden, Ruth Hillo, Mary Bachman 1917; Grace Conrey 1918; Lena Whitlatch 1919; Fern Smith, Lois Bachman 1920; Mary E. Spaur 1921; Miriam Fletcher 1922; Ruth Larson 1923; Blanche Boven 1924; Cleo Grimes, Edith Agan 1925; Edith Agan 1926; Joye Black 1928; Thelma Agan 1930-31; Oletha Lenning 1932-33; Vera Kincaid 1934; Oletha Lenning 1937-38; Merrill Whitlatch 1938; Georgia Hubler 1939-40; Nora Loynachan 1941; Mary L. Hindman, Lois McCormick 1942; Lois McCormick 1943; Kathryn Crandall

1944-45; Eunice J. Bingaman 1947; Dorothy Carruthers 1948-49; Mrs. Freda Chamberlain 1951; Freda Chamberlain 1954; Mrs. Ada Brees 1955-56; and Zelma Beebout 1957-58.

Fillmore (9)

Filmore, 1940 – Teacher Olive McVey. Front row: Bertrand Dennison, Donald Busick, Delores Childers, ___Busick, Phyllis Dennison, and Colleen Hendrix. Back row: Melvin Dennison, Richard Hendrix, Robert Busick, Arlo Busick, Pauline Beem, Ruby Busick, and Marjorie Lamb. (Alberta Finarty absent.)

IF THIS SCHOOL were still standing, it would be about midway on 94th Place, which is the short stretch of north/south road connecting Rutledge Street and Story Drive. I am guessing that it was named for our 13th president Millard Fillmore, who served between 1850 and 1853. As the vice president for Zachary Taylor, he became president when Taylor died in the summer of 1850, and Fillmore finished out his term. Although he is not a well known president, naming a school for him seems appropriate. He came from a large family of nine children and had little time for an education. When he was fourteen, his father apprenticed him for seven years to a cloth maker. Realizing that he needed more education, Millard studied on his own, memorizing words from the dictionary as he worked. Before his apprenticeship ended, he bought his release for thirty dollars. He also bought a dictionary, the first book he ever owned. He was the first president to have a library in the White House.

The only mention I found about Fillmore School from early days was this entry in the February 18, 1886, *Knoxville Journal*. "Teacher Elisa Croft was surprised by patrons of school who came with baskets as she completed a 3 month term."

Beverly Jones told me that she began attending Fillmore as a first grader in the spring of 1944 and went to school there until the school closed the following spring. After that she went to Dallas. She remembers three girls taking doll furniture and staying overnight with teacher Ruth Kinney. She believes the other two were Patty Finarty and Colleen Hendrix. (I don't know if this was a common practice among teachers, but I do know that such special overnight stays were long remembered by students. Some of my mother's students from the North Porterville School (1926-27) have told me that my mother used to take one or two students home with her on weekends. They thought this was a real adventure as my grandparents lived "far away" across the river near Knoxville.)

Beverly Jones also recalls the winter day that

Patty Finarty hooked up her dog to a sled to take her to school. And when the snow melted during the day, Patty had a real problem getting the sled back home.

Teachers included Miss Maggie De Moss 1879; Miss Ella Hammond, Katie Bonebrake 1880; Miss Ella Hammond, Della Smith 1881; Miss Della Smith 1882-83; Miss Della Smith, Miss Johnson 1884; Miss Elisa Croft 1885; Lizzie Smith, D. W. McKinnis 1889; Miss May Bishop 1893; Lora Myers 1895; Mary Pringle, Bernice Maddy 1898; Mary Pringle, Bernice Maddy, Ida Staggs, Anna Bush 1899; Ida Staggs, Anna Bush, Nina Pringle 1900; Nina Pringle 1901-02; Elsa Moon 1903-04; Nora Welch 1905; Gerald Hunerdosse, Gertrude Mallory 1906; Gertrude Mallory, Mayme Lahman 1907; L. May Miller 1908; Della Ridenour, Mabel De Witt 1909; Ira E. Houser 1910; Anna Bingaman 1911; Orba L. Moore 1912; Gladys Witt, Gretta Noftsger 1913; Margie Shives, Orba L. Moon 1914; Liva Barrett 1915-17; Helen How 1918; Nora Harty, Ruth Perry, Dimmie Hart 1919; Lois Bachman 1920; Bessie Hixenbaugh 1921; Winifred Brillhart 1922; Daisy Black 1924; Thelma Maddy 1925; Ella Johnson 1927; Cleo Black 1930; Thurlene Agan 1931-32; Icel L. Miller 1933; Wilma Madley 1934; Margaret Agan 1935; Joye Black 1936-39; Olive McVey 1940; Lida McMannis 1942; Luella I. Beebout 1943; and Mrs. Ruth Kenney 1944.

Gosport (22)

Gosport – Teacher Charlene Scheele Bryan.

THE WEATHERED SCHOOL BUILDING stands on its original site in the former town of Gosport, one mile north of Columbia, eight miles south of Knoxville, one-half mile west of Highway 14. The town of Gosport was platted in 1853 as New Town, but the name was changed a few years later to Gosport. (Why, I wonder, when there is no large body of water for miles around.) A post office served this small village from 1854-1905. In 1875, it had several general stores, two churches, a blacksmith shop, and a wagon-making establishment—everything needed to serve the residents of what promised to be a growing town. In 1884, the town had a population of seventy-one. All gone.

From the archives of the Knoxville newspapers I found several references to the early days of the Gosport school:

Iowa Voter 1869: The county superintendent reported A. C. Keithly hired at thirty dollars a month. Sixty-nine were enrolled with thirty-eight present. All the branches were taught except history. They needed a larger house. Scholars were studious and orderly with considerable proficiency in arithmetic.

Knoxville Journal 1874: There was a singing

class concert on December 12 conducted by Mrs. Samuel Kennedy. There were vocal music classes for four courses of two weeks each.

1879: J. W. Collins had sixty students. The correspondent commented that three or four students were seated in a seat designed for two. Teacher Della Smith received eighteen dollars per month.

March 13, 1880: Voted down levy for a new school building. School had more scholars than anyone in the township.

September 1882: The new school was ready for plasterers the following week. (Patrons must have recognized the need for a new school.)

December 1882: Question for debate at Gosport was "Resolved that free trade would be good for the U. S." (Early schools often held these debates during evenings or on Saturdays to help inform the public on current issues.)

February 4, 1884: "We cast our rough and ready physiognomy in on the Gosport School one day last week and found the teacher and scholars busy as may be seen in any of our ungraded schools. Our teachers are all crowded as to be unable to do justice to their pupils."

February 1889: Schools in the area were closed because of scarlet fever.

April 1890: Della Smith had forty students. I visited by phone with Marjorie Agan Clark, who taught at the Gosport School from 1945-47 and walked a mile and a half from her home to school each day. I asked if she rode to school when the weather was bad. "No," she said, "if the weather was bad we either couldn't get the car started or the roads were too muddy to drive to school. It was a good time to be a teacher as they were good kids and there was much learning." Marjorie also taught in 1962 and 1963, the final year Gosport was open.

Carol Lou Hall, whose husband Orville and daughter attended Gosport, has been instrumental in organizing the annual Gosport School reunions for many years. This year (2010), Julie Irving and Betty Clark are planning the event. What a great tradition.

Teachers included: A. C. Keithley, A. H. Parks 1869; Miss Lizzie McKern 1874; J. W. Collins, Della Smith 1879; H. F. Conroy, J. F. Rutherford 1880; Mrs. McGinnis 1882; Clark J. Jones, J. W. Elder 1883; W. L. Jones 1884; Della Smith 1885; Eva Elder, J. W. Elder, Della Smith 1886; Della Smith, Millie Bebout 1889; Della Smith 1890; Mr. Elder 1891; N. E. Venable 1892; A. G. Spaur 1893; Larry Morrow 1894; Josie Smith 1895; Josie Smith, Corda Venable, Floyd Stotts, Lacy Morrow 1896; Floyd Stotts, Miss Morrow 1897; Floyd Stotts, Owen Whitlatch 1898; Owen Whitlatch 1899; Ethel W. Elder 1900; Floyd Stotts 1901; John Stotts, Mary Irons 1902; Mary Irons 1903; W. P. Wells, A. J. Welch 1904; Beniti May, Nora Welch 1905; Nora Welch, Mabel De Witt 1906; Frank Crawford, L. May Muller 1907; Maude De Raat 1908; Mabel Shook 1909; Gladys Kerr 1910-11; Eva Agan 1912-14; Marjorie Cooper 1915; Ada Alexander 1916; Gladys Garnett 1917; Mary Bachman, Gladys Witt 1918; Charlene Scheele 1919-20; Cleo Grimes 1922; Daisy Black, Cleo Grimes 1924; June McCorkle 1925; Mildred Moon 1926; Mrs. Charlene Bryan 1927; Mrs. Charlene Bryan, Edna Neal 1928; Cleo Black 1929; Joye Black 1930; Fern Rietveld 1932-33; Jessie Shives 1934-35; Clarice V. Hall 1936; Luella I. Shore 1937-39; Aletha Shore 1940-41; Julia Dunmire 1942; Lida McMannis 1944;

Marjorie Agan 1945-47; Glenna L. Smith 1948-49; Thelma Little 1950; Thelma Little, Zelma Beebout 1951; Mrs. Zelma Beebout 1952-53; Maxine Adams 1955-56; Mrs. Margery D. Dennison 1957-58; Zelma Beebout 1959-61; and Marjorie Agan Clark 1962-63.

Liberty (30)

LIBERTY WAS STRAIGHT WEST of Columbia with half the district being in Washington Township and the other half in Dallas Township. It would have been near the intersection of 70th Avenue and Virginia Street.

Teachers were Dr. Kirk 1877; Miss Jennie Wilson 1880; Miss Lottie Rutherford 1881; Ella Gaass 1886; Miss Harvey 1891; Dale Witt 1895-96; G. W. Morrison 1898; Floyd Stotts 1899-1900; S. B. Wolfe, G. W. Morrison 1901; Mary Irons 1902; Ida Long 1904; Elsa Mason 1905; Mattie Long 1906; Frankie Carruthers 1907; Anna Bingaman 1908; Edith Stotts 1909; Arvilla Hayes 1910; Neva Wilson 1911; Beatrice Lundy 1912-13; Ethel Deskin 1914; Edith Agan 1915; Forest Bonifield, Mary Sirus, Florence Newman 1916; Violet Blue 1917; Edith Agan 1918-20; Lucille Miller 1921-23; Mrs. Mary McCombs 1914; Leota D. Hall 1925; Jay Hawkins 1926; Leila Hancock 1929; Mabel McNeish 1930; Mabel McNeish 1932; Mabel Lee 1933; Maxine Carson 1934; Freda Elwood 1935-36; Mary M. Carson 1937-38; Elizabeth Dawson 1939; Loveda Hill 1941; Mrs. Loveda Shore 1942; Miss Dorothy Foster 1944-45; Mrs. Edna Mendenhall 1948-49; Marlene Stevenson 1951; and Luella Beebout 1955.

New Albany (11)

New Albany, 1947 – Right side from back: Teacher Ruth Kenny, Robert Quigley, Richard Mathes, Dolores Mathes, and Ronald Shives. Left side: Myrtle Condra, Jeena Mae Condra, and Wayne Shives.

THIS SCHOOL, now being used as a farm building, is six miles south of Knoxville at 2028 Highway 14 on the John Frakes property. It originally stood on the farm just north of this one.

A *Knoxville Journal* article of 1880 reported there was a Valentine spelling at the school. Also a new branch (subject), card playing, had been introduced at the school. (Let's hope this was studied at recess.)

According to a record book, the value of the school in 1884 was $300.

From The *Knoxville Journal* of August 1885, we note that J. H. Moore had a contract to dig a well at the Albany School.

In September 1887, the newspaper correspondent said that "The directors of New Albany are awake to the interests of the school. In addition to cleaning, white washing, and papering the school they have purchased a set of anatomical charts."

"One of the Albany school boys carries a black eye caused by a collision with the teacher" (*Knoxville Journal*, March 1888).

In February 1889, the correspondent expressed a resistance to change in writing that Liz Wilson closed with an "old fashioned hop"—something new but hardly worthy of imitation.

In 1923, the teacher reported there were eight volumes in the library. (Not nearly enough, but the teacher probably checked books out of the public library for the students.)

In the spring of 1936, 8th grade grads were Mary Catherine Fortner, Dana Oenida Beebout, and Wilma Jones. Helen and Charlene Rinehart graduated in 1938.

I talked with sisters Dolores Schuring and Rose Marie Briggs, who, along with brother Richard Mathes, attended this school. Here are some excerpts from the e-mail which Rose Marie sent: "One time as I was excused to go to the bathroom, as I started to sit down, I noticed a huge snake in the hole. I ran screaming back to the schoolhouse and teacher sent one of the boys out to survey the situation. All they did was get the snake to wrap around a stick and threw it over the fence. 'A harmless bull snake' they said. I honestly think I waited until I got home to relieve myself."

"As I look back, we got to do things that kids today don't even get to do: enter things in the fair, entertained our parents with skits on the holidays, had family potlucks, and even go on field trips. Mrs. Kenney took us to the new Hy-Vee store in Knoxville, right across from what was the old Junior High building. As we entered the store, the door opened for us, but then all of a sudden, it started to close behind me. I didn't want to get stuck in the store all by myself so I took a dart back out the 'in door' and almost got stuck. Modern inventions!"

"Once there was a furious storm outside and my folks came to pick me up. Every time we would open the door to go out the coat room and get outside, the coat room would move away from the schoolhouse. We finally opened a window and crawled outside to the car." Dolores recalls that Rose Marie was so small that the wind lifted her off her feet and their father had to carry her to the car. (Since most country schools lacked a basement people often asked what teachers and students did if there was a tornado. I remember being told that we should seek cover in the ditch. If such a storm had been spotted, I'm sure our parents would have been there to rescue us. They didn't always have radio warnings but they kept a close eye on the sky.) Rose Marie closes with this sentence: "Country school was like being on a field trip every day, out in the country enjoying nature and fresh air. I thank God every day for the opportunity I had to enjoy country school and for the wonderful teachers who worked so very hard for all of us and especially for the valuable 'lessons' learned."

Teachers who taught at this school were Mr. A. C. Keithley 1879; Mrs. Charles Griffin, Mrs. Frank Conrey 1880; Miss Maggie De Moss, Mr. David McGinnis 1881; Miss Alice Scales 1882; Miss Addie Burnett, Nellie Boyston 1883; W. C. Jones 1884; Clarence Cole, Eva Elder 1885; I. G. Agan 1886; Della Smith 1887; Della Smith, Surrie S. Wilson

1888; Liz Wilson, Cora Venable, Della Smith 1889; Della Smith, Adda Young 1890; Nora Venable, Maude Spiren 1891; Nora Venable, Dora Heavner 1892; Julia Ruckman 1894; Corda Venable 1895; Mary Roller; Julia Ruckman 1896; Julia Ruckman 1898; Julia Ruckman; Fannie Gelderblom 1899; Lulu Townsend, Art Betterton 1900; Julia Ruckman, Art Betterton, Maude Inskeep 1901; Maude Inskeep 1902; Nora Pringle 1903; Mae Moon 1904; Fannie Benifield 1905; W. H. Conrey 1906; Maude Brubaker, Gertrude Dykstra 1907; Mabel De Witt 1908-09; Beulah Stuff 1910; Jo Mendenhall 1911; Birdie Fast 1912; Clella Andrews 1913; Clella Andrews, Rhea Wilson 1914; Rhea Wilson, Mrs. Marshall 1915; Laura Taggart 1916; Grayce Rowland 1917; Hester Hyslop, Ruth Flanders 1918; Ruth Flanders 1919; Gladys Schelle 1920; Faye Kerney 1921; Avis Van Loon 1922; Ellen Fitzpatrick 1923; Merle Witt 1924-25; Thelma Maddy 1926; Edith Agan 1927; Theo Witt 1928-29; Ruth Dennison 1930; Madge Wilson 1931; Iva Bingaman 1932; Faye Wynn 1933; Oletha Lenning 1934; Ruby C. Finarty, Ruby Seaman 1935; Theo Witt 1936-37; Mrs. Ruby Ver Steeg 1938-39; Bernice Dennison 1940-43; and Mrs. Ruth Kenney 1946-53.

Pleasant Ridge (25)

PLEASANT RIDGE was east of Columbia at the intersection of 120th Avenue and Virginia Street. Teachers were Nannie Redisill 1886; Miss Kate Derry 1887; Kate Derry 1889; Herbert Curtis 1891; Edith Fountain 1895; F. W. Parker 1901; Minnie Vannoy 1902; John Stotts 1903; Mary Irons, Beniti May 1904; Ida Long 1905; Olive Hunnerdosse 1906; Mabel De Witt 1907; Mayme Lahman 1908; Susie Truwent 1909; Birdie Fast 1910; Frank Crawford, Gretta Noftsger 1911; Eva B. Jones, Edith Agan 1912; Edith Agan, Alma Love 1913; Gladys Witt, Ferne Rowland 1914; Gladys Witt 1915; Fannie Pierson 1916; Marie Tucker 1917; Gladys Witt 1918-20; Merle Witt 1922-23; Veneti Grimes 1925; Ruby Clatt 1927; Marie Cayne 1929; Maxine Robinson, Clarice Hall 1930; Duane Bingaman 1936; Irene Vriezelaar 1927; Marlene L. Shore 1938; Kathleen Roberts 1940; and Kathryn Crandall 1941-42.

Union (19)

UNION SCHOOL was one of three schools in Marion County named "Union." From older plat maps it looks as if the school would have been in the northeast corner of section 19, placing it on the west side of what is now 80th Avenue. Teacher Thelma Straup, who taught there in the late 40s, describes its location as being just south of the Crandall Corner (from the Melcher and Dallas History Book). She says in earlier days the room was arranged with benches around the outside walls with higher benches in front of them for desks. When Thelma taught there the benches had been replaced by modern desks but the stove still stood in the middle of the room.

Recently I talked with John Pierce and his mother, Mrs. Marlene Stevenson, who followed Mrs.

Straup as teacher. That coal-burning stove also made a lasting impression on Marlene, who remembers having to keep the fire going. She said that once a month the families held an evening potluck with the Thomas family usually providing the music.

John Pierce, owner of Pierce's Pumpkin Patch, writes that when his mother was teacher there, she picked up several kids on the way to school. The state mandated that the car or pickup had a school bus sign on the bumper. The sign was homemade and held onto the bumper with rubber straps made from an inner tube.

He remembers going to Leo and Etta Goodes to get a pail of drinking water. At recess, he says, it was always fun to play ante over or tag. They played baseball if there were enough kids. "We were always nervous when the County Superintendent came."

Teachers were Miss Litton 1880; Miss Alta De Moss 1881; George Clark, Mr. J. W. Elder 1884; Emma Johnston 1886; F. W. Shultis 1889; William Stevenson 1890-91; Miss Kate Derry 1892; Floyd Stotts 1895-96; Beatrice Nye 1898; F. W. Parker 1899; Owen Whitlatch, Beatrice Nye 1901; Leota Tice 1902; Ida Long 1903; E. A. McCoy, Mae Moon 1904; Vera Witt, Mattie Gray 1905; Mattie Gray 1906; Mayme Lahman, Mattie Gray 1907; Arnetta Hayes, Idella Graves 1908; Cluna Karns, Idella Graves 1909; Mayme Lahman 1910; Birdie Fast 1911; Mabel Wilson, Rachel Wilson 1912; Eva B. Jones, Orba L. Moore 1913; Orba L. Moore 1914-15; Mrs. Minna Oldham 1916; Minna Oldham, Gladys Witt 1917; Cluna Brown 1918; Cluna Brown, Mrs. Mary Spaur 1919; Lois Bachman 1921-22; Cleo Grimes 1925; Veneti Grimes 1926; Ruby Miller 1927; Mildred Patterson 1929; Clara Ridlen 1930-31; Joesphine Roberts 1932; Robert Dougherty 1933; Thurline Agan 1935; Malvina Neely 1936-37; Miss Opal I. Caulkins 1938-41; Luella Beebout 1942; Anna Bingaman 1944; Clena L. Beebout 1945; Thelma Straup 1947-51; and Mrs. Marlene Stevenson 1952-56.

Union – Older students: Marjorie Bingham and Jack and Carolyn Fortune with Teacher Thelma Straup.

Washington (6)

WASHINGTON SCHOOL was about two miles east of Dallas. If the records are correct, this picture was taken the last year this school was in session. One wonders why they did not continue, as there were certainly enough pupils to support a school. Did the building burn down? Did they consolidate with Dallas or another neighboring district? The school was known locally as the Sheepskin School, and I'm sure there's a story there as it's far from its very patriotic name of Washington.

In *The Journal* of November 1889 is a reference to the fact that the older farm boys were going back to school after corn harvest. Because they often stayed home for spring planting as well as harvesting, some of them were nearing twenty before they finally completed their education. "The boys gladly leave corn husking for a year and while their sore fingers are healing in the school house, their heads will be taking in knowledge for future use."

Teachers were Etta Steele 1883; Miss Johnston 1884; B. F. Kirk 1885; Emma Johnston, Maggie Shawner 1886; Laura Essex 1889; Laura Essex, Miss Letitia Keefer 1893; Miss Mary Maddy 1894; May Maddy 1895; Lora Myers 1898; Mary Kelley 1899; Mary Kelley, Ella McKinney 1900; Lizzie McKinney, Lora Myers 1901; Lizzie McKinney, Carrie Hunt 1902; Elaine Stillwell, Efffie McIntire, Carrie Hunt 1904; Anna Ridenour, Mrytle Brauner 1905; Myrtle Brauner 1906-08; Myrtle Brauner, Nora Willis 1909; Ruby Palmer, Ida Fenon, Chas. Leavengood 1910; Chas. Leavengood 1911; C. H. Leavengood, Nora Willis Wener 1912; and Grace Patterson, Eva B. Jones 1913-15.

Washington, 1915 – Row one: Dee Ward, Mervin Leavengood, Iva Klootwyk, Bill Harvey, Lois Harvey, Pearl Carter, and Geraldine James. Row two: Oliver Harvey, Glen Brawner, Clarence Klootwyk, Lois Carter, Alice Klootwyk, Opal Cain, and Perry Harvey. Row three: Lester Klootwyk, Robert Wood, Forrest Brawner, Bill Cain, Goldie Harvey, Teacher Eva Jones, George Cain, and John Carter.

Teachers of Marion County Country Schools

In the following list, school names that are repeated in multiple townships are followed by the initial in parentheses of the appropriate township.

A

Abernathy, Maude – Ladoga, Stringtown, Burch
Abrahamson, Miss Lavone – Fairview (D)
Abram, Florence – West Pella
Abrams, Gladys – Flagler South
Acklin, Ona – Brush Creek, White Walnut, Bunker Hill (Sw)
Acklin, Virginia – Bunker Hill (LP)
Adair, Helen – McMillan North, Flagler North, Liberty (K), Pleasant Grove (K), Rising Star, Amsterdam East, Mt. Vernon
Adair, Mary – Lincoln (K)
Adams, Bette – Buckeye, Flagler South
Adams, Ida May – European # 1
Adams, Maxine – McMillan North, Victory Central, Burr Oak, Flagler, Flagler North, Liberty (K), Gosport
Adams, P. E. – Des Moines Valley
Adams, P. Edgar – Black Oak, Pleasant Hill
Adams, Queene – Liberty (S)
Adamson, Ruth I. – Pleasant Ridge (I)
Adonis, P. Edgar – Lincoln North
Adrian, Martha – Pleasant Grove (LP)
Agan, Edith – Freedom, Sunnyside, Simmons, Pleasant Ridge (K), Spring Hill, Columbia, Elm Grove, Liberty (W), New Albany, Pleasant Ridge (W)
Agan, Mrs. Esther – Marion
Agan, Eva – Round Grove, Gosport
Agan, F. M. – Round Grove
Agan, I. G. – New Albany
Agan, Lois – Round Grove, Willow Grove
Agan, Maggie – Simmons
Agan, Margaret – Fillmore
Agan, Marjorie – Columbia, Gosport
Agan, Martina – Burr Oak
Agan, Thelma – Columbia, Elm Grove
Agan, Thurlene – Fillmore, Pleasant Ridge (W), Union (W)
Albertson, Henry – Horstman
Albertson, W. E. – Freedom
Alexander, Ada – Liberty (K), Otley, Gosport
Alexander, Jno – West Pella
Alexander, Kate – Oak Ridge
Alexander, Miss – Otley
Alexander, Nora M. – Pleasant Hill, Fairview (R)
Allen Frances – River Ridge West
Allen, Franie – Coal Ridge (I)
Allen, Sylvia – Springfield, Spring Hill
Allen, Dr. W.W. – Pleasant Grove (LP)
Alley, Dorothy – Bend
Allfree, Elva – Pleasant View
Allsup, Effie – Clark
Almach, Gertrude – Marion, Ladoga, Pleasant Valley
Ammer, H, F. – Hickory Grove
Amos, Leulah Stuff – Pleasant Grove (K)
Amsberry, A. L. – Iola
Amsberry, Mr. – Highland
Amsberry, Mrs. Merle – Flagler North
Anderson, Anna – Fairview (P)
Anderson, Cleo – River Ridge West
Anderson, Dorothy – Des Moines Valley
Anderson, Elsie – Liberty Corner, Red Rock, Summit
Anderson, Gertrude – Porterville South
Anderson, Lelia – Liberty Corner
Anderson, Mrs. Lois – Simmons
Anderson, Miss – Otley
Anderson, Wilma – Caloma, Oradell
Anderson, Virgie Shinn – Flagler, Maple Grove, Fairview (P), Blaine
Andrew, Clella – Willow Grove, New Albany
Andrews, Prof. – Otley
Angel, J. O. – Virginia, Union (U)
Anspach, Mary – Virginia
Anthony, Edith – Porterville South
Anthony, Mrs. Hazel Kading – Fairview (F)
Applegate, Alda – Indiana, Prairie College, Salem
Applegate, C. D. – Carlysle, Black Oak, Cedar Valley (L)
Applegate, Georgia – Highland
Applegate, Nannie – Union (I)
Arens, Leona – Amsterdam East, Porterville South, Richland
Armstrong, Cora – Flagler North
Armstrong, Emma – Brush Creek

Aschenbrenner, Ruth – Pleasant Grove (LP), Porterville North
Ash, Evelyn – Collins
Ash, Ida – Sunnyside, Conn, Wheeling
Atherton, L. Y. – Elm Ridge
Augustine, Bertha – Iola, McMillan North, Hazel Ridge, Flagler North, Rising Star
Auld, Miss Mary – Flagler North
Ausberry, Edith – Bunker Hill (K)
Auspach, Mary L. – Vigilance
Avery, Marjorie – River Ridge East
Avery, Pauline – Bethel
Ayers, Mable – Fairview (P)

B

Bachman, Lois – Dallas Center, Fillmore, Union (W)
Bachman, Mary – Elm Grove, Gosport
Badgley, Oneida – Fairview (D)
Bailey, Addie – Shiloh
Baker, Flora – Otley
Baker, Kenneth – Cedar Valley (I)
Baker, Leah – Coal Ridge (I), Shiloh
Baker, Leona – Shiloh
Baldridge, Frank – Bunker Hill (Sw)
Ball, Maxine – Sunnyside
Ball, Samuel T. – Caloma
Ballard, Freda – Fair Oak
Ballard, Miss – Liberty Corner
Ballenger, Agnes – European #3
Balmer, Laura – Oak Ridge, Pleasant Grove (S), Pleasant View
Balmer, Ruth – Cincinnati
Bane, L. D. – Black Oak
Bane, Leonard – Lincoln (K), Pleasant Ridge
Bane, Myrtle Brown – Ladoga
Banes, Mrs. Anna – Dallas Center
Banifield, Leta – Des Moines Valley, Mt. Vernon, Union (U)
Banks, Clara – Clay Center, McMillan North, Victory
Banks, Wm. – Elm Ridge
Barber, Anna – White Breast
Barendregt, Anna – Silver Grove East
Barker, Erma – Iola
Barnes, Miss Alice – Washington (K)
Barnes, Lina – Clark
Barnes, Linda – Core
Barnes, Miss – Elm Ridge
Barnes, Sylvia – Union (C)
Barnett, Elretta – Highland (F), Sunnyside

Barnett, Louis – Valley View
Barnwell, Gladys – Porterville South, Rock Island
Barr, Ethel L. – Buckeye, Pleasant Valley
Barr, Grace – Burch
Barrett, Jennie D. – Hazel Ridge, Pleasant Ridge (K)
Barrett, Liva – Fairview (F), Sunnyside, Liberty (K), Core, Fillmore
Barringer, De Lana – Willow Grove
Barton, Clara – Virginia
Barton, Violet – Newbern
Batten, Cora – Cedar Valley (I)
Batten, Flora – Buckeye, Fee, Pleasant Grove (K), Pleasant Ridge (K), Rising Star, Spring Hill
Batten, Florence – Thornton
Battles, Mertie – Hawkeye
Bauer, Geneva – Dallas Center
Beall, Mary – Pleasant Grove (S)
Beaman, Lillian – Pleasant Ridge (K)
Bean, Dorothea – Eureka
Bearden, Alice B. – Columbia
Bearden, E. G. – Red Rock
Bearden, Emma – Fairview (D), Marion, Newbern
Bearden, V. M. – Fairview (D), Newbern
Beardon, E. – Pleasant Valley
Beardon, M. E. – Pleasant Valley
Beary, Anna Ruth – Burr Oak, Fairview (P)
Beary, Cecilia – Rees
Beary, D. J. – Simmons
Beary, Helen – Fairview (C)
Beary, Kathryn – Cedar Valley (I)
Beary, Madonna – Fairview (K)
Beary, Mary – Red Rock
Beary, Mary L. – Flagler
Beary, Mildred – Buckeye, Fairview (K)
Beaver, Arlene – Fairview (C)
Beaver, Arlys J. – Des Moines Valley, Eureka
Beaver, Mrs. Maryellen Johnson – Des Moines Valley
Beaver, Wilma – Eureka
Beckwith, Florence – West Pella
Beckworth, Ethel – Rees
Beckworth, Florence – Burr Oak (Sw)
Beebout, Mrs. Carl – Columbia
Beebout, Clinna – Columbia, Union (W)
Beebout, Miss Ellen – Elm Grove
Beebout, Louella – Caloma, Spring Hill, Liberty (W), Union (W)
Beebout, Luella I., – Fillmore
Beebout, Maric – Fairview (P), Columbia

Beebout, Millie – Gosport
Beebout, Rachel – Columbia
Beebout, Zelma E. – Pleasant Ridge (K), Elm Grove, Gosport
Beedle, Virgie – Cedar Valley (I)
Beem, Mrs. Helen – Franklin Center, Fairview (K), Fee
Beem, Helene – Pleasant Valley
Beem, Pauline – East River Ridge
Beem, Viola – O.K.
Beeman, Pearl – Pleasant Hill, Valley at Percy, Oak Ridge
Beers, C. – Porterville North
Beckwith, Beulah – Pleasant Hill
Behner, Laura – Fairview (R), Oak Ridge
Behnock, Miss Anna – Virginia
Beintema, Birdy – Amsterdam West
Bell, Lucy – White Walnut
Bell, Maxine – Dallas Center
Bell, Sister M. Martha – Chicago
Bellamy, Irene – Pleasant Grove
Belson, Agnes C. – Pleasant Valley
Beltzell, Kate – O.K.
Belvill, Marnie – Eureka
Benge, Catherine – Franklin Center, Ladoga, Oradell
Benifield, Fanny – New Albany
Bennett, Mrs. Cleo – Des Moines Valley
Bennett, Jacob – Hickory Grove
Bennett, Mrs. Lillian – Burr Oak, Pleasant Ridge (K)
Bennett, Olla – Burr Oak, Bennington
Bennick, Lucy Hoksbergen – Battle Ridge
Bennink, Gertrude – Silver Grove East
Bennink, Nellie – Porterville North, Valley
Bensink, Agnes – European #1, Pleasant Grove (S)
Benson, Ethel – Buckeye
Berg, Leona – Porterville North
Berkenbosch, Catherine – Pleasant Grove (S)
Berkenbosch, Pauline – Oak Ridge
Berley, Miss Vivian – Lincoln South
Bernett, Lillian – Mt. Vernon
Berns, Auria – Liberty (S)
Betterton, Art – Vigilance, Buckeye, Liberty (K), Pleasant Grove, Salem, Scott, Spring Hill, Black Oak, Elm Grove, New Albany
Bevin, Darlene Vinson – Caloma, European #3, Pleasant Grove (L), Richland
Beyer, Alta – Richland
Beyer, Marie – European #2
Beyers, Gideon – European #3
Bicklehaupt, Miss Kate – Liberty Corner
Biddle, Geraldine – Flagler North, Flagler South

Biddle, S.T. – Caloma
Biggs, Virginia – Pleasant Hill
Billingsley, Sadie – Highland, Stringtown, West Pella, Clark, Oradell
Bingaman, Anna – Simmons, East River Ridge, Columbia, Fillmore, Liberty (W), Union (W)
Bingaman, Bert – Elm Grove
Bingaman, Duane – Columbia, Pleasant Ridge (W)
Bingaman, Eunice J. – Elm Grove
Bingaman, Mrs. H. C. – White Walnut
Bingaman, Ina – Columbia
Bingaman, Iva – New Albany
Bingaman, Nannie – Iola
Bishop, May – Hawkeye, Fillmore
Bishop, Nellie – Liberty (K)
Bishop, Violet – Oak Ridge
Bissett, Nellie – Freedom
Bittenbender, Alice – Freedom, Fairview (F), Brownlee
Bivans, Etta – West Bethel, Fairview (K)
Bivans, Lula – Coal Ridge, River Ridge East
Black, Mrs. Catherine – Brush Creek
Black, Cleo – Columbia, Fillmore, Gosport
Black, Daisy – Marion, Silver Grove West, Valley, Fillmore, Gosport
Black, Edna – Maple Grove
Black, Elizabeth – Iola
Black, Hallie – Springdale, Hawkeye
Black, Janie – Spring Hill
Black, Jennie – Hazel Ridge
Black, Joye – Horstman, Maple Grove, Salem, Union (U), Elm Grove, Fillmore, Gosport
Black, Kate – Elm Grove
Black, Miss Mary E. – Pleasant Ridge (K)
Blackman, Miss Elizabeth – McMillan North
Blackman, Mrs. Mary – Simmons, Buckeye, White Breast
Blackman, Mrs. – Rising Star
Blain, Miss D. – Core
Blair, Emma – Franklin Center
Blair, Ve Lola – Fairview (C), Union (C), Vigilance, Indiana, Springfield, Bunker Hill (K), Pleasant Ridge (K), Black Oak
Blake, Beulah – O.K.
Blake, Miss Inez M. – Pleasant Ridge (K)
Blakely, Mr. – Otley
Blanche, Sister Mary – Chicago
Blom, Marjorie – Bend, Fair Oak
Blue, Violet – Liberty (W)
Bogaard, Leona – Union (C), Shiloh, Richland

Bogaard, Mabel – European # 1, Richland
Boland, Katherine – Amsterdam West, Plainview, Valley
Bone, Lou – Pleasant Ridge (K)
Bone, Walter – Burr Oak, Scott, Blaine
Bonebrake, Katie – Fillmore
Bonebrake, G. E. – Elm Grove
Bonifield, Forest D. – Highland, Georgia Ridge, Liberty (W)
Bonifield, Pearl – Eureka, Fairview (C), Fairview (D), Flagler, Salem, Washington (K)
Bookman, Helen – Amsterdam East
Boot, Marjorie – Richland
Booth, Lucy – Indiana
Bootsma, Bessie – Silver Grove West
Bootsma, Helene – Amsterdam East, Pleasant Grove (LP), White Breast
Borden, Blanche – Maple Grove, West Pella
Bos, Beulahdean – Richland
Bos, Garrett – Amsterdam West, Valley, Liberty (S)
Boswell, Iscle – Horstman, Hazel Ridge
Boswell, Nora – Plainview
Bourek, Esther Brown – Dallas Center
Boven, Blanche – Elm Grove
Bowens, Gladys – Fairview (R)
Bowery, Gladys – Caloma, Liberty (K)
Bowman, Evelyn – Flagler, Flagler South
Bowman, Hilda L. – Brownlee, Lincoln North, Flagler South
Boyd, Betty Lou – Dallas Center
Boydston, Mella – Liberty (K)
Boydston, Miss – Fairview (K)
Boyston, Nellie – New Albany
Boylau, Martha – Victory
Braam, Lena – Bunker Hill (L)
Brack, Nellie – Amsterdam West
Braden, Nellie – Elm Grove
Brady, James – Thorntown
Brady, Mrs. – Pleasantville South
Brager, Ella – Porterville North
Brass, James – European #2
Braun, Irmagarde – Caloma, Elm Ridge, Flagler South, Scott
Brauner, Myrtle – Freedom, Washington (W)
Brause, Anna – Burch
Brause, Fern – Scott, Valley at Percy
Brees, Ada – Elm Grove
Breese, Olive – Georgia Ridge, Weston, Pleasant Valley
Bremmer, Dora – European #3
Brenman, C. M. – Cedar Valley (I)
Brenna, Charles – Cedar Valley (I)
Brennan, A.C. – Cedar Valley (I), Willow Grove

Brennan, Beatrice – Coal Ridge (I)
Brennan, Mrs. Charles – Coal Ridge (I)
Brennan, Conner – Prairie College, Shiloh
Brennan, Connie – Scott
Brennan, Kate – West Bethel, Empire, Cedar Valley (I), Round Grove, Robuck, Scott, Victory
Brennan, Paul – Oak Ridge
Brennan, Tom – Round Grove
Brenniman, Bertha – Black Oak
Brewer, W – Sunnyside
Bridges, Cora – Cedar Valley (I), Springfield
Bridges, Miss Colleen – Union (C)
Bridges, Mary – Victory
Bridges, Nellie – Sunnyside, Liberty (L), Bennington
Brightwell, E. P. – Newbern
Brillhart, Mr. J. W. – Flagler
Brillhart, Winifred – Fillmore
Brimmer, Matha – European #3
Britton, Hettie – McMillan North, Burr Oak, Elm Ridge
Brock, Velta – Fairview (R)
Brockett, Nellie – Valley at Percy
Brodigum, C. T. – East Bethel
Brodigum, Charlie – East Bethel, West Bethel
Boekenoogen, Louisa – Silver Grove West
Brooks, Bessie – European #1, European #3, Pleasant Grove (L)
Brooks, Frances – Franklin Center, Caloma
Brooks, Helen – European #2, European #3, Porterville North, Valley, White Breast
Brooks, Lois – Pleasant Grove (LP), Porterville South
Brous, Mede B. – Valley at Percy
Brouse, Anna – Coal Ridge (I), Willow Grove, Liberty (K), Bend, Mt. Vernon
Brown, Amanda – Georgia Ridge, Ladoga, West Pella, Blaine, Clark, Rees
Brown, Armanda – Buckeye, Pleasant Valley
Brown, Beatrice – Buckeye, Liberty Corner
Brown, Cluna – Union (W)
Brown, E.E. – Iola
Brown, Esther – Dallas Center, Fairview(F), Horstman, Marion, Newbern, Sunnyside
Brown, Frankie – Pleasant Hill
Brown, Jessie – Iola
Brown, Juanita – Horstman
Brown, Loretta – Fairview (K)
Brown, Miss Maggie – Fairview (K), Weston
Brown, Mrs. Wilma – Porterville North
Browne, Herman – Maple Grove

Brownfield, Merle – Marion, Black Oak
Brubaker, Estella – Round Grove, Elm Ridge, Rising Star, Scott, Washington (K)
Brubaker, Ivey – Union (C)
Brubaker, Maude – Vigilance, New Albany
Brubaker, Rosa – Clay Center, Vigilance, Carlysle, Liberty (K), Pleasant Grove (K), Summit
Brubaker, Stella – Fairview (C), Union (C), Indiana, Prairie College, Round Grove, Willow Grove, Pleasant Ridge (K), Scott, Liberty North (L)
Brubaker, Velma – Mt. Vernon
Bruce, Ethelle – Brownlee
Bruce, Catherine – Pleasant Valley
Bruce, Jessie – Red Rock
Bruce, Mrs. – Fee
Bruce, Vera K. – Pleasant Grove (S)
Bruere, Harvey – Des Moines Valley
Bruere, Mary J. – Des Moines Valley
Bruett, Mary E. – Salem
Bruge, Catherine – Marion
Bruitt, Jennie – Hazel Ridge
Brummel, Anna – Richland
Brummel, Caroline – Valley View
Brummel, Cornelia – Battle Ridge
Brummel, Elva – Plainview
Brummel, Marie – Cincinnati
Brunia, William – River Ridge East
Bryan, Charline – Gosport
Buckingham, Mammie – Oak Ridge
Bucklew, Eloise – Springfield
Bucklew, Esther – Burr Oak
Bucklew, Iantha – Dallas Center, Caloma, Pleasant Ridge (K)
Buckley, Laura – Highland, Buckeye, Bennington, Spalti, Thorntown, Clark
Buckner, Edna – Hawkeye
Bump, Gwyneth – Valley View
Bunting, Ruby – Simmons
Burch, Roxie – Spalti
Burdan, Blanche – Cedar Valley (I)
Burdick, June – Liberty (K), Washington (K)
Burggraff, Edith Cummings – Bunker Hill (LP), European #1, Valley
Burke, Ella – Des Moines Valley
Burkley, Bettie – Liberty (K)
Buckley, Laura – Clark
Burnett, Miss Addie – New Albany
Burnett, Elretta – Bend
Burns, Alice – Porterville North

Burns, Margaret – Battle Ridge
Burrows, Alice – Pleasant Ridge (K)
Burt, Miss Carrie – Fairview (D), Liberty (K), Washington (K)
Burt, Esther – Horstman
Burt, Nellie – Georgia Ridge
Burton, Miss Doris – Brownlee, Burr Oak
Burton, Edna I. – Columbia
Burton, Ethel E. – Virginia
Burton, Miss – Columbia
Bush, Anna R. – Empire, Fairview (K), Pleasant Grove (K), Burch, Fillmore
Bush, Byron – Caloma, Rock Island
Bush, Ethel L. – Pleasant Valley
Bush, Mabel – Chicago, Fairview (D), Hazel Ridge, Buckeye, Burr Oak, Rising Star, Salem, Washington (K), Collins, Pleasant Hill, River Ridge West, Fairview (R), Oak Ridge, White Walnut, Fair Oak, Union (U)
Bussey, Pearl – Liberty (L), Liberty South (L)
Butcher, Emma – Sunnyside, Clark
Butcher, Dean – Valley at Percy, Burr Oak (Sw), Oradell
Butcher, Mary – Oak Ridge
Butterfield, J. K. – Highland
Butterfield, L. – Lincoln (K)
Bye, B. D. – Salem
Bye, D. O. – Maple Grove
Bye, Will – Maple Grove
Bybee, Kathryn – Willow Grove, Brownlee
Bybee, Mildred – Willow Grove
Byram, Hollis L. – Porterville North
Byram, K. L. – Amsterdam West
Byram, Kenneth – Porterville North

C
Caffrey, J. P. – Carlysle
Caffrey, John P. – Fairview (K), Georgia Ridge, Burch
Caffrey, Juno – Fairview (D), Pleasant Valley
Caffrey, Laveda – Burch
Caffrey, Mary – Highland, Sunnyside, Fairview (K), Georgia Ridge, Stringtown, Burch, Oradell, Elm Grove
Caffrey, Nellie – Dallas Center
Cain, Nellie – Porterville South, Cedar Valley (L), Virginia
Cain, Ruby – Franklin Center
Cain, Zelma – Burr Oak
Calhoun, Betty Mae – Newbern
Cambrion, Echo – Hazel Ridge, Springdale
Cambrion, Fern – Hazel Ridge
Cambrion, Fran – Hazel Ridge

Cambrion, Leona – Springdale, Pleasant Ridge (K)
Campbell, W. D. – Caloma, Valley at Percy, Pleasant Valley
Camppen, M. C. – Fairview (D)
Canon, Miss – Fairview (K)
Carlson, Mary Osborne – Union (C)
Carnahan, Mrs. – Brush Creek
Carnahan, George – Battle Ridge
Carney, May – Hickory Grove
Carr, Lula M. – Otley
Carr, Margaret – Pleasant Valley
Carr, Nellie – Union (C)
Carrington, Mary – Shiloh
Carruthers, Dorothy – Simmons, Elm Grove
Carruthers, Frankie – Simmons, Liberty (W)
Carson, Anna – Horstman
Carson, Mary – Fairview (D), Liberty (W)
Carson, Maxine – Liberty (W)
Carson, Thelma – Pleasant Ridge (F)
Cart, Wilma – Wheeling, Burr Oak (Sw), Bunker Hill (Sw)
Carter, Frankie – Collins
Carter, Lizzie – Pleasant Valley
Carter, Marie – Dallas Center
Carter, Norma – Pleasant Hill
Case, Mont. E. – Core
Cash, Ruth – Summit
Castor, Mrs. Della – Shiloh
Caswell, Maude – Newbern, Mt. Vernon
Catrenich, Mrs. Betty – Scott
Caulkins, Opal I. – Fee, Fair Oak, Bunker Hill (Sw), Union (W)
Cayne, Marie – Pleasant Ridge (W)
Chadwick, Miss – Wheeling
Chamberlain, Ferol – Des Moines Valley, River Ridge West
Chamberlain, Freda – Spring Hill, Elm Grove
Chamberlain, Mrs. – Simmons
Chambers, Mamie – Fairview (D), Valley at Percy, Oak Ridge, Valley View
Charles, Catherine – Cincinnati
Charles, Mrs. Eileen – Pleasant Hill
Charles, Elsie – Otley
Charles, Mary – Liberty Corner
Charles, Mary L. – Pleasant Valley
Cheetham, Miss Ruth – Pleasantville South
Cherrie, Alice – Flagler, Flagler North
Childers, Nellie – Fair Oak
Chivers, Hazel – Hazel Ridge, Round Grove, Flagler, Scott, Shiloh, White Breast, Rees
Chivers, Mrs. Ruth – River Ridge West

Chrisman, Marie – Franklin Center
Chrismore, Irene – Brownlee
Chrismore, Mary Pringle – Round Grove
Christiansen, Mrs. Maud – Spring Hill
Churchilll, Miss – White Walnut
Claire, Dorothy – Union (U)
Claire, Estelle – Victory
Clark, A. D. – Lincoln (K)
Clark, Callie – Burch
Clark, Cassa – Sand Ridge
Clark, Charles – Clark
Clark, Dorothy – Eureka, McMillan North, Mt. Vernon
Clark, Elsa M. – Wheeling
Clark, Elsie – Conn, Ladoga, Clark
Clark, Frances – Willow Grove, Pleasant Hill
Clark, George – Union (W)
Clark, Gordon – Valley
Clark, Hazel – Freedom
Clark, Mrs. J. C. – Washington (K)
Clark, James – Lincoln (K)
Clark, Jessie – Bennington, Fairview (R)
Clark, Marjorie Agan – Gosport
Clark, Mary – Fairview (C), Georgia Ridge, Porterville North, Bennington, Collins, Otley, Burr Oak (Sw)
Clark, Mary C. – Bennington, Collins, Burr Oak (Sw)
Clark, Mary E. – Bennington, Collins
Clark, Mary J. – Bennington
Clark, Mattie Belle – Summit
Clark, Mollie – Clark
Clark, Molly – Georgia Ridge
Clark, Nettie Belle – Flagler South
Clark, Rhea – Hazel Ridge, Buckeye, Oak Ridge
Clark, Stella B. – Porterville South
Clark, Wanda C. – Fair Oak
Clark, Wilma – Pleasant Ridge (K), Brush Creek
Clarke, Daisy – Fairview (C)
Clarke, Pearl – Flagler South
Clatt, Ruby – Pleasant Ridge (W)
Cleair, Dorothy – Georgia Ridge, Maple Grove
Clevenger, Ulric – Brush Creek
Clifford, Elizabeth – Sand Ridge, Cincinnati
Clifford, Lizzie – Valley at Percy, Hickory Grove, Cincinnati
Cline, Blanche – Elm Ridge
Cline, Leona – Springfield
Cline, Lula – Pleasant Grove (K)
Cline, Ruth – Brush Creek
Cline, Sadie – Ladoga
Clingan, Bertha – Fairview (D), Coal Ridge (I), Bend, Blaine

Cloe, Alma – Spring Hill, Bend
Cloe, Maude – Liberty South (L)
Cloe, Rhea – Pleasant Ridge (K)
Clutter, Minnie – Silver Grove West
Coakley, Myrtle – Cincinnati
Cochrane, J. L. – Bennington, Valley at Percy, White Walnut
Coding, Arthur – Fairview (R)
Coffey, Clara – Burr Oak (Sw)
Coffey, Leo – Cincinnati
Coffrey, Rae – Oradell
Coffman, Barbara – McMillan North
Coffman, Mrs. Donna – Columbia
Coffman, Miss Fannie – Durham
Coffman, H. – Pleasant Hill (K)
Coffman, Tunnie – Amsterdam East
Cole, Clarence – New Albany
Cole, Cyrenus – Pleasant Grove (LP)
Cole, Samuel – Valley
Collins, Ella – Horstman, Fairview (F)
Collins, Fern – Bethel, Hazel Ridge, Maple Grove, Elm Grove
Collins, Fran – Sunnyside
Collins, Grace – Caloma
Collins, Izah – Flagler North, Mt. Vernon
Collins, J. – Round Grove
Collins, J. W. – Gosport
Collins, Wilbur – Union (C)
Columba, Sister M. – Chicago
Colyn, Evelyn – Bennington
Colyn, Minnie – Amsterdam East
Comer, Lois – Porterville South
Comer, Lola – Richland
Compton F. M. – Pleasantville North
Compton, Permella – European #1, Porterville
Conant, Hazel – Eureka, Springdale
Concepta, Sister Mary – Chicago
Conn, A. F. – Cedar Valley (I)
Conn, Mrs. – Fairview (K)
Conn, Sarah – Carlysle, Ladoga
Connaway, Mary – River Ridge East
Conner, Alice – Collins
Conner, Junior – Bethel
Conny, T. L. – Mt. Vernon
Conrey, C. W. – Black Oak
Conrey, Charles W. – Spring Hill, Burr Oak (Sw)
Conrey, Charlie – Liberty (L)
Conrey, E. A. – Red Rock
Conrey, Francis – McMillan North, Buckeye, Elm Ridge, Bend

Conrey, Mrs. Frank – New Albany
Conrey, Grace – Bend, Elm Grove
Conrey, T. L. – Liberty (K), Black Oak, Shiloh
Conrey, W. G. – Pleasant Ridge (K)
Conrey, W. H. – Elm Grove, New Albany
Conrey, Willie – Pleasant Ridge (K)
Conroy, H. F. – Gosport
Conway Grace – Horstman, Sunnyside
Conway, Maggie – Fairview (K)
Conway Margaret – Franklin Center, Georgia Ridge, Stringtown, Burch
Conway, Martha – Highland, Fairview (K), Clark
Cook, Mrs. C. P. – Otley
Cook, Mable – European #3
Cook, Mrs. O. P. – Summit
Cook, Ruby – Liberty Corner, Liberty (S)
Cookley, Kate – European #1
Cooley, Twylah – Iola, Clay Center
Coon, Jennie – Bethel
Coons, Ella – Robuck
Cooper, Bonnie – Des Moines Valley
Cooper, Carolyn – Spring Hill
Cooper, Florence – Burch
Cooper, Mrs. Hazel – Collins
Cooper, Helen – Fairview (C), Freedom, Sunnyside, Bend, Fairview (P), Columbia
Cooper, Mrs. Jean – Simmons, Elm Ridge, Maple Grove
Cooper, Mae – White Breast
Cooper, Maggie – Des Moines Valley, Elm Ridge, Valley, Bennington, Pleasant Hill, Oak Ridge, Otley, Rees
Cooper, Marjorie – Bethel, Horstman, Hazel Ridge, Springfield, European #1, European #2, Black Oak, Fair Oak, Pleasant Grove (S), Gosport
Cooper, Miss – Mt. Vernon
Cooper, Nellie – Clay Center, LibertyNorth (L)
Cooper, Thomas – Bethel
Cooper, Thos. – Cedar Valley (L)
Copland, Emily – McMillan North
Core, Alberta – Red Rock, Blaine
Core, Berneice – Oradell, Rees
Core, Elizabeth – Burch
Corey, Eva – Rock Island
Cornelius, Anna – River Ridge East
Cornelius, Edith – Pleasant Grove (LP)
Cornell, Dixie M. – Spring Hill
Cornell, Ella – Clark
Cory, Eva M. – McMillan North, Elm Grove
Coster, Bertha – Lincoln South

Coster, Lela – Rock Island
Coster, Leta – West River Ridge
Coster, Lizzie – Lincoln North
Cotter, Kate – Burch
Cottrell, Annie – Des Moines Valley
Couch, Ethel – Bunker Hill (Sw)
Couch, Jessie – Red Rock
Coulson, Frances – Pleasant Valley
Coulson, Helen – White Walnut
Coulson, Sadie A. – Pleasant Hill, Fairview (R)
Courtney, Miss – Georgia Ridge
Covey, Arlene – Liberty (K), Scott
Covey, Juanita – Brownlee
Covey, Maxine – Scott
Covey, Mildred – Fee, Washington (K), Red Rock
Covey, Vera – Iola, Fairview (K)
Cowles, Bess – Hickory Grove, Cincinnati
Cowles, Hal – Cincinnati
Cowman, Maggie – Valley at Percy, Oak Ridge
Cox, Elizabeth – European #2
Cox, Lonice – Rising Star
Cox, Louise – Sunnyside, Lincoln (K), Washington (K)
Cox, Mary – Rising Star
Crabtree, Vida Davis – Georgia Ridge
Craig, Alma Cloe – Union (I)
Cramer, Bessie – Bunker Hill (K)
Crandall, Kathryn – Elm Grove, Pleasant Ridge (W)
Crandall, Pauline – Marion
Crawford, F. E. – Simmons
Crawford, Frank – Fairview (P), Elm Grove, Gosport, Pleasant Ridge (W)
Crawford, Jo Ann – Richland
Crawford, Lula – Newbern
Crawford, Wilma – Fairview (D), Marion, Newbern
Crew, Miss Ella – Pleasant Valley
Crew, Mr. F. – Dallas Center
Crew, Fred – Liberty Corner
Crew, Miss – Spring Hill
Crippen, Vera – Union (C), Fairview (D)
Cristy, Lora – Cedar Valley (I), Coal Ridge (I)
Croft, Miss Eliza – Fillmore
Croft, Liza – Empire, Maple Grove, Columbia
Croft, Miss – Hazel Ridge
Crone, Florence – West Pella
Cronkhite, Mrs. Abe – Pleasant Grove (K), Blaine
Cronkhite, Augusta – Pleasant Grove (K), Pleasant Ridge (K)
Cronkhite, Eunice – Pleasant Grove (K)
Cronkhite, Grace – Fair Oak, Core
Crosby, A. H. – Des Moines Valley, Eureka, Carlysle, Bunker Hill (L), European #2, Porterville South, White Breast, Liberty Corner, White Walnut, Pleasant Grove (S), Core
Crosby, Albert – Durham, Vigilance, Newbern, Bunker Hill (LP), White Breast, Liberty Corner
Crosby, Alice – Liberty (K), Maple Grove, Washington (K), Coal Ridge (Polk), River Ridge East
Crosby, Dorothy – Victory Central
Crosby, Miss Ella – Bunker Hill (K), Liberty (K), Core
Crosby, Eleanor – Carlysle, Simmons, Liberty (K), Pleasant Grove (K)
Crosby, Lulu – Sunnyside, Bunker Hill (K), Maple Grove, Rising Star, Fairview (P), Mt. Vernon, River Ridge West
Cross, Nancy – Shiloh
Crouch, Josephine – Washington (K)
Crouch, Mrs. Lena – Flagler
Crouch, Mary – Buckeye, Maple Grove
Crowder, Maude – Pleasant Grove (K), Pleasant Ridge (K), Pleasant Grove (S), Clark
Crowdson, Miss Ollie – Liberty (K)
Crowley, Fannie L. – Horstman
Crozier, Mr. E. – Rousseau
Crozier, Elizabeth – Bend
Crozier, Ella – Bend
Crozier, Lucille – Bend
Crozier, Madge – Spring Hill, Bend
Crozier, Marilyn – Fairview (P)
Crozier, Otis – Georgia Ridge, Sand Ridge, River Ridge West
Crozier, Zelma – Fairview (C), Vigilance
Crue, Effie – Springdale
Crue, Ella – Brush Creek
Crum, Betty M. – Pleasant Grove (LP)
Cue, Ruby – Caloma, Round Grove
Culbertson, Mrs. Gladys J. – Horstman
Culbertson, Henry – Horstman
Culbertson, Rhoda – Highland, Willow Grove, Sand Ridge
Cully, Miss Eleanor – Liberty (K), Pleasant Grove (LP), Porterville North, Liberty Corner
Cully, Nora – Porterville
Culver, Edna – Fairview (K)
Culver, Ruth – Hickory Grove
Cunningham, Alleta – Lincoln South, Maple Grove, Spring Hill
Cunningham, Florence – Elm Ridge
Cummings, Edith – European # 1, Summit
Cummings, Faye – Eureka, Fairview (C), Iola, McMillan North, Bunker Hill (K), Pleasant Grove (K), Pleasant Hill
Cummings, Ida – Highland

Cummings, Ina – Victory
Cummings, Norma Jean – McMillan North
Curry, Mabelle – Union (C)
Curtis, Elsie – Prairie College
Curtis, Ethel – Pleasant Ridge (K), Fair Oak
Curtis, H.J. – Spring Hill
Curtis, H. T. – East Bethel
Curtis, Herbert – Pleasant Ridge (K), Pleasant Ridge (W)
Curtis, Hiram – Valley at Percy
Curtis, J.H. – Newbern
Curtis, J. T. – Fairview (R)
Curtis, Lee – Elm Ridge, Highland, Pleasant Grove (LP)
Curtis, Margaret – Highland, Flagler North
Cuthbertson, Margaret – Newbern, Buckeye, White Walnut

D

Daggey, Gloria – Plainview
Daily, Eva – Clay Center, Cedar Valley (I), Cedar Valley (L)
Daily, John – Flagler
Dainty, Fern – Pleasant Ridge (F), Flagler South, Victory
Dale, Paul – Ladoga
Daly, Elsie – Collins
Daly, Grace – Caloma
Dana, Miss A. M. – Plainview
Danihy, Nora – Conn
Danks, Margaret – Oak Ridge
Danks, Nettie – Pleasant View
Danks, Peter – Valley at Percy, Hickory Grove, Liberty Corner
Danks, Stella – Collins
Danthy, Nannie – Rees
Dark, Rhea – Dallas Center
Darnell, Alythe – Liberty (L)
Darnell, Anna – Victory
Darnell, Aura – Carlysle, Fairview (K)
Davenport, Altha – Buckeye, Plainview, Rees
Davenport, Lydia – Bend
Davenport, Miss Madge – Burch
Davenport, Maria – Plainview
Davenport, Mary – Iola, Bend
Davenport, Miss – Spring Hill
Davenport, Mr. – Otley
Davenport, Nora – Valley
Davidson, Clara – Black Oak
Davidson, Edres – Fairview (F)
Davis, Blanche – Brush Creek
Davis, Miss Charlotte – Flagler North
Davis, Cora B. – Vigilance, Pleasant Ridge (F), Black Oak

Davis, Dora – Indiana
Davis, Elizabeth – Victory
Davis, Eulice – Shiloh
Davis, Ferne – Cedar Valley (I), Cedar Valley (L)
Davis, India B. – Liberty (K)
Davis, Mrs. J. M. – Highland
Davis, Leah – Coal Ridge (I)
Davis, Mae – Carlysle, Shiloh, Bennington
Davis, Mae Ida – Elm Ridge
Davis, Mae Parker – Sunnyside
Davis, Mrs. Minnie – Flagler, Otley
Davis, Mrs. Minnie McDonald – Scott
Davis, Miss – Fee
Davis, Nora E. – Shiloh
Davis, Nora F. – Clay Center, Vigilance
Davis, Ollie – Fairview (C)
Davis, Ruby – Fairview (P), River Ridge West
Davis, Vida – Maple Grove, Clark
Davis, Virgie – Victory
Dawson, Edith – Brownlee, White Breast, Blaine
Dawson, Elizabeth – Liberty (W)
Dearth, Alice – White Walnut
De Bruin, Mrs. William – Plainview
De Bruyn, Mrs. A. A. – Amsterdam East, Silver Grove East
De Cook, Arie – Porterville South
De Cook, Cornelia – Plainview
De Cook, John P. – Valley
De Graff, Bernice – Pleasant Hill, Fair Oak
De Haai, Hazel – Valley at Percy
De Haai, Mrs. Helen Shaffer – Fairview (R)
De Haai, Myrtle – Pleasant Grove (LP)
De Haan, Ada – Eureka, Pleasant Grove (LP)
De Haan, Anna – Amsterdam East, Plainview, Valley
De Haan, Jennie – Bunker Hill (LP)
De Haan, Kate – Plainview
De Heer, Mrs. Opal – Bunker Hill (LP), West Pella, Union (U)
De Joode, Mrs. Evelyn – McMillan North
De Jong, Edna – Valley, Liberty (S)
De Jong, Janet M. – Porterville North
De Jong, Jeanette – Sand Ridge
De Jong, Mabel – European #2
De Kock, Eva Mae – Liberty Corner
De Long, Allen – Porterville North
De Moss, Alta – Union (W)
De Moss, Miss Maggie – Elm Grove, Fillmore, New Albany
De Nooy, Lena – European #1
De Pringer, Mrs. Lillian – Porterville North

De Pringer, Velma – Amsterdam West
De Raat, Maud – Round Grove, Elm Ridge, Salem, Gosport
De Ronde, Mrs. Margaret – Sand Ridge
De Vany, Stella – Bennington
De Viny, J.R. – Flagler, Burr Oak (Sw), Bunker Hill (Sw)
De Viny, Ross – Conn, Hawkeye, Bunker Hill (Sw), West Pella, Oradell
De Vries, Agnes – European #3
De Vries, Leona – European #2
De Wit, Tillie – Amsterdam West, Plainview
De Witt, Cleo – Pleasant Ridge
De Witt, Mrs. Emily – Clay Center, Eureka
De Witt, Mabel – Clay Center, Spalti, Bend, Fillmore, Gosport, New Albany, Pleasant Ridge (W)
De Witt, Musa – Weston
De Witt, Roxie – Ladoga, Spalti, Stringtown, Weston, Wheeling
De Witt, Tomie – Conn, Ladoga, Stringtown
De Zwarte, Lorene – Washington (K)
Decker, Ella – Iola, Bunker Hill (K), Rising Star, Bend, Fairview (P)
Deitrick, Faye – Freedom
Deitrick, Wanda C. – Fair Oak
Dekker, Jeanette – Silver Grove West
Delaplane, Mrs. Jennie – Iola
Den Adel, Edward – European #1, Porterville North
Den Beston, Betty Vriezelaar – East River Ridge
Den Burger, Margaret – Bunker Hill (LP)
Den Hartog, Janet – European #1, European #2, European #3, Brush Creek
Dennison, Bernice – New Albany
Dennison, Grace – Flagler North
Dennison, Marjorie – Gosport
Dennison, Mildred – Highland
Dennison, Ruth – New Albany
Denny, C. E. – Washington (K)
Denny, E.E. – Flagler North
Denny, Mr. – Spring Hill
Denotter, Miss Lois – Summit
Derry, Cleumeria – Fairview (K)
Derry, Kate – Highland, Burr Oak, Pleasant Ridge (K), Salem, Spring Hill, Pleasant Ridge (W), Union (W)
Deskin, Ethel – Liberty (W)
Dewey, Earl – Fair Oak, Rees
Dickenson, Adda – Rees
Dickerson, Aura – Victory
Dickey, Aura – Eureka, Buckeye, Liberty Corner, Otley
Dickey, Grace – Amsterdam East

Dickey, Mable – Flagler, Fairview (P), Brush Creek
Dickey, Minnie – European #2, Sand Ridge, Fairview (P), White Breast, Fair Oak
Dickey, Miss – Newbern
Dillon, Nannie M. – Liberty (S)
Dinwiddie, Kate – Fairview (D), Marion, Newbern, Indiana, West River Ridge, Red Rock, Fair Oak
Dinwiddie, Miss – West Bethel
Ditto, Ethel – Core
Dixon, Dorothy E. – Burch
Dixon, Eva – Rock Island
Dodd, Ella – Liberty (L)
Dolan, Mrs. Susie N. – Lincoln South, Porterville South
Donnally, Naureen – Hazel Ridge
Donway, Grace – Clark
Dooley, Mildred – Flagler North, Spring Hill
Doolittle, Laura – Flagler South
Doolittle, Miss – Plainview
Doran, Mollie – Vigilance
Dotson, Ione – Brownlee
Dougherty, Robert – Union (W)
Doughman, Burch – Union (C), Virginia
Doughman, Mrs. T. F. – Lincoln North
Douglas, Mrs. Faye – Clay Center, Vigilance, Washington (K)
Douwstra, George – Richland
Douwstra, Simon – European #2
Dowden, Ernest T. – Pleasant Hill
Dowley, Lorie – Highland (F)
Drake, Ollie – Ladoga
Draper, Grace – Clark
Dulen, Margaret – Rock Island
Dumville, Inez – River Ridge West
Duncan, Clinna – Fairview (D), Horstman
Duncan, Lettie – Rising Star, Blaine
Duncan, Miss – Salem
Dunlap, Helen – Rees
Dunlap, Miss – Otley
Dunmire, Julia – Gosport
Dunn, Ida – Plainview
Dunn, Mrs. Velda – Iola, West Pella
Dunnick, Gretchen – Liberty (S)
Dunnink, Anna – Plainview
Durham, Alice – Des Moines River Valley
Durham, Cora M. – Coal Ridge (I)
Durham, Florence – Iola, Porterville North
Durham, G. A. – Clay Center, Iola
Durham, Irene – Pleasant Grove (S)
Durham, J. P. – Iola

Durham, Kenneth – Iola
Durham, Mary E. – East Bethel, Iola, Amsterdam East, Porterville North
Durham, Mattie J – Iola, North Lincoln
Durham, Myrtle – Fairview (D)
Durham, Preston – Durham
Duvey, Earl – West River Ridge
Dyer, Thurza – Pleasant Ridge, Stringtown
Dykstra, Bertha – Plainview, Silver Grove East
Dykstra, Faye – Cincinnati
Dykstra, Mrs. G. – Carlysle
Dykstra, Gertrude – Pleasant Valley, New Albany
Dykstra, Helen – Cincinnati
Dykstra, Laura Fisk – Battle Ridge
Dykstra, Mable L. – Pleasant Ridge (K), Fairview (P)

E

Easter, Olive – Lincoln (K), River Ridge East
Eberhart, Fannie – Iola, Horstman, Hazel Ridge, Bunker Hill (K), Elm Ridge, Georgia Ridge, Salem, Blaine
Eberhart, Miss Freddie – Elm Grove
Eberhardt, Miss – Liberty (K)
Eddy, Rhonda E. – Bunker Hill (K), Thorntown, Core
Edman, Minnie – Fairview
Edmonds, Mae – Otley
Edmonds, Miss – Fairview (K)
Edwards, Mary – Otley
Eide, Fanny – Far Oak
Elder, Ellen – Bethel
Elder, Ethel – Coal Ridge (I), Gosport
Elder, Eva – Gosport, New Albany
Elder, J. W. – Dallas Central, Highland, Flagler, Battle Ridge, Gosport, Union (W)
Elder, Mrs. J. W. – Flagler
Elder, Mr. – Donley
Eldridge, Rose – Sunnyside, Springfield
Ellinwood, Mollie – Iola
Elliot, F. V. – White Walnut
Elliot, Mary – Mt. Vernon
Ellis, Dorothy Alley – Pleasant Valley
Ellison, Florence – Red Rock, Fair Oak
Elrod, Alice – Fairview (R)
Elwood, Freda – Liberty (W)
Elwood, Miss – Columbia
Ely, Mary Myers – Spring Hill
Emerson, Eula – Pleasant Grove (K), River Ridge West
Emerson, Helen – Lincoln (K), Washington (K)
Emerson, Norma Jean – McMillan North, Washington (K)

England, Elizabeth – Dallas Center
Entler, Mary – Collins, Oak Ridge
Erb, Beatrice – Burr Oak, Fairview (K)
Erb, Cloa – Springdale
Erb, Dorothy – Fairview (R)
Erp, Mariah – Valley
Erskine, Kate – Pleasant Hill
Ervin, Doris – Pleasant Ridge, Scott
Eshom, Myrtle – Cedar Valley (I), Shiloh
Essex, Laura – Burr Oak, Elm Ridge, Spring Hill, Washington (K), Washington (W)
Essex, Miss – Burr Oak, Coal Ridge (Polk)
Estella, Sister M. – Chicago
Estes, Caroline – Franklin Center
Etcher, Fern – Liberty (K)
Etcher, Guy – Robuck
Evans, Clare – Liberty Corner
Evans, Jennie – Des Moines Valley, Victory Central, Cedar Valley (I)
Evans, Lue – Des Moines Valley
Evans, Luella – Iola
Evans, Ollie – Willow Grove, Salem
Everett, Tessie – River Ridge West
Exley, Wayne – Simmons
Exline, Mrs. Rose Ellen
Eyerly, Miss Nannie – Cincinnati
Eysink, Lois Jean – European #3
Eysink, Norma – Georgia Ridge

F

Failor, Hazel Nell – Valley at Percy
Fairley, Geraldine – Caloma
Fairley, Ola – Collins, Hawkeye, Burr Oak (Sw), O.K., West Pella
Fairley, Phyllis – Union (C)
Fall, Bessie L. – Virginia, Otley, Pleasant View, Columbia
Fall, Minnie – Otley
Fassen, Joe – Pleasant Grove (LP)
Fasset, Mr. – Elm Grove
Fasset, W. H. – Elm Grove
Fast, Birdie – Highland, New Albany, Pleasant Ridge (W)
Fast, Ruth – Victory, Washington (K)
Fawcett, Fonda – Fee, Pleasant Hill, Valley at Percy
Faye, Ruth – Simmons
Feagins, Virgie – Liberty (K)
Fedro, Mary – Franklin Center
Fee, Blanche – Buckeye, River Ridge East
Fee, Edgar – Union (U)

Fee, Florence – Buckeye, Flagler, Flagler South, Maple Grove
Fee, Grace B. – Rees
Fee, Imogene – Rising Star, Columbia
Fee, Norma – Flagler South
Fee, Rena – Maple Grove
Feight, Doris – Horstman
Feight, Gertude – Springdale
Fellers, Miss – Iola
Fennema, Alice – Core
Fennema, Beatrice – Otley
Fennema, Bess – Pleasant Grove (S)
Fennema, Cattolina – Bunker Hill (LP)
Fennema, Gertrude – European #3
Fennema, Gladys – Pleasant Grove (L), Silver Grove West
Fennema, Julia – Pleasant Valley
Fennema, Lawrence – Silver Grove West
Fennema, Lena – Valley View
Fennema, Margaret – Amsterdam East, White Breast, Hickory Grove
Fennningkeit, Ida – Collins
Fenon, Ida – Washington
Fergison, Mabel – Horstman, Round Grove
Ferguson, Arminda – McMillan North, Pleasant Grove (K), Victory, Fairview (P)
Ferguson, Inez – Clay Center
Fernerod, Eunice – Sunnyside, Pleasant Grove (K)
Ferrume, Alice – Fairview (R)
Fetters, C. Ella – Newbern
Fike, G.A. – Pleasantville North
Fillman, Marie – Washington (K)
Finarty, Ruby C. – New Albany
Finch, Anna – Empire
Finch, Charles D. – Coal Ridge (I)
Finnesay, Katherine – Collins, Pleasant Hill, White Breast, Hickory Grove
Fisher, Ed. T. – Valley View
Fisk, Cynthia – Pleasant Grove (L), Valley
Fisk, Laura – Bunker Hill (LP), Otley
Fisk, Mae – European #3, Valley, Liberty (S), Richland
Fitzpatrick, Ellen – Elm Ridge, Flagler, Flagler North, Pleasant Grove (K), New Albany
Flanagan, Joy – Pleasant Ridge (K), Bend
Flanders, Hollie – Round Grove
Flanders, Laura – Brownlee
Flanders, Lora – Iola, Burr Oak
Flanders, Mary E. – Willow Grove, Prairie College, Spring Hill
Flanders, Ruth – Lincoln (K), New Albany

Flanegan, Kate – Sand Ridge
Fleming, Nellie – Bunker Hill (Sw), O.K.
Flesher, Myrtle – Springdale
Flesher, Nellie – Springdale
Fletcher, Miriam – Union (C), Pleasant Ridge (K), Richland, Elm Grove
Fletcher, Thelma – Dallas Center
Flockhart, Lillian – Rees
Floreberta, Sister M. – Chicago
Foot, Miss Maggie – Hickory Grove
Ford, Anita – Otley
Ford, Eva – Franklin Center, Simmons
Forgery, Mrs. Albert – Prairie College
Forgy, Dorothy – Fee, Blaine
Foridell, Grace – Burr Oak
Fornerod, Eunice – Mt. Vernon
Forsythe, Jankia – Otley
Forsythe, Minnie – Durham, Plainview, Otley
Foster, Dorothy – Springfield, Columbia, Liberty (W)
Foster, M.A. – Clark, Rees, Columbia
Fountain, Edith – Pleasant Ridge (K), Pleasant Ridge (W)
Fouts, Mable – Valley at Percy
Fowler, Winifred – European #2, Pleasant Grove (LP), Liberty (S)
Fox, Helen – White Walnut
Frank, Jas D. – Sand Ridge, White Walnut
Frazier, Adah – Blaine
Freel, Grayce – Conn, Hawkeye, Spalti, West Pella
Freel, Nadina – West Pella
Freeman, Frances – Collins
Freeman, Ida – Hazel Ridge, Bennington, Fair Oak, Bunker Hill (Sw), Blaine
Freeman, Olive – Fairview (F), Springdale, Collins, Oak Ridge
Freeman, Ollie – McMillan North
French, Beulah – Union (U)
French, Lilly – Pleasant Hill (K)
Frey, R. W. – Flagler North
Fridlington, Mrs. Daisy – Union (C)
Fridlington, Ruth – Fairview (C)
Frobosa, Elsie – Horstman, Pleasant Ridge (F)
Frost, Mary – Flagler South, Georgia Ridge
Fry, Clara – Hickory Grove
Fry, Tressa L. – Washington (K), Bend, Fairview (P)
Fuller, Miss Mae – Empire
Funk, Anna – Union (C)
Funk, James – River Ridge West
Furgy, Dorothy Mae – Fairview (C)

G

Gaass, Alice – O.K.
Gaass, Eleanor Ver Ploeg – Battle Ridge
Gaass, Ella – Liberty (W)
Gaass, Gertie – Silver Grove East
Gaass, Henrietta – Sand Ridge, Silver Grove East, Liberty (S), Valley View
Gaass, Minnie H. B. – Porterville South, Liberty (S), Pleasant Grove (S), Valley View
Gaass, Nellie – Otley
Gable, Pearl – Willow Grove, Round Grove
Galain, Jack – Oradell
Gardener, Eva – Dallas Center, Newbern, Fairview (K)
Gardener, Verna – Victory
Gardner, Brownie – Fairview (K)
Gardner, Jen – Brownlee, Mt. Vernon
Gardner, Marcia – Spalti
Gardner, Nellie – Highland, Burr Oak
Garnett, Gladys – River Ridge West, Gosport
Garnett, Ruby – Mt. Vernon
Garrison, L.A. – Bunker Hill
Gaston, Minnie – Des Moines Valley, Caloma, Burch
Gaston, Myrta – Caloma, Springdale, Franklin Center
Geelhoed, Nettie Lankelma – European #3
Gehring, Darlene – Horstman
Gelderblom, Fannie – Rising Star, Rock Island, New Albany
Gelderblom, M. E. – Rock Island
Gelderblom, M. G. – Liberty Corner
Gelderblom, Ollie – McMillan North, Highland, Elm Ridge, Rising Star, Rock Island, Shiloh, Coal Ridge (Polk), River Ridge West
Gerling, Eleanor – Rees
Gezel, Caroline – Valley, Pleasant Grove (S), Richland
Gezel, Elizabeth – Porterville North, Silver Grove East
Gezel, Gertrude – Silver Grove East
Gheist, Thane – Pleasant Valley
Ghrist, Ethel – Iola, Rock Island
Ghrist, Jennie – Shiloh
Ghrist, Laura – Maple Grove, Washington (K)
Ghrist, Mary – McMillan North, Elm Ridge
Ghrist, Thayne – Burch
Gibbons, Laura – Shiloh
Gibbons, Lulu – Newbern, Virginia
Gibson, Florence – Simmons
Gibson, Hazel – Iola, Union (C)
Gifford, Lela – Franklin Center
Gifford, Lizzie – Valley at Percy
Gilbert, Annette – Valley View
Gilchrist, Emma – McMillan North, Cedar Valley (L)
Giles, Mary – Marion
Giles, Rose – Simmons, Bend
Gill, Mabel – Pleasant Ridge (K)
Gillaspie, Grace – Conn, Hawkeye, Ladoga, Clark
Gillaspie, Lena – Burr Oak (Sw)
Gillaspie, Leona – Valley, Rees
Gillogly, Phyllis – Pleasant Grove (S)
Gilson, C. M. – Rising Star
Glass, Myrtle – Fairview (F)
Glenn, Alice – E. Bethel, Des Moines Valley, Flagler North
Glenn, George – West Bethel
Glenn, Jeanie – East Bethel
Glenn, Jennie – Fairview (C)
Glenn, Miss – Des Moines Valley
Goble, Pearl – Brush Creek
Godfrey, Leota – Pleasant Hill, Bend
Goering, Vera – Union (I)
Goering, Viola – Union (C), Dallas Center, Franklin Center
Goldizen, Mae – Des Moines Valley
Goldsmith, M. M. – Porterville North
Golfrey, Jean – Maple Grove
Goode, Mr. – Caloma
Goodenough, L. – Porterville
Goodenough, Lee – Georgia Ridge, Valley at Percy
Goodwin, Cora – Springfield
Gosselink, Anna Mae Vande Noord – Amsterdam East
Gosselink, Clara – Porterville North, Porterville South, Liberty (S)
Gosselink, Cornelia – European #2, Valley
Gosselink, Mrs. Dale – Sand Ridge
Gosselink, Elizabeth – Richland
Gosselink, Geraldine – Porterville South, Silver Grove West, Fair Oak
Gosselink, Mildred – Plainview, Summit
Goughnour, Mrs. Ruth – Rising Star
Graham, Miss Lena – Oradell
Grandia, Ardella – Plainview
Grandia, Beulah – Plainview
Grandia, Esther – European #1
Grandia, Junella – Porterville North
Grandia, Lois – Liberty (S)
Grandia, Thelma – Plainview, Porterville North, Silver Grove West
Grant, Alice – E. Bethel
Grant, Anna – European #1, European #2, European #3
Grant, G. – E. Bethel
Graves, Anna L. – Fairview (D), Newbern

Graves, Hella L. – Freedom
Graves, Idella – Rees, Union (W)
Graves Mr. – Rising Star
Graves, Nellie – Otley
Graves, Vera M. – Cincinnati
Graves, W. A. – Freedom, Newbern
Graves, W. N. – Newbern, Fairview (F)
Gray, Delia M. – Pleasant View
Gray, Lucie – Virginia
Gray, Mattie – Dallas Center, Horstman, Union (W)
Gray, Vera Lucille Beck – White Breast
Greenaway, Mary – Fee, Flagler North, Lincoln (K), Pleasant Grove (K), Salem, Spring Hill, Washington (K), Fairview (P), Mt. Vernon, White Breast, White Walnut, Elm Grove
Greenwood, Jonia – Wheeling
Greer, Mrs. Chester – Georgia Ridge
Greer, Ruth Perry – Georgia Ridge
Gregory, Duinie – Iola, Flagler South, Liberty (K)
Gregory, Mildred – Flagler North, Lincoln (K)
Griffin, Mrs. Charles – New Albany
Grimes, Cleo – Elm Grove, Gosport, Union (W)
Grimes, Inez – Salem
Grimes, Veneti – Pleasant Ridge (W), Union (W)
Groenenweg, Mary – Washington (K)
Grootveld, Esther – Plainview
Grootveld, Janet – European #3, Plainview
Grootveld, Helen – European #1
Grundman, Bertha – European #3
Grundman, Lydia – Silver Grove East
Grundman, Ruth – Bunker Hill (L), European #1, European #2
Guerner, Helen – Victory Central
Gullion, Stanley – Cedar Valley (I)
Gurney, Evelyn – Spring Hill, West Pella, Burch
Gurney, Mrs. Mildred – McMillan North, Victory Central

H

Haas, Lola B. – Springdale
Hackert, Edna – Porterville North
Hackert, Florence – Bunker Hill (LP), Pleasant Grove (LP)
Hackert, G. L. – Battle Ridge, Bunker Hill (LP), Porterville North, Porterville South, Valley, River Ridge West
Hackert, Garrit – Porterville South
Hackert, Govert – Eureka, McMillan South, Pleasant Grove (L), Pleasant Grove (S)
Hackert, N. – Liberty (S)
Hahn, Nellie – Sand Ridge
Haigh, Gertrude – Highland
Haines, Edith – Porterville South
Haines, Effie – Eureka, Shiloh
Haines, Mr. – Otley
Hakes, Mrs. Joan East – Elm Ridge
Hall, Clarice V. – Gosport, Pleasant Ridge (W)
Hall, Mrs. Cleta – Fee
Hall, Ida C. – Bethel, Springfield, Liberty (L), Liberty South (L), Elm Grove
Hall, Leota T. – Liberty (W)
Hall, Lizzie – Cedar Valley (I)
Ham, Avis – Fairview (R)
Hamilton, Anna Rose – Des Moines Valley
Hamilton, Charles – Indiana
Hamilton, Clara – E. Bethel, Coal Ridge (I)
Hamilton, Cora – Bunker Hill (Sw)
Hamilton, Edith – Salem
Hamilton, Effie – Pleasant Ridge (F), Union (I), Conn
Hamilton, Flossie – Valley at Percy
Hamilton, J. R. – Union (I)
Hamilton, James – Cedar Valley (I), Liberty (K), Liberty North (L)
Hamilton, Jennie – Oak Ridge
Hamilton, Jim – Cedar Valley (L)
Hamilton, Mary – Porterville North, Valley
Hamilton, May – Lincoln South
Hamilton, Ruth – Fairview (R)
Hamilton, Miss Tillie – Clay Center, Shiloh
Hamilton, Viola – Valley at Percy
Hamm, Mae – Pleasant Grove (K)
Hammer, Della – Pleasant View
Hammer, Florence – Sand Ridge, River Ridge East, White Breast, Brush Creek, Red Rock, Fair Oak, Oradell
Hammond, Miss Ella – Fillmore
Hammond, Miss Fannie – Clay Center
Hammond, J.J. – Pleasant Hill
Hammond, Mr. – Clay Center
Hamrick, Lorraine – Springfield
Hancock, Leila – Liberty (W)
Hand, Marie – Spring Hill
Hankock, Irene – Fairview (D)
Hanks, Miss Ida – Clay Center
Hanley, Alta – Flagler North, Blaine
Hanna, June – Victory
Hanson, C.A. – Ladoga
Harden, Gladys – Buckeye, Elm Ridge
Hardin, B. A – Donley, Fee
Hardin, Byron – Liberty (K)

Hardin, C.C. – Lincoln (K), Clark
Hardin, E. S. – Clark
Hardin, Faye – Springdale
Hardin, Marie – Oradell
Hardin, Nora – Thorntown
Hardin, R. A. – Highland, Fairview (K)
Hardin, Vera C. – Pleasant Ridge (K)
Harding, C.C. – Core
Harding, Genevieve – Fairview (D)
Harding, Nannie – Maple Grove
Harding, Nora – Valley at Percy, Spalti, Wheeling
Harkin, Beatrice – Chicago
Harkin, Hazel – Fairview (K), Georgia Ridge, Fairview (P), Clark, Burch
Harkin, Joy – Dallas Center
Harland, Mary T. – Chicago
Harlow, Charles – Shiloh
Harms, Effie – Shiloh
Harmsen, Hattie – Amsterdam East, Amsterdam West, BunkerHill (LP), Pleasant Grove (LP), Porterville North, Porterville South, Sand Ridge, Liberty (S), Richland
Harmsen, Jennie – Pleasant Grove (LP), Porterville North
Harned, May – Freedom
Harnet, Mary – Chicago
Harp, Della – Pleasant Valley
Harp, Ona – Pleasant Hill, Oak Ridge, White Walnut
Harp, R. A. – Pleasant Grove
Harrington, Edith – Clay Center
Harrington, Hattie – Des Moines Valley
Harrington, Helen – Eureka, McMillan North, Flagler
Harrington, Holly – E. Bethel
Harrington, Mildred – Highland, Flagler North
Harrington, Stella – Prairie College
Harris, Carolyn Mae – Otley
Harris, Mr. J. P. – White Walnut
Harrison, Ruth – Union (C), West Pella
Harsin, A. Jeanne – Victory
Harsin, Helen – McMillan North, Elm Ridge, Flagler
Harsin, M. – Flagler
Harsin, Mendela – Flagler
Harsin, M. F. – Iola
Harsin, M. V. – Liberty (K), Burch
Harsin, Mr. – Springdale
Harsin, Pauline – Clay Center, Elm Ridge
Hart, Dimmie – Fillmore
Hart, Sara – Shiloh
Hartness, Edith – Vigilance
Hartness, Edythe – Bunker Hill (K), Liberty (K), Scott

Harty, Nora – Fillmore
Hartz, Nora – Hazel Ridge
Harvey, Bertha – Clay Center, Rock Island, Valley at Percy
Harvey, Mrs. Dwight – Red Rock
Harvey, Miss Hattie – Clay Center
Harvey, Loureen – Fairview (C)
Harvey, Miss – Liberty (K), Liberty (W)
Harvey, Reefa – Des Moines Valley, Eureka
Harvey, Sara Jane – Red Rock
Hase, Mr. – Highland
Hasselman, Artie – European #3
Hatfield, Bessie – Rees
Hawk, Mrs. Ethel – Rock Island
Hawk, Ruth – Caloma, Sunnyside, Pleasant Ridge (K)
Hawkins, Beulah – Fairview (D), Buckeye, Shiloh
Hawkins, Jay – Liberty (W)
Hawkins, Selma – Freedom, Pleasant Valley
Hawthorne, Grace – Richland
Havley, Alta – Flagler, Salem
Hayes, Arnetta – Union (W)
Hayes, Arvilla – Willow Grove, Maple Grove, Oak Ridge, Elm Grove, Liberty (W)
Hayes, Bertha – Hawkeye, Stringtown, Thorntown
Hayes, Beulah E. – Brownlee, Fee, Porterville North
Hayes, Beulah Jones – Fee, Lincoln (K)
Hayes, Helen – Caloma
Hayes, Nora – Battle Ridge
Hays, Beulah – River Ridge West
Hays, Ethel – West Pella
Hays, Lillie A. – Union (U)
Hazen, Esther H. – Fairview (C)
Hazen, Hester – Fairview (D)
Heaberlin, Betty – Bend
Heaberlin, Pauline – Bennington, Collins
Headlee, Mrs. Bessie R. – Fairview (R)
Headlee, Mrs. Leo – Bennington
Heavener, Dora – Caloma, Sunnyside, New Albany
Hedrick, Floyd – Elm Grove
Hedrick, Lucille – Highland
Hege, Miss – Washington (K)
Hegwood, Leah – Franklin Center, Bend, River Ridge West
Hegwood, Lenora – River Ridge West
Hegwood, Marie – West Pella
Hegwood, Nora – Mt. Vernon, River Ridge East
Heinke, Minerva – Springdale
Heinke, Minnie L. – Freedom, Caloma, Fairview (F)
Heisel, Walter P. – Collins
Heki, Meda – Plainview

Held, Hazel – European # 1
Heller, Anna – Dallas Center, Springdale, Franklin Center, Pleasant Ridge (F)
Heller, Clara – Franklin Center
Helm, Elva – Valley at Percy
Henby, Bell – Eureka, River Ridge West
Henby, Billie – Oradell
Henderson, Miss Mae – Bunker Hill (Sw)
Henderson, Marie – Pleasant View
Hendrix, Vione – Fairview (P), Burch
Henning, Pauline – Highland
Henry, Claudia – Burr Oak, Valley at Percy, Fairview (R), White Walnut
Henry, Cora – Valley at Percy
Henry, Lizzie – Vigilance, Flagler North, Pleasant Hill
Herny, Claudia – Bethel
Herny, Kathryn – Amsterdam East
Herrick, Helen – Brownlee
Herschauer, Elizabeth – Dallas
Herweh, Adeline – Collins, Pleasant Hill
Hesselink, Elizabeth – Silver Grove West
Hester, Mrs. Mary – Franklin (K)
Heston, Doris – Columbia
Hetherington, Fern – Coal Ridge (I)
Hickey, David – Red Rock
Hiemstra, Effie – Elm Ridge, Valley, Valley View
Hiemstra, Emily – Plainview, Richland
Hiemstra, Leona – Porterville South
Hiemstra, Mable – Liberty Corner
Hiemstra, Margaret L. – Pleasant View
Hiemstra, Margaret M. – Bunker Hill (LP), Cincinnati
Hightman, Lizzie – Burr Oak
Hildman, Beulah – Sunnyside
Hill, Cleo – Spring Hill, Porterville South, Columbia
Hill, Cora – Burr Oak, Pleasant View, Elm Grove
Hill, Garneth – Fee, Fairview (P)
Hill, Harriet L. – Freedom
Hill, Loveda – Liberty (W)
Hill, Miss – East Bethel
Hill, Ruth – Eureka, Flagler, Rees
Hillabolt, Nora – Spalti
Hillo, Ruth – Elm Grove
Hilsabeck, Mrs. Thelma – Fairview (K)
Hindman, Helen – Flagler North, River Ridge East, White Breast
Hindman, Lelia – Flagler North
Hindman, Mary L. – Elm Ridge, Elm Grove
Hines, B.F. – Oak Ridge

Hines, Martha – Des Moines Valley
Hixenbaugh, Bessie – Fillmore
Hixenbaugh, Marie – Franklin Center
Hixson, Flossie – Marion
Hocking, Julia – Iola, Liberty (K)
Hodege, Mary – Iola
Hodges, Miss – Victory
Hodgson, Eula – Washington (K)
Hodgson, Irene – Cincinnati
Hoefker, Carl – Otley
Hoge, Eva – Brush Creek
Hogue, Eva – Elm Ridge
Hohl, Thelma – Fairview (C), Victory Central
Hoksbergen, Gertrude Den Hartog – Battle Ridge, Fair Oak, Pleasant Grove (S)
Hoksbergen, Henrietta – White Breast
Hoksbergen, Lena – Sand Ridge, Summit
Hoksbergen, Lucy – Battle Ridge
Hol, Miss Marie – Bunker Hill (LP)
Holden, Alice – Black Oak
Holdsworth, Reefa – Eureka
Holland, Hazel – Simmons, Summit
Hollister, Adelaide – Burch, Union (U)
Hollister, Alvira – Rees
Hollister, Olivia – Bunker Hill (LP), Collins, Valley at Percy, Oradell
Hollingshead, Miss Betty – Flagler North, Liberty (K), Maple Grove, Blaine
Hollingshead, C. M. – Liberty (K)
Hollingshead, Carroll N. – Mt. Vernon
Hollingshead, E. T. – Porterville North
Hollingshead, G. W. – Bunker Hill (LP)
Hollingshead, Gene – Liberty (K)
Hollingshead, Glen – Iola, Elm Ridge
Hollingshead, Jeanne Harsin – Victory
Hollingsworth, Mary – Franklin Center
Hollingsworth, Marie – Freedom
Hollowell, Cora – Round Grove, Shiloh
Hollowell, Flossie – Conn, Burch, Oradell
Hollowell, Will – Round Grove
Holst, Ricka – Porterville North
Holt, Clifford A. – Valley at Percy
Hon, Cora – Caloma, Franklin Center, Hazel Ridge, Springdale, Buckeye
Hon, Leora – Springdale
Hon, Mrs. – Spring Hill
Honnold, Ina L. – Bennington
Honnold, Ira – Liberty Corner, Pleasant View

Hoogenakker, Cora – Amsterdam West, Battle Ridge, Bunker Hill (L), Plainview
Hook, Ina – Thorntown
Hopaman, Allen – Bunker Hill (LP)
Hopson, Flora – Porterville North
Hopson, Nora – Amsterdam East
Horn, Van – Elm Ridge
Horney, Eva – Clay Center
Horsman, Mrs. Gail – Fairview (K)
Hospers, Anne – Silver Grove West, Valley
Hospers, Anthony – Battle Ridge
Hospers, Cornelia – Amsterdam East, Bunker Hill (LP), Silver Grove East
Hospers, Jeanette – Silver Grove East
Houck, Miss Minnie – Pleasant Valley
House, Margaret – Union (C)
Houser, Ada – Round Grove, Fairview (P)
Houser, Bertha – Caloma, Hazel
Houser, G. B. – Round Grove
Houser, Ira E. – Fillmore
Houser, Isa E. – Shiloh
Houser, Isa F. – Highland
Houser, Iva – Willow Grove
Houser, Mrs. – Clay Center
How, Helen – Fillmore
How, Lucille – Willow Grove
Howard, Ella – Newbern
Howard, Guy – Marion
Howard, M. J. – Pleasantville South
Howard, Wanda – Union (U)
Howell, Mary – Battle Ridge, Porterville
Howser, C. B. – Rising Star
Hoyt, Rolla – Shiloh
Hubler, Georgia – Elm Grove
Huckaby, Hattie – Collins, Hickory Grove
Hudson, Kate – European # 1
Huff, Jennie – Caloma, Amsterdam East, Brush Creek
Huff, Mrs. – Victory
Hughes Bertha – Fairview (C), Coal Ridge (I), Amsterdam East, Liberty (L), Virginia
Hughes, Dora – Pleasant Valley
Hughes, Edith – Fairview (P)
Hughes, Emma – Valley at Percy, Oak Ridge
Hughes, Fern Orcutt – Burr Oak
Hughes, Lydia – Collins
Hughes, Maude – Cedar Valley (I)
Hughes, Myrta – Prairie College
Hughes, Vada Jane – Bunker Hill (L)

Huigen, Miriam – Pleasant Grove (S)
Hukill, Echo – Caloma, Springdale, Cedar Valley (I)
Hukill, Maxine – Fairview (F), Pleasant Ridge (F), Sunnyside, Clark
Hukill, Oma – Springdale
Hunnerdosse, Della – Newbern, Caloma
Hunnerdosse, Gerald – Fillmore
Hunnerdosse, Glen – Horstman
Hunnerdosse, Olive – Dallas Center, Horstman, Franklin Center, Pleasant Ridge (W)
Hunnerdosse, Oscar – Horstman
Hunt, Bess – O.K.
Hunt, Carrie – Bunker Hill (K), Washington (W)
Hunt, Cordye – Elm Grove
Hunt, Florence – Caloma
Hunt, Mary – Collins
Hunt, Roy – Bunker Hill (Sw)
Hunt, Miss Ruth – Buckeye
Hunt, Mrs. Velta – White Walnut
Hunter, Jessie – Highland, Bennington, Mt. Vernon, East River Ridge
Hutchings, Eva – Black Oak
Hutchison, Anna – Victor
Huyser, Helen – Silver Grove West
Hyatt, Helen – Wheeling
Hyatt, Mattie – Columbia
Hyatt, Minnie – Fairview (K), Lincoln (K), Bennington, White Breast
Hyatt, Mrs. – Blaine
Hyatt, Nannie – Des Moines Valley, Union (I), Flagler, Liberty (K), Rising Star, Salem, Scott, Collins, Fairview (P), White Breast, Red Rock, White Walnut, Fair Oak
Hyslop, Hester – New Albany

I

Iddings, Jeanie – Stringtown
Iddings, Jessie – Stringtown
Iddings, Ruby – Stringtown
Immel, Nora – Highland
Ingle, Miss Pauline – Collins
Inskeep, Florence – Vigilance, Liberty (K)
Inskeep, Jennie – Blaine
Inskeep, Jessie – Rock Island
Inskeep, Maude – Fairview (C), Lincoln North, Freedom, Rock Island, Shiloh, Virginia, Collins, West Pella, Elm Grove, New Albany
Inlow, Vivian – Hawkeye

Iowina, Sister M. – Chicago
Irma, Mary – Carlysle
Irons, Mary – Freedom, Liberty South (L), Thorntown, Gosport, Liberty (W), Pleasant Ridge (W)
Irwin, Edith – Pleasant Grove (S)
Isley, Isabel – Des Moines Valley

J

Jabaai, Matilda – Oak Ridge, Summit
Jack, Edna – Cincinnati
Jackson, Mamie – Coal Ridge (I), Rock Island
Jacobs, Cora – Freedom, Georgia Ridge
James, Eva – Valley at Percy, Fairview (R)
Jansen, Mrs. W. A. – Porterville South
Jarman, Flora – Fairview (P), White Breast
Jarnigan, Marie – Cincinnati
Jemison, Anna – Virginia
Jenkins, Estella – Salem
Jenkins, Lucia – Rising Star
Jenkins, Mable – Burr Oak
Jenkins, Mary – White Walnut, Clark
Jenkins, Stella – Union (C), Liberty (K)
Jennings, John – White Walnut
Jennings, Lora – Pleasant Valley
Jennison, Clarence – River Ridge West
Jennison, Howard – Marion
Jesse, Georgia Jane – Conn, Ladoga, Pleasantville South
Johnson, Beatrice – River Ridge West
Johnson, Bertha Augustine – Iola, Columbia
Johnson, Edna – Horstman, Pleasant Ridge (K)
Johnson, Ella – Simmons, Fillmore
Johnson, Emma – Columbia
Johnson, Fay – Hawkeye
Johnson, Helen – Hazel Ridge
Johnson, Henry – West Pella
Johnson, Mrs. Jean – Des Moines Valley, Eureka
Johnson, Jennie – Durham, Lincoln South, McMillan South, Elm Ridge, Bennington, Bend, Mt. Vernon, West Pella
Johnson, Jennie K. – Elm Ridge
Johnson, Mrs. Mabel – Valley at Percy
Johnson, Mary – Virginia
Johnson, Maryellen – Fairview (C)
Johnson, May – Union (C)
Johnson, Miss – Mt. Vernon, Fillmore
Johnson, Nellie – Lincoln (K), Scott
Johnson, Nita – Brush Creek
Johnston, Emma – Union (W), Washington (W)
Johnston, Louise – Columbia

Johnston, Miss – Washington (W)
Jones, Betty – Brush Creek, Oak Ridge
Jones, Beulah – McMillan North, Union (C), Burr Oak, Pleasant Grove (K)
Jones, Clark J. – Gosport
Jones, Dorothy – Bunker Hill (Sw)
Jones, Emma – McMillan North, Vigilance
Jones, Ethel – Scott, Brush Creek, Red Rock, White Walnut, Blaine, Core
Jones, Eva – Otley, Pleasant Ridge (W), Union (W), Washington (W)
Jones, Florence – Valley at Percy
Jones, Katie – Caloma, Maple Grove, River Ridge East
Jones, Lulu M. – Shiloh
Jones, Marie – Fair Oak
Jones, Mary – Liberty (K), Fair Oak, Clark, Rees, Union (U)
Jones, May – Fairview (P)
Jones, Velta – Bend, Mt. Vernon
Jones, W. C. – New Albany
Jones, W. L. – Gosport
Jones, Wanda – White Breast, Valley View, Blaine, Rees, Union (U)
Jones, Wm. – Victory
Jordan, Ada – Spalti, Fairview (R)
Jordan, Ima – Weston
Jordan, Velma – Core
Judd, Miss Myrtle – Pleasant Valley
Juline Ellen – Fairview (F)
Juline, Grayce – Sunnyside
Juline, Rena – Franklin Center, Pleasant Ridge (F)
Juventine, Sister – Chicago

K

Kading, Carol – Pleasant Ridge (F)
Kading, Hazel – Franklin Center, Hazel Ridge, Springdale
Kading, Naomi – Round Grove
Kading, Ruth – Franklin Center, Highland
Kading, Vera – Hazel Ridge, Round Grove
Kain, Emma – Pleasant Hill
Kain, Marjorie – Valley at Percy
Kain, Mary – Fairview (R), Pleasant Valley
Kaldenberg, Alice Postma – Battle Ridge
Kaldenberg, Emma – Pleasant Grove (LP)
Kaldenberg, Esther – European #1
Kaldenberg, Theo H. – Pleasant Grove (LP), Rock Island
Kamerick, Gertrude Ver Steeg – Battle Ridge
Kamp, Loveda – Bend, White Breast, Bunker Hill (Sw)
Kamp, Zora – Oradell

Kane, Elizabeth – Fairview (R), Oak Ridge
Kane, Marjorie – Fairview (R)
Karns, Cluna – Burr Oak, Salem, Washington (K), Bend
Karns, Pearl – Pleasant Ridge (K)
Karns, Velta – Burr Oak, Elm Ridge, Maple Grove
Karr, Blanche – White Breast, Fair Oak
Karr, Ellen – Red Rock, Fair Oak, Liberty (S), Richland
Karr, Gladys – Liberty Corner
Karr, Grace – Brush Creek, Fair Oak
Karr, Leah – River Ridge West
Karr, Nellie – White Breast, Cordova, Liberty (S)
Karrbedding, J. M. – River Ridge West
Keables, Kate – Silver Grove West
Kearney, Elizabeth – Coal Ridge (I)
Kearney, Ella – Franklin Center, Springdale, Simmons, Clark
Kearney, Francis – Fairview (K)
Kearney, Margaret – Cedar Valley (I)
Kearney, Patrick – Cedar Valley (I)
Kearney, Tressa – Simmons
Kebiddle, Frany – Dallas Center
Keefer, Jennie – Bunker Hill (K), Elm Ridge, Flagler North, Flagler South, Washington (K)
Keefer, Letttie – Mt. Vernon
Keefer, Letitia – Elm Ridge, Burr Oak, Flagler North, Flagler South, Salem, Washington (W)
Keefer, Miss – Elm Ridge, Salem
Keene, Alta M. – Marion, Rising Star
Keifer, Flossie – Franklin Center
Keifer, Jennie – Lincoln (K)
Keithley, A. C. – Gosport, New Albany
Keller, Anna – Hazel Ridge
Kelly, Esther – Maple Grove
Kelly, Florence – Pleasant Ridge (F)
Kelly, Mary – Franklin Center, Empire, Burr Oak, Salem, Washington (W)
Kelsey, Algie – Richland
Kemper, Karl – Pleasant Hill
Kendall, Minnie – Vigilance, Bunker Hill (K), Flagler North
Kendall, Miss – Bunker Hill (Sw)
Kendrick, Hazel – Liberty (LP)
Kennedy, David – Lincoln (K)
Kennedy, Ethel – Thorntown, Core
Kenney, Mrs. Bessie Robuck – Shiloh
Kenney, Miss Coline – Marion
Kenney, Faye – Marion, New Albany
Kenney, Ruth – Georgia Ridge, Maple Grove, Pleasant Ridge (K), Fillmore, New Albany
Kentz, Jeanette – Richland

Keran, Minnie – Silver Grove West
Kerr, Gladys – Gosport
Kerr, Mrs. Leah – East River Ridge
Kersbergen, Bert – Battle Ridge
Kertz, Eunice – Round Grove, Willow Grove
Kester, Flora – Eureka, Burr Oak, Liberty (K), Elm Grove
Kester, Jennie M. – Vigilance, Prairie College, Liberty (K), Rising Star
Kester, Walter E. – Brownlee, Scott, River Ridge West
Keuning, Anna – Summit
Keuning, Celia – Bunker Hill (LP), Pleasant View
Keuning, Jennie – Pleasant View, Valley View
Keuning, Margaret – Amsterdam West
Kime, Marjorie – Caloma
Kimmell, G. W. – Plainview
Kimmell, George – Battle Ridge, Pleasant Grove (LP), Porterville North, Silver Grove West, Valley
Kincaid, Atha – Brownlee
Kincaid, Emmet – Coal Ridge (I), Prairie College, Simmons, Rising Star, Elm Grove
Kincaid, Vera – Vigilance, Elm Ridge
Kincaid, W. J. – Cedar Valley (I), Round Grove, Simmons, Shiloh, Columbia
King, Anna – Elm Ridge, Maple Grove, Pleasant Grove (K), Blaine
King, Emma – Pleasant Hill
King, Mary – Elm Ridge, Fee, Flagler North
King, Ora – European #1
King, Verna – Brownlee
Kingery, Miss Dena – Fairview (K)
Kingery, Marjorie – Pleasant Hill
Kingery, Marie – Flagler, Fairview (R), Pleasant Valley
Kingery, Marie Snider – Pleasant Valley
Kingman, Bess L. – Burr Oak (Sw)
Kinsell, Jessie B. – Collins
Kinser, Erma – McMillan North
Kirby, Mary – Springdale
Kirk, B. F. – Washington (W)
Kirk, B. S. – Pleasant Ridge (K)
Kirk, Dr. – Liberty (W)
Kirk, Miss Laura – Pleasant Ridge (K)
Kirkpatrick, Beulah – Flagler, Liberty (K), Rising Star
Kirkpatrick, Nellie – Wheeling, Bunker Hill (Sw)
Kirriday, Wm. – Chicago
Kirton, Mabel – Fairview (D), Newbern
Kise, Inez – Bunker Hill (Sw)
Kissinger, Lillian – Flagler
Kitch, J. W. – Shiloh

Klein, Almira – Valley
Klein, Lavina – European # 1
Klein, Mrs. Nellie – Summit
Klein, Rena Marie – Amsterdam East, Bunker Hill (LP), Liberty (S), Otley
Kleinendorst, Miss – Fairview (K), Otley
Kline, Mr. – Lincoln North
Klinker, Ernest – Des Moines Valley, Collins, Valley at Percy, White Walnut
Klyn, Mrs. Margaret – European #2
Klyn, Sara – European #2, Valley
Knolten, Gertrude – Caloma
Knowles, Evelyn – Buckeye
Kolenbrander, Rosetta Walraven – Battle Ridge
Koob, Mrs. Naomi – Valley
Kooi, Mrs. Ed – Bunker Hill (LP)
Kooi, Mrs. Esther L. – Valley
Kool, Betty Louise – Valley at Percy, Liberty (S)
Kool, Dorothy – Fairview (R)
Kool, Faye Wynn – Round Grove
Kool, Marilyn Nadine – Summit
Koons, Anna Slocum – Battle Ridge, Otley
Koopman, Lottie – Amsterdam West
Kruse, Mrs. Ruth – Marion
Kuhn, Stella – Thorntown
Kuiper, Ida – Amsterdam West
Kunkle, Charles – Simmons, Cedar Valley (I)
Kuty, Berneice – Columbia
Kutz, Eunice – Maple Grove, Pleasant Ridge (K), Collins
Kutz, Lois – Iola, Fairview (R)
Kuyper, Jennie – Plainview

L

Lacken, Myrtle – Salem
Lacy, Sadie – Plainview
LaFayette, Ina – Hawkeye
Lahman, Mayme – Fillmore, Pleasant Ridge (W), Union (W)
Laird, Phyllis – Cedar Valley (I)
Lake, Ora L. – Freedom, Pleasant Grove (K)
Lamb, Mr. D. W. – Lincoln North
Lamme, Maude – Lincoln (K)
Lammere, Maude – Elm Ridge
Lammie, W. H. – Vigilance
Lancaster, Helen – Eureka
Landhow, Helen – Highland
Lang, Maude – Freedom
Lang, Minnie – Marion

Langebartels, Clara – Caloma, Fairview (F), Pleasant Ridge (F), Collins
Langebartels, Nora – Franklin Center, Pleasant Ridge (F)
Langebartels, Sophia – Franklin Center, Hazel Ridge
Langebartels, Sylvia – Fairview (F)
Langerak, D. W. – Bunker Hill (LP)
Langerak, Ruth – Silver Grove West
Lanham, Alice – Sunnyside
Lanham, Miss Grace – Buckeye, Fee, Flagler
Lanham, Miss Helen – Flagler South
Lanham, Miss – Simmons
Lankelma, Peter – Silver Grove West
Larew, Catherine – Fairview (C)
Larew, Grace – Des Moines Valley, Eureka, Flagler North
Larew, Mrs. C. T. – Eureka
Larson, E. E. – Cedar Valley (L)
Larson, Ed – Liberty Corner
Larson, Ruth – Elm Grove
Lash, Nora – Des Moines Valley
Laske, Myrtle – Porterville South
Laughlin, Estella – Lincoln South
Laummer, Maud – Eureka
Lautenbach, Marie – Pleasant Grove (LP), Silver Grove East
Lautenbach, Sarah – European #3, Silver Grove East
Lawrence, Sister Mary – Chicago
Lawther, Verona – Oak Ridge
Layman, Mamie – Marion
Lazey, George – Valley
Le Cocq, Margret – Amsterdam West, European #3
Le Grande, John Jr. – Brush Creek
Le Grande, Mary – Pleasant Grove (S), Pleasant View
Le Grande, Nellie – Brush Creek
Leach, Hattie – Oak Ridge
Leamime, W. H. – Black Oak
Leavengood, C. H. – Washington (W)
Leavengood, Chas. – Dallas Center, Washington (W)
Lee, Doris – Fair Oak, Otley, Summit
Lee, Mabel – Liberty (W)
Leeper, Maggie – Brush Creek
Leffler, Christina – Iola
Leighton, A. – White Walnut
Lemme, Maude – Lincoln (K)
Lemmon, Aletha – Eureka, Pleasant Grove (K), Core
Lemmon, Hattie – Fairview (K)
Lemmon, Irma – Oak Ridge
Lemmon, Jennie – Fair Oak, Pleasant Grove (S), Core
Lemmon, Mabel – Fairview (F), Porterville South
Lemmon, MaBelle – Porterville North

Lemmon, Mattie – Brush Creek, Blaine
Lemmon, Oletha – Amsterdam West, Spalti, Burch
Lenning, Oletha – Elm Grove, New Albany
Lenzine, Dorothy – Springfield
Leonard, Arthur – Elm Ridge
Leonard, Lizzie – Franklin Center, Highland, Sunnyside, Pleasant Ridge (K), Spring Hill
Leonard, Margaret – Vigilance, Georgia Ridge
Lerr, Beulah – Burch
Leuty, Camille – Elm Ridge, Pleasant Grove (K), European #1, River Ridge East
Leuty, Jennie – Fairview (C), Pleasant Grove (K), Rising Star, Pleasant Hill, Valley at Percy, Blaine
Leuty, Mable – Liberty (K), Valley at Percy
Leuty, Martha – Core
Leuuvin, Marjorie – Bennington
Lever, Beulah – Fairview (K), Washington (K)
Levin, Marjorie – Pleasant Valley
Lewis, Lorna – Battle Ridge
Lewis, Roberta – White Walnut
Lewis, Sarah – Fair Oak, White Breast
Leydens, Joyce – Plainview
Liebert, Ceola – Iola, Rising Star, Silver Grove West
Lillard, Mrs. Elizabeth – Dallas Center, Caloma
Lindley, Fannie – Iola
Line, Mabel – Round Grove
Linn, Beulah – Liberty (K)
Linscott, Ruth – Dallas Center, River Ridge West
Lion, Mable – Springfield
Litchfield, Blanche – Hawkeye, Weston, Clark, Burch, Oradell, Rees
Litchfield, Miss – Oradell
Liter, M. B. – Porterville North
Liter, Mary Belle – Valley
Little, Lydia – Pleasant Ridge (K)
Little, Ruth – Buckeye
Little, Thelma – Gosport
Litton, Marjorie – Pleasant Ridge (K), Scott
Litton, Miss – Union (W)
Livingston, Miss M. E. – Flagler
Logan, Ethel – River Ridge West
Logan, Miss – Empire
London, R. W. – Highland
Long, Ada – Carlysle
Long, Carrie – Weston
Long, Evalyn A. – West Pella
Long, Georgia – Springfield, Rising Star, Shiloh
Long, Ida – Liberty (W), Pleasant Ridge (W), Union (W)
Long, Martha B. – Columbia
Long, Mattie – Freedom, Liberty (W)
Long, Maud – Pleasant Ridge (K)
Long, May – Marion, Shiloh
Loomis, Mrs. Bessie – Rees
Louster, R. N. – Pleasant Ridge (K)
Love, Alma – Pleasant Ridge (W)
Loynachan, Alberta – Round Grove
Loynachan, Neva – Round Grove
Loynachan, Nora – Elm Grove
Loynachan, Sarah Jeanette – Clay Center
Lubberden, Cornelia – Valley
Lubberden, Mrs. W. – Summit
Lubberden, Mrs. Wayne – Valley View
Lucas, W. H. – McMillan South, Lincoln South, Elm Ridge, Fee, Lincoln (K), Pleasant Grove (K), Cedar Valley (L)
Lukin, Lila – Caloma
Lukin, Vera – Franklin Center, Pleasant Ridge (F), Springdale
Lumn, Earnest – Springdale
Lundy, Beatrice – Liberty (W)
Lundy, Mrs. Mildred – Des Moines Valley, Coal Ridge (I), Brownlee, Elm Ridge, Fee, Lincoln (K)
Lundy, Mrs. Wm – Buckeye
Lusk, Edna L. – Collins
Lust, Opal – Valley View
Lyman, Betty – Burr Oak, Shiloh
Lyman, Cora – Carlysle, Coal Ridge (I), Victory, Liberty North (L), Virginia
Lyman, Sarah – Cedar Valley (I), Liberty (K)
Lyman, Tabitha – Shiloh
Lyon, Evelyn – Bend
Lyons, Nina – Clay Center

Mc

McArthur, Myrtle – Coal Ridge (I), Brownlee, Pleasant Ridge (K), Black Oak, Cedar Valley (L), Liberty South (L), Shiloh, Red Rock, Oradell
McAtee, Miss Daisy – Maple Grove
McBride, Nellie – Bennington, Valley at Percy
McCallister, Sara – Amsterdam East
McCarthy, Max – Newbern
McClark, Elsie – Bunker Hill (Sw)
McClary, Blanche – Pleasant Ridge (K), Shiloh
McCleary, Irene – Otley
McCleary, Zerilda – Brush Creek
McClelland, Caroline – Bunker Hill (K)
McClelland, Mrs. R. G. – Porterville North, Valley View

McClure, Hazel – Columbia
McClure, Helen – Columbia
McClure, Miss – Elm Ridge
McClymond, J. P. – Springdale
McClymond, Lottie – Des Moines Valley, Willow Grove, Browlee, Bunker Hill (K), Rising Star, Bend
McClymond, Lula – Pleasant Ridge (F)
McClymond, Mary – Iola, Burr Oak
McClymond, Miss – Burr Oak
McColleren, Mary – Flagler
McCollough, Gertrude – Des Moines Valley, Scott, River Ridge West, Blaine
McCollum, Isabell Hayes – Red Rock
McCollum, Mattie – Flagler
McCollum, May – Amsterdam East, Fairview (K)
McCollum, Phena – Iola
McCollum, Robert – Mt. Vernon
McCollum, Zella – Flagler, Flagler North
McCombs, Mrs. Gene – McMillan North, Victory Central
McCombs, Mary W. – Dallas Center
McCombs, Mrs. Mary – Coal Ridge (I), Liberty (W)
McConahey, Helen – McMillan South, Carlysle, Cedar Valley (I), Coal Ridge (I), Burr Oak, Black Oak, Brush Creek
McConahey, Junior – Bunker Hill (K)
McConeghey, Arlene – Pleasant Valley
McConeghey, Cecil – Pleasant View
McConeghey, Eileen – Brush Creek
McConeghey, Mable – Pleasant View
McConeghey, Ruth – Liberty Corner
McConnell, Faye – Red Rock
McConoughey, Jennie – Highland, Burr Oak, Victory
McCorkle, Cora – Newbern
McCorkle, Cordia – Horstman, Marion
McCorkle, June – Gosport
McCormick, Eulalia – Buckeye
McCormick, Lois – Elm Grove
McCown, J. S. – River Ridge West
McCoy, E. A. – Union (W)
McCoy, Molly – Collins
McCoy, Thelma – Collins
McCreary, Lillie – Columbia
McCully, Bonnie L. – White Breast
McDaniel, Mrs. Norma – Valley at Percy
McDillon, Nannie – Amsterdam East
McDonald, John – Hickory Grove
McDonnell, Darlene – Eureka, Pleasant Grove (S)
McDonnell, Marie – Horstman, Otley
McDonnell, Minnie – Fairview (C), Union (C), Scott, White Breast
McDonnell, Violet – Des Moines Valley, Brownlee, Elm Ridge, Flagler, Spring Hill
McDonnell, Myrtle – Horstman
McDowell, Arilla – Columbia
McDowell, Minnie – Horstman, Newbern
McDowell, Sevilla – Columbia
McEdrea, Nellie M. – Thorntown
McFarland, Hazel – Summit
McFreel, Grayce – Clark
McGinnis, David – New Albany
McGinnis, Ethel – Horstman
McGinnis, Mrs. – Gosport
McGovern, Nell – North Flagler, Pleasant Grove (K)
McGowen, Nell – Flagler, Washington (K)
McGraw, F. I. – Burch
McGraw, J. R. – Burch
McGraw, Robert – Fairview (P), Valley View
McGreery, Kathryn Wessels – Oak Ridge
McGrew, Annie F. – Columbia
McGrew, J. M. – Red Rock
McGrow, J. Roscoe – Fair Oak
McGuire, Murl – Liberty (K), Pleasant Grove (K)
McIntire, Caroline – Bunker Hill (LP)
McIntire, Effie – Willow Grove, Salem, Washington (W)
McIntyre, Laverda – O.K.
McKee, Miss Mollie – Clay Center
McKeigh, Mamie – Spring Hill, Liberty (L), River Ridge East
McKenny, Ella – Fairview (F), Hazel Ridge, Maple Grove, Pleasant Grove, Pleasant Ridge (K), Washington (W)
McKenny, L. H. – Highland, Valley at Percy, White Walnut
McKenny, Lizzie – Caloma, Franklin Center, Highland, Springdale, Buckeye, Bunker Hill (K), Burr Oak, Fairview (K), Maple Grove, Pleasant Ridge (K), Scott, Bennington, West River Ridge, Oak Ridge, Washington (W)
McKenzie, Eugenia – Fairview (C)
McKenzie, Flora – Fairview (C), Union (C)
McKern, Charles – Salem
McKern, Miss Lizzie – Gosport
McKillip, Ella – Union (C)
McKinney, L. H. – Valley at Percy
McKinnis, D. W. – Fillmore
McKinnis, Dave – Elm Grove
McLaughlan, Cecilia – Fair Oak
McLaughlin, Lou – Porterville North
Mclrea, Mrs. Nellie – Highland

McMannis, Ida – Willow Grove, Columbia, Fillmore, Gosport
McMichael, Amelia – Liberty Corner, Cincinnati, Otley
McMillan, Anna – McMillan South, Porterville North
McMillan, Fern – Cedar Valley (I)
McMullen, Annie – Prairie College
McMurphy, Mae – Georgia Ridge
McNeil, Mary – Franklin Center
McNeish, Mrs. Mabel – Marion, Liberty (W)
McPheter, Wm. – Bend
McQuerry, Emma – Burch
McQurney, Emma – Valley View
McRae, Alice – Valley at Percy
McRae, Alta – Bunker Hill (Sw), O.K.
McRae, Jeanie – Weston
McRae, Lulu – Caloma
McReynolds, Elsie – Otley, Summit, Valley View
McReynolds, Lillian – Otley
McReynolds, Ruby – Pleasant Valley
McTaggert, Blanche – Lincoln (K), Pleasant Grove (S)
McVay, Edith – Vigilance
McVay, S. – Clay Center
McVey, Olive – Fillmore

M

Maasdam, Sarah – European #1, European #2
Macbeth, Anna – Fair Oak
Mach, Candace – Liberty (K)
Maddy, Alice – Union (C)
Maddy, Berneice – Indiana, Fillmore, Pleasant Ridge (W)
Maddy, Miss Clara – Springfield, Bunker Hill (K)
Maddy, Ella – Round Grove, Victory, Liberty North (L), Shiloh
Maddy, Emma – Carlysle, Round Grove, Victory, Elm Grove
Maddy, Frank – Springfield
Maddy, Hollare – Spring Hill
Maddy, Marie – Eureka, Clark, Rees
Maddy, Mary – Elm Ridge, Washington (W)
Maddy, Maude – Rees
Maddy, May – Washington (W)
Maddy, Mildred – Blaine
Maddy, Miss Ollie – Elm Grove
Maddy, Pearl – Fairview (D)
Maddy, Roy – Round Grove
Maddy, Thelma – Lincoln (K), Rising Star, Fillmore, New Albany
Maddy, Zella – Victory
Madley, Wilma – Fillmore

Main, Wanda – River Ridge West
Mair, Mrs. – Iola
Maiter, Odessa – Eureka
Mallory, Gertrude – Burr Oak, Fillmore
Manix, Agnes – Empire, Fairview (K), Fee, Georgia Ridge
Manix, Alice – Freedom
Manix, Annie – Fairview (K)
Manle, Agnes – Hazel Ridge
Manley, Elsie – Coal Ridge (I), Shiloh
Mann, Josie – Lincoln North
Mann, Margaret – Pleasant Ridge (K)
Mann, Rose – West Bethel, Durham
Manners, Mr. B. – Georgia Ridge
Manners, R. M. – Flagler, Flagler North
Marble, Florence – Horstman
Marlky, R. G. – Rising Star
Marmon, Ina – Springfield
Marquis, Belva – Horstman
Marquis, Beulah – Horstman
Marsch, Florence – Porterville North
Marsh, Alta – Bethel, McMillan North, Springfield, Bunker Hill (K), Burr Oak, River Ridge East, Red Rock, Clark
Marsh, Ava – Union (U)
Marsh, Bertha H. – Ladoga, Thorntown, Weston, Wheeling
Marsh, Claudia – Highland
Marsh, Dora – Donley, Liberty (K), Washington (K)
Marsh, Dow – Highland
Marsh, Grace – Burch
Marsh, Ida – White Breast
Marsh, Iva B. – Pleasant Grove, Spring Hill, Conn, Stringtown, Wheeling, Core
Marsh, Marie – Spalti
Marsh, Maude – Wheeling
Marsh, Miss – Mt. Vernon
Marsh, Nora – Horstman
Marshall, Eva B. – Carlysle, Cedar Valley (I), Black Oak, Elm Grove
Marshall, Frances – Pleasant View, Valley View
Marshall, Lucinda – Willow Grove, Rising Star, Shiloh, Fairview (P)
Marshall, Lulu – Pleasant Grove (S), Richland
Marshall, Mae – Bunker Hill (LP), Hickory Grove, Pleasant Grove (S), Summit
Marshall, Mary – Pleasant Grove (S)
Marshall, Mrs. – New Albany
Marshall, Winifred – Bunker Hill (LP), Pleasant View
Martin, D. W. – Bunker Hill (K), Bennington, Wheeling, Burr Oak (Sw), Bunker Hill (Sw), O.K., West Pella

Martin, Loyt – Washington (K), Bunker Hill (Sw), O.K.
Martin, Maude – Black Oak, Liberty (L), Pleasant Hill
Martin, Miss – Fee
Martin, Pluma – Washington (K)
Martin, Reda – Porterville North, Red Rock, Rees
Martin, Sallie – Iola, Plainview
Mason, Clara – Dallas Center, Horstman, Spring Hill
Mason, Elsa – Liberty (W)
Mason, Elsie – Dallas Center
Mason, Etha – Horstman, Marion, Newbern
Mason, Fern – Union (U)
Mason, Laura – Dallas Center, Fairview (D), Freedom, Newbern, Caloma, Hazel Ridge, Sunnyside, Burr Oak
Mason, Rose – Durham
Masteller, Miss – Fairview (C)
Masteller, Sara – White Breast
Masteller, Sylvia – Spring Hill
Mathena, Ed – Newbern
Matheney, H. M. – Bennington
Mather, Mrs. C. W. – Virginia
Mather, Clara – Cedar Valley (L)
Mathes, Cora – Rock Island
Mathes, Johanna – East River Ridge
Mathews, Cora – Sunnyside
Mathews, Mary – Des Moines Valley, Lincoln North, Maple Grove
Mathias, Mabel – Cincinnati
Mattox, Clara – Sand Ridge
Maulry, Mrs. C. – Shiloh
May, A. J. – Flagler
May, Benita – Columbia, Gosport, Pleasant Ridge (W)
May, John – Cedar Valley (I)
Mayberry, Mrs. Bertha – Des Moines Valley
Meade, Elizabeth – Pleasant Grove (S)
Meek, Ada – Spring Hill
Meek, Mr. – White Walnut
Meek, Mrs. – White Walnut
Meekma, Marvel – Porterville North
Mendenhall, Edna – Liberty (W)
Mendenhall, Jo – Sunnyside, Brownlee, Salem, New Albany
Mendenhall, Marie – Clay Center
Menninga, Yella
Meppelink, Mae – European #3
Mercer, Howard – Highland
Merris, Ruth – Buckeye
Metcalf, June – Iola
Metcalf, Katheryne Ann – East River Ridge, West River Ridge

Metcalf, Marie – Georgia Ridge, White Breast, O.K., Burch, Union (U)
Metcalf, Mr. – Highland
Metz, Chester A. – McMillan North, Fairview (D)
Metz, Daisy – Hazel Ridge
Metz, E. L. – Cedar Valley (I)
Metz, Grace – Willow Grove, Fairview (P), O.K.
Meyers, Blanche – Cedar Valley (I), Cedar Valley (L)
Mick, Lilly – McMillan South, Virginia, Red Rock
Millard, W. J. – Elm Ridge
Miller, Alta – Eureka
Miller, Dick W. – Otley
Miller, Gertrude – Lincoln North
Miller, Icel L. – Freedom, Highland, Fillmore
Miller, L. May – Round Grove, Willow Grove
Miller, Lavada – Marion
Miller, Lena – Willow Grove
Miller, Lucille – Liberty (W)
Miller, Lulu – Pleasant Ridge (F)
Miller, May – Marion, Hazel Ridge, Elm Grove, Fillmore
Miller, Mrs. – Durham
Miller, Mrs. Myrta – O.K.
Miller, Nora – Dallas Center
Miller, Ruby – Lincoln South, Highland, Pleasant Ridge (F), Washington (K), Cedar Valley (L), Columbia, Union (W)
Miller, Sally – Porterville North
Miller, Mrs. Selma – Columbia
Miller, W. H. – Dallas Center
Miner, A. L. – O.K.
Miner, Ira – Oradell
Minor, A. R. – Freedom
Mitchell, Kenneth – Fairview (D)
Mix, Mary – Bunker Hill (Sw)
Moberry, Bertha – Victory Central
Mobswarth, Lois – Columbia
Moffatt, Christina – Black Oak, Shiloh
Moffatt, Marguerite – Bend
Mohler, Miss Almira – Hawkeye
Mohler, Mrs. Anna – Bunker Hill (Sw)
Mohler, Bernice – Liberty Corner, White Walnut
Mohler, Mrs. Clarence – Bend
Mohler, Daisy A. – Bunker Hill (Sw)
Mohler, Eleanor – White Walnut
Mol, Cornelia – White Breast
Momyer, Ella – Iola, Flagler, Pleasant Hill (K)
Momyer, Mary – Durham, Iola, Elm Ridge, Flagler North
Monahan, Adda – Porterville North
Moneysmith, Maxine – Maple Grove

Monroe, Anna – Coal Ridge (I), Indiana, Prairie College, Victory
Monroe, Fonda – Springfield
Monroe, Orah – Burr Oak (Sw)
Monroe, Pearl – Pleasant Grove (S), O. K., West Pella, Blaine
Monsma, Mrs. Dorothy Witzenburg – European #3, Pleasant Grove (LP)
Mood, R. J. – Dallas Center
Mooman, Pearl – Pleasant Grove (S)
Moomaw, Harry – Cordova
Moon, Elsa – Fillmore
Moon, Mrs. Etha C. – Fairview (P), Blaine
Moon, Mae – Prairie College, New Albany, Union (W)
Moon, Mildred – Gosport
Moon, Rickey – Round Grove, Simmons
Moon, Ruby – Wheeling
Moon, Wilma – Willow Grove
Moore, Bertha – Des Moines Valley, Lincoln North
Moore, Ernest A. – Indiana
Moore, Forest A. – Carlysle, Rising Star, Collins
Moore, Gay – Flagler
Moore, Mrs. Helen – Scott
Moore, Manford – Porterville North
Moore, Mark – Flager
Moore, Maude – Wheeling
Moore, Myrtle – Blaine
Moore, O.K. – Buckeye (K)
Moore, Obra L. – Vigilance, Freedom, Burr Oak, Fillmore, Union (W)
Moore, Vela M. – Fairview (R)
Moore, W. F. – Iola
Moose, Con – Pleasant Ridge (K)
Moose, Gay – Sunnyside, Rees
More, Myrtle – Buckeye
Moreyes, Ella – West River Ridge
Morgan, Allie – Pleasant Hill
Morgan, Eleanor – Sunnyside, Oak Ridge
Morgan, Fern – Franklin Center
Morgan, Henry – Valley
Morgan, Mrs. Lucille – Des Moines Valley, Eureka, Georgia Ridge
Morgan, Opal – Flagler North, Liberty (K), Victory, Mt. Vernon, River Ridge West, White Breast, White Walnut
Morgan, Ruth – Bennington
Morgensen, Lela Galvin – West Pella
Morris, Grace – Highland, Liberty (K)
Morris, Lizzie – Porterville South
Morris, Mabel – Liberty (S)

Morrison, G. W. – Fairview (D), Freedom, Liberty (W)
Morrison, George – Round Grove
Morrison, Maggie – Buckeye
Morrison, R. M. – Fee
Morrissey, Mary – Burch
Morrow, Kelly – Bend
Morrow, Lacy – Gosport
Morrow, Lara – Round Grove
Morrow, Larry – Marion, Gosport
Morrow, Laura – Newbern
Morrow, Mary – Round Grove
Morrow, Miss – Marion, Simmons, Gosport
Morrow, Nellie – Burr Oak, Liberty (K), West Pella
Morse, Mrs. Geneva – Brownlee
Mosier, Nettie – Shiloh
Moss, Effie – Fairview (F)
Mott, Catherine – Sunnyside, Brownlee
Mott, Evelyn – Fairview (C), Union (C), Victory Central
Mowery, Tina K. – Flagler, Rising Star
Muilenberg, Marie – Fair Oak, Otley
Mulby, Edith – Burr Oak
Muller, May – Gosport
Muller, N. F. – Liberty (K)
Mulley, Edith – Pleasant Ridge (K)
Mullins, Lola – Fairview (R), Liberty Corner
Mullins, Lucille – Brush Creek, Pleasant Valley, White Walnut
Mullins, Sadie D. – White Walnut, Summit
Mullins, Sadie K. – Round Grove, Fairview (R), Hickory Grove, Liberty Corner, Pleasant Valley, Otley
Mullins, Sarah K. – Pleasant Valley, Summit
Murdy, Ellen – White Breast
Murphy, Alice – Dallas Center, Flagler, Flagler South
Murphy, Dora – Liberty (K)
Murphy, Everet – Fairview (K)
Murphy, Lucille Grace – Union (C), Fairview (R), Fair Oak
Murphy, Mamie – Chicago, Fairview (F), Weston, West Pella, Blaine, Clark
Murphy, Mayme – Oradell
Murr, Donald – Columbia
Murray, Marjorie – Fairview (D)
Musgrove, Daisy – Fairview (C), Union (C)
Musgrove, Garnet – Union (C)
Myers, Lora – Caloma, Brownlee, Fairview (K), Fillmore, Washington (W)
Myers, Miss Mary E. – Liberty (K), Fair Oak

N

Nace, Augusta – Fee
Nace, Ava – Blaine
Nace, Gusta – Pleasant Grove (K)
Nace, Mrs. Gustin – Fee
Nace, Myra – Empire
Nace, R. C. – Buckeye
Nace, Prof. Robert – Liberty (K)
Neal, Edna – Buckeye, Fairview (K), Victory, Hawkeye, River Ridge West, Oradell, Gosport
Needles, Darell D. – Newbern
Neels, Antionette – European #1, European #2, European #3
Neels, Nellie – Silver Grove West
Neely, Inez – River Ridge West
Neely, Malvina – Fairview (C), Flagler South, Maple Grove, Rising Star, European #3, Fairview (P), Clark, Oradell, Union (W)
Neff, Hazel – Fairview (R)
Neifert, Lillian – Vigilance, Springfield
Nell, Hazel F. – Fairview (R)
Nelson, Eunice Jane – Columbia
Nemer, Frances – Pleasant Valley
Newman, Florence – Newbern, Liberty (W)
Newman, Gary – Newbern
Newman, Nellie – Dallas Center, Fairview (D), Marion, Newbern, Brush Creek
Newton, George W. – Caloma
Neyenesch, Hattie – Silver Grove East, Silver Grove West
Neyenesch, Helen – Des Moines Valley, Amsterdam East, Silver Grove East, Valley
Nichols, Bonnie Jean – Flagler South, Spring Hill, Fairview (P), River Ridge West
Nichols, Jimmy – Bend
Nichols, Susanna – Bend
Nicholson, Alberta – Round Grove, Springfield
Nicholson, Miss – Shiloh
Nicholson, Phyllis – Pleasant Ridge (K)
Nicholson, Ruth – Clay Center
Nicholson, Wilma L. – Clay Center, Vigilance, Shiloh
Nickeru, Miss Lizzie – Victory
Niemeyer, George P. – Battle Ridge, European #2
Nieuwsma, Mrs. Gladys Leusink – European #3, Sand Ridge
Nimmo, Letha – Pleasant Valley, Summit
Nittel, Genevia – Brownlee
Noah, Wilma – Union (C), Coal Ridge (I), Round Grove, Shiloh
Noe, Edith S. – Bunker Hill (K)
Noe, Edna S. – Rising Star
Noesges, Marguerite – Chicago
Noftsger, Gretta – Columbia, Fillmore, Pleasant Ridge (W)
Noftsger, Minnie – Columbia
Noftsger, Victoria – Vigilance, Brownlee, Brush Creek
Nolan, Mollie B. – McMillan South
Nolin, Elvin M. – Pleasant View, Valley View
Nolin, Floyd – Clay Center
Norman, Ernest – Weston, Pleasant Valley
Norris, Amy E. – Fairview (C), Fairview (D), Newbern, Springdale, Caloma, Hazel Ridge, White Walnut
Norris, Blanche – Springdale
Norris, Kathleen – Shiloh
Norris, Kathryn – Newbern, Cedar Valley (I), Round Grove
Norris, Nina – Porterville South
Norris, Susie – Vigilance
Nossaman, Allen – Porterville North
Nossaman, Miss Wilma – Porterville North
Nugteren, Lena – Sand Ridge, West Pella
Nutt, Kathryn – Burr Oak, White Breast
Nutter, Eva – Liberty (K), Fairview (P)
Nutter, Olive – Bunker Hill (Sw)
Nye, Beatrice – Core, Rees, Union (W)
Nye, Mabel – River Ridge East, Oradell
Nye, Orville – Pleasant Ridge (K), Sand Ridge, Cordova, Red Rock, Rees

O

O'Berg, Mollie P. – Collins
O'Brien, Catherine – Fairview (K)
O'Brien, M. J. – Oradell
O'Dell, Beryl – Clay Center, Des Moines Valley, Bennington, Mt. Vernon
O'Dell, Harold – Fairview (C)
Odom, Evelyn Stevenson – Flagler North
Oldham, Mrs. Minnie – Caloma, Union (W)
Oliver, Helen – Burr Oak (Sw)
O'Mella, Mrs. Florence – Lincoln (K), Fairview (R), Blaine
Onstine, William – Battle Ridge
Orcutt, Grace – HIghland (F), Otley
Orcutt, Susie – McMillan North, Freedom, Salem
Orenburg, Grace – Flagler South
Orr, Charlene – Brownlee
Osborn, Mrs. Helen – Fairview (C), McMillan North
Osborn, Mr. – Eureka
Oster, Viola – Pleasant Hill
Overton, Belle – Springfield, Prairie College
Overton, Mrs. Helen – Lincoln (K)
Overton, Laura Belle – Fairview (C)

Owens, Estalline – Pleasant Ridge (K), Bend
Owens, Etta – West Bethel
Owens, Neola June – East River Ridge
Oxenrider, Jennie – Newbern

P

Pace, Birdie – Elm Ridge
Pace, Miss Ella – Virginia
Pace, Miss – Durham, Elm Ridge
Painter, Dora – Pleasantville South
Palmer, Fessie M. – Clay Center, Buckeye, Pleasant Grove (K), Washington (K), Bend
Palmer, Frank – Liberty (K)
Palmer, Gracie – Caloma
Palmer, Ruby – Freedom, Empire, Washington (W)
Palmquist, Hilda – Eureka
Palmquist, Mabel – Coal Ridge (I), Bend, River Ridge East
Palmquist, Olive – Amsterdam East, Sand Ridge
Pannekoek, Grayce – Richland, Summit, Valley View
Pardee, Abigail – Pleasant Hill
Park, Lena – Valley at Percy
Parker, Alice – Liberty (L)
Parker, F.W. – Buckeye, Blaine, Pleasant Ridge (W), Union (W)
Parker, Lillie – Elm Grove
Parker, Mary – Round Grove, Porterville North, Liberty South (L)
Parker, May – Weston, Pleasant Grove (S)
Parker, Worth – Springdale
Parks, A. H. – Gosport
Parks, Ila – Fairview (D)
Parks, Mary – Eureka, Iola, Flagler, Flagler North, Washington (K)
Parnel, Villa – Hazel Ridge, Liberty (K)
Parson, Miss Josie – Fee
Passmore, Mollie – Pleasant Hill
Patch, Berneice – Caloma, Pleasant Ridge (F), Oradell
Patchen, Miss Connie – Fairview(R)
Patchen, Corney – Liberty Corner
Patchin, Camela M. – Red Rock
Paterson, Johanna – Flagler
Patrick, Miss Mabel – Victory
Patten, Mrs. Jennie – Vigilance, Washington (K)
Patten, Mrs. Jennie Huff – Amsterdam West
Patterson, Agnes – Thorntown
Patterson, Edna – Amsterdam West
Patterson, Grace – Brownlee, Mt. Vernon, Washington (W)
Patterson, Mildred – Union (W)

Patton, Ruth – Georgia Ridge
Paulding, Thelma – Columbia
Pearson, Mr. – Otley
Peas, A. T. – Dallas Center
Pegram, Blanche – Fairview (K)
Penland, Ruby – McMillan North, Horstman, Burr Oak, Liberty (K), Fairview (P)
Pense, A. F. – Pleasant Ridge (F)
Perkey, Mrs. Boyd – Oak Ridge
Perkey, Mrs. Mary – Red Rock, White Walnut
Perkey, Ruth – Brush Creek, Fairview (R), Red Rock, Union (U)
Perrin, Mrs. Jeanette – Summit
Perry, Blanche – Pleasant Hill
Perry, Mrs. Hazel – Dallas Center, Marion
Perry, Ruth – Georgia Ridge
Peterson, Miss Johanna – Flagler South
Phelps, Alice – Lincoln South, Flagler North
Phelps, Bernice – Spring Hill, Rock Island
Phelps, Clara – Virginia
Phelps, Clova – Carlysle, Indiana
Phillips, D. I. – Bend
Phillips, Nytha V. – Freedom
Pickett, Bertha – Oradell
Pierce, E. F. – Otley
Pierce, Mattie – Pleasant Grove (LP)
Pierson, Fannie – Pleasant Ridge (W)
Pierson, Lulu – Simmons, Columbia
Pietenpol, Henry W. – Pleasant Grove (LP)
Pinnick, Estelle – Summit
Platt, Jacqueline – European #3, Pleasant Grove (LP), Summit
Platt, Lynn – Battle Ridge, European #2, Otley
Platt, Sylvia – European #1, European #2, European #3, Plainview, Pleasant Grove (L), Porterville South, Sand Ridge, Otley
Plette, Henrietta – Silver Grove West
Plummer, Maude – Sunnyside, Pleasantville North, Spalti, Stringtown, Wheeling, Burr Oak (Sw), Bunker Hill (Sw)
Poe, Arthur – Union (C)
Poe, Pearl Bonifield – Fairview (C), Buckeye
Poffenbarger, Alta – Flagler South, Fairview (P), West River Ridge
Pomeroy, Ida – White Walnut
Pomeroy, Mrs. Leo – Oak Ridge
Pope, Mrs. Alta – Pleasant Grove (LP), Porterville South
Pope, B. D. – Liberty (K)
Porter, Alberta – Round Grove

Porter, Mattie – Fairview (D), Newbern
Porter, Roy K. – Fairview (D)
Porter, Ruth – Cedar Valley (I)
Postma, Bertha – Liberty Corner
Poush, Cleo – Fairview (D)
Powell, Minnie – Stringtown, West Pella, Rees
Powell, Violet Lucille – White Walnut
Powers, Mabel B. – Washington (K)
Prentice, Emma – Ladoga, Pleasantville North, Spalti, Clark, Oradell
Presser, Fannie – Horstman
Prewitt, Josa – Burr Oak (Sw), Core
Prewitt, Nora – Ladoga
Prickett, Emma – Caloma
Prickett, Gertie – Richland
Prickett, Gertrude – Elm Grove
Pringle, John – Fairview (K), Summit
Pringle, John W. – Indiana, Liberty (K), White Breast, Liberty (S), Pleasant Grove (S), Pleasant View
Pringle, Mary – Fillmore
Pringle, Nina – Freedom, Black Oak, Fillmore
Pringle, Nora – New Albany
Printz, Ione – Pleasantville North, Stringtown, West Pella
Printz, Myrtle – O.K.
Pritchett, Bertha – Sunnyside, Burch
Pritchett, Gertrude – Highland, Rising Star, Hawkeye
Profitt, Adah – Ladoga, Weston, West Pella
Profitt, Iva – West Pella
Pruit, C. S. – Plainview
Pruitt, Josa – Fair Oak
Pugh, Minerva – Amsterdam East, Battle Ridge, European #3, Sand Ridge, Silver Grove West
Putnam, Berda – Fee, Rees
Putnam, Floyd – Burr Oak
Putnam, Gerda – Liberty (K)
Putnam, Ida – Valley at Percy
Putnam, Lloyd – Fairview (K), Flagler, Georgia Ridge
Putnam, Loren – Liberty (K), Burch
Putnam, Lorence – Fee

Q

Quam, Mons S. – Battle Ridge
Quante, Annie – Horstman
Quick, Mabel – Pleasant View
Quiener, Gertrude – Oak Ridge
Quillen, Alice – Liberty North (L)

R

Radcliff, J. L. – Wheeling
Ragan, Irene – Brush Creek
Rales, Lillian V. – Springfield
Ramage, June – White Breast
Rambo, Alma – Otley
Ramsey, Bernice – Collins
Ran, Alice – McMillan North
Randell, Edith – Burr Oak
Randolph, G. T. – Core
Rankin, Cora – Carlysle, Indiana, Liberty (K), Rising Star, Scott, Spring Hill, Black Oak, Pleasant Hill
Rankin, Edna M. – Simmons
Rankin, Genevieve – Victory
Rankin, Helen – Union (C), Vigilance, Springfield
Rankin, Kenneth – Vigilance
Rankin, Lorraine Henrick – Clay Center
Rankin, Mattie – Union (C), Springfield
Rankin, Mary Woody – Bunker Hill (K)
Rankin, Maude W. – Victory
Rankin, Mella – Bethel, Eureka, McMillan North, McMillan South, Lincoln North, Lincoln South, Fair Oak
Rankin, Miriam – Springfield, Victory
Rankin, Miss – Otley
Rankin, Pauline – Clay Center, Victory
Rankin, Sylvia – Otley
Ray, Gladys – Bennington
Ray, Mabel – Eureka
Ray, Mildred – River Ridge West
Ream, Imogene – Rising Star
Ream, Marie – Victory Central, Vigilance, Victory
Ream, Pauline – Victory
Reasoner, W. J. – Freedom
Rebertus, Darlene – Pleasant Valley
Recktenwald, Wanda – Valley at Percy
Redding, Clara – Porterville North
Redding, Minnie – Durham
Redisill, Nannie – Pleasant Ridge (W)
Reed, A. I. – Hawkeye
Reed, A. J. – West Pella
Reed, D.S. – Hawkeye
Reed, Dorothy – Oradell
Reed, Gerry – Burr Oak (Sw)
Reed, Miss Gertrude – Valley at Percy
Reed, Johanna – Ladoga, Pleasantville North, Clark
Reed, Mary – Fairview (R)
Reed, Nadine – Mt. Vernon
Reece, Rena – Fairview (P)

Reece, Ruby – Highland, Flagler North, River Ridge West
Reed, Albert – Elm Ridge
Reep, Mrs. Norma – Des Moines Valley
Rees, Genevieve – Fairview (R)
Rees, Vane – Burch, Rees
Reese, Angie – Elm Ridge, Fee, River Ridge West
Reese, Genevieve – West Pella
Reese, Henderson – Brush Creek
Reese, Marcie Gardner – Round Grove
Reese, Winifred – River Ridge West
Reeser, Ruth – Coal Ridge (I)
Reeves, Alpha – Bennington, Oak Ridge
Reeves, Bessie B. – Oak Ridge
Reeves, Daisy – Franklin Center
Reeves, Edith – Wheeling
Reeves, Hazel – Fair Oak, Otley
Reeves, Prof. J. H. – Eureka
Reeves, Rena – O.K.
Reichard, Miss Beatrice – Clay Center
Reichard, Georgia – Highland, Flagler
Reider, Agnes – Cedar Valley (I)
Reins, Estella – Coal Ridge (I), Maple Grove, Core
Reiser, Hazel – Pleasant Grove (K)
Reiter, Frances – Franklin Center, Highland
Reius, Roman – Georgia Ridge
Relph, Susie M. - Columbia
Renaud, Clarence – Amsterdam East
Renaud, Gertrude – Amsterdam East, Battle Ridge, European # 1
Render, Agnes – Elm Grove
Reser, Ruth – Liberty Corner
Reuvers, Leona – Bunker Hill (LP), Valley
Reynolds, Birdie – Ladoga, Spalti
Reynolds, E. M. – Otley
Reynolds, Mabel – Springdale, Carlysle, Brownlee, Liberty (K), Maple Grove, Rising Star, Bend, Mt. Vernon, Blaine
Rhinehart, May – Hickory Grove
Rhinehart, Velma – West Pella
Rhynsbergen, Jeanie – Bunker Hill (LP)
Rice, Ethel – Union (C)
Rice, Dora – Horstman, Black Oak, Virginia, Valley at Percy, Red Rock
Rice, Hazel – Carlysle, Flagler North, Bennington, Pleasant Hill, Otley
Rice, Lon – Shiloh
Rice, Richard – Prairie College, Pleasant Ridge (K)
Rice, Rosa – Fairview (C), Iola, Weir City

Rice, Wilson – Shiloh
Richard, Arthur – Red Rock
Richard, Miss Mattie – Clay Center, Eureka, Pleasant Hill
Richards, Daisy – Hawkeye, Oradell
Richards, Grayce Ann – Iola, Franklin Center, Sunnyside
Richards, Lois – Collins
Ridenour, Anna – Lincoln South, Horstman, Carlysle, Prairie College, Simmons, Pleasant Ridge (K), Scott, Black Oak, Shiloh, Elm Grove, Washington (W)
Ridenour, Della – Victory Central, Round Grove, Salem, Fillmore
Ridenour, Ella – Vigilance
Ridenour, S. – Brush Creek, Pleasant Valley
Ridenour, Samuel – White Walnut
Ridlen, Anistacia – Mt. Vernon
Ridlen, Clara – Elm Ridge, Scott, Union (W)
Ridlen, Ruth – Caloma, Elm Ridge
Ridpath, Curtella E. – Fairview (P)
Rietveld, Alma K. – Bunker Hill (LP)
Rietveld, Antionette – Bunker Hill (LP)
Rietveld, Bertha – Fair Oak, Pleasant Grove (S), Pleasant View, Summit
Rietveld, Clarence – River Ridge West, Bunker Hill (Sw)
Rietveld, Delia – Des Moines Valley, Eureka, Iola, Amsterdam East, Amsterdam West, Silver Grove East, White Breast
Rietveld, Fern – Amsterdam East, Gosport
Rietveld, Jennie – Silver Grove West, Valley
Rietveld, Katherine – Liberty (S), Otley
Rietveld, Katie – Porterville North, Fair Oak
Riggle, Grant – Caloma
Riggs, Ada Mae – Marion, Caloma, Sunnyside
Riggs, Miss – Freedom, Simmons
Riggs, Rena – Horstman, Newbern, Hazel Ridge
Riggs, Rosella – Newbern
Riherd, Ruby – Brush Creek, Red Rock
Rinehart, Eva – Elm Ridge, Blaine
Rinehart, Flossie – Clark, Rees
Rinehart, Wilma – Buckeye, Blaine
Ringrose, Albertine – Sunnyside
Risse, Hal – Lincoln (K)
Risser, Hazel – Bend
Rithchie, Elizabeth – Caloma, Hazel Ridge, Highland, Sunnyside
Roach, Georgia – Liberty Corner, Pleasant View, Summit
Roberts, Della – Flagler, Coal Ridge (Polk)
Roberts, Elsie – Marion
Roberts, Edna M. – Fairview (F)

Roberts, Edna Neal – Elm Ridge
Roberts, Josephine – Union (W)
Roberts, Kathleen – Columbia, Pleasant Ridge (W)
Roberts, Miss – Dallas Center
Roberts, Nellie – Scott
Roberts, Prof. – Elm Ridge
Robertson, Belle – Eureka
Robinson, Betty – Pleasant Valley
Robinson, Ellen – Fairview (P), Fairview (R)
Robinson, Grace – Pleasant Ridge (F), Liberty (K)
Robinson, Gretchen – Collins, Pleasant Valley
Robinson, Jane Ann – Bend
Robinson, Maxine – Pleasant Ridge (W)
Robinson, Miss – Caloma, Fairview (K)
Robinson, Pearl – Pleasant Ridge (F), Flagler South
Robinson, Ralph – Simmons
Robison, Helen – Pleasant Grove (S)
Robuck, Bessie – Elm Ridge, Shiloh
Robuck, Jessie – Union (C)
Robuck, Virginia – Willow Grove, Buckeye
Roe, Fae A. – Caloma
Roff, Lorraine – Maple Grove
Roff, Velma – Brush Creek
Rogers, Jean – Union (C), Buckeye (K), Spring Hill, Cedar Valley (L), Hickory Grove
Rogers, Jessie – Collins
Rogers, Mary – McMillan South, Newbern, Empire, Indiana, Springfield, Victory, Shiloh, Fairview (P)
Rogers, Nellie – Vigilance, Cedar Valley (I), Highland, Round Grove, Willow Grove, Bunker Hill (K), Burr Oak, Salem, Victory, River Ridge West, White Walnut
Rogers, Miss R. F. – Rising Star
Rogers, Rachel L. – Union (I), Bunker Hill (K)
Rogers, Roscoe – Bunker Hill (K)
Rogers, S. M. – Carlysle, Prairie College, Simmons, Black Oak
Roland, Helen Hayes – Caloma
Rolfe, Bernice – Bethel, Virginia, Mt. Vernon, Blaine
Roller, Mary – Iola, Lincoln South, Highland, Prairie College, Elm Ridge, Pleasant Grove (K), Washington (K), Cedar Valley (L), Liberty North (L), Pleasant Valley, Core, Columbia, New Albany, Weir City
Roller, Miss – Rising Star
Romans, Will H. – Cincinnati
Romansis, Pearl – Pleasant View
Roorda, Dora – European #1, European #2, European #3
Roorda, Georgia – Eureka, European #2, European #3, West Silver Grove
Roorda, Joyce – Porterville North
Roorda, Marie – Amsterdam West
Roorda, Wilma – Eureka
Roose, Irene – Sand Ridge
Roozeboom, Minnie – Otley
Rose, Kate – Shiloh
Rose, Ruth – Union (C), Vigilance
Rose, Sadie – Shiloh
Rose, Sarah – Stringtown
Ross, Nellie – Battle Ridge
Roue, J.J. – Shiloh
Roush, Vada – Fairview (R)
Rouwenhorst, Bertha – European #1, Valley View
Rouwenhorst, Jeanette – Richland
Rouwenhorst, Johanna – Flagler, European #2, Sand Ridge, Liberty (S)
Rouze, A. W. – Burr Oak (Sw)
Rouze, Lloyd – River Ridge West, West Pella
Rovaart, Ethel – Amsterdam West, Valley
Rowland, Alta – Valley at Percy
Rowland, Cora – Shiloh
Rowland, Fern – Freedom, Scott
Rowland, Grace B. – Flagler, New Albany
Rowland, Grayce – Brownlee, Flagler
Rowland, Hazel – Eureka
Rowland, Helen – Vigilance
Rowland, Leona M. – Vigilance
Rowland, Mrs. Lillian – Vigilance, Victory
Rowland, Mrs. – Cedar Valley (I)
Rowland, Zella M. – Red Rock
Rowley, Emma – Weston
Rowley, Erma – Fairview (P)
Rozenberg, Miss Ida – Hazel Ridge
Rozendaal, Mrs. John H. – Richland
Ruckman, Della
Ruckman, Dora – Marion, Valley at Percy
Ruckman, Florence – Fair Oak
Ruckman, Julia – Union (I), Buckeye, Burr Oak, Liberty (K), Rising Star, Scott, Spring Hill, Victory, Liberty North (L), New Albany
Ruckman, Miss – Fairview (P)
Ruckman, Mrs. Nellie D. – Blaine
Ruckman, Ruth – Rees
Runnels, Minnie – Liberty South (L), Oak Ridge
Runyan, Willie – Shiloh
Rupalo, Miss Louise – White Breast
Ruple, Grace – Bethel
Rushing, Letha – Flagler South

Russel, Emma D. – Empire
Rutherford, Addie – Coal Ridge (I), Pleasant Ridge (K), Liberty North (L)
Rutherford, J. F. – Gosport
Rutherford, Miss Lottie – Liberty (W)
Rutherford, Mrs. – Bunker Hill (Sw)
Rutherford, Ora – Prairie College, Round Grove
Ryan, Olive L. – White Walnut
Rysdam, Miss Helen J. – Buckeye

S

Sammons, Ida – Fee, Ladoga, Weston
Sanders, Ella – Cedar Valley (L)
Sanders, Lydia – Vigilance
Sanders, R. A. – Round Grove
Sargeant, Wilma – Pleasant Valley
Sarver, Alta Miller – Eureka
Sarver, Berlita – Cedar Valley (L)
Sarver, Bertha – Clay Center, Fair Oak
Sarver, Bessie – Fair Oak
Sarver, Mary – Fairview (C), River Ridge East
Sarver, Pauline – Union (C), Fairview (C), Buckeye, Pleasant Valley, Red Rock, Fair Oak
Sarver, Percie – Red Rock, Fair Oak
Sarver, Ruby – Willow Grove
Savage, Clara – West Pella
Savage, Minnie – Fairview (C), Empire
Savage, Minta – Springdale
Saville, Melvina – White Breast
Savool, J. – Oak Ridge
Saxson, Miss – Caloma
Scales, Miss Alice – New Albany
Schakel, Grace – Liberty Corner, Cincinnati, Pleasant Grove (S)
Schakel, Norma – Amsterdam West
Schakel, Olive – Battle Ridge
Scarborough, Miss – Liberty Corner
Scarbro, Paul – Cincinnati
Schalk, Emma – Cincinnati
Scheele, Charlene – Scott, White Walnut, Gosport
Scheele, Gladys – Core, Union (U), New Albany
Schell, Mrs. Dorothy – Highland
Schippers, Joyce – Bunker Hill (L), Silver Grove West
Schippers, Mrs. Lena – Richland
Schmidt, Jessie – River Ridge East
Scholistica, Sister M. – Chicago
Schrieber, Rev. William – Horstman
Schroder, Mrs. Faye – Caloma

Schroder, Miss Zelma – Buckeye
Schuack, Fae – Hawkeye
Schultis, C. A. – Pleasant Valley
Schultis, Clarence – Rising Star
Schultz, Jeanette – Pleasant Hill
Schultz, Mr. – Rising Star
Schurbring, Lily – Porterville North
Scott, Abram – Liberty (K)
Scott, Edna Townson – Victory
Scott, Eva – Iola, Salem, Shiloh
Scott, Tracie – Oradell
Seaman, Ruby – McMillan North, Pleasant Ridge (K), Spring Hill, Blaine, New Albany
Seifken, Marilyn – Victory Central, Georgia Ridge
Sellers, Bertha – Hickory Grove
Sels, Arthur – Battle Ridge
Sels, Gertrude – Amsterdam West
Serena, Sister M. – Chicago
Sexton, Hannah – Empire
Shadle, Chris – Franklin Center
Shadle, John – Pleasantville South
Shadle, Miss – Pleasantville South
Shannon, Robert – Brush Creek
Shannon, Miss Rose – Shiloh
Shannon, Willard – Clark
Sharib, Mary – Flagler South
Sharon, Mary – Durham, McMillan North
Sharon, Meria – Virginia
Sharon, Myrtle – Clay Center, Iola, McMillan North, McMillan South, Shiloh
Sharpe, Edith – Hazel Ridge, Red Rock, Core
Shaver, Mary – Clay Center
Shaw H. – Porterville North
Shaw, Luella – European #3
Shawner, Maggie – Washington (W)
Shawver, Belle – Conn, Thorntown, Bunker Hill (Sw), Burch
Shawver, Jennie – Flagler South
Shellady, Miss – Brush Creek
Shephard, Martha – River Ridge East
Shephard, Mildred – Burch
Shera, Hallie – Blaine
Sherlock, Huldah – Flagler North
Sherman, Henry – Maple Grove
Sherman, Mrs. S. M. – Liberty (K)
Sherwood, Edna – Springfield
Sherwood, Martha E. – Flagler North, Victory
Sherwood, Mary May – Sunnyside
Shields, Marie – Sunnyside

Shinn, Airie – Liberty North (L)
Shinn, Katherine – Cedar Valley (I), Cedar Valley (L)
Shinn, Noel D. – Cedar Valley (I)
Shinn, Orrie A. – Prairie College
Shinn, Virgie – Franklin Center, Elm Ridge, Fairview (K), Fee, Flagler, Maple Grove, Spring Hill, Porterville South, Liberty (L), Bend, Oak Ridge
Shinlow, Suzanne – Fairview (P)
Shives, Bessie – Pleasant Ridge (K)
Shives, Dorothy – Gosport
Shives, Margie – Horstman, Fillmore
Shives, Mrs. Woodrow – Flagler North
Shivers, Dorothy – Fairview (F)
Shivers, Lena – Hazel Ridge
Shivers, Mary – Lincoln (K)
Shivvers, Grace – Caloma, Highland, Springdale
Shivvers, Mary – Highland, Sunnyside
Shoemaker, Marie – Burr Oak (Sw), West Pella
Shoemaker, Mildred – Bend
Shook, Miss Mabel – Round Grove, Pleasant Grove (K), Gosport
Shook, Maude – Highland, Burr Oak
Shore, Aletha – Fairview (D), Gosport
Shore, Mrs. Loveda – Liberty (W)
Shore, Luella – Caloma, Gosport
Shore, Marlene L. – Pleasant Ridge (W)
Shore, Raymond E. – Fairview (D), Columbia
Shovelain, Kathryn – Simmons, Fee, Rock Island
Shriner, Olive – Fee
Shroder, Marye – Cincinnati, Burr Oak (Sw)
Shultis, F. W. – Union (W)
Shutts, Mary – Pleasant Grove (S)
Shuy, Jean – Victory Central
Simbro, Cleta – Brush Creek, Liberty Corner
Simmers, Miss Hazel – Oak Ridge
Simmons, Julia – Georgia Ridge
Simmons, Mary – Round Grove, Springfield, Union (I)
Simms, Mary – Liberty (L)
Simpkins, Dale – Pleasant Grove (LP)
Simpkins, Jennie – Iola, Porterville North
Simpkins, Lydia – Pleasant Grove (LP)
Simpkins, Miss – Elm Ridge
Simpkins, Miss Pearl – Flagler, European #1
Simpkins, W.W. – Pleasant Grove (LP)
Simpson, Edna – Caloma
Simpson, Nettie – Iola
Simpson, Nora – Flagler North, Sumpter, Pleasant View
Sims, Alma – Silver Grove West
Sims, Mrs. Eulice – Shiloh
Sims, Mary – McMillan North
Sirus, Mary – Liberty (W)
Slack, Miss – Wheeling
Slattery – Fairview (P)
Slayman, Evelyn – Shiloh, Bend, Pleasant Grove (S)
Sloan, J. A. – Otley
Slocum, Anna – Fair Oak
Slocum, Erma – Fairview (P)
Slykhuis, Henry – Flagler South, River Ridge East, Brush Creek, Rees
Slykhuis, Mamie – Sunnyside
Smith, Agnes C. – Rees
Smith, Alice Edna – Shiloh
Smith, Beatrice – Lincoln South, Sunnyside, Brownlee, Georgia Ridge, Cedar Valley (L), Weston, Mt. Vernon, Pleasant Valley
Smith, Clarence – Prairie College
Smith, Cornelia – Hawkeye
Smith, Della – Spring Hill, Fillmore, New Albany, Gosport
Smith, Mrs. Don – Washington (K)
Smith, Elretta – Pleasant Grove (K), Mt. Vernon
Smith, Emma – Valley at Percy, Thornton, Dallas Center, Freedom, Horstman, Marion, Newbern
Smith, Fannie – Highland, Springdale, Caloma, Sunnyside, Bunker Hill (Sw)
Smith, Fern – Round Grove, Springfield, Willow Grove, Elm Grove
Smith, Fred – Donley, Liberty (K)
Smith, Gail – Cincinnati
Smith, George – Georgia Ridge, White Walnut
Smith, Glenna L. – Gosport
Smith, H.G. – Carlysle
Smith, H. O. – Carlysle, Washington (K), Cedar Valley (L)
Smith, Harry – Coal Ridge (I)
Smith, Helen L. – Round Grove
Smith, Iris – Pleasant Ridge (F)
Smith, Josephine – Round Grove
Smith, Josie – Round Grove, Gosport
Smith, Julia – Hawkeye
Smith, Kate Erskine – Fairview (R)
Smith, Kathleen Norris – Round Grove
Smith, Kathryn – Spring Hill
Smith, Katie – Pleasant Grove, Washington (K)
Smith, Lizzie – Spring Hill, Fillmore
Smith, Mrs. Mamie – Valley
Smith, Mrs. Mamie B. – Pleasant Valley

Smith, Mamie C. – Spring Hill, River Ridge West, White Breast
Smith, Mrs. Mamie G. – Summit
Smith, Mary V. – Union (C)
Smith, Miss Minnie – Salem
Smith, Myrtle E. – Dallas Center, Marion, Pleasant Ridge (F), Willow Grove
Smith, Nellie – Iola, Red Rock
Smith, Perry – Sand Ridge
Smith, Mrs. Rosa – Carlysle, Indiana, Prairie College, Willow Grove, Brownlee, Pleasant Grove (K), Spring Hill, Black Oak
Smith, Ruth – Pleasant Grove (K), Clark
Smith, Ruth Marie – Willow Grove, Buckeye
Smith, Miss S. S. – Oak Ridge
Smith, Miss Sadie – Hickory Grove, Pleasant Valley
Smith, Sara S. – Hickory Grove
Smith, Mrs. Tomie – Burch, Oradell
Smith, Violet – Pleasant Valley
Snider, Cora – Fairview (K), Weston
Snider, Marie – Oak Ridge
Sniff, Bula – Brownlee
Snow, Dorothy – Clay Center
Snow, Edna – Burr Oak
Snow, Mrs. – Cedar Valley (I)
Snowden, Elizabeth – Bend
Snyder, Cora – Maple Grove
Snyder, Emma – Oradell
Snyder, Joyce – Amsterdam East
Snyder, Lizzie – Springdale, European #2, European #3, Black Oak, Collins, White Breast, Oak Ridge, Burr Oak (Sw)
Snyder, Myrtle – Pleasant Ridge (K), Blaine
Snyder, Nellie – Porterville South
Snyder, Rena – Liberty (K), Washington (K), Rees, Union (U), Elm Grove
Snyder, W. S. – Brush Creek
Solder, Bert – Brush Creek
Sorenson, Sara – Eureka
South, C. A. – Horstman
South Miss – Highland
Spalti, Maude – Conn, Hawkeye, Spalti, Stringtown, Wheeling, Oradell
Spalti, May – Spalti
Spalti, Mildred Lyman – Hawkeye
Spalti, Nora – Des Moines Valley, Pleasantville North, Stringtown, West Pella, Oradell, Rees
Spaur, A. G. – Gosport

Spaur, Mrs. Mary – Union (W)
Spaur, Mary E. – Elm Grove
Spaur, Odessa – Union (C)
Speed, Berneice – Prairie College
Speed, Mrs. Eugene – Liberty (K)
Spence, Hannah – Maple Grove, Pleasant Ridge (K)
Spence, Miss – Franklin Center, Pleasant Ridge (K)
Spencer, Miss Hannah – Burr Oak
Spencer, Myrtle – Springdale, Sunnyside, Mt. Vernon
Spicer, Miss Maud – Burr Oak
Spiren, Maude – New Albany
Spires, Edna – Collins, Bunker Hill (Sw), West Pella
Spratt, Francis – Otley
Spruit, C. – Porterville North
Staggs, Ida – Blaine, Fillmore
Staley, Beatrice – White Walnut
Staley, Darlene – Horstman
Staley, Meryle – Bend
Stallings, Elsie Frobasue – Dallas Center
Stan, Dora – Red Rock
Stanberry, Grace – Fee, Rees, Union (U)
Stanger, Florence – Pleasant Ridge (F)
Stanger, Lulu – Hazel Ridge, Pleasant Ridge (F)
Stanger, Marjorie – Burr Oak
Stanger, Minnie – Columbia
Stanger, Mr. – Simmons
Stanley, Mr. J. B. – Highland
Starr, Miss Donna – White Walnut
Starr, Miss Dora – Flagler
Starr, Hattie – Red Rock
States, Mrs. Grace – Columbia
Steele, A. L. – Rising Star
Steele, Abe – Rising Star
Steele, Etta – Union (U), Columbia, Washington (W)
Steele, Lena – Pleasant Grove (S), Summit
Steele, Miss – Flagler North
Steele, Prof. – Liberty (K)
Steen, Bessie – Scott, Wheeling, Pleasant View
Steenhook, Janet Grootveld – Battle Ridge, European #3, Silver Grove West, River Ridge East
Stegeman, Marie – European #3
Steinkamp, Pearl – Battle Ridge, European #3, Valley View
Stenz, Angeline – Maple Grove
Stenz, Angie – Elm Ridge, Flagler South
Stentz, Miss Mattie – Flagler South
Stentz, Myrtle – Fairview (P)
Stentz, Nettie – Union (I)
Stephens, Gladys – Carlysle

Stephens, Miss – Lincoln (K)
Stephenson, Mrs. Arlene – Scott
Sterenberg, Grace – Vigilance
Sterling, Meryl – Fairview (F), Spalti, Fairview (P), West Pella
Sterret, Carrie – Pleasant View
Stevens, Bertha – Thorntown
Stevens, Cleta – Fee
Stevens, Jno. – Pleasant Valley
Stevens, Myrtle – Pleasant Ridge (F)
Stevenson, Evalyn A. – Highland, Coal Ridge (I)
Stevenson, Grace – Round Grove
Stevenson, Fern – Marion
Stevenson, Fred – Empire, Pleasant Ridge (K)
Stevenson, Marlene – Liberty (W), Union (W)
Stevenson, W. S. – Core, White Breast
Stevenson, William – Union (W)
Steves, J. A. – Blaine
Stewart, Della – Fee
Stewart, Freda – Oak Ridge
Stewart, Vera E. – Simmons
Stickle, Bernice – Empire, Highland, Prairie College, Buckeye, Georgia Ridge
Stienerman, Leulah – Liberty (S), Summit
Stillwell, Blaine – Empire, Hazel Ridge
Stillwell, Elaine – Washington (W)
Stine, Bessie – Fairview (P)
Stittsworth, Fern – Pleasant Grove (K), Mt. Vernon
Stittsworth, Inez – Flagler North, Georgia Ridge, Spring Hill, Bend, Blaine
Stittsworth, Paulina – McMillan North, Flagler North, Liberty (K), Pleasant Grove (K), Pleasant Ridge (K), Scott, Blaine
Stittsworth, Ruth – Georgia Ridge, Core
Stockholm, Estella – Conn
Stoddart, J.J. – Plainview
Stone, Edna Mae – Shiloh
Stone, Howard – Union (U)
Stone, Mary – Springdale, Springfield
Stone, Sue – Caloma, Sunnyside, Cedar Valley (I), Elm Ridge, Flagler, Flagler South, Georgia Ridge, Liberty (K), Lincoln (K), Rising Star, Pleasant View, Columbia
Stoops, Hattie – Sunnyside
Stotts, Edith – Liberty (W)
Stotts, Floyd – Union (C), Columbia, Gosport, Liberty (W), Union (W)
Stotts, John – Gosport, Pleasant Ridge (W)
Stotts, Mary – Columbia

Stout, Mary – Iola
Stower, Iva – Highland
Stradley, Myrtle – Burr Oak (Sw), Bunker Hill (Sw), Oradell
Straup, Mrs. Luree – Dallas Center
Straup, Thelma – Freedom, Columbia, Union (W)
Stroud, Almee – Buckeye
Stroud, Edith – Union (C), Vigilance, Victory
Stroud, Helen – Vigilance
Stout, Mary – Flagler North
Stuart, Faye – Fairview (D), Columbia
Stuart, Martha – Fair Oak
Stuart, Maude – River Ridge West
Stuart, Nannie – Flagler, Flagler South
Stubbs, Areole – Fairview (K)
Stubbs, Orin – Clark
Stuff, Beulah – Des Moines Valley, Eureka, Pleasant Ridge (F), Cedar Valley (L), River Ridge East, Liberty (S), Blaine, New Albany
Stuff, Leulah – Bunker Hill (L), Liberty (S), Otley
Stunenberg, Grace – Iola, Elm Ridge
Sturgeon, Katherine – Bethel, Highland, Burr Oak, Liberty (K), Victory
Suelson, Mrs. Mary – Lincoln (K)
Sullivan, Anna – Eureka, Flagler, Rising Star
Sullivan, Ella – White Breast
Sullivan, Eleanor – Buckeye, Flagler, River Ridge West
Sullivan, Ethelle – Liberty South (L)
Sullivan, Nora – Durham, Bunker Hill (K), Flagler
Summy, Anna – Pleasant Ridge (F)
Summy, Bessie – Thorntown, Clark
Summy, Blanche – Spalti
Summy, Edna – Conn, Wheeling
Summy, Iva – Pleasant Ridge (F), Conn, Pleasantville South
Summy, Nora – Burch
Summy, Ruth – Oradell, Rees
Surder, Bertha – Bethel
Sutton, Bertha R. – Fair Oak
Swain, A. J. – Pleasant Hill
Swain, Holly – Pleasant Ridge (F), Valley View
Swain, Mrs. John – Blaine
Swanson, Victoria – Columbia
Swartz, Edith – Des Moines Valley
Swayne, Carol – Brownlee
Swayne, Pearl – Willow Grove, Indiana, Prairie College, Buckeye, Washington (K), Mt. Vernon
Swearingen, R. L. – Summit
Swearingen, Robert L. – Pleasant Hill
Sweem, Mrs. Carolyn – Scott

Sweem, Esta – Pleasant Grove (K), Virginia, Conn
Sweem, Esther – Freedom
Sweeny, Hazel – Fairview (R)
Synhorst, Dorothy – Amsterdam East, Amsterdam West

T

Tade, Lola E. – Bunker Hill (LP)
Taggart, Blanche W. – Lincoln North
Taggart, Gladys – Georgia Ridge
Taggart, Laura – Washington (K), European # 1, Fairview (R), Liberty Corner, Red Rock, Pleasant Grove (S), New Albany
Taggart, Lena Fern – Pleasant View
Taggart, Martha – Pleasant Valley, Cincinnati
Talbot, Verna – Bunker Hill (LP)
Tandy, Ethel – Vigilance, Porterville South
Taylor, Clarice – Fairview (D)
Taylor, Miss Ellie – Maple Grove
Taylor, Gertrude – Valley at Percy
Taylor, Gladys – Springfield
Taylor, Lila – Burch
Taylor, Mabel – Round Grove, O.K.
Taylor, Mary – Oak Ridge
Taylor, Merle – Pleasant Hill, Pleasant Valley, O.K.
Taylor, Miss – Otley
Taylor, Nellie – Burr Oak (Sw)
Taylor, Virginia – Columbia
Teeter, Josephine – Elm Ridge
Tellet, Pansy – Eureka
Templeton, Alice – River Ridge East, Brush Creek, Liberty Corner, Pleasant Valley, Burch
Templeton, Ed – Fairview(R)
Templeton, Elizabeth – Brush Creek, Oak Ridge, Red Rock
Templeton, Florence – Pleasant Hill, Fairview (R)
Templeton, Jessie – Fair Oak
Templeton, Josephine – Fairview (R)
Templeton, Mary – Fairview (R), Pleasant Valley
Templeton, Ruth – Brush Creek
Templeton, S.S. – Hickory Grove, Pleasant Valley, White Walnut, Pleasant View
Templeton, Sarah Jane – Pleasant Valley, Red Rock, Rees
Templeton, Stephen – White Walnut
Ter Louw, Anna – Valley View
Ter Louw, Christina – European #1, Rock Island, Pleasant Grove (S), Valley View
Terrell, Cora – Coal Ridge (I)
Terrell, Walter – Pleasant Ridge (K)
Terwilliger, Ada – Stringtown, Clark, Burch

Teter, Grandville – Union (U)
Teter, T. W. – Blaine
Thomas, Mrs. – Shiloh
Thomas, Ruth – McMillan North
Thomassen, Dora – Plainview
Thomassen, Josie – European #1, European #2
Thompson, Mrs. Betty – Caloma
Thompson, Frances – Maple Grove
Thompson, Irene – Victory
Thomson, Inez Schroder – Pleasant Valley
Thondale, Sara – Oradell
Thornberg, Florence – Bunker Hill (Sw)
Thornberg, Iva – Rees
Thornberg, Lee – Rees
Thornberg, Pansy – Conn
Thornton, Gertrude – Valley at Percy, Pleasant Valley
Thorpe, Irene – Coal Ridge (I)
Thron, Burline – Marion
Tice, Hattie M. – Porterville
Tice, Leota – Horstman, Marion, Union (W)
Tidball, Miss Cassie – Flagler, Flagler South
Timmerman, Miss – Lincoln (K)
Timmerman, Miss Ruth – Pleasant Grove (K)
Timmins, Hazel – Fairview (R)
Tinkey, Kate – Columbia
Toche, Miss Celgo Mylet – Empire
Todd, Mrs. J. – Porterville
Todd, Loraine – Dallas Center
Todd, Mary E. – Porterville North
Todd, Maud – Battle Ridge, Porterville North, Porterville South
Todd, Miss – Clay Center
Todd, Mrs. – Porterville North
Todd, Sarah – Porterville South
Tonda, Catherine – Brush Creek, Fairview (R)
Tool, Victoria – Hickory Grove
Toom, Grace – Iola, Flagler North, Amsterdam West, Bend, Fairview (P), Mt. Vernon, River Ridge East, River Ridge West
Toom, Harriet – Amsterdam East, Richland
Toom, Maggie – Bend
Totten, Bertha – Liberty North (L), Liberty South (L), Virginia
Totten, Georgia – Cedar Valley (L), Blaine
Towne, Helen – Buckeye
Townsend, Edna – Fairview (C), McMillan North, Liberty (K), Victory, Washington (K)
Townsend, Lora – Red Rock

Townsend, Lula – Fairview (C), Rising Star, Scott, Victory, Washington (K), New Albany
Tracy, Albert – Columbia
Tromp, Mrs. Cornie – Liberty (S)
Troutman, Eunice – Freedom
Truer, Ethel – Springdale, Amsterdam West, Rees
Truman, Mary L. – Highland
Truwent, Susie – Pleasant Ridge (W)
Tucker, Alicia – Coal Ridge (I)
Tucker, Josephine – Fairview (P)
Tucker, Marie – Mt. Vernon, Pleasant Ridge (W)
Tucker, Miss Mollie – Springfield
Tugie, S. – Flagler South
Tuinstra, Elizabeth – Sand Ridge
Tuinstra, Kathryn – Pleasant View
Turner, Miss Doris M. – Georgia Ridge
Turner, Mary L. – Burr Oak, Washington (K), Collins, Bend
Tuttle, Mrs. Vyola – Richland
Tyrell, Faye – Hazel Ridge, Pleasant Grove (K), Porterville, Fair Oak
Tysseling, Alice – Plainview
Tysseling, Edna – Rising Star, Weston
Tysseling, Lucille – Salem, Victory, Weston, Fairview (P)
Tysseling, Minnie – Des Moines Valley, Lincoln North, Lincoln South, Maple Grove

U

Umble, Ina L. – Valley at Percy, Fair Oak
Umpleby, Myrtle – Rees
Updegraff, Abe – Maple Grove

V

Van Arkel, Edgar – Eureka, Union (C), Valley, Red Rock
Van Benthuysen, H. L. – Bethel
Van Benthuysen, J. W. – Black Oak
Van Benthuysen, Luisa – Liberty (L)
Van Benthuysen, P. – Liberty South (L)
Van Den Berg, Helen – Summit
Van Donselaar, Cornelia Gosselink – Plainview
Van Donselaar, Frances – Maple Grove, Amsterdam East, Pleasant Grove (L), River Ridge West
Van Doren, Loveda – Horstman, European #3, Liberty South (L), Shiloh, Fair Oak, Liberty (S)
Van Duren, Dorothy – European #2
Van Dusseldorp, Ada – Liberty Corner, Richland
Van Dusseldorp, Mrs. Evelyn – Summit
Van Dyke, W. J. – Durham, Flagler, West River Ridge
Van Dyne, Martin – Newbern

Van Emmerick, Cunera – European #2
Van Essen, Ruth – Richland
Van Gorp, Bess – Bunker Hill (LP), Collins, Oak Ridge, Red Rock
Van Gorp, Blanche – Pleasant Hill
Van Gorp, Florence Hackert – Battle Ridge
Van Gorp, Irene – Des Moines Valley
Van Gorp, Lucie – White Breast, Liberty Corner, White Walnut, Summit, Valley View
Van Gorp, Marie – White Breast, Fair Oak
Van Gorp, Minnie – Bunker Hill (LP)
Van Haaften, Irene – Liberty (S)
Van Hemert, Greta – Silver Grove West
Van Hemert, Mary Jane – Pleasant View
Van Hemert, Thelma – Valley, White Breast
Van Heukelom, Alda – Pleasant Grove (LP)
Van Heukelom, Marjorie – Porterville South, Liberty (S)
Van Heukelom, Thressa – Bunker Hill (LP)
Van Liew, Iva – Willow Grove
Van Loon, Avis – Scott, Brush Creek, New Albany
Van Loon, Geneva – Buckeye, Scott, Clark
Van Loon, Iva – Flagler South, Rising Star
Van Loon, Myrtle – Sunnyside, Scott
Van Loon, Vernon – Cedar Valley (I), Elm Grove
Van Maaren, Harold – River Ridge East
Van Maaren, Nellie – Fairview (R)
Van Ness, Ila – Amsterdam West
Van Nimwegen, E. – Amsterdam West
Van Nimwegen, Elizabeth – Sand Ridge, Silver Grove East, Richland
Van Ommen – Bunker Hill (LP)
Van Pelt, John – Bunker Hill (LP)
Van Pilsum, Gesiena – Sand Ridge
Van Polen, Allie – Silver Grove West
Van Rees, Leona Arens – Battle Ridge
Van Rheenen, Lena Hoksbergen – Battle Ridge
Van Rheenen, Nellie – Oak Ridge, Otley, Pleasant Grove (S), Valley View
Van Roekel, Harriet – Pleasant Grove (S)
Van Roekel, Henrietta – European #3, Pleasant Grove (S), Pleasant View, Richland, Valley View
Van Roekel, Johannah M. – European #1, European #3, Porterville South
Van Sittert, Florence – Otley
Van Spankeren – Otley
Van Veen, Hattie – Porterville North, Rock Island, West Silver Grove, Summit

Van Winkle, Elmer – Cedar Valley (I), Coal Ridge (I), White Walnut
Van Winkle, Rev. J. E. – Mt. Vernon
Van Wyk, Hattie Neyenesch – Battle Ridge
Van Wyk, Jacob – European #1
Van Wyk, Mrs. Johnita – Bunker Hill (LP), Valley View
Van Wyngarden, Eva Mae – Porterville North, West Silver Grove, Valley
Van Zante, Mrs. A. D. – Valley View
Van Zante, Agnes – Bunker Hill (LP), Liberty (S)
Van Zante, Bertha – Pleasant Grove (LP), Rock Island, Otley
Van Zante, Dick C. – Summit
Van Zante, Elizabeth – Porterville South
Van Zante, Mrs. Henrietta L. Van Roekel – Battle Ridge
Van Zante, Jennie Van Osstrum – Battle Ridge
Van Zante, Julia – Porterville South, Sand Ridge
Van Zante, K – Porterville South
Van Zante, Mabel – Porterville South
Van Zee, Artie – Bunker Hill (LP)
Van Zee, Bertha – Porterville South
Van Zee, Cora – Fairview (F), Springdale, Sunnyside
Van Zee, Louise – European #3
Van Zee, Maggie – European #2, Porterville South, Valley, Richland
Van Zee, Marcile – Silver Grove West
Van Zee, Matilda – Summit
Van Zee, Pearl – European #1, Porterville South
Van Zomeran, Avis Van Houweling – Des Moines Valley, Battle Ridge
Van Zomeran, Miss Joan – Summit
Vance, Mr. – Maple Grove
Vande Gaard, Besse – Amsterdam West
Vande Kieft, Mrs. Ruth – Amsterdam East
Vande Kieft, Wilma – Union (C), Amsterdam East
Vande Ven, Frank – Plainview
Vanden Berg, Joe – Valley
Vanden Berg, Velma – Brownlee
Vander Beek, Betty – Plainview
Vander Burce, Marie – Amsterdam West
Vander Busse, Marie – Liberty (S), Richland
Vander Hart, Agnes – Battle Ridge, European #2, Plainview
Vander Hart, Annette – Iola
Vander Hart, Etta – European #3, Porterville
Vander Hart, Evelyn – Summit
Vander Hart, Marie S. – Amsterdam East, European #1, Sand Ridge, Liberty (S), Otley, Summit
Vander Kieft, Johanna – Valley
Vander Kraan, Florence – Pleasant Valley
Vander Linden, Alta M – Amsterdam East, Amsterdam West, Porterville South
Vander Linden, Bessie – Amsterdam East, Battle Ridge, West Silver Grove
Vander Linden, Irene – European #3
Vander Linden, Leona – Iola, Valley
Vander Linden, M. – Amsterdam West
Vander Linden, Margaret – Battle Ridge, Pleasant Grove (L)
Vander Linden, Marinus – Porterville North, Richland
Vander Linden, Ray – Union (C)
Vander Linden, Ruth – Bunker Hill (LP), European #1, European #3, Silver Grove West, Liberty (S)
Vander Ploeg, Albert – Otley, Pleasant Grove (S)
Vander Ploeg, Annie – Valley, Summit
Vander Sluis, Nellie – Plainview
Vander Voort, Miss Christina – Valley View
Vander Wal, Antoinette – Battle Ridge, Bunker Hill (LP)
Vander Wal, Jeanette – European # 1
Vander Zyl, Alice – Amsterdam East, Pleasant Grove (LP), Valley
Vander Zyl, Cornie – Valley View
Vander Zyl, Jennie – Sand Ridge
Vander Zyl, Mary (Marie) – Silver Grove East, West Silver Grove
Vannoy, Minnie – Columbia, Pleasant Ridge (W)
Varenkamp, Lydia – Amsterdam East, European #2
Vaughn, Miss Mary – Clay Center, Valley at Percy
Vaught, Evelyn – Pleasant Grove (S)
Veenscholer, Alice – Amsterdam West
Veenschoten, Avis – Plainview
Veenstra, Minnie – Amsterdam East, Amsterdam West
Veenstra, Orrissa – Amsterdam East
Venable, Cora – New Albany
Venable, Corda – Elm Grove, Gosport, New Albany
Venable, Cordye – Elm Grove
Venable, N. E. – Gosport
Venable, Nora – New Albany
Ver Dught, Mrs. Betty – Union (U)
Ver Dught, Dorothy – Porterville South, Fair Oak, Pleasant Grove (S)
Ver Dught, Edna – Pleasant View
Ver Heul, Edna – European #3, Plainview, Otley
Ver Heul, Elizabeth – European #3, Plainview
Ver Heul, Henrietta – Porterville North
Ver Heul, Kate – Valley, Richland
Ver Heul, Martha – Fairview (K), European #1, Porterville North, Bend
Ver Meer, Jeanette Vander Wal – Battle Ridge

Ver Ploeg, Alma Rietveld – Battle Ridge, European #1, European #2
Ver Ploeg, Arlene – Valley View
Ver Ploeg, Hester – Porterville, Silver Grove West
Ver Steeg, Christine – European #1
Ver Steeg, Dena – European #1, Summit (S)
Ver Steeg, Gertrude – European #1, Fair Oak
Ver Steeg, Hester – Amsterdam East
Ver Steeg, Ruby – Liberty (K), Lincoln (K), Fairview (P), New Albany
Ver Steeg, Sam – Bunker Hill (L), Silver Grove West
Verhey, Anna – European #3
Verhey, Dena – Valley
Verhey, James – Battle Ridge
Verhoef, Mrs. Ruth – Valley
Vernon, Fred – Empire
Vernon, Leslie – Fairview (K)
Vernon, Martha – Freedom
Vernon, Nytha L. – Freedom
Vernon, T. L. – Bethel, Highland, Cedar Valley (I)
Verrips, Laura – Battle Ridge
Verwers, Irma Mae – White Breast
Vickers, Laura – Summit
Viers, Rosa Blodgett – Bunker Hill (Sw)
Viers, Thelma – Bunker Hill (K)
Viers, Velda Lucille – Simmons
Vierson, Etta – European #2
Vierson, Josie – Amsterdam East
Vierson, Lula – Valley, Columbia
Vierson, Mabel – Elm Ridge, Pleasant Grove (K), O.K.
Villant, Clarence – Coal Ridge (I)
Vincent, Miss – Spring Hill
Vingari, E. – Plainview
Vinson, Alice – Washington (K)
Vinson, Darlene – Caloma, Springdale
Vinyard, Emily – Silver Grove West
Visser, Berneice – Bunker Hill (Sw)
Visser, Irma – Amsterdam East
Visser, Mrs. Katheryne – East River Ridge
Vogelaar, Mrs. Elmer – Bunker Hill (L)
Vogelaar, Mae M. – Battle Ridge, Otley, Richland, Summit
Vogelaar, Margaret M. – Summit
Voorhis, Fred – Bunker Hill
Vos, Carolina – Fair Oak
Vos, Gertrude – White Breast
Vos, Johnita – Pleasant View, Valley View
Vos, Marjorie Boot – Battle Ridge, European #1
Vos, Raymond – Richland

Vriezelaar, Betty – Plainview
Vriezelaar, Gradus – Battle Ridge, Liberty Corner, Pleasant View
Vriezelaar, Irene M. – Clay Center, Liberty Corner, Otley, Richland, Valley View, Pleasant Ridge (W)
Vriezelaar, Kathryn – Liberty Corner
Vriezelaar, Leona Bogaard – Union (C)
Vroom, Gertrude – Valley

W

Waddle, Claude C. – Marion
Waddle, Dora – Fairview (R)
Waddle, Dorothy – Oak Ridge
Waddle, Nellie Caffery – Dallas Center
Waddle, Paul J. – Dallas Center
Wadell, Miss Beulah – Fee
Wagaman, Allen – Bunker Hill (LP)
Wagner, Bernice – Silver Grove West, Pleasant View
Wagner, Geneva – Franklin Center
Wagner, Mrs. Lila Lukin – Franklin Center
Wagner, Mary B. Mills – Georgia Ridge
Wagoner, Florence – Flagler
Wahls, Miss Sallie – Durham
Wald, Miss – Valley at Percy
Walker, Dorothy – Buckeye
Walker, Eva M. – Liberty South (L)
Walker, Everett – Ladoga, Wheeling, West Pella
Walker, Lavonne – Valley at Percy
Walker, Mamie – Bennington
Waln, Miss A. E. – Clay Center
Waln, Miss Alice – McMillan North
Waln, Miss Amanda – Clay Center
Waln, Miss Sadie – Durham, Lincoln North
Waln, Miss Sarah – West Bethel
Walraven, Rosetta – Richland
Walstra, Mrs. Jeanne – Sand Ridge
Walter, Mary Esther – Elm Ridge
Walton, Joel T. – Bend
Ward, Helen J. – Burr Oak
Ward, John P – Fairview (K), Brush Creek
Ward, John W. – White Breast
Ward, Kate – Fairview (K)
Ward, Lucy – McMillan South, Lincoln (K), Pleasant Ridge (K), Spring Hill
Ward, Pauline – Highland, Sunnyside
Ward, T. E. – Liberty (K)
Ward, Thurman – Hazel Ridge, Highland, Sunnyside, Buckeye, Lincoln (K), Pleasant Ridge (K)

Warder, Marea – Flagler North
Warner, Jeanette – Hickory Grove
Warner, Jessie – European #2, Porterville North, Collins, Conn, Thorntown, Mt. Vernon
Warren, Alice – Des Moines Valley, Lincoln South, Lincoln North, Durham
Warren, Margaret – Cincinnati, Summit
Warren, Pauline – Pleasant Grove (S)
Warren, Mrs. – Des Moines Valley
Wassenaar, Gertie – Bennington, Pleasant Valley
Wassenaar, Nellie – Valley at Percy
Wasson, C. M. – Liberty (K), Rising Star, Brush Creek
Watkins, Miss Carrie – Wheeling, Oradell
Watkins, Inez – River Ridge East
Watkins, Jennie – Freedom
Watkins, Lela – Buckeye
Watkins, Mable – Indiana, Oak Ridge
Watkins, Miss Media – Highland, Rising Star
Watkins, Miss Maggie – Des Moines Valley, Highland, Rising Star, Spring Hill, Rousseau
Watson, M.C. – Highland
Watson, Mamie Lucille – Hawkeye
Way, Cecil F. – Bethel, Prairie College, Valley at Percy
Way, Mrs. Gertrude – White Walnut
Way, Gretchen M. – Indiana
Wcbb, Clara – Porterville
Webb, Gladys – Pleasant Hill
Webb, Lulu – Porterville North
Webb, Marie – Pleasant Hill
Weed, J. B. – Red Rock, Fair Oak
Weir, Agnes – Freedom
Weishar, Lucille – Dallas Center
Welch, A. J. – Gosport
Welch, Bessie – Bunker Hill (K)
Welch, Beulah – Cedar Valley (I), Fee, Spring Hill
Welch, Blanche – Prairie College, Round Grove, Simmons, Union (I), Scott, Victory
Welch, Bressa – Buckeye, Bunker Hill, Oradell
Welch, Ethel M. – Otley
Welch, Fern – Horstman, Hazel Ridge, Highland, Simmons, Springfield
Welch, Julia – Summit
Welch, Maude – Prairie College, Spring Hill, Blaine
Welch, Nora – Prairie College, Springfield, Fillmore, Gosport
Welch, Norue – Prairie College, Springfield
Welch, Rena Fee – McMillan North, Burr Oak, Fee, Spring Hill, White Breast
Welch, Rose Ellen – Clark, Union (U)
Welch, Vera – Elm Ridge, Flagler South
Welch, Vinnie – Flagler, Flagler North
Welcher, Ethel – Eureka, Round Grove, Fairview (K)
Welcher, Miss – Highland, Flagler North
Wellons, W. E. – Newbern, Valley at Percy, O.K.
Wells, F. E. – West Pella
Wells, W. P. – Gosport
Welsher, Ella – Hazel Ridge
Welsher, Helen – Salem
Welsher, Mrs. Liza – Hazel Ridge
Wener, Nora Willis – Washington (W)
Werts, Marvel – Freedom
West, Electra – Oradell
West, Miss – Pleasantville North
West, Oletha – Burr Oak
Westner, Nora M. – Lincoln (N or S?), Cedar Valley
Westphalia, Mary E. – Dallas Center
Weston, Mary – Pleasant Ridge (F)
Weyman, Mrs. Martha – Vigilance
Weyman, Mrs. – Liberty (K)
Whaley, A. – Eureka
Whaley, Alex – Coal Ridge (Polk)
Whaley, Betty – Liberty (K), Pleasant Ridge (K), Scott, White Walnut
Whaley, Francis – Coal Ridge (I)
Whaley, Martha Louise – McMillan North, Brownlee, West Pella
Wheatcraft, Edith – White Walnut
White, Aggie – Coal Ridge (I)
White, Agnes – Flagler North
White, Basil – Liberty (K), Red Rock
White, Beatrice – Blaine
White, Hazel – Springdale
White, Helen – White Walnut
White, Lavere – Horstman
White, Lola – Collins
White, Miss – McMillan North, Fairview (K)
White, Nora – Iola, Elm Ridge, Flagler, Flagler North, Victory, Coal Ridge (Polk)
White, Raymond – Elm Ridge
White, S.J.O.G. – Newbern
Whitlach, Ida – Elm Grove
Whitlach, Lena – Elm Grove
Whitlach, Leona – Round Grove
Whitlach, Merrill – Springfield, Elm Grove
Whitlach, Orlan – Columbia
Whitlach, Owen – Prairie College, Simmons, Columbia, Gosport, Union (W)

Whitney, Mrs. Mary – Prairie College
Whitney, Mrs. – Washington (K)
Wicker, Nina – Oak Ridge
Wiegand, Almeda – Iola
Wiegand, Emily – Des Moines Valley
Wiegand, Miss M. – Eureka
Wiegand, Mary – Caloma
Wilcut, Ada – Pleasant Ridge (K), West River Ridge
Willcox, Mary Esther – Elm Ridge
Wilkin, Eleanor F. – White Walnut
Wilkins, Velma – Fairview (C), Fairview (D)
Willene, Margaret – Flagler South
Willets, Lena – Brownlee
Williams, Alice – Maple Grove
Williams, Bertha – Fairview (D), Fairview (F), Springdale
Williams, Bess L. – Freedom, Franklin Center, Fairview (F)
Williams, Bessie – Georgia Ridge, Pleasant Ridge (K), Black Oak, Hawkeye, Weston, Cincinnati, Otley, Rees
Williams, C. O. – Liberty (K)
Williams, Duane – Des Moines Valley
Williams, Flavia – Thorntown, Weston, Oradell
Williams, Florence – Fair Oak
Williams, Jessie – Burr Oak, Red Rock, White Walnut
Williams, Marie – O. K.
Williams, Ruth – Clark
Williams, John – Caloma, Franklin Center, Pleasant Ridge (F), Springdale, Lincoln (K)
Williamson, C. O. – Franklin Center, Washington (K)
Williamson, H. C. – West Pella
Williamson, Mr. – Franklin Center, Burr Oak
Willis, Florence – Horstman, Salem
Willis, Nora – Empire, Hazel Ridge, Marion, Washington (W)
Wilson, Bethine – Collins
Wilson, Miss E. – Pleasantville North
Wilson, Edna – Bunker Hill (Sw), O. K.
Wilson, Eva – Des Moines Valley, Carlysle, Bend, White Walnut, Pleasant Grove (S)
Wilson, Hazel – Georgia Ridge
Wilson, Miss Jennie – Liberty (W)
Wilson, Kathleen – Newbern, Franklin Center
Wilson, Lizzie – Empire, Marion, New Albany
Wilson, M. L. – Pleasant Hill, Valley at Percy
Wilson, Mable – Freedom, Union (S)
Wilson, Madge – Sunnyside, Salem, New Albany
Wilson, Marion – Bennington
Wilson, Mary – Newbern, Rock Island
Wilson, Maude – Iola, Vigilance, Victory, Valley at Percy

Wilson, Miss – Highland, Plainview
Wilson, Nellie – McMillan North, Liberty (L), Liberty North (L), Liberty South (L), Shiloh, Weir City
Wilson, Neva – Freedom, Liberty (W)
Wilson, Newt – Pleasant Grove (LP)
Wilson, Rachel – Dallas Center, Union (W)
Wilson, Reefa – Rock Island
Wilson, Rhea – Brush Creek, New Albany
Wilson, Sherman – Burr Oak, Columbia
Wilson, Surrie S. – New Albany
Wilson, Thelma – Freedom
Wilson, W. S. – Pleasant Ridge
Winegardner, Stella – Eureka, Springdale, Brownlee, Elm Ridge
Wines, Mr. Rolland – Highland
Wing, Betty – Scott, Washington (K)
Wing, Loren D. – Otley, Rees
Winters, Alice – Rising Star, River Ridge East
Wise, Mildred – Porterville North
Wise, Katherine – Simmons
Witt, Dale – Liberty (W)
Witt, Gladys – Round Grove, Pleasant Ridge (K), Fillmore, Gosport, Pleasant Ridge (W), Union (W)
Witt, Lizzie – Columbia
Witt, Merl – Highland, Pleasant Grove (K), Washington (K), New Albany, Pleasant Ridge (W)
Witt, Theo – New Albany
Witt, Vera – Cedar Valley (I), Indiana, Union (W)
Wittmer, Bertha – Otley
Witzenberg, Dorothy – Amsterdam East, European #3
Witzenberg, Luedna – Silver Grove West, Pleasant View, Valley View
Wohler, Daisy – O. K.
Wolf, Cora D. – Eureka, Elm Ridge
Wolfe, A. – Prairie College
Wolfe, Atha – Union (C), Springfield, Weir City
Wolfe, B. D. – Elm Grove
Wolfe, S. B. – Elm Grove, Liberty (W)
Wood, Mrs. Hazel M. – Columbia
Wood, Helen M. – Marion
Wood, Nadine – Amsterdam East
Woodcock, Mr. B.F. – Fee
Woodcock, Mabel – Fairview (F), Thorntown
Woodle, Ruth – Springdale, Spring Hill
Woods, Lizzie – European #2
Woods, Luella – Des Moines Valley
Woody, Bertha – Fairview (C), McMillan North, Vigilance
Woody, Ellen – Pleasant View

Woody, Mary – Clay Center, McMillan North, Iola, River Ridge East, River Ridge West
Woody, Orpha – Clay Center, Iola, McMillan North, River Ridge East
Woody, Suska – Iola, McMillan North, River Ridge East
Woody, Sylvia – Lincoln South, Sunnyside, Amsterdam West
Woody, Tressa E. – Burch
Woody, Tressa Faye – Bend
Woodyard, Caroline – Caloma
Woodyard, J.H. – Highland
Woodyard, Nellie – Horstman
Workerman, Lillie – Des Moines Valley, Bend
Workman, Cora – Fee
Worley, Minnie – Marion
Wormhoudt, Dirkie – European #1, European #3
Wormhoudt, Dorothy – European #2
Wormhoudt, Kamp – Pleasant Grove (LP)
Worrall, Hazel – Eureka, Buckeye, Burr Oak, Pleasant Valley, Fair Oak, Burch
Worsted, Beulah – Iola
Worstell, Beulah – Burr Oak, Georgia Ridge, Porterville South, Conn, Blaine, Carlysle
Worstell, Eva – Eureka, Fee, Maple Grove, Pleasant Grove (K), Spalti, Blaine
Worth, Merle – Hickory Grove
Wortham, Pearl – Lincoln (K)
Worthington, A. D. – Oradell
Worthington, Fay – Rees
Worthington, Margorie – Victory
Worthington, Maycie – Burr Oak, Stringtown, Red Rock
Wren, Agnes – Georgia Ridge, Burch
Wren, Charles – Buckeye, Georgia Ridge, Blaine, Rees
Wren, Elizabeth – Clark
Wren, Kathryn – Fairview (K), Georgia Ridge
Wren, Margaret – Porterville, Rees
Wright, Ariel – Horstman, Hazel Ridge
Wright, Bess – Lincoln (K), Pleasant Grove (K)
Wright, Edith – Lincoln North
Wright, F. – Fairview
Wright F. M. – Flagler, Red Rock
Wright, Frank – Spring Hill, Battle Ridge
Wright, Jacquetta – Fairview (P)
Wright, L. Bess – Maple Grove
Wright, Lois – Bend, Mt. Vernon
Wright, Luella – Fairview (D), Washington (K)
Wright, Nellie – Iola
Wright, Ola – Liberty South (L)
Wright, Olga – Empire, Liberty Corner
Wright, Willa – Iola
Write, Franklin Milton – Silver Grove West
Write, Sarah – Fairview (D)
Wynia, Margaret – Rock Island, Liberty (S)
Wynn, Faye – New Albany

X

Y

Yetter, Aaron – Elm Ridge
Young, Miss Adda – Union (I), Spring Hill, New Albany
Young, Anna – Union (C), Shiloh
Young, Miss Fannie – Springfield
Young, Fern – European #3, Liberty North (L)
Young, Geneva – Collins
Young, Mrs. Geraldine – Columbia
Young, J. R. – Maple Grove
Young, Lida – Liberty (L)
Young, Roy – Clay Center
Young, Ruth – Pleasant Hill, Oak Ridge
Young, Yella C. – Liberty Corner

Z

Zeigler, Edna M. – Fairview (C)
Zerley, Lula – Pleasant Grove (S)

Photo Enlargements

Clay Township, Eureka, 1912 – Back row: Jeanette Roorda, Luella Millard, Pearl Millard, Ollie Parson, Reifa Lancaster, Beulah Lancaster, Sylvia Millard, Blanche Lerew, and Teacher Faye Cummings. Middle row: Susie Leighton, Violet Lancaster, Milton Redding, Marion Toom, Ilo Roberts, Gertrude Roorda, Bessie Millard, (small girl behind Bessie not identified), Gertrude Parson, Oral Adair, and Jennie Van Engelenhoven. Front row: (unidentified), Robert Roorda, David Roorda, Lester Redding, Lizzie Millard, Ester Redding, John Van Engelenhoven, Lloyd Parson, Arie Van Engelenhoven, and Lester Bryant.

Union School, May 10, 1935 (last day of school) – Some preschool children were visitors. Row 1: Martin Johnson, Leona Schimmel, Kenneth Knox, Aaron Knox, Shirley Fridlington, Junella Harkness, Dale Vos, and Gilbert Schimmel. Row 2: Dora Schimmel, Melvin Vos, Herbert Laird, William Schimmel, James Schimmel, and Teacher Daisy Fridlington holding Henry Dirk Schimmel. Row 3: Marguerite Knox, Faith Fridlington, "Little Bertha" Schimmel, Jacob Vos, and Loren Johnson. Row 4: Helen Laird, Jennie Schimmel, Gertrude Vos, "Big Bertha" Schimmel, Lucille Johnson, and Pete De Jong.

Dallas Township, Fairview, 1904 – Back row: Dora Frueh, Rena Riggs, Letta Mason, Dora Mason, Alma Pearl Wilson, Emma Smith, Mary Frueh, Sade Graves, Elsie Mason, Nora Smith, Myrtle Smith, Oliver Hunnerdosse, Clara Mason, Ollie Wilson, Katherine Dinwiddie, Robert Riggs, Harry Poush, Edgar Smith, and Grant Riggs. Middle row: Loren Riggs, Lloyd Riggs, Thomas Merl Graves, Ernest Hunnerdosse, Walter Mason, Mathew Smith, John Whitemy, (unknown), Edward ____, (unknown), and Giles Smith. Front row: (unknown), Vera Mason, Ruth Smith, Avis Mason, and Pearl _____.

Indiana Township, Cedar Valley – Postcard picture given by teacher around 1910. Row one: Blanche Nickell, (unknown), Grace Caulkins, Floyd Pearson, Mabel Nickell, Flossie Sanders, (unknown), Billie Booth, and Mary Ross. Row two: Clarice Schellinger, Beulah Caulkins, Thelma Booth, Ivan Nickell, Earl Booth, Glenn Ross, and Paul Pearson. Row three: Faye Ross, Desie Sanders, Bud Pearson, John Booth, Thlema Sanders, Gertie Booth, and Teacher Mary Roller.

Indiana Township, Prairie College, 1897 – Front row: Cresco Applegate, Lois Applegate, Chas Coolley, Kerns Applegate, Teacher Elsie Curtis, Paul Applegate, Nellie Applegate, and Aura Brause. Back row: Loren Robuck, Park Robuck, Stanley Smith, Elma Coolley, Etta Applegate, Laura Robuck, Mary Coolley, Fannie Robuck, and Frank Robuck.

Indiana Township, Round Grove – Souvenir booklet typical of those given to students at the end of the year.

ROUND GROVE
Public School
INDIANA TP., MARION CO., IOWA.

ETHEL WELSHER, TEACHER.

Pupils

Kinne Smith
Amos Smith
Grace Smith
Fern Smith
Ernest Smith
Nettie Smith
Earl Smith
Clark Smith
Emma Ridnouer
Electa Hulgan
Omie Hulgan
George Whitlatch
Arlos Morrow
Fary Elliott
Florence Pack
Loyd Hedrick
Arthur Hedrick
Ray Coolley
Grace Coolley
James McCarty

Jennie Smith
Ben Smith
Tellus Smith
Fred Smith
Ray Smith
Mary Smith
Loyd Smith
Della Ridnouer
Mamie Hulgan
Grace Hulgan
Ruth Whitlach
Frances Whitlatch
Rolla Jordan
Belle Pack
Ernest Antrim
Forest Hedrick
Clifford Hedrick
Ward Coolley
Vera Maddy
Beulah McCarty

SCHOOL BOARD:
M. S. Coolley, - - W. C. Coolley,
F. E. Whitlatch, - James Jordan,
J. T. Maddy.

Indiana Township, Simmons, 1897 – The students between five to twenty years of age were Nora, Bessie, Maude, Loren, Clement, and Fred Welch; Bertha, Dessie, Austin, and Frank Davis; Ann, Ada, Laura, Willie, George, Emmett, John, and Naomi Kincaid; Lulu, Jim, and Lawrence Mart; Lillie, Mary, Bernice, Lola, Fred, and Cecil Jeffers; Mary, Asberene, Robert, and Vint Allen; Lola, Arch, and Lewis Maddy; Loren and Curtis Guillion; Anna and George May; and Alice Sherwood.

Knoxville Township, Burr Oak – Taken by Pearl Adams when Maycie Worthington was teacher from September 1, 1910, to February 24, 1911. Students were Pearl Adams; Clifton and John Cathcart; Esther and Marie Conner; Mamie Clark; Grace and Fred Houser; Selma, Beulah, and Mary Hawks; Roxie and Cleo Wright; Ruby, Esther, and Jessie Wilson.

Knoxville Township, Fee, 1947 – Teacher Mildred Lundy standing in back of classroom. Front row: Ardan Graves, Jerry Stone, Lew Arl Brent, and Jimmie Herman. Second row: Virginia Sams, Janice Fee, Dick Stone, and Roger Bryan. Third row: Twyla Little, Marilyn Herman, Ron Sherman, and Larry Little. Fourth row: Evelyn Shewmon, Carol Fee, Melvin Sams, and Lawrance Stone.

Knoxville Township, Flagler, 1914 – Row one: James Wignall, Frank Mitchell, Casey Zoutte, Bessie Barr, Rose DeCrotus, Elizabeth Dainty, Almeda Cooper, Francis Horton, Harry Nichols, and Thelma Wignall. Row two: Louis Dainty, William Horton, Rena Fortner, Germaine Zoutte, Louie Zoutte, Alfred Wignall, Irvin Pace, Frank Dainty, William Henderson, and Clabber Des Planges. Row three: Harvey Cecil, (unknown), Lois Dainty, Jess Nichols, Ronald Simpson, Marshall Des Planges, Henry Delpace, Arthur Chivers, and Henry Saville. Row four: Mary Murphy, Wilbert Dainty, Adolph Herduin, Robert Nichols, Fred Saville, Avis Chivers, Clara Fortner, Laura Murphy, Edith Simpson, and Zetella Herduin. Row five: Beulah Horton, Gladys Freeman, Blanche Fortner, Leona Pace, Ferne Dainty, Clarence Thompson, William Chivers, Cyprene Zoutte, Charles Nichols, and Walter Des Planges. Row six: Teachers Ruth Hill and Andy May.

Knoxville Township, Liberty, 1935 - Students included Douglas, Bob, and Betty Barnett; Wilbur Tull; Wallace Thomas; Juanita and Harriet Hartshorn; Rose Ellen Welch; Oscar and Tommy Barnes; Hoyt, Glenna, Wilma, and Wanda Monroe; Bernice and Doris Waits; Betty Reeves; Ruby Gilchrist; and three Applegate children. Teacher Arlene Covey.

Knoxville Township, Pleasant Grove, 1917 – Teacher Leulah Stuff Amos. Row one: Esther Jones, Agnes Wren, Edith Smith, Sarah Vander Linden, Fern Booth, Paul Jones, Thomas Wren, and Ted Sterling. Row two: Edith Bowery, Madeline Crozier, Agnes Jones, Glenn Booth, Worth Booth, and Everett Sterling. Row three: Edna Booth, Frances Smith, Mary Vander Linden, Matilda Barnes, and Lois Talbott.

Knoxville Township, Pleasant Ridge, 1909 – Teacher Bessie Williams. Front row: Pearl Karns, May Ellison, Grace Ellison, Ward Colwell, and Johnie Sylvanus. Back row: Dale Woodle, Lloyd McConeghey, Wrex Colwell, Dick Sylvanus, and Van Merriman. Peeping out of the window: Hally Clark and Helen Sylvanus. Student Pearl Karns became the teacher at Pleasant Ridge in 1917 and 1918.

Knoxville Township, Spring Hill, 1892 – Row one: Loren McKern, Carl McConaughey, Effie Shields, Lyman Masteller, Bert James, Howard Conrey, John Proudfoot, and Forest James. Row two: Cora Caulkins, E. Baty, Earl Brady, Pearl Proudfoot, Ella Moore, Cora Conrey, Cleo McKinney, Walter Caulkins, Isaac Brady, and Ed Harvey. Row three: Teacher Sylvia Masteller, E. Baty, Gertie Elder, Babe Fortner, Lewis Cloe, Earl Jones, Amos Ross, Delno Brady, May Brady, Charles Brady, Bert Conrey, and Caleb Moore. Row four: Earl Brees, Carre Brees, Florence Bowman, Belle McConaughey, Carrie McKern, Anna Hunt, Lillie Fortner, Eva Harvey, and Alta Conrey. Row five: Rinda Roff, Lottie McConaughey, Mary McConaughey, Mattie Harvey, Minnie Spicer, Jessie Young, Ann Harvey, Mossie Brady, and Nancy Conrey.

Knoxville Township, Washington – End of the year school picnic, May, 1950. Row one: Alice Smith, Marlys Fee, Carol Tonda, Johnny Sharp, Donald Fast, Terry Keever, Ted Dykstra, Phillip Langstraat, and Dale Dixon. Row two: Keith Dixon, Floyd De Moss, Larry Smith, Patty Dykstra, Ronald Fast, John De Moss, and Jerry Sharp. Row three: Teacher Frances Thompson, Joyce Langstraat, Dorotha De Moss, Janice Dixon, Gloria Langstraat, Calvin Smith, and Tom De Moss.

Lake Prairie Township, European #1, 1907 – Front row: Dick Vander Wilt, John Den Adel, Pauline Ver Ploeg, Lonnie Ver Ploeg, Bill Den Adel, Henry Ver Ploeg, Sunny Van Baale, Dick Ver Ploeg, Mamie Boat, Nettie Van Helton, and Dave Van Haaften. Back row: Johnie De Kock, Lewis Vander Wilt, Dean Van Helten, Betha Den Burger, Nelis Bensink, Grace Vos, John Boat, Gertie Bensink, and Deila Van Zee.

Lake Prairie Township, European #3 – Pupils of Lois Eysink on a field trip. She taught from 1948-51.

Lake Prairie Township, Plainview – Parents and children gather for the last day of school celebration in 1907.

Lake Prairie Township, North Porterville, 1909 – Row one: Tone Blom, (unknown), and Dave Van Steenis. Row two: (unknown), (unknown), ____De Vries, (unknown), Will Van Zante, Sarah Van Steenis De Haan, and (unknown). Row 3: Lester Lankerak, (unknown), (unknown), Clara Van Steenis Van Zee, Teacher Geraldine Ashenbrenner, Gertie Van Zante Huyser, (unknown), Martha Ver Ploeg Dykstra, Josie Ver Ploeg Blom, Tryne Ver Ploeg Bloem, and Gradus Van Zante.

Lake Prairie Township, Sand Ridge, 1909 – Row one: Vernie De Briun, Herman Westerkamp, Gerrit Van Gorp, Arie M. Van Haaften, Edgar Vander Hart, Neal Ver Steegt, Lester Van Gorp, Nellie Westerkamp, Sara Ter Louw Van Hemert, Marie Eeling Dykstra, Walter Vander Hart, Roy Van Haaften, Clarence Sheehy, Herman Zwank, Marion Klyn, Arie Klyn, and John Eysink. Row two: Josie Van Haaften Groenendyk, Sophia Vos Geurts, Maggie Eysink Vander Pol, Jennie Vos Zwank, John S. Ter Louw, Minnie Eeling Ostrum, Tryna Eeling Beyer, Teacher Nelle Hahn, Anna Ter Louw, Bennie Zwank, Jacob Eeling, Ed Vos, John Boertje, Arie H. Van Haaften, Louis Van Haaften, and Lydia Ter Louw.

Lake Prairie Township, Silver Grove West, 1901 – Row one: Freda Marinus, Hattie Klein, Margaret Vander Garde, Jennie Klein, Jeanette Onstine, Bessie Vander Garde, Bessie Van Houten, Emma Van Houten, Reka Van Houten, and Henry Martinus. Row two: James Van Loon, Art Klein, Gerrit Dykstra, John Van Peursem, Tunis Witzenberg, and John Slot. Row three: Jennie Van Peursem, Luedna Witzenberg, Blanche Witzenberg, Lois Van Loon, Sarah Vander Leest, Tone Klein, Gradus Vander Linden, Gradus Dykstra, Andrew Van Houten, and Andrew Mersbergen. Row four: Anna Marinus, Gerrit Klein, Richard Klein, Yella Witzenberg, Gertie Van Peursem, Lucy Witzenberg, Jennie Mersbergen, Maggie Slot, and Mille Van Peursem. Row five: John Vander Leest, Dora Van Loon, Gertie Dykstra, Teacher Bessie Vander Linden, Martin Vander Linden, Richard Vander Leest, and Ed Kooinegor.

Perry Township, Collins, spring 1899 – Left to right: Teacher Maude Inskeep, Louella Spencer, Roxy West, Frank Morrison, Georgia Spencer, Alfred Spencer, Mable Ball, Sadie West, Cordis West, Flossie Morrison, Henry West, Benjamin West, and Grace West.

Perry Township, Pleasant Hill, spring term 1915 – Teacher Sadie Coulson. Row one: Leo Wilson, Cleo Cowman, Maude Kain, and Coral Kain. Row two: Keith Cowman, Clarence Cowman, Lorene Cowman, Roy Schrader, Paul Tidball, Fay Wilson, Mildred English, Oleta Rinehart, and Dorothy Cowman. Row three: Gladys Kain, Margaret Umble, Letha Cowman, Floyd Wilson, Marie Rinehart, Harry Schrader, and Vernie Umble. Row four: Robert Schrader, Harold Wilson, Tommy Schrader, and Ransom Rinehart. (Ivan Hughes was absent.)

Perry Township, Valley – Front row: Ray Mikesell, Pearl Manning, Loren Owens, Jennie Bullington, Free Walker, Jennie Leuty, Camille Leuty, Bertha Keller, Zuella Walker, and Pearl Mikesell. Back row: Rachel Mikesell, Henry Wagner, Lorenzo Bullington, Minta Brown, Hazel Flory, Emma Keller, Della Bullington, Chase Keller, Martha Leuty, Ethel Walker, Lizzie Keller, and Izora Manning. The date is probably early 1900s. The teacher is listed as Effie Hanes, but she is not in the official list. MCHS has a souvenir booklet from Walter E. Wellons, who taught the first term of 1905. Many of the same students are listed in that booklet along with others named Holmes, Schafer, Robinson, Carter, and Colyn.

Polk Township, Coal Ridge, 1887 – Row one: Bill Neely, Wessie Poffenbarger, ___Vander Werf, ___Vander Werf, Joe Pifer, and Clyde Davis. Row two: Cora Dickey, Ollie Poffenbarger, Emily Blackman, Grace Davis, Georgia Poffenbarger, ___ Vander Werf, Lucy Woodyard, Lida Woodyard, Edith Smith, and Dick Smith. Row three: Will Dickey, Roy Dickey, Emma Armstrong, Warren Woodyard, Vick Obrian, Teacher Laura Essex, Orve Reynolds, Brade Davis, Della Wheeler, Annie Robinson, Addie Smith, Alma Poffenbarger, Alta Poffenbarger, and Sarah Franklin in back.

Polk Township, West River Ridge, 1913 – Lloyd Rouze, teacher. Note clothing styles and everyone frowning into the sun.

Red Rock Township, Oak Ridge, 1922 – Teacher Eleanor Morgan. Row one: Doyle Carter, Dea Owens, Lester Miller, Delbert Kain, Garry Vander Mann, and Paul Brown. Row two: Janette De Haai, Olive Kain, Marie Owen, and Herbert Carter. Row three: Janette Vander Mann, Merle Owens, Ona Owens, and Carl Miller.

Summit Township, Otley, November 8, 1935 - Row one: Ivan Kaldenberg, Wilma Pol, Darlene Postma, Robert Schuring. Row two: Harold Pothoven, Lawrence Dykstra, Henrietta Schuring, Evelyn Kool, Eva Van Baale. Row three: Gerald Veenendal, Gene McKeever, Edward Van Ee, Marion Pol, Ralph Poortinga. Row four: Billy Vriezelaar, Jake Schuring, Leonard Pol, Luella Vos, Norma Dykstra, Betty Longdin. Row five: Ralph Van Vliet, Nedra Neely, Webb Neely, Hubert Postma, Raymond Robus, Betty McKeever. Row six: Clarence Van Buren, Bernie Van Ee, Cora Heeren, Lois Van Vliet, Geraldine Van Wyk. Teachers: Dick Miller and Doris Lee.

Union Township, Rees – After the October 1923 snowstorm. Teacher Reda Martin. Front row: Alberta Slykhuis, Grace Slykhuis, John Able Dickenson, Waldo Dickenson, and Gracie De Moss. Back row: Donald Rees, Cynthia De Moss, Tommy De Moss, and James Rees.

Washington Township, New Albany, 1947 – Right side from back: Teacher Ruth Kenny, Robert Quigley, Richard Mathes, Dolores Mathes, and Ronald Shives. Left side: Myrtle Condra, Jeena Mae Condra, and Wayne Shives.

Washington Township, Washington, 1915 – Row one: Dee Ward, Mervin Leavengood, Iva Klootwyk, Bill Harvey, Lois Harvey, Pearl Carter, and Geraldine James. Row two: Oliver Harvey, Glen Brawner, Clarence Klootwyk, Lois Carter, Alice Klootwyk, Opal Cain, and Perry Harvey. Row three: Lester Klootwyk, Robert Wood, Forrest Brawner, Bill Cain, Goldie Harvey, Teacher Eva Jones, George Cain, and John Carter.

Washington Township, Washington, 1915 – Row one: Dee Ward, Mervin Leavengood, Iva Klootwyk, Bill Harvey, Lois Harvey, Pearl Carter, and Geraldine James. Row two: Oliver Harvey, Glen Brawner, Clarence Klootwyk, Lois Carter, Alice Klootwyk, Opal Cain, and Perry Harvey. Row three: Lester Klootwyk, Robert Wood, Forrest Brawner, Bill Cain, Goldie Harvey, Teacher Eva Jones, George Cain, and John Carter.

Bibliography

Bussey Centennial Committee. *Bussey Centennial - Bussey, Iowa 1875-1975*. Marceline, MO: Walsworth, 1975.

Clark, Betty and Bob; Clarke, Donna and Tom. *Flagler Iowa Area History 1877-1998*. Knoxville, IA: Clark and Clarke, 1998.

Heusinkveld, Emma Lou. *Pella School History 1847-1980*. Pella, IA: Pella Printing Co., 1980.

Heusinkveld, Harriet. *Red Rock, Iowa, Annals of a Frontier Community 1843-1969*. Pella, IA: Pella Printing Co., 1993.

Melcher and Dallas Committee. *Melcher and Dallas History Book, 1855 - 1982*. Marceline, MO: Walsworth, 1982.

Nollen, Carl. *Silver Grove School, History of a Country School West of Pella, Iowa, in Marion County*. Pella, IA: self-published, 2004.

———. *Liberty Corner School, History of a One-Room Country School Southeast of Otley, Iowa, Summit Township, Marion County*. Pella, IA: self-published, 2010.

———. *Marion County Country Schoolhouses, Photographs of Remaining Schools, In Conjunction With the Iowa Convention for Country School Preservation, October 1, 2004*. Pella, IA: self-published, 2004.

———. *Silver Grove School Update to the 2004 History*. Pella, IA: self-published, 2006.

———. *Valley School, History of a Country School Southeast of Pella Iowa, Lake Prairie Township, Marion County*. Pella, IA: self-published, 2007.

Pella Historical Society Committee. *History of Pella Iowa 1847-1987 Vols. I and 2*. Dallas, Texas: Curtis Media Corporation, 1988 and 1989.

Pleasantville Committee. *Pleasantville Past and Present*. Marceline, MO: Walsworth, 1976.

Tracy Committee. *Tracy Centennial—100 Years of History from Tracy and Surrounding Area*. Oskaloosa, IA: Gene Phillips, 1974.

William, Donnel, and others. *The History of Marion County*. Des Moines, IA: Union Historical Company, 1881.

Wright, John W. *History of Marion County Vol. 1*. Chicago: S. J. Clark, 1915.

www.ingramcontent.com/pod-product-compliance
Lightning Source LLC
Chambersburg PA
CBHW062126160426
43191CB00013B/2213